# SIMPSON

IMPRINT IN HUMANITIES

The humanities endowment
by Sharon Hanley Simpson and
Barclay Simpson honors
MURIEL CARTER HANLEY
whose intellect and sensitivity
have enriched the many lives
that she has touched.

*The publisher gratefully acknowledges the generous support of the Simpson Humanities Endowment Fund of the University of California Press Foundation.*

*Violette Nozière*

# Violette Nozière

## A STORY OF MURDER IN 1930S PARIS

### Sarah Maza

UNIVERSITY OF CALIFORNIA PRESS

BERKELEY   LOS ANGELES   LONDON

University of California Press, one of the most distinguished
university presses in the United States, enriches lives around
the world by advancing scholarship in the humanities, social
sciences, and natural sciences. Its activities are supported by
the UC Press Foundation and by philanthropic contributions from individuals and institutions. For more
information, visit www.ucpress.edu.

University of California Press
Berkeley and Los Angeles, California

University of California Press, Ltd.
London, England

Library of Congress Cataloging-in-Publication Data

Maza, Sarah C., 1953–
    Violette Nozière : a story of murder in 1930s Paris /
Sarah Maza.
        p.   cm.
    Includes bibliographical references and index.
    ISBN 978-0-520-26070-2 (cloth : alk. paper)
    1. Nozière, Violette, 1915–1966.   2. Women
murderers—France—Paris—Biography.   3. Murder—
France—Paris—Case studies.   4. Women—France—
Paris—Social conditions—20th century.   5. Paris
(France)—Social conditions—20th century.   I. Title.
    HV6248.N7M39 2011
    364.152'3092—dc22                          2010028603

Manufactured in the United States of America
20   19   18   17   16   15   14   13   12   11
10   9   8   7   6   5   4   3   2   1

This book is printed on Cascades Enviro 100, a 100% post
consumer waste, recycled, de-inked fiber. FSC recycled
certified and processed chlorine free. It is acid free,
Ecologo certified, and manufactured by BioGas energy.

FOR JULIETTE

# CONTENTS

ILLUSTRATIONS

ACKNOWLEDGMENTS

Any merit to be found in this book must surely come from the two extraordinary places in which I had the good fortune to carry out the bulk of the
work on it, Paris and Stanford. I completed most of the research during a
yearlong sabbatical leave in France, for which I thank Northwestern University. As I was finding out about neighborhood life in the 1930s, Paris
worked its magic and my family made lasting connections with people in
our patch of the city, the *quatorzième*. For those Tuesday mornings in the
café on Rue Boulard and much else since, I thank Alain and Clotilde
Policar, Hélène Teussard, Kirill Zaboroff, Jean Nirouet, and Olivier
Basso. Working on the *douzième* has also strengthened long-standing ties
to the friends through whom I first encountered the Picpus area of Paris,
Barbara and Patrick Genevaz.

I was also lucky the day I walked into the Bibliothèque des Littératures
Policières in Paris. The library itself is a treasure, and its director, Catherine
Chauchard, generously shared with me her extensive knowledge of French
crime history. She has helped me at every turn in subsequent years. M. Yves
Ozanam at the Bibliothèque de l'Ordre des Avocats went out of his way to
track down biographical information on members of the legal profession for
me. I am grateful to Mme Simone Mayeul for talking to me about her early
years in the apartment next door to the Nozières, and to M. Philippe de
Vésinne-Larue for sharing with me his memories of his cousin René.

As I began work on a project in a field, the twentieth century, to which I was new, I had to rely on the advice of friends much more knowledgeable than I. For crucial leads, ideas, and bibliographic advice, I thank Pierre Birnbaum, Carolyn Dean, Laura Lee Downs, Sarah Farmer, Nancy Green, Laura Hein, Gabrielle Houbre, Dominique Kalifa, Tessie Liu, Philip Nord, Mary-Louise Roberts, and Tyler Stovall. I was also lucky to have Brad Reichek's research assistance as I got started. Mi Gyung Kim provided helpful information on a crucial point of medical history. Jonathan Eburne gave me excellent leads as well as access to his work on Surrealism and crime when it was still unpublished, and Stephen Kern saved me from a number of mistakes by reviewing my chapter on the subject. Anne-Emmanuelle Demartini has been exceptionally generous in sharing with me from the start her own very fine work-in-progress on the Nozière case.

The book began to take shape thanks to support from the Alice Berline Kaplan Institute for the Humanities at Northwestern. I thank the institute's director, my longtime colleague and friend Holly Clayson, and Elzbieta Foeller-Pituch, then its assistant director, for helping me get the project off the ground. The bulk of the manuscript was written in the beautiful setting of the Center for Advanced Studies in the Behavioral Sciences in Stanford. The center more than lived up to its reputation as a utopia for scholars, thanks to Claude Steele, Anne Petersen, Linda Clark, and the congenial staff and fellows with whom I was privileged to spend a year. Mickey Dietler, Miles Kahler, Jessica Riskin, Vicki Schultz, and Fred Turner had their part in the year's social and intellectual pleasures. I especially thank the gang of four "historicist" scholars with whom I shared weekly lunch discussions, Gail Herschatter, Julie Hochstrasser, Paula Findlen, and Katie Trumpener, for their warm support and acute readings of my early drafts. I received constructive criticism from audiences at presentations I gave at the Center for Advanced Studies as well as at Northwestern, Stanford, Berkeley, and Harvard. Longtime friends and colleagues in the North Carolina Triangle French History Group offered me especially pertinent reactions and advice during a session arranged by Lloyd Kramer.

My greatest thanks go to four readers of the penultimate draft of the manuscript: Carolyn Dean (again), Caroline Ford, and Ruth Harris reviewed the manuscript for the press and generously identified themselves, thereby giving the author occasion to importune them further with questions. My friend and colleague Ken Alder also read a full draft and gave me excellent suggestions and a crucial morale boost when my energy for the project was beginning to flag. Family helped out too: Jim LoScalzo performed editorial miracles with my inexpert photos (several of which originally included my feet), while Monica, Jonathan, and Suzy Maza reassured me that the book in progress was not unreadable. My thanks extend to my agent, Christy Fletcher, for excellent feedback as the book was taking shape and for shepherding it to a publisher. This project has allowed me to appreciate once again Sheila Levine's outstanding qualities as an editor and friend; Kate Marshall's competence and patience have been a blessing in the book's final stages, and it has been a pleasure to work once again with Rose Vekony.

Nobody has given me more confidence in the project and joy in carrying it out than Sean Shesgreen, who moved to France, learned French, cooked endless dinners, moved again, and heard the story of Violette Nozière many more times than anyone should have to. For all of this and his perceptive readings of my chapters, I am deeply in his debt. Our daughter Juliette responded with characteristic spirit, resilience, and wit when her life was twice upended in aid of her mother's research. She, if anyone, will appreciate the irony of being at thirteen the dedicatee of a book about a teenage parent-slayer.

# Introduction

If we had a keen vision and feeling of all ordinary human life, it would
be like hearing the grass grow and the squirrel's heart beat, and we
should die of that roar which lies on the other side of silence.

GEORGE ELIOT
*Middlemarch*

AUGUST 21, 1933. It is late summer and late at night. The city is unusually
quiet because every Parisian who can afford to has gone on vacation. The
scene is a two-room apartment on the sixth floor of a working-class building on the far eastern end of the city. The rooms are well appointed, over-
furnished with imitation antiques, curtains, doilies, and family photographs, though the tiny kitchen between the two main rooms is shabby
and primitive. Violette Nozière, a fashionably dressed young woman of
eighteen, is in the bedroom, lying awake on the massive double bed. In
the dining room, the bodies of her father and mother are sprawled on a
folding cot. Just before midnight, Violette gets up and searches the apartment for money. When she finds it, she crams it into her purse. She looks
in one last time on her parents; then, after checking to make sure no neighbors are awake, she exits, closing the door with utmost care, and creeps
down the stairs.

She first heads over to Paris's eastern park, the Bois de Vincennes, less
than a mile from the apartment, and spends a few hours there in the dark.
Then she travels to the Latin Quarter in the center of the city and books
a room in a modest hotel near the Boulevard Saint-Michel. The next day,
August 22, she sends a cable from the Latin Quarter to her parents' address
explaining that she will be out for dinner and will only get home late that
night.

How do you spend the day after you have handed each of your parents a glass of water laced with poison and encouraged them to drink it on the pretext that it is medication? Violette drops by the home of her best girl-friend and convinces her to join her later for an evening of dancing, drinking, and flirting. Then she heads for the city's biggest and most elegant department store, where she buys herself a set of glamorously fashionable evening clothes: a long black dress, matching elbow-length gloves, a gray shrug, black beret, and costume jewelry. Come evening, Violette and her friend Madeleine are seated in the famous Montparnasse café La Coupole, on the lookout for interesting encounters. Is Violette able to put out of mind, as she sips a cup of hot chocolate, the two bodies lying inert in a flat at the other end of the city?

Around one o'clock the next morning, August 23, a car driven by a wealthy young man pulls up in front of the Nozières' apartment building. Violette gets out and thanks her escort. She heads up the stairs, again very quietly. Does her heart sink before she opens the door to the flat, or is she beyond all that? The bodies are there, still motionless but separate: her mother's now lies on the big double bed. Violette goes straight to the kitchen and opens the gas main, turns on the stove burners, then quickly goes out and stands in the hallway. The smell is soon overpowering. She goes to the neighbor's door and pounds on it, screaming, "Help, help! I think my parents have committed suicide!" Four days later everyone in France will know her name.[1]

In 1933–34, Violette Nozière was probably the most famous woman in France and certainly the most hated. Contemporaries in Paris and throughout the country were for a time obsessed with her. They read about her daily in the papers, crowded around the prison where she was held, sang songs about her wicked deeds, and wrote hundreds of letters to the judge who was investigating her case. They argued about her father, her mother, her boyfriends, her clothes, and her behavior. They compared the Nozière affair—with much exaggeration, to be sure—to the Dreyfus case, which had torn the country apart in the 1890s.

Conspicuous and controversial at the time, the Nozière affair remains alive in the memory of contemporaries—octogenarians in France still remember it—but has otherwise mostly fallen into oblivion. Violette's story was briefly revived in the 1970s, when a popular book on the case was published, inspiring a movie directed by one of France's preeminent filmmakers, Claude Chabrol, but it then was largely forgotten again. In retrospect, the general amnesia about something that once loomed very large seems understandable. The actions of an ordinary girl who poisoned her parents look trivial in comparison to the 1933 Nuremberg Rally (which was held at exactly that time), the right-wing violence that erupted in Paris in February 1934, the Popular Front, or the Spanish Civil War, not to mention international events unfolding after 1939.

But the Nozière case deserves our attention precisely because it directs us to aspects of experience that have been obscured by the importance conferred by later developments on organized politics and international relations. Looking back on France in the 1920s and 1930s, strikes, right-wing rallies, paramilitary organizations, and a perilous international scene loom large because we know what happened a few years down the road.[2] But what about all those aspects of social and cultural life that have little bearing on the subsequent grim story of defeat, occupation, collaboration, and resistance? A central purpose of this book is to recover and describe aspects of the lives of middle- and working-class Parisians in the twenties and thirties that have been overshadowed by our focus on World War II. The Nozière affair opens up vistas on features of this period that often go unmentioned: the stories of migrants from the countryside making a life for themselves in the city, of working-class girls and boys getting an education in school and in the city's streets and workplaces, of families struggling to get by on modest salaries in tiny apartments, of strange crimes like Violette's that crowded international events off the front page of popular newspapers.

This book centers on a crime that was also a scandal, what the French call an *affaire*. The value of "big cases" for contemporaries and subsequent historians is not just that scandal is intrinsically fascinating, but that *affaires* allow for the articulation of values and ideologies. The most resonant *affaires* are those that achieve something close to a tragic dimension because they involve two sharply defined but seemingly incompatible systems of belief. The Dreyfus case in the 1890s, for instance, caused a rift between, on one side, French people who saw themselves as defenders of the army and national honor and, on the other, those who cared passionately about Republican ideals of justice and religious tolerance. A century later in the United States, warring narratives in the O.J. Simpson case highlighted—and artificially separated—on the one side the scandalous persistence of racial prejudice and on the other the horror of domestic violence.

What is remarkable about the Nozière case, by contrast, is that it never became a clear contest between sharply defined ideological camps. Though public opinion seemed at first united in its outrage at the teenage parent-killer, there soon emerged complicating factors that made the case increasingly murky and unsettling. The story of Violette's crime could not be made to fit into neat ideological packages, no matter how hard various parties in the media and the judicial system tried to press it into familiar scenarios. And yet people at all levels of society argued about it, read about it, and wrote about it. In this book, I propose that the meaning of the case for contemporaries resided precisely in its troubling ambiguity. I argue that Violette's deed and its aftermath took on the importance they did because the controversies they elicited mirrored important aspects of French city life in the 1930s: this was a time when class divisions were eroding and the status of women was especially fluid, when children stayed in school longer and were often better educated than their parents, when young working girls could buy clothes that looked like those worn by society women.

To understand all the associations evoked in contemporaries by the story of Violette and her parents, we must turn first to the place where it all started: 9 Rue de Madagascar in the twelfth arrondissement at the far eastern end of the City of Light.

ONE

# A Neighborhood in Paris

WHEN PEOPLE TODAY THINK ABOUT women in Paris between the wars, the names that come to mind are those of glamorous figures who created lasting works while building scandalous reputations: Coco Chanel, the pauper from Normandy who turned high fashion upside-down; the African-American Josephine Baker whose half-naked dancing titillated the city and the world; the openly bisexual best-selling author known as Colette; Simone de Beauvoir, who turned her back on a stiff-necked family to become the companion of Jean-Paul Sartre; American expatriates and sexual nonconformists like Gertrude Stein, Alice B. Toklas, and Janet Flanner. These women inhabited the center of the city, both physically and metaphorically: the stages of Montmartre, the theaters and couture houses of the Right Bank, the publishing offices and literary salons of the Latin Quarter. To understand the world that created an obscure young woman like Violette Nozière, we must first move out of the center of Paris and travel east to a neighborhood where, in the 1930s, famous people and tourists never set foot.

Violette and her parents lived in the twelfth arrondissement, a district on the southeastern edge of the city. Moving east from Notre Dame and the heart of Paris past the Place de la Bastille, one crosses the oldest and most famous working-class district, the Faubourg Saint-Antoine. Saint-Antoine is where joiners, cabinetmakers, goldsmiths, tanners, and other skilled artisans took to the streets in July 1789 to besiege a hated prison-fortress, the Bastille, and tear it down stone by stone. Farther east is the twelfth arrondissement. The district became part of Paris only in 1860, an item in Baron Haussmann's plan to expand, unify, and recast the city into a marvel of modern urbanism. After presiding over the 1853 completion of Paris's biggest railway station, the Gare de Lyon, Haussmann took over the villages of Bercy and Picpus, which lay east of the station on the way to the castle and woods of Vincennes. The area that Baron Haussmann's plans gobbled up was still mostly composed of farms and convents into which the city's violent history had only once notoriously intruded. During the Revo-lution, the bodies and severed heads of some thirteen hundred of the guil-lotine's victims—nobles, priests, nuns, and commoners—were tossed into pits in the burial grounds of a convent in Picpus, and sometime later the remains of one of the heroes of that time, the Marquis de Lafayette, were interred nearby. In the decades after 1860, boulevards and apartment build-ings sprang up where fields had been, but in the early twentieth century farms were still numerous in the area, and many inhabitants got their milk straight from a nearby cow. As late as the 1950s, some streets had no side-walks, cars were few, and horse-drawn carriages were a common sight.[1]

The twelfth was a popular neighborhood but not a poor one. Wretched poverty could still be found in the northern areas of the city, in the heights around and beyond Père Lachaise Cemetery, where factory work-ers put in backbreaking days and got drunk at night, and whole families lived in roach-infested flophouses known as *garnis*.[2] Belleville, la Goutte d'Or, and other northern districts had earned a place in the mythology of revolution when their most radical inhabitants poured south to reclaim the city during the Paris Commune of 1871, eventually setting aflame monuments in the heart of Paris. For many in those areas, daily wages barely covered the cost of rent and food. But the city contained even greater degrees of poverty. In the 1930s Paris was ringed by shantytowns, in the area known as *la zone*. In the no-man's-land where the city walls had been torn down, hundreds of jobless and marginally employed people lived in shacks within a subculture, the world of the "fortifications" or *fortifs*, rife with addiction and violence. "A stench comes out of this strange country," wrote a contemporary, "which, at the gates of the most refined city on earth, offers a sprawling spectacle of a regression to savage life."[3]

A far cry from all this, the *douzième* was a "good" neighborhood of working-class and lower-middle-class families with its own set of distinctive cultures. Down by the river in Bercy stood the great wine depots for the city of Paris, where reds and whites from all over France were unloaded from trains and barges, then barreled, bottled, and shipped into the city and farther afield. The Bercy men started work at daybreak after an alcoholic breakfast, and paused midmorning to cook the huge steaks known as *entrecôtes de Bercy* and drink some more. At lunchtime, female office workers hurried to avoid the unwelcome attentions of the ever-inebriated depot men. At night hobos roamed around drilling holes in the barrels, filling up on high-octane Algerian reds. There were a few small factories in the area, such as the tobacco manufacturer's on the Rue de Charenton, where women known locally as "Carmens" rolled cigars.[4]

Mostly, people worked at steady, respectable jobs in workshops, offices, and stores. In the summer, kids swam off the quays of the Seine, buying horse-meat sausages for a snack when they had a few coins; in the winter, they played on the ramps and staircases of the train stations.[5] On Sundays, families went for a stroll in the Bois de Vincennes, where you could play tennis, as Violette and her father did, by stretching a string between two trees. The arrondissement had fifteen cinemas, which drew gaggles of children on Thursdays when school was out, families and young couples on the weekends. Sometimes the people of Picpus or Bercy took the metro or tramway into the heart of the city, to a world so distinct from their own that they often said, "We're going to Paris."[6] For the most part they remained in a district that was very much its own world, a village on the edge of the big city. As Albert Tourneux, who grew up not far from the Nozières early in the century, put it proudly, "I was born on Rue Crozatier. I went two hundred meters to school, three hundred to go work, four hundred to get married. I married a girl from Avenue Crozatier. After my service, we went to live on Boulevard Diderot, about one kilometer away. In the neighborhood everyone knew me."[7]

For neighborhood people, major excitement came once a year. During the three weeks after Easter, circus performers and exotic animals took over the enormous Place de la Nation (formerly Place du Trône) at the northern end of the district, drawing crowds from all over the city. The extravaganza known as the Foire du Trône claimed origins in the twelfth century, when the monks from a local abbey held a yearly sale of spiced pastries, but the fair had really taken off in the nineteenth century as a post-Lent blowout for the Parisian working classes.[8] Esmeralda, "queen of the gypsies," opened the fair in a crown and white dress, riding sidesaddle on a horse; in the following weeks, over two thousand acrobats, jugglers, and animal tamers showed off their skills amid a profusion of food and drink. A leading draw until her death in 1929 was the entertainer known as La Goulue ("the She-Glutton"), once immortalized in posters by Toulouse-Lautrec, who now eked out a scanty living as a dancer-cum-lion-tamer.[9] One woman from the twelfth remembered going to the fair every afternoon as a child to watch the parades with her uncle, enjoying an event "that seemed natural, integrated into the life of the neighborhood." She was surprised that some of her friends were not allowed to do the same: "That is how I learned about social cleavages: there were those who went to the Foire du Trône, and those who did not."[10]

More than the wine depots or the fair, however, the institution that gave the twelfth its identity was the railway. Between the wars the district was home to several smaller railway stations—at Bastille, along the quays at Bercy and La Rapée—all of them dwarfed by France's most famous train station, the Gare de Lyon. Located at the western edge of the arrondissement, the Gare de Lyon had opened under Napoleon III and reached its pinnacle in 1900, when the huge, ornate Art Nouveau building we know today was opened to coincide with Paris's Universal Exposition.

As the hub of France's north-south line, the Gare de Lyon was not just a national railway station but an international one. In pre–World War II Europe, if one traveled by train from London to Nice, Antwerp to Madrid, Berlin to Rome, the route would almost inevitably go through it. Before 1937, France's railways were in the hands of six private companies, the largest of which, based in the Gare de Lyon, had a name that said it all: Paris-Lyon-Marseille. The PLM owned the line that linked France's three biggest and richest cities, its locomotives chugging south along the country's oldest trade route, the Rhône valley. Inside the Gare de Lyon, one can still admire, adorning the famous turn-of-the-century brasserie Le Train Bleu, splendid murals showing the cities served by the PLM on the banks of the mighty Rhône and the shores of the Mediterranean. At the other end of the line, the Saint-Charles station in Marseille, with its monumental staircase and statues of nude women representing France's colonies, was planned as a southern echo of the great Parisian station.

The twelfth arrondissement was shaped, in large part, by movement into the city: barges docking at the quays, trains shrieking into the stations. A large part of its population was made up of railway workers and their families, people of modest origins born outside Paris, for whom a job with the

PLM and a move to the big city offered a way out of provincial poverty. Germaine and Jean-Baptiste Nozière were among them.

Germaine Hézard did not work for the railway company; she married into it. Germaine was born in 1888 in the small town of Neuvy on the Loire River, just over a hundred miles south of Paris. The Hézards had lived in Neuvy for generations, as had other large local peasant families, such as the Boutrons and the Desbouis. Germaine's mother, Philomène, born in 1849, was a Boutron. When she was twenty-one, she and her husband, Alcime Hézard, had a daughter, also named Philomène, who married a Desbouis. Their daughter was an only child until nineteen years later. In 1889, having perhaps become careless about contraception, they had another daughter, to whom they gave the much more fashionable name Germaine.[11] Germaine grew up like an only child in what must have been a poor family. Her father worked the land, though the 1906 census listed him as a roadworker. Her mother had no official occupation, but probably toiled in and out of the house all of her life. In 1926, widowed and living with her in-laws, the seventy-seven-year-old continued to work as a day laborer. When Germaine was eighteen and still living with her parents, she was a seamstress, probably taking in commissions at home.[12]

Neuvy had a little over fourteen hundred inhabitants in 1901 and two hundred fewer in 1931. It was a poor place but not an isolated one, located on one of France's main thoroughfares. A river village on the Loire, Neuvy was once a postal relay on the ancient highway from Paris to Antibes. During the interwar years, trucks and cars whizzed by on the *Nationale 7,* as did trains on the PLM line. Neuvy had never been cut off from the rest of France, and especially not from national politics—for one thing, its inhabitants, unlike those of most French villages, had long spoken French rather than a local dialect. The Nièvre Department in which it is located has a tradition of leftism stretching back to the Revolution. In 1789 Neuvy had a National Guard unit, in 1792 a Popular Society that decreed the local church was now a "temple of Reason," and in 1793 a Surveillance Committee that promised "the death of tyrants and the execution of despots." In 1851 the inhabitants of Neuvy rose up with the rest of the French Left against Louis-Napoléon Bonaparte, in 1871 they hoisted a red flag in sympathy with the Paris Commune, and throughout the twentieth century Socialist candidates in the area regularly trounced their right-wing opponents.[13]

Within the community, however, things changed slowly, with opportunities gradually contracting. Neuvy had once been famous for its pottery, but mass production had killed the craft. Located next to Burgundy, the area traditionally boasted great wine; vine growers still assembled every year in Neuvy to celebrate their patron, Saint Vincent, by ceremonially sucking on a Gamay-soaked vine stock and partying their way though a hundred-liter barrel over a couple of days.[14] The Boutrons and Hézards still worked the vine, but that trade had been hit hard by the last century's phylloxera epidemic; by 1900 there were only a couple dozen small vine growers left in the village. In the late nineteenth century, a man named Fougerat had opened a rubber factory, so Neuvy now had a few industrial workers, but for most of the unskilled, there was little besides hard, unprofitable work on the land.[15] A child who did well in school and whose parents could afford to keep him there longer than age twelve might aspire to the most coveted situation: steady employment with the post office or the railway. With options so limited and with river, rail, and road so close, it is hardly surprising that the more enterprising ended up in Paris.

Germaine left Neuvy twice. At age eighteen, she escaped the drudgery of sewing at home by wedding a man named Louis Arnal, a gilder whom she followed to Paris. The marriage lasted only thirteen months, reportedly because Arnal started seeing an old girlfriend. She returned to Neuvy for a while, then moved back to Paris, where she managed a wine store.[16] Germaine Hézard was tall and elegant with pale skin, brown hair, and a classically handsome face, and her status as an "experienced" divorcee probably added to her allure. In June 1913 she met Jean-Baptiste Nozière, whom everybody called Baptiste. There was nothing remarkable about Baptiste's looks: he was on the short side, with thinning hair, a weak chin, and a hangdog expression that his full mustache only accentuated. He came from even poorer peasant stock than Germaine. But he had one big thing going for him: a high-paying, stable job as an engine driver for the PLM.

If you follow the Loire River several hundred miles south from Neuvy, upstream, you get to the part of Auvergne called the Haute-Loire, in the heart of France's central mountain range, the Massif Central. Here Baptiste was born in 1885 in a village called Prades. With a population of around three hundred at the turn of the century, Prades made Neuvy look downright cosmopolitan. A journalist in 1933 described the hamlet as nestled in "a desolate setting of arid hills, its fifty houses with red-tiled roofs dwarfed by a haughty rock that bears the ruins of an ancient seigneurial chateau."[17] The village stood in a gorge of the Allier River, a tributary of the Loire, which ran through a jagged volcanic plateau. Down in the river-bed, land was scarce and poor, and to make matters worse, the river regularly overflowed when the snows melted, laying waste the crops.[18] It was all the local farmers could do to grow enough barley, rye, and potatoes to survive on. Rough bread, cabbage, and the lard from a few pigs barely fed the population through long, snowbound winters.[19]

Prades was located in one of those areas that urban visitors at the turn of the century considered barely French. While most of the locals understood the French language, they spoke the local patois, a mixture of Provençal and Auvergnat dialects. Stocky and weather-burned, they wore a distinctive costume, the men in wide breeches, striped waistcoats, and broad-brimmed felt hats, which they took off only to sleep, the women in headscarves topped with a smaller version of the felt hat, and clogs on everyone's feet. Clothes were washed as they had been for centuries, scrubbed with ashes twice a year. Houses were more like huts, small and dark with scant light and heat provided by smoky peat fires. Floods ate away at the feet of the rare pieces of furniture, so everything of value had to be stowed high up.[20] The writer George Sand, who visited the area in the mid-nineteenth century, told of the suffocating stench she encountered in one such hut, where every piece of clothing and every item of food was hung from the ceiling, sweat-soaked hose and rotting sausage alike.[21] An image of the Virgin or of the Sacred Heart usually hung on one of the walls, but Catholic devotion coexisted with witches and soothsayers in many places, and adults as well as children feared the *loup-garou*, the wolf from hell who roamed at night with his diabolical lupine acolytes.[22] Many adults died young, and when a child got sick, you didn't fetch a doctor. How would you pay him, since there was no trade and therefore no money? Only women could earn a pittance in the scant daylight hours of the winter months. They made lace as they had for generations, juggling spools over a frame to produce intricate creations, breathtaking designs floating on invisible backgrounds that would be scooped up for a few coins by a traveling *leveur de dentelles* once the roads became passable.[23] Unlike the people of Neuvy, the inhabitants of places like Prades, isolated and focused on survival, neither knew nor cared about politics, and the revolutions, empires, and republics of the nineteenth century passed by mostly unnoticed.[24]

The men in Prades worked their smallholdings, even when they listed another occupation, such as grocer or innkeeper or, in the case of Baptiste's father, baker. Félix Nozière, born in 1858, came from Saint-Julien, an equally tiny place a couple of miles downstream. His mother, whose name is recorded as Naugère, had conceived him out of wedlock "of father unknown," then found a husband. In January 1884, twenty-six-year-old Félix, a rural laborer, a bastard child raised by his stepfather, married seventeen-year-old Marie-Constance Bernard from Prades.[25] They had three children, the oldest of whom, Baptiste, was born a year into their marriage.

Baptiste seems to have distanced himself emotionally as well a physically from his family over the course of his life. His mother had died by the time he reached adulthood, and his sister, Marie-Juliette, five years his junior, figured nowhere in his life. Was she dead too, or married and living elsewhere? His brother wed a woman also named Marie, and the young couple lived with the widowed Félix. Baptiste's younger brother went off to war in 1914 never to return, and Marie continued to live with her father-in-law. It was no doubt a sensible arrangement: Félix needed someone to keep house, and it must have been difficult in those years for a woman either to remarry or to survive on her own. Whatever really went on between Félix and this Marie thirty years his junior, their cohabitation fueled much village gossip and was later to lead to a rift between the baker and his oldest son.[26]

Life in Prades and Saint-Julien was grim, escape routes few. But Baptiste Nozière had an odd manner of fairy godmother looking out for him even before his birth. When Félix and Marie-Constance wed in January 1884, three of their witnesses were rural laborers who could barely scrawl something resembling a signature. The fourth was a railway employee from distant Langeac who signed his name, Pierre Plantin, with labored elegance, all curlicues and paraphs. Thirteen months later another railway worker served as witness on Baptiste's record of birth.[27] There was nothing unusual about a poor peasant couple inviting men of higher status—literate folks with enviable jobs—to serve as witnesses, but it is also tempting to see in these choices a harbinger of Baptiste's later trajectory. A railway ran past Prades and Saint-Julien, just as it did by Neuvy.

The line was built in the 1860s by the PLM company, first cutting westward into the Massif Central from Lyon to the major towns of Saint-Étienne and Le Puy. Another line, completed in 1870, crossed the region from northwest to south, part of it running along the gorges of the Allier past Prades and stopping in Saint-Julien. An old-timer living in a nearby village remembered the arrival in the 1860s of men who dynamited their way through the mountains: "They were hard workers and brought some life into the village. They danced, smoked, drank. Some of them married girls from the Auvergne." But she also recalled resistance to the building of a station from villagers who feared it would "disturb their habits." Peasants said the smoke would kill their crops and the coals set fire to the fields, and anyway since they had no money to take the train, they didn't see the point of it.[28] They did get the point eventually, especially when railways brought status to the village and work to the luckiest among them.

The few railway jobs available in Prades were hardly glamorous or easy: a handful of men in the village made a living as diggers or road menders for the company.[29] When it came to survival, though, the PLM was surely a safer bet than the local soil and weather; and there were better company jobs out there, in other hamlets and towns. The village schoolteacher must have known to look out for the brightest boys, those who might have a shot at a good job linked to the most striking symbol of the modern world. Though we know nothing of Baptiste's trajectory, we know plenty about what drew boys like him into working for the rail company.

Railway jobs demanded a lot of a man but gave a lot in return.[30] The six companies that the French state took over in 1937 offered many forms of security and, for certain kinds of work, excellent pay, but the company also "owned" your life in a way that comparable jobs did not. The world of rail companies was huge—about four hundred thousand workers in the early twentieth century—and far more complex than the "workers and bosses" structure of other contemporary workplaces. There were road-workers, ticket controllers, and crossing guards at the bottom, mechanics, maintenance men, firemen, and drivers in the middle, then stationmasters and other bureaucrats, and at the top engineers trained in elite schools.

Railway companies were good to their employees for self-interested reasons. Training a man for the specialized work involved in the running of trains was a long and expensive process, and worker instability had to be avoided for reasons of cost. They recruited young men from the two groups most likely to guarantee loyalty, those whose fathers already worked for the company and provincial peasant boys. Urban workers typically did not apply for railway jobs, nor did the companies especially want them: to have a good career in the railway you had to be willing to be displaced and then submit to the company's erratic schedules and elaborate regulations. City boys were too independent and rebellious, too attached to where they came from, to be worth the training.[31] Baptiste was probably a good student in elementary school, and someone—more likely the schoolteacher than his illiterate father—must have helped him secure a scholarship to continue his postelementary studies in a nearby town in the specialized Arts and Crafts (*Arts et Métiers*) School, which prepared students for the lower end of the technical professions; Baptiste trained initially as a locksmith.[32]

We can understand Baptiste's origins and experiences through those of a close fictional counterpart, Antoine Bloyé. In 1933, the year of Violette's crime, the novelist Paul Nizan published a fictionalized account, *Antoine Bloyé,* of the life of his own father, a railwayman who rose to middle-class respectability from poor rural origins. Antoine grows up deep in the countryside in western France, in a village where his father works as a mailman and then a ticket controller for the Paris-Orléans line and his mother does washing for the local bigwigs. Nizan describes the ways in which the railroad disrupted life in the French countryside, opening up a new sense of space, time, and possibilities for youngsters: "More than one country boy is drawn to the chugging of copper-bodied locomotives, to those metal bees buzzing over the decks of the new iron bridges. . . . One day they pack their bags and make their ways to the towns on the railway line, towns where the Company is hiring." Unlike his sharecropper grandparents or his own brutal and pessimistic father, whom he compares to a goat moving only as far as his tether allows, Antoine understands, thanks to the railway, that his future is not predetermined.[33]

Urged by his primary-school teacher, Antoine gets a scholarship to attend secondary school in a nearby town, in a technical education track. Antoine is not to study Latin or Greek, of course, for what would a worker's boy do with that kind of useless knowledge? The classics were a class marker at the time, and in his first year "Antoine gropingly understands that he will never possess the same passwords and rallying signs" as his wealthier classmates.[34] Even his own curriculum seems strangely irrelevant, since the history and geography he learns, the tragedies of Racine and Corneille he is made to memorize, have nothing to do with "Father's night shift, his cigar smuggling, the steaming blood of butchered pigs . . . and cleaning up the crud of rich folks." But he learns to write essays on Pascal and earn prizes, since he "could act the trained monkey as well as the next fellow."[35] Success leads to three years in a craft school in the bigger town of Angers, one of those institutions that "train subaltern officers for the great armies of French industry."[36] Out of trade school, a young man would learn his way around the stations and their great roaring beasts by doing metalwork, then repairing machines before he was allowed to ride and drive them. Antoine spent a few years rusticated in the small city of Tours doing maintenance and repairs before he was sent, as was Baptiste, to headquarters in Paris. The upper end of the workforce, firemen and engine drivers, earned a fixed monthly salary rather than a daily wage, which put them in a league with middle-class workers like civil servants.

Despite the grime on their clothes, engine drivers probably earned more than many white-collar workers: a driver made several times what a beginning office worker did, and that was just in base pay.[37] Railway incomes from that time are difficult to evaluate because the companies controlled their workforce—which was, after all, on the move and away from direct supervision—through a complicated system of bonuses and penalties. There were *primes,* or bonuses, for timely arrivals, for saving on coal and oil, for the number of kilometers covered. And even before the companies were gobbled up by the French state, they provided better disability and retirement benefits than any other employer at the time. As a young boy from Prades, what better goal than driving an engine? It made the worker part of the labor aristocracy, the job was safe and well-paid, and one had a fair amount of control and autonomy on the job. As a bonus, one got to look like the embodiment of grimy, heroic working-class masculinity, like Jean Gabin in the 1938 movie *La Bête humaine.* The men who worked on the engines were admiringly called *gueules noires,* "black mugs," though it must have been a stretch for the mousy-looking Baptiste to live up to the image. Railwaymen could even flex their political muscle for real, by joining, as most railway workers did, one of the two left-wing unions, the Socialist CGT or the Communist CGTU. The age of great railway strikes was over by 1933—the last big one was in 1920—but, as we shall see, the union and party could still do a lot for their members in a time of crisis. Railway work placed an employee securely in the upper tier of the working class and earned enough that workers did not have to fear falling back into the ranks of the real proletariat.[38]

To work for the railways in France between the wars was to enter a distinctive world, one that was privileged, to be sure, but also bureaucratic, paternalistic, and isolating. There were the myriad regulations for every job, and endless paperwork to go with them—workers joked that if they really started following the rules every train in France would come to a stop.[39] The price paid for a good job was isolation, both from one's roots and to some extent from the world at large. Like Baptiste and Antoine, most railway employees—about six in ten—lived and worked far from their provinces of origin. While this may not be unusual in the United States today, it was atypical of French life between the wars, when people expected to live out their lives close to home. In most cases, geographical displacement was compounded by social estrangement, with parents and their better educated children inhabiting different cultural worlds as well. Finally, the men who worked on the trains had odd schedules and shifts that made it difficult to socialize with anybody, much less workers in other occupations.[40] All of this is related to the tragedy that befell the Nozières: whatever pathologies prevailed on the sixth floor of 9 Rue de Madagascar, they were at the very least magnified by the fact that the family lived in a social vacuum.

When Baptiste arrived in Paris, he settled in the twelfth arrondissement, just as the semifictional Antoine did in the thirteenth. Every small or middle-sized town had a "station neighborhood," and in Paris there were two main eastern *quartiers de la gare:* the one around the Gare de Lyon, just north of the Seine, and to the south a section of the thirteenth around the Gare d'Austerlitz. These neighborhoods were both heavily populated by railway employees, many of them young single men who rented a room, worked hard at the depot, and caroused with their bachelor colleagues when they were off duty. Sex was available from the sort of women who catered to travelers and workers around every railway station. The fictional Antoine made their acquaintance in Tours, "those bareheaded, slipper-wearing girls who paced the endless walls of the railway lines under the green haloes of the gaslights." The women's rooms were in earshot of the engines, they knew the train schedules by heart, and they charged little for their services.[41]

Did Baptiste visit prostitutes? We know little of his life outside work until, at the age of twenty-eight, he met Germaine and moved in with her. Before entering domestic life, he most likely rented a room from a landlady who did his washing and cleaning; he would have been a regular at lunch with other men, ordering the stewed meat with vegetables because it was cheaper than a steak or a cutlet, washing it down with a quarter-liter of red wine, sharing in the sexual or anticlerical banter that would make a whole table of men hoot with laughter: "If a church collapses, you'll only get a bunch of dead ignorants, imbeciles, or crazies!"[42]

Political attitudes in these neighborhoods were divided between traditional left-wing loyalties and truculent skepticism. Railway workers read the Socialist *L'Œuvre,* the Communist *L'Humanité,* or the ostensibly apolitical (it hid its right-wing leanings) mass daily *Le Petit Parisien.* Baptiste, probably a *L'Humanité* reader, could never have imagined that one day his photograph would appear on the cover of all three. Some workers were naively hopeful: "In the new regime, we will take turns being engineers, stationmasters." Most, according to one observer, signed up with radical parties as a matter of habit and tradition: "They would have been radical [Republicans] forty years ago; they were socialists twenty years ago; they are giving in to Bolshevist pressures today. They're a docile flock."[43] Cynical as it is, this comment accurately describes what we know of Baptiste's politics. He belonged to a Communist trade union, but there is no evidence that his membership amounted to anything more than simply what was expected in the workplace. Nothing suggests that he harbored concerns about anything beyond his job and his family. As one of his colleagues put it after his death, "He was a rose-water Communist who signed up with the party just so they'd give him some peace."[44]

By the 1920s France had been living for half a century under the Third Republic, a heavily parliamentary political system that offered a modicum of stability while its political class lurched from scandal to scandal. In the late 1880s a presidential son-in-law was caught peddling political access from the Élysée palace; in the early 1890s the French learned that deputies were paid off handsomely to support the French company that was planning the Panama Canal; at the turn of the century, the treachery and cover-ups that led to the unjust conviction of the Jewish Captain Dreyfus besmirched the whole French army; in 1899 President Félix Faure died of a stroke in his office, pinning his mistress under his considerable bulk, and in 1914 the wife of center-left politician Joseph Caillaux was acquitted after shooting and killing a newspaper editor who had printed her husband's personal letters. The last great charismatic voice on the left, the socialist Jean Jaurès, who had been calling for the country to resist the rush to armed conflict, was murdered at the end of July 1914, three days before France declared war on Germany. The war left France depopulated and demoralized, and after the Russian Revolution the French Left split in two. Cynicism and disengagement in many quarters may have been inevitable.

Workers in the thirteenth arrondissement were quick to denounce all politicians, especially prominent figures on the left, such as Aristide Briand, Alexandre Millerand, or "that pig of a Caillaux," who got rich playing ball with all those other bigwigs. "Those people, they just used us!" was a typical refrain. "Politics is just a bunch of deal-making. Our sort don't really get it, they don't tell us what's really going on. . . . Then there's those that want to have a revolution! Well, buddy, I'm not wishing their revolution on you or me or anyone else." As for the unions, they took your money, all right, but where were they when you really needed them? A contemporary described politics in the district as "many indifferents and a few revolutionaries."[45] Things were not very different across the river. Pierre Toulon, born in 1908, son of a factory worker and a concierge in the twelfth arrondissement, looked back on his childhood and said that his father never talked politics, never said whom he voted for: "Actually, I think he didn't give a damn." His wife's brother was a militant Communist, but the rest of her family was equally indifferent: "Dad was sort of a socialist, but he never went on strike. . . . The truth is, we really weren't that interested." The family read the ostensibly apolitical *Le Petit Parisien*, which gave pride of place to sensational crimes over worker unrest.[46]

Baptiste built his career in his twenties, rising through the ranks from mechanic to the coveted, well-paid position of engine driver. Only at the age of twenty-eight did he settle down with the handsome twenty-four-year-old divorcee Germaine Hézard. They met as neighbors living on the same landing of a building at 10 Rue Montgallet, very near the Gare de Lyon. In the spring of 1913 Baptiste and Germaine moved from their separate quarters on the sixth floor of the building to a three-room flat on the third floor.[47] They may have encountered some disapproval from the neighbors, but their families were far away and in any case in the French countryside premarital sex and even conception had long been tolerated if the couple was clearly headed for the altar. Pregnancies before marriage were not uncommon among railway couples at the time.[48] Besides, Germaine's divorce did not come through until January 1914. She was four months pregnant when the couple married in their Paris neighborhood on August 17, 1914, two weeks after France entered the war. They returned to Neuvy for the birth, and Germaine's widowed mother was there to welcome the little girl who arrived on January 11, 1915. She was baptized Violette—a flower name, fashionable but not all that common, for a pretty little girl.[49] Only later were some people to see a grim coincidence in the fact that it began with *viol*, the French word for rape.

Baptiste's job saved him from the killing fields of World War I. The country needed its trains running more than ever now that soldiers and weaponry had to be transported to and from the front. Railway employees usually avoided combat duty, to the annoyance of other workers, who sometimes unfairly branded them as shirkers, *planqués*.[50] Even if Baptiste had to be away a lot more, the couple and their baby were able to settle into life in a new apartment at 9 Rue de Madagascar.

Rue de Madagascar, about three hundred feet long, is today entirely residential and devoid of street life, but in the 1920s and 1930s it was lined with no less than twenty-five shops. Simone Mayeul, who grew up next door to Violette and her parents, told me there was everything you needed on the street—butchers, grocers, dairy stores, shoemakers, sewing and notions shops. On Tuesdays and Fridays you could go to the big market on Rue de Charenton a few blocks away, but mostly all you might want was right there on the street.[51] Another old-timer confirmed, "Those people lived just about in autarky, with every shop they needed right there. You'd have thought you were in the provinces." Because everyone shopped in the same small emporia, they learned much about each others' business— who was entertaining big, for instance, because they rushed their roasts over to the baker's oven.[52] There was a lot of on-street sociability, especially in the summer months, when people set chairs on the sidewalk to watch the children play; in the evenings groups of men spent hours standing together smoking pipes and talking.[53]

The street was a world unto itself, with its own character and reputation. Rue de Madagascar was "serious," Simone Mayeul insisted, a respectable place, very well considered. With 676 inhabitants in 1931, the street's population was twice the size of Prades', half that of Neuvy's. Germaine and Baptiste were back in a village of sorts, but its inhabitants were city people. The men were railroad employees, office workers, electricians and plumbers, shopkeepers. The women worked as seamstresses, secretaries, or shop attendants, or kept house.[54] "Serious" meant that the street included few factory workers and no bars or prostitutes.

Much can go on, of course, in the tranquil lives of ordinary people on a "serious" street. Take Ernest Landry, a middle-aged grocer on Rue de Madagascar in 1933 who had a lovely wife, Marcelle, and a small daughter. A single woman named Yvonne Mercier began to spend a lot of time in the store chatting with Mme Landry. Yvonne was the object of local gossip because at thirty-four she had neither a husband nor a boyfriend, nor did she project the image of a future old maid. In fact, her "silhouette" was described by local denizens as that of a *garçonne,* a 1920s-style androgynous flapper—not a common sight in a popular neighborhood. Ernest soon had an unpleasant feeling about Yvonne and his wife's friendship: "The rumor, at first remote, got closer and closer: every day neighbors brought new information that confirmed the abominable truth," and one day Landry caught the two women in flagrante. When—by his account—he asked Yvonne to leave his wife alone, she laughed and taunted him like a film noir villain: "Wherever you go, I'll manage to see her." He shot her with a revolver he had just purchased. The neighborhood closed ranks around the murderer.[55] Yvonne Mercier lived in the same building as the Nozières and was shot two months before Violette committed her crime.

The grocer couple had one child. So did the Nozières, as well as a majority of families in the neighborhood.[56] In 1931, when Violette was sixteen, 9 Rue de Madagascar, a six-floor building with a front and back unit, housed forty families. Eleven of them had a single child; only five had two. The only large brood, the four Maunet boys, belonged to a poor family; their father was a deliveryman. The parents of single children, by contrast, were railway or office workers, or skilled craftsmen: Simone Mayeul next door was the only child of an electrician. The pattern extended to the street as a whole, where in 1931 the dominant family model by far was a couple or a widowed parent with a single child. There were one hundred and six such families on Rue de Madagascar, as opposed to only thirty-four with two or more offspring. Baptiste and Germaine, who practiced birth control by means of coitus interruptus, chose deliberately to have only one child, and in this they were utterly typical of people of their class and time.

In the late nineteenth century, the French stopped having big families: between 1900 and 1939 the population grew only by 3 percent, while that of Germany increased by 36 percent and that of Italy by 33 percent. The First World War compounded a difficult situation: with a million and a half Frenchmen dead and hundreds of thousands incapacitated, many French-women were unable to marry.[57] But the war alone cannot be blamed for the demographic "hollow years" of the 1930s, since birthrates had dropped precipitously starting in the 1890s, especially in cities. Suddenly poorer people had started behaving like richer folks and limiting births for the sake of a better life. A third or more of the families of craftsmen, railway workers, office workers of both sexes, and generally families where women went out to work at better jobs chose to have only one child; only a tiny proportion had more than two. Even for factory workers, the average number of children per family was slightly under two.[58]

There were probably many reasons why a couple like the Nozières decided to have only one child. For one thing, there was nobody to forbid it: even practicing Catholics in France had few qualms about birth control, and nothing suggests that the Nozières were religious. Most of all, the motive seems to have been social ambition. With Baptiste expecting to earn good money, there would be no need to send children out to work in their teens; on the contrary, it would be best to have one child, so you could comfortably support a lengthy course of studies and bask in the re-

Figure 1. The dining room at Rue de Madagascar after the crime, with Violette's sleeping cot. (Courtesy Archives de Paris, D2 U8 379 and 380.)

flected glory of having raised a teacher, doctor, or engineer. Even a girl could enter the professions, and if she did not, with a good education and a dowry she might snare a well-heeled son-in-law.

Yet another reason to have a single child was a severe lack of space, a common problem in Paris at this time. Nine Rue de Madagascar is made up of two buildings separated by an inner courtyard, each composed of six floors with three flats per floor. The Nozières moved into a cramped two-room apartment on the sixth floor of the back building, which, over the course of the investigation, was to become the best known flat in Paris. A tiny entrance hall opened to the right onto a front room taken up by a dining-room set—table, chairs, and sideboard—in the heavy, faux-Renaissance style popular then in the middle classes (fig. 1). The back room, where the couple slept, was similarly crammed with furniture: a double bed, a dresser, and a closet fronted by a curtain that the crime was to make notorious. Between the two rooms were a tiny galley kitchen that doubled as a bathroom and an unusual luxury for such a place—the family's

Figure 2. The kitchen at Rue de Madagascar. (Courtesy Archives de Paris, D2 U8 379 and 380.)

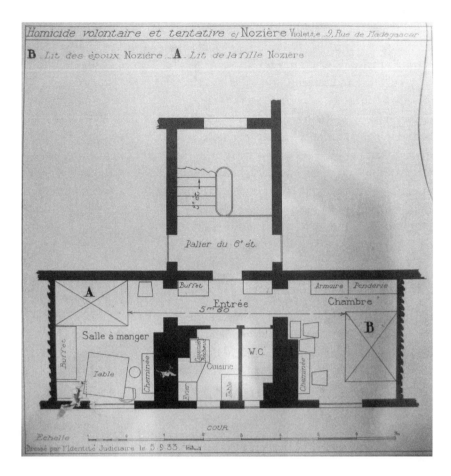

Figure 3. Floor plan of the Nozières' apartment from the case records. (Courtesy Archives de Paris, D2 U8 379 and 380.)

toilet (figs. 2 and 3). Violette did not have any space to herself: she slept on a folding cot set up every night in the dining room by the sideboard. Busy wallpaper and the family's decorative possessions—antimacassars, lace curtains, family portraits, and a calendar—add to the claustrophobic feel of the place.[59] Birth control seems an understandable response to these cramped surroundings, which must surely, later on, have exacerbated Violette's feeling of entrapment.

Lack of space was near universal in interwar Paris, which was experiencing a citywide housing shortage. Inflation, long leases, and government-mandated rent control made housing affordable but by the same token discouraged both new building and even upkeep by landlords, so that dwellings, even for workers of some means, tended to be small and decrepit.[60] Parisians who grew up between the wars reminisce about folding cots, curtains and screens, and toilets on the landing or outdoors.

Aline Tourneux, the concierge's daughter, recalled sharing the concierge lodge with her parents and sister. The single room contained a big bed, a mirrored armoire, a coal stove, and a table. At night the girls' folding cot went up, as did a screen in front of the parents' bed. There was no water in the lodge: you washed in the courtyard. "We lived on top of each other, but my sister and I never saw anything that might have shocked us. I don't know how my parents managed it." A few blocks away, her future husband lived the same way, sharing a dark two-room flat with his parents and brother: "In the dining room everything folded, I mean the table for meals and the cot where my brother and I slept, as the room was very small." If you needed to wash, you went to the nearby public showers.[61] Similarly, a woman in the neighboring eleventh recalled an apartment much like the Nozières': thirty-three square meters for a family of four, a minuscule kitchen, and a toilet but no bathroom. The girls shared a folding bed in a room as wide as the span of one's arms. "We had no shower. In those days if you'd had one put in, it would have been pretty darn expensive for one thing, and then we would have seemed pretentious."[62]

Like their neighbors, the Nozières led a life that was cramped, modest, and economical. They were reasonably well off and could have been more so had Germaine gone back to work, as did so many women in her situation. Six out of ten single French women worked at the time, as did four out of ten wives, a higher proportion than anywhere else in Europe.[63] Germaine chose, however, to remain a housewife. Her choice was dictated by both logistics and tradition. The wives of engine drivers were usually, like Germaine, of very modest origins: they came from villages or small towns, most often from peasant families, and had worked as seamstresses, domestics, or laundresses. Almost always, they stopped working after marriage, even before having children, and they rarely took a job after the kids were grown. Their husbands' schedules were erratic, and custom decreed that a woman had to be home to feed her man, no matter what. Since their families of origin were far away and their husbands traveled for days at a time, work and child-rearing together would have been impossible.[64] And then it was the custom, the way it had always been for railway families: there was even an expression, *faire la cheminote,* which referred to staying home if you were married to the rail. On the Rue de Madagascar, there were twenty-three families of PLM workers; only one included a working wife.[65] According to a neighbor, Germaine rarely went out; she "was always doing housework, too much of it really, always throwing dust and shaking rags out the windows."[66]

Though Germaine's stay-at-home status was dictated by her husband's work, there was more to it. The nonworking wife has frequently been a status symbol among the upwardly mobile of modest origins, a sign of the husband's ability to provide, and certainly at the time in France it served as a claim to bourgeois identity.[67] Germaine was an aloof and difficult woman, but some of the hostility she drew in the neighborhood before and in the wake of the crime had to do with her nonworking status. If she was going to be so high and mighty as to stay home without working, shouldn't she have done a better job of raising the girl? Jealousy and resentment in the building and beyond were palpable in the weeks after the crime.

The housebound nature of Germaine's existence balanced her husband's peripatetic job; he was away for days at a time driving engines on the Vichy line. Other than that, the Nozières led a circumscribed life devoid of distractions beyond a Sunday stroll in the Bois de Vincennes and annual summer vacations, courtesy of the PLM, in either Neuvy or Prades. Baptiste did have one hobby: like other senior railwaymen, he grew vegetables in the victory garden bestowed on him by the company near the Porte de Charenton at the eastern end of the district.

The policy of giving rail workers access to urban gardens was either a progressive contribution to worker well-being or yet another canny form of paternalistic control. An official of the northern line explained in a 1922 speech that the policy was a way of reconnecting railwaymen from peasant backgrounds with the soil they came from, while providing them with a healthy alternative to bars and other vices: "Nothing has the moralizing force of nature, and I know of no other sport equal to that of gardening. . . . Don't you believe, gentlemen, that thus we are able to reconcile nature with its most cruel enemy, the railroad?"[68] Symbolically, the railwaymen's gardens acknowledged that the men who worked them were country boys whose jobs had put them on a fast track into the urban future. For all of its consoling power, the garden could not always compensate for the kind of social dislocation that led the fictional Antoine Bloyé eventually to commit suicide. Baptiste loved his garden, loved cultivating vegetables and with them, no doubt, his memories of a hamlet in the mountains of central France. As we shall see, however, there may have been evil slithering across Baptiste Nozière's little patch of Eden.

Germaine and Baptiste Nozière lived in a village in the city, a few miles distant but still far, far away from the skullduggery of Third Republic politics and the Paris of André Gide, Pablo Picasso, and Coco Chanel. When the world came to their doorstep, did they even venture out to explore it? From May to November 1931, the Bois de Vincennes, barely a mile from their apartment, was the site of Paris's huge International Colonial Exposition, timed to coincide with the centennial of France's conquest of Algeria. For six months some eight million visitors, half of them Parisians, came to visit the 272 acres of an extravagant theme park mostly devoted to France's colonial possessions. The centerpiece of the exposition was a huge reproduction, bigger than Paris's own Sacré-Cœur, of the Cambodian Angkor Wat temple. From there you could stroll down a broad and handsome Colonial Avenue to visit a West African village, a Moroccan souk, and a market in Martinique. Nothing that France owned was left out, not even Saint Pierre and Miquelon, represented by a lakeside fisherman's hut and a lighthouse. Other sovereign nations were invited to represent themselves, and although some demurred, Herbert Hoover reluctantly agreed to contribute a replica of Mount Vernon staffed with bewigged extras.[69]

Did the Nozières ever visit the exposition? It would have been hard not to, unless Baptiste was enough of a true believer to heed the Communist Party's call to boycott the extravaganza. Opponents of colonialism were invited instead to an exhibition jointly organized by Communists and Surrealists, "The Truth about the Colonies," which offered photographic evidence of exploitation as well as statues of the Virgin Mary labeled "European Fetishes."[70] The International Colonial Exposition was aimed precisely at people like the Nozières and their neighbors in the twelfth, as a lure away from unpatriotic leftism. The direction of the exposition fell to Marshal Hubert Lyautey, the officer most conspicuously identified with colonial ventures. Before the First World War, Lyautey had served in Indochina, Madagascar, and North Africa, energetically "pacifying" Algerian resistance and maintaining a balance between rival tribes in Morocco. Even with his colonial career behind him, Lyautey seemed unable to kick the habit of pacification, which is why he opted for the exposition's eastern location: the exhibition was designed to bring "social peace" to the working-class districts of eastern Paris by offering them access to the wonders of colonialism and thus diverting them from Communist sympathies.[71]

The Bois de Vincennes, where the colonial exposition took place, marked the eastern end of Paris, the farthest of a series of places on the edge of the city where Violette's journey into notoriety began: Rue de Madagascar and the working-class neighborhoods around it, the Gare de Lyon with its influx of immigrants and travelers, the garden at Porte de Charenton where her father tended his patch of vegetables. In 1933 France's capital was still a constellation of separate neighborhoods, and many Parisians spent their life mostly within the confines of their villagelike *quartiers*. That was not to be the case for Violette Nozière. Ambition, desire, and a need to escape would eventually make hers a trajectory that embraced a wide span of the city's separate worlds.

TWO

# Interwar Girlhoods

VIOLETTE'S CHILDHOOD WAS UNREMARKABLE. She was the cherished only child of a family well integrated into its surroundings—decent people from the heart of France perfectly poised to achieve their modest ambitions. If anyone knew that Germaine had been divorced and that her child arrived a few months "early," none of that would have stacked up against the Nozières' blatant domestic propriety. Baptiste earned good money and was visibly devoted to the handsome, strong-minded woman he had married; not one to linger in cafés, he came straight home after work and handed over his paychecks to his wife. There was no sign of marital discord, and the uxorious Baptiste wanted nothing more than to trail along to the market with his wife or take walks in the Bois de Vincennes with the little family.

Violette was duly cosseted and coaxed. Her mother breast-fed her until she was almost two, and never left her side until the little girl entered the public primary school on nearby Rue de Wattignies at age five, staying there until she graduated at age twelve with a primary school certificate. Six years later, teachers had positive if somewhat indistinct memories of her: "She was a nice little girl, industrious, quite intelligent, worked well, she gave me entire satisfaction. She was an average student who never stood out." Not standing out was evidently a good thing: "She was all-around average," recalled another teacher. "She never got noticed in any way and left only a good impression." One teacher did remember that she was very spoiled, especially by her mother, who tolerated no criticism of her darling, even when the teachers thought the girl deserved them.[1]

Schooling for everyone was a core value of Republican France. The Revolution of 1789 aimed to wrest education away from the clergy, but it took a century of struggle through the regime changes of the nineteenth century for Republicans to attain their goal of free, universal, state-sponsored education for girls and boys aged six to thirteen, thanks to the Ferry Laws of 1881–82.[2] The monuments to that triumph can still be seen in the streets of every French town: the solid old stone buildings where today, decades after coeducation has become the norm, the French flag surmounts a lintel still inscribed "École de Filles" or "École de Garçons." Although in theory public schools dispensed a democratic and neutral education, they were staffed by teachers loyal to the state, and their curriculum boosted secular Republicanism by, for instance, presenting the French Revolution as a positive event or teaching moral and civic values with no reference to religion. Private religious schools were still available for a fee, but they were deemed academically inferior, especially for boys.

The elites of the Third Republic were far from indifferent to female education, since women were considered vulnerable to the retrograde influence of priests. An 1880 law created state-sponsored secondary education for girls, although it was fee-paying and, of course, optional. Its proponents argued that properly educated mothers could raise sons as patriotic citizens and help avoid another defeat by Germany.[3] The regime thus paradoxically continued the Republican tradition of encouraging female education while refusing to give women voting rights, which they achieved only in 1944.

Germaine and Baptiste were evidently good Republicans, but their focus on Violette's education surely had more to do with the pursuit of social and professional success than with ideology. For the Nozière parents and the unremarkable student Violette, the next step after primary school seemed perfectly clear: she would attend what was called an *école primaire supérieure,* a higher primary school, for a few years in preparation for going out into the workforce. Extended primary schooling for girls was also created in 1880, providing what amounted to a female alternative to hands-on apprenticeships for boys; the extra schooling for girls served as preparation for office or retail work or as a lower-class "finishing school" for domestic life. The upper primary school curriculum lasted three years and offered a combination of home economics, shorthand and typing, the basics of commerce, and foreign language instruction.[4]

There were no upper primary schools for girls in the twelfth; Violette attended, along with at least one friend from her primary school, the École Sophie Germain in the center of Paris. The young girl had to travel a few districts westward, no doubt by metro and in her mother's company, to the Saint-Paul neighborhood on the right bank, just a few blocks away from the Île Saint-Louis and the medieval heart of Paris. The areas along the Seine between the Marais and the Hôtel de Ville, nowadays expensively gentrified, were still shabby working-class neighborhoods in the 1930s, but the experience of the city must have left its mark on Violette: this was her first extended encounter with life outside the urban village around the Rue de Madagascar. A head shot of Violette from around the time she entered Sophie Germain shows a quintessential "good girl": demurely attractive, serious looking, wearing an elegant blouse and a gold medal on a chain (fig. 4).

Had her parents not entertained higher aspirations for her, Violette's educational trajectory would probably have been similar to that of her friend Madeleine Debize, her companion on the night after the crime, whom she knew from elementary school. Madeleine lived a short distance from Violette, in a family also typical of its place and time. She was the only child of a father who did interior painting and carpentry and an office-worker mother. She had a few years of post-primary training, also at Sophie Germain, which included shorthand and typing, the basics of commerce, and language instruction. Her parents encouraged her to work up her language skills with trips to England, an extensive stay in Germany, and even conversation sessions with a German student upon her return. By her late teens Madeleine held down a rather glamorous job as a trilingual secretary for an impresario in Montmartre.[5]

Madeleine Debize and her mother embodied the most important trend in employment, especially women's employment, in France between the wars: the rise of the office worker. Over the course of the Third Republic, from the 1880s to the 1930s, the number of white-collar workers in France tripled, while that of factory workers did not even double. The emblematic figure of this change was the typist-secretary: there were fifty of them in Paris in 1886, three thousand by 1900, and tens of thousands between the wars, when the job became massively feminized. The mouthful of a word *sténodactylographe* was early on shortened to *dactylo,* always assumed to be female. In the nineteenth century, the so-called *midinette* was an emblematic

Figure 4. Violette in her early teens. (Courtesy Archives de Paris, D2 U8 379 and 380.)

figure of Parisian life—the young, attractive female garment worker immortalized in the figures of *La Bohème*'s Mimi and Musetta. The *dactylo* was her direct descendant: the sexy, stylish, working Parisienne.[6]

Office workers like Madeleine lived where they had grown up but stood out from the bulk of the population of their districts because they wore chic, citified clothes. One contemporary observer described a Saturday lunchtime in a restaurant in the thirteenth arrondissement. At one table were railway workers in drab garments; at another sat an office worker, "a woman of about thirty wearing an elegant outfit with an open collar; her carefully waved hair . . . [was] piled atop her head." Nearby a male employee with a haughty expression, wearing rings on his fingers and an open-collared suit, waited with a bouquet of carnations; he was soon joined by two loud young women in black dresses and velvet high-heeled shoes. Descriptions like this remind one of how important and striking *actual* white collars and cuffs could be in a working-class area, especially in a sea of off-gray working clothes of "the hue that betrays a poor laboring crowd." With their "starched collars and cuffs, fashionable suits, furs, feathered hats, gold rings and chains," office workers were the nouveaux riches of their plebeian neighborhoods, sniffed the middle-class man who recorded these scenes.[7]

But what worker would not want this for his or her child—a sit-down job, elegant clothes, and regular pay? At a time when youngsters could start bringing home money by their mid-teens, education beyond elementary school was considered, for poorer folks, "a sacrifice." In the generation before Violette's, the goal of poorer parents was typically for a child to get an elementary school certificate at age twelve or thirteen. Aline Lucas, born in 1904, explained: "My mother was a worker, she wanted us to be happier than she was. She sent me to school up to the [elementary] certificate." Between the wars, extended primary schooling was seen as the way out of the working class, for girls as well as boys; in 1881 under a quarter of students in upper primary schools were female, and by 1938 girls outnumbered boys. In 1932 a female shopkeeper in Lyon said of her daughter, an only child: "I did not hesitate to send her to the upper primary school, even though it cost me. . . . I wanted her to have a commercial degree to get a good job."[8]

The small size of families and high incidence of only children in early-twentieth-century France must be among the main reasons why girls as well as boys were pushed to excel in their studies. There are plenty of instances, even at the turn of the century, of working-class families saving up and encouraging a single daughter to rise above them socially, for instance by studying to become a schoolteacher.[9] For the kind of family Violette came from, in a social world where school rather than church conferred prestige and set social norms, educational ambition was gender-blind.[10]

So it was only natural for Violette to go on with her studies, though at this stage things did not go as well as before. After breezing through primary school, the young girl had to repeat her first year at Sophie Germain, not strictly for academic reasons but because of failing health. A delicate child, she had suffered a ruptured appendix at age ten, but her health deteriorated around the time she changed schools. By her own account, when she got her first periods between the ages of twelve and thirteen, she suffered from incessant hemorrhaging, which led to anemia and occasional fainting spells. A short time later, she developed sinusitis and stomach aches. At the time, the family doctor explained these as "growth-related" problems.[11] Later on, physicians who examined her health history in the context of the police investigation came to believe that most of these illnesses were much exaggerated or psychosomatic in origin.[12]

In the three years she spent at Sophie Germain, these were not the only problems the young girl developed. When she left the school in May 1930, her teachers took a dim view of the fifteen-year-old: "Fairly good conduct, good behavior in class, must be watched outside," one of them wrote. "Good-tempered but lacks energy and straightforwardness," noted another. "Average intelligence, does not apply herself. Left for health reasons." A third teacher was more explicitly damning: "Lazy, devious, hypocritical, vain, avoids work, questionable behavior."[13] According to a schoolmate, Violette had been "frequenting" the boys at the nearby Lycée Charlemagne.[14]

Germaine and Baptiste's next decision for their daughter's education was a surprising one. Was it concern for her health or her morals, or social ambition? They brought her closer to home but enrolled her in secondary school. There was no girls' lycée in the area, but secondary classes for girls were offered at the local boys' high school, the Lycée Voltaire.[15]

It was around this time that Violette probably became sexually active. Her first lover may have been a certain Jean G., a childhood friend in Neuvy, or Raymond Rierciardelli, a boy six years older than she who worked as a mechanic and lived across from her on Rue de Madagascar. Violette and Raymond were an item in the summer and fall of 1931, though whether they actually slept together is unclear. After Violette's arrest, Raymond told the police he "frequented" her for a few months, using a French verb which, like "date," can refer either to going out as a couple or more specifically to sexual intercourse. He downplayed their relationship and insisted it was platonic, but others around them were not so sure.[16] Baptiste's friend, colleague, and fellow building resident Arsène Chausse said that "everyone in the neighborhood knew of the liaison except for the parents" and that he took it upon himself to inform Violette's father of what was going on.[17] Under pressure from her parents, Violette produced a letter to Raymond in which she broke off the relationship to "focus on her studies." Raymond's memory of Violette was that "she was not very consistent. One day she said she wanted to become a doctor, the next day it was a teacher." Violette's parents must have been horrified that their sixteen-year-old had a boyfriend, let alone a man in his twenties with grease on his clothes who hailed from a poor Italian family.[18]

Violette soon found a more glamorous suitor, probably the first boyfriend who mattered to her. Around Easter of 1932, she met the older brother of a girl she went to school with. Pierre Camus, a medical student, said he had been struck by the young girl's interestingly melancholy demeanor—no doubt also by her pale, slender good looks. The son and grandson of doctors, this young man was a real bourgeois. Photos of Camus later published in the newspapers show him sporting the look fashionable among the middle-class student youth of the time and familiar from pictures of the young Sartre: hair parted sideways and slicked down, horn-rimmed glasses, a debonair pipe and ironic smile. He treated Violette to drinks in cafés; she was reserved and mysterious, and suffered from inexplicable bouts of depression and crying jags. Later, when Violette was in serious trouble, Pierre asserted, as Raymond had done, that he never had sex with her.[19]

Where Violette's parents were concerned, however, neither Pierre's social and educational credentials nor the nature of the relationship would have made any difference: Violette was sixteen, still in school, and not supposed to be seeing boys at all, platonically or otherwise. Although by the spring of 1932 Violette already had quite a reputation in the neighborhood, her mother claimed that it was only around this time that she became suspicious. One day she found a note in the pocket of the smock Violette wore to school, which read: "Pierre, my Pierre, what is to become of me? What should I do, I have no idea, after what I've learned, but I forgive you and still love you."[20] It was typical of Violette that she calmly told her furious mother that the note was a rough draft for a school writing exercise. It was typical of Germaine that, even though there was a phone number scribbled on the paper, she made herself believe her daughter's lie.

Violette was often absent from class with another of her mysterious illnesses, a form of "typhoid fever." A schoolmate, Betty Gajiecky, later reported that Violette did well in school and was usually near the top of the class despite her absences; Violette had told Betty that her mother wanted her to become a mathematics teacher.[21] Violette's teachers were not so sanguine. She worked hard in the fall trimester and then was increasingly absent from classes in the next two quarters. The headmistress advised her parents to withdraw her from school. She had been spotted outside the lycée with a young man, and the school administration told her father she should be sent away from Paris. The reports on the young girl were strikingly similar to those from her previous school: "Conduct quite good, good behavior in class, must be watched outside. Good natured, lacks energy and forthrightness, average intelligence, insufficient diligence, left for health reasons."[22]

At the end of the 1931–32 school year, Germaine and Baptiste, who seemed to regard ever more schooling as the solution to problems with their daughter, made an extraordinary move: they enrolled her in the oldest and most prestigious girls' lycée in Paris. They were able to do so thanks to a lucky personal connection. A M. Duchemin, who taught mathematics in a famous boys' lycée in Paris, happened to spend his summers in Neuvy-sur-Loire. Duchemin later told a Paris newspaper, "One day Violette Nozière's mother brought her to me. She was happy and proud and looked at her child with wonder." Madame Nozière said that Violette had some "big plans" for her education, that she was preparing for the prestigious École de Sèvres, and would Duchemin help her work on her mathematics. M. Duchemin gave the girl some geometry problems, was impressed by her mathematical talent, and suggested the classes at Lycée Voltaire. Later on, it was he who, at the Nozières' request, recommended Violette to the headmistress of the Lycée Fénelon.[23]

The Lycée Fénelon was founded in 1883, the very first institution to provide public secondary education to girls. It is located in the heart of the Latin Quarter on the quaint Rue Saint-André-des-Arts, a short walk from the great fountain of Archangel Michael, where the Boulevard Saint-Michel meets the Seine. Violette was back in the heart of the city, mingling with middle-class students and other more dubious denizens of the Latin Quarter.

Girls' lycées, which opened slowly in France—there were only forty-one of them nationwide at the turn of the century—had two constituencies. As fee-paying institutions, they were aimed at the well-to-do. France had a long tradition of respect for the literate and cultivated upper-class woman, and the school curriculum had always included figures like the seventeenth-century Mme de Sévigné, author of witty and poignant letters.[24] The literary elites of the Third Republic specifically resurrected and cultivated the memory of eighteenth-century France, the era of the *salonnière,* as an age of both enlightenment and elegant womanhood.[25] Girls' lycées were aimed at providing young upper-middle-class women, in a secular context, with an education that would give them social and intellectual polish before they entered marriage. A prominent educator explained that young women in lycées might not memorize endless facts but would become cultivated. They would know the style of a monument and how to appreciate a painting or a statue; they would be given access to a range of books, and the "morals" class would familiarize them with Buddha and Marcus Aurelius, English utilitarianism and Kantian rationalism: "Their minds [will] become critical and tolerant."[26] There was no thought, initially, that girls would ever compete with boys, and the crowning examination of the lycée system, the baccalaureate, was offered to girls only in 1902.

The politicians who devised and implemented the laws considered, however, that it would be untoward if a republican educational institution were not in principle open to everyone on a meritocratic basis. Hence, girls' lycées always included a minority of scholarship girls, accomplished students from lower-middle-class families. In 1905, the bulk of them had parents who were schoolteachers (the largest group), white-collar workers, or shopkeepers. Only 3 percent each of scholarship students were the children of workers or peasants.[27] Even so, conservative parents feared that girls' lycées were dangerously democratic. Around 1900 a nun in Nice told a lady of her acquaintance not to send her daughter to a state secondary school: "She'll only meet butchers' daughters there." Even a liberal gentleman balked, on gendered grounds: "I don't mind if a concierge's son says *tu* [the familiar form of address] to my son in the lycée classroom, but I don't care to think of his sisters being *tutoyées* by schoolmates of lesser breeding."[28] In the early twentieth century, as the baccalaureate was opened to girls and, in 1925, girls' programs were aligned with those of boys, the female lycée remained a socially hybrid institution, a cultural finishing school for daughters of the Republican upper classes on the one hand, and a path to a career, especially school-teaching, for girls from modest backgrounds on the other. As late as 1939, only sixty-four thousand girls were enrolled in them.[29]

As for the Lycée Fénelon, it was more socially exclusive than most. Fénelon was the oldest such school and the only one that trained girls for the prestigious École Normale Supérieure, the apex of French higher education. The best in Paris and hence in the nation, with teachers all holding the coveted *agrégation,* Fénelon enrolled mainly the daughters of professors and teachers, professionals, and high civil servants.[30] Violette began classes there in October 1932. Out of her depth both socially and academically, she lasted only a few weeks, but her immersion in the life of the Latin Quarter was to prove a turning point.

Parents with girls to raise are usually concerned about two things: formal education on the one hand, sexual safety and propriety—the two are always linked—on the other. Both are understood to determine a girl's future, though the more traditional the social setting, the larger the second looms. To understand Violette's adolescence, and the reactions of others after she became notorious, we need to understand the norms of contemporaries from different social classes. How much emphasis was placed on educational achievement, how much, in theory or in practice, on decent sexual behavior? And did the norms differ from class to class?

*Vicieuse* was the word applied in interwar France to a girl of any age who showed too much knowledge of or interest in sex. The term means not "vicious" but prone to (sexual) vice, and it came to be applied routinely to Violette Nozière. In the upper classes, girls could more easily be kept ignorant of such matters, but in peasant or working-class families living conditions could expose them early to dangerous information. In modest households "vice"—inappropriate interest in sex—was a prime consideration in judging girls under thirteen: precocity was universally condemned. Other qualities expected from girls included obedience (being "docile" and "submissive" were good traits), good manners, and performance in school. Peasants were the least concerned about their daughters' intelligence and studies, but workers and middle-class parents cared a great deal about schoolwork. Parents in the lower middle classes were especially eager that their girls do well in their studies.[31]

Childhood sexual innocence was vigorously enforced in the upper classes. The twentieth century's pioneering feminist philosopher, Simone de Beauvoir, was born in 1908 to a conservative family of upper bourgeois and lower aristocrats. Her mother, although apparently happy as a young bride, considered everything having to do with the body sinful and so repellent that she never informed her daughters about what to expect at puberty. Mme de Beauvoir carefully monitored her children's reading, allowing them nothing but the safest and blandest fare; she even snatched a novel by Colette from the family maid. Simone's mother walked her two daughters to school and back, and opened and read all their letters. The Beauvoir girls prayed twice daily, went to confession twice a month, took communion three times a week, and were directed to look away if they saw a couple being affectionate on a park bench. A maid the family hired was dismissed because she went out in the evenings with men from the nearby fire station. Françoise de Beauvoir may have been more controlling than other young bourgeois matrons, but Simone suggested in her memoirs that her mother's principles and attitudes were typical of her class and time.[32]

The First World War affected in many different ways both the lives of young girls and attitudes toward them. One in ten adult Frenchmen died in the hecatomb, and many others were disabled; by the 1920s there were a million more French women than men between the ages of twenty and forty. During the conflict, women were needed for men's jobs, and they stepped in as factory hands, post office workers, and office clerks. But the war also opened up the professions to upper-class women. More of them got diplomas, since fewer were likely to wind up with husbands: both the war and its aftermath violently disrupted the balance of the sexes in France.[33]

Mary-Louise Roberts has argued that the war produced a widespread cultural crisis experienced, in large part, as tension between men and women. Veterans returned from the conflict embittered, contrasting their own shattered lives to their image of the privileged and protected existence of civilians, especially women, who had been spared the nightmare of the trenches. Writers and politicians scapegoated women for France's declining population. In July 1920, the French Chamber of Deputies ratified a bill imposing stiff penalties on anyone advocating or advertising any form of contraception or abortion. The law was the harshest of its kind in Europe in its punitive stance toward nonprocreating women. German shells were held less to blame for population decline than the selfishness of postwar women, intent on their own work and pleasure, determined to "live their life" rather than "give life." A popular novel of 1924 was entitled *Madame Does Not Want a Child*.[34]

The runaway publishing success of the early 1920s was Victor Margueritte's *La Garçonne,* which gave dramatic form to anxieties about depopulation and female emancipation. (*Garçonne* means tomboy, but in the twenties it referred to the bobbed and short-skirted flappers whose scandalous behavior was often assumed to include lesbianism.) *La Garçonne* tells the story of Monique Lherbier, a young woman from a wealthy family whose life is shattered when she discovers that the fiancé to whom she has given herself was only interested in her dowry. Disgusted by the hypocrisies of bourgeois society, especially its bartering of women, Monique rebels by embracing a life of vice that includes promiscuity, an open affair with a woman, and opium addiction. Intent on having a child, she discovers that she is sterile. In the end, the young woman is redeemed by the love of a serious young man, a veteran who likens Monique's desperate plunge into a lonely existence of soul-numbing pleasures to his own experience of the horrors of the trenches.[35]

There was plenty in the novel both to offend and to excite contemporaries—not only its scenes of the steamy goings-on in the pleasure dens of Paris but its radical author's denunciation of bourgeois sexual hypocrisy and his open advocacy, in this and other works, of equality and freedom for women. A massive success, *La Garçonne* sold twenty thousand copies in a few days upon publication and ten thousand a week in the following month; after several reprintings, one million copies were in circulation by the end of the decade despite—or perhaps because of—condemnation by the Catholic hierarchy. By one reckoning, up to a quarter of the literate public eventually read it.[36] The novel's success, beyond what it owed to voyeurism and scandal, testifies to deep worries about female independence, national sterility, and the cultural havoc caused by the war's distortion of gender expectations.

On the surface, the lives of young women from different social classes were becoming more similar between the wars. Girls from better-off working-class families were urged to stay in school longer and become city-smart office workers. Meanwhile, the worsening economic climate of the twenties and the shortage of marriageable men were pushing the daughters of bourgeois families into the professional, or even clerical, workforce. Both kinds of girl would wind up, in Paris at least, riding the metro together in their black dresses and fur-trimmed coats.

Simone de Beauvoir was of the same social class as the fictional Monique Lherbier, but her life growing up was in some material aspects more similar to Violette Nozière's. Simone's parents also came from the provinces but were solidly upper-class—landowners of minor nobility on her father's side, upper-bourgeois bankers and civil servants on her mother's.[37] If Violette grew up affluent by the standards of her milieu, Simone was impoverished compared to her bourgeois peers. Simone's mother came from a family whose fortunes had declined so sharply during the war that they were never able to make good on her dowry. Her father was a younger son with few resources, a charming, cultivated, self-indulgent man who found it hard to put his mind to gainful employment.

For Simone and her sister Hélène, especially in the years after the First World War, daily life was about deprivation and keeping up appearances.

Though the family's first apartment in Montparnasse was reasonably comfortable, like the flats of workers it featured a folding cot where little Hélène slept in a hallway while Simone shared a tiny room with the family maid. When Simone was about ten, the family was forced to move to a smaller and grimmer apartment in the same neighborhood, a fifth-floor walk-up with no balconies, where the girls shared a room so tiny there was barely enough space to get out of bed. The Beauvoirs had no running water, little heat in winter, and no live-in help. Simone bitterly resented the lack of privacy, as she was unable to escape her mother's constant surveillance.[38] The girls wore embarrassingly graceless outfits and got new clothes only when the old ones wore out. At home nothing was wasted, "not a crust of bread, a bit of string, a ribbon, or a chance to eat or drink for free." Once, when Simone was going through an especially ungainly early adolescence, she was not bought a new dress for a family wedding; her mother simply bound her growing breasts tightly with strips of cloth so she could fit, just barely, into her old one.[39]

In material terms, the lives of Violette and Simone, housed in tight quarters, wearing homemade clothes, and watching every sou, were not so different. Culturally, however, the two girls belonged to different universes. Violette spent her provincial summers in the company of illiterate rural workers, while Simone stayed in large houses named Meyrignac and La Grillière that had been in the family for generations. Violette saw her father pull off his shirt and wash at the kitchen sink every night, while Simone barely looked at her own body, having been taught that everything physical was vulgar and offensive. In Simone's world, sexual purity was a class marker: "I had been told over and over that the lower classes have no morals: the misconduct of a washerwoman or a flower girl seemed to me so self-evident it did not even scandalize me." She felt oddly "sad" when she came upon the family maid sitting on the lap of her fiancé.[40]

Schooling also drew the line between social classes. It was a given that the Beauvoir children would not go to public school: the best lycées offered primary as well as secondary classes, but Simone's father feared that the girls would be contaminated by companions of a lower class.[41] Moral corruption by lower-class children was a major concern for the bourgeoisie, as Berthe Bernage explained in her 1928 etiquette book. Children should be placed in good private schools whenever possible, Bernage wrote. Where circumstances make a public elementary school the only choice, "choose one where the teachers have the best moral stature; watch out whom your child chooses as companions; use family training and good examples to undo any bad habits in speech and deportment that unrefined schoolmates might communicate."[42]

While Françoise would have liked to enroll her daughters in an exclusive convent school like the one she had attended, she had to compromise and send them merely to a Catholic lay academy, the Cours Adeline Désir. In the early years of schooling at the Cours Désir, mothers accompanied their daughters to the school and stayed in the classroom knitting and embroidering while the little girls were instructed in history, geography, languages, and the tenets of the Catholic faith. The school was quite rigorous academically, but teachers assumed that their pupils were destined either for marriage and motherhood or for the convent. The "general culture" course taught young ladies how to curtsy, preside over tea parties, and address an important person in the correct manner. The yearly prizes were given out not for academic achievement but for piety, devotion to duty, and deportment.[43]

Georges de Beauvoir was no feminist, but ironically he encouraged his daughters' careers for the most conservative of reasons: "You girls will not get married, he often said. You have no dowry, so you will have to work."[44] To people in the Beauvoirs' world, marriage without a dowry was unthinkable, and Georges was enough of a religious skeptic to rule out the convent. The most obvious and acceptable job for an unmarried woman was teaching, preferably in a private school, and Simone was accordingly allowed to sit for the academically demanding baccalaureate, which had just recently been opened to girls. Her sister Hélène had artistic inclinations and was able to enroll in art school, also with a view to a possible teaching career. For women lower down the social scale, work and motherhood were not incompatible: Violette's mother did not work, but her friend Madeleine's did. For daughters of the bourgeoisie, a job as a teacher of younger children or a librarian was acceptable only as an alternative to marriage, if a shortage of men or money made the latter impossible. Simone de Beauvoir had to wear down her parents before they gave her permission to take university classes and to concentrate in philosophy as a path to more specialized lycée teaching.

In yet another area the lives of upper-middle-class girls differed from those of lower-middle-class women like Violette: the nature and structure of social life. A family like the Nozières lived in a world where social ties, such as they were, grew out of proximity on the job and in the neighborhood. There is no indication that such links were in any way consciously cultivated through visits and invitations. One of the neighbors who spoke to the police in September 1933, Arsène Chausse, had known Baptiste Nozière since 1909. The two men had been colleagues for twenty-four years, had lived in the same building for eighteen, and considered each other friends. Chausse described their relationship using an unusual verb: "We 'neighbored' [voisinions] a lot"—they interacted as neighbors.[45] From all of the descriptions of life on Rue de Madagascar, it appears that social contact was a matter of regular but unplanned encounters in the stairway or courtyard, at the concierge's lodge, on the sidewalk, and in neighborhood stores. As for the wider city, it was pretty much a social desert to those who lived in the twelfth.

In the upper classes, by contrast, social life and connections were the object of diligent intelligence-gathering, planning, and cultivation, most of it carried out by the women of the family. Nothing was left to chance. At the age of ten, Simone became fast friends with a little girl named Élisabeth Le Coin (called Zaza in Beauvoir's memoirs) who, like her, attended the exclusive Cours Désir. The girls' friendship prompted the Beauvoir parents immediately to try to figure out who the Le Coins were. They happily discovered that the father was a highly placed engineer for the railways, that the mother hailed from a "dynasty of militant Catholics," and that they shared common acquaintances. The little girls were allowed to play.[46] Nine years later, Zaza's family forbade her from marrying the man she loved because upon investigation it turned out that his mother, who lived in a distant provincial town, had entertained an adulterous affair—a debacle that Simone believed to have precipitated Zaza's death from an unspecified illness.

Participation in social duties with their mothers was one of the foremost responsibilities of upper-class young girls, although by the interwar years they were more likely to grumble openly about rituals such as the endless round of afternoon visits. Because her family's lack of money made marriage prospects unlikely, Simone was spared the worst of this, but her friend Zaza was not. In her later teens, the latter endured constant hectoring by her mother, who chided her for spending too much time on studies, reading, and music at the expense of her "social duties." One summer, Zaza expressed her anger by gashing her own leg with an ax to escape the constant round of social occasions and have a chance to read. Most of the time, however, Zaza and Simone's friends "easily played their role in the social world; they were present for their mother's 'day,' served tea, smiled, and pleasantly spoke of nothings."[47] Georges de Beauvoir's ambiguous attitude toward his older daughter's unusual intelligence and academic success was a function of his class-bound view of women as social creatures and his reverence for the traditional aristocratic *femme d'esprit:* "In his view, a woman's place was in the home or the salon." Both of Simone's parents tried to convince her that intelligence and learning were a good thing for a woman if they enabled her to "shine in the salons." Her father, she later reflected, would have been happy for her to be "exceptional" if she were not "eccentric."[48] A quick mind and wide culture could be assets if they allowed a young woman to reinforce her own and her family's place in the semipublic world of upper-class society.

As for the real public world, it was forbidden territory to bourgeois girls, except on a few highly supervised occasions, such as a family outing to the theater. Upper-class girls were still chaperoned by mothers, brothers, or other reliable surrogates when they left the house, day or night. Only in their late teens did Simone and Zaza have permission to go out walking together on Sunday mornings so that they could chat privately. It never occurred to them to go to a café, an institution whose purpose mystified them: "What are all those people doing in there?" Zaza once asked Simone outside a café, "Don't they have a home?" When she began her university studies, Simone initially met male students of her social class who invited her for tea in bakeries: "They did not go to cafés and at any rate would never have taken a proper young woman to one."[49] The difference between upper- and lower-middle-class young women in France between the wars could thus be conveyed by the ways they became public persons: in drawing rooms and country houses for one group; in shops, offices, cafés, and on neighborhood streets for another.

Like Simone but earlier in her life, Violette broke the rules of her class and time. The working and lower middle classes also enforced rather strict sexual propriety for young girls, though it was combined with greater frankness and pragmatism. Aline Tourneux, a concierge's daughter in the *douzième,* described the history of her meeting with and courtship by her future husband, Pierrot. In 1928, when she was seventeen, Aline was invited to go to a dance with a friend of her mother's, Mme Soulier, and the latter's nineteen-year-old daughter, Jeanne. The ball was a very proper affair: a Sunday afternoon event organized by the Republican Youth of the eleventh arrondissement, where most young girls were chaperoned. "You did not misbehave there," Aline later commented. "In a way the socialists are just as puritanical as the churchy types; there's strict morality in the working class." When she caught the eye of a young man of twenty named Pierre Toulon, he knew not to ask her directly to dance but to approach the older lady she was with for permission.[50]

Aline was impressed by the youth, who worked as an office boy for a stockbroker: "That fellow's not a factory worker," she thought. "He's one of those who wear a tie."[51] Their courtship began cautiously, since it was improper for the young girl to have a boyfriend who was not an official fiancé. When she went on a day-trip with the Republican Youth, he jumped on his bicycle and pedaled to meet her, and they held hands, "nothing improper." Eventually they fell into a pattern of "frequentation" that involved kissing, though all this was still hidden from her parents. He came to meet her when her work let out but stood across the street so people would not notice; he waved at her in the evening outside her bedroom window until her mother became suspicious.[52]

Aline and Pierrot thought of themselves as a steady, serious item, even though the relationship was clandestine, probably because of Aline's youth. Then one day Pierrot forced a serious change. He felt unwell and had pimples on his face, and he told Aline that the family doctor had advised him that he needed to have sex, possibly by visiting a prostitute. What was he supposed to do? Aline does not seem to have wondered, even in her later reminiscences, if this was a ruse to get her into bed. "I was in such a state when he told me about this prescription. He had to go with a girl for his pimples to get better. What was to be done? Well, there were not a whole lot of options, I had to go through it. And so I did. On a first of April, just a year after we first met." They went to a hotel, and as they were setting off, Mme Soulier's daughter, who had somehow caught on, grimly wished Aline, " 'Good bye, and good luck.' I swear, she must have read my face."[53]

It was not a romantic occasion; Aline came out of it aching both morally and physically, wondering why young married women did not walk about like cripples. Once the deed was done, however, there seemed no point in further resistance, and they kept going back to the same hotel. By September Aline was pregnant. They planned to get married, of course, and faced the unpleasant prospect of telling their parents about the pregnancy. Aline's mother went into "deep mourning." Pierrot's mother "yelled and screamed as usual that one did not marry one's mistress. Aline, my mistress! Incredible." Each set of parents probably believed that their child had been manipulated, and that this boded ill for the future. After the initial scandal, their parents came around, and the pair got married in the town hall. When they looked for a place to live, their landlady insisted that they could not rent a room from her unless they first had a church wedding. For the ceremony, Aline and all of her family were dressed in black: "It was not very cheerful."[54]

Aline and her boyfriend caused an initial scandal by breaking the rules, though they eventually remedied matters to everyone's satisfaction. Their story conforms to what we know of the norms of urban courtship in early-twentieth-century France. Girls under the age of eighteen were closely watched, especially by their mothers. They were not expected to have social lives outside those of their families: while work did afford some independence to older teens, in general it was understood that unmarried young girls should not go out unsupervised, especially not in male company. After eighteen, the age of legal emancipation, standards relaxed somewhat, especially if a girl was making her own money.[55]

Working-class girls who came of age were much freer to choose a mate than their upper-class sisters were. Most couples got acquainted either in the neighborhood, at work, or, like Aline and Pierrot, at dances, which were acceptable venues for courtship. A chambermaid in 1925 could deliver a whole sociology of dances in Paris: there were the famously wild dances on the Rue de Lappe, near the Place de la Bastille, where respectable shopkeepers and office workers went to gawk at the pimps and prostitutes. The "Blue" Ball in the north of the city had a very mixed clientele, and at the Breton Ball you met employees from Brittany and Auvergne: café and restaurant waiters, hotel maids, and dairymaids. Many balls were regionally or professionally selective, such as the very formal dances of cooks and house servants. By one estimate, about one-half of all working-class couples in Paris met at a dance.[56]

Once a couple had met, they would be allowed to "frequent" each other only if there had been an explicit promise of marriage. If the pair were undecided or too young, they had to meet, as Aline and Pierrot had done or Violette with her boyfriends, in deep secret. It was perfectly acceptable for an engaged couple to be seen together in public, but for young people to go out together without the knowledge and consent of their parents was a transgression of widely accepted norms. If a boy regularly came to see a girl outside her window without first talking to her father, he would compromise her.[57]

Naturally, a serious "frequentation" quite often led to sex. In Paris, many modest families like the Nozières had come straight from the countryside, where premarital sex was quite common. In a small rural community, an imprudent swain could easily be forced to marry the girl he impregnated, so there was no great harm as long as everyone involved was equally poor. A mother in Normandy whose daughters both got pregnant before marriage commented, "I'm very happy, it proves they can do it [bear children]."[58] As we have seen, Germaine and Baptiste lived together before they married. In the city, for a girl to accept physical intimacy was a much bigger gamble, since young men were far less accountable. Whether eager like Violette or reluctant like Aline, working-class girls in any case had a good idea of what sexual congress was about ("Good luck"), unlike Simone de Beauvoir, who until quite late believed that the mystery of marriage involved a blood transfusion that made the bride and groom into kin.[59]

Among the urban working classes, premarital sex was so widespread that between the wars one in five brides was pregnant and 12 percent already had a child.[60] In the earlier decades of the Third Republic, girls who gave themselves before marriage were censured on the grounds that yielding to your fiancé showed a lack of principle that might result in later adultery. In the early twentieth century, tolerance for such behavior increased greatly, but only if the pair was genuinely headed for the town hall. But how was a girl to know? If parents were involved, the matter was simple, and some women carefully kept letters that announced the man's intentions. In many cases women had only their beau's word for it, and pressure or emotional blackmail on the part of men was frequent. "I'll leave you if you don't" was the most common weapon but far from the only one. A soldier in the Great War, for instance, came up with a much nobler-sounding rationale than Pierrot's story about clearing up pimples: if his girl did not sleep with him then she did not love him, and he would find a way to get himself killed.[61]

Unlike in the upper classes, where the sexual act was laden with religious and moral taboos, among more modest people carnal relations before marriage were tolerated as long as the man then agreed to right the situation. The initial panic and scandal that attended the pregnancy of Aline and girls like her seem merely to have reflected the fear that this might not happen. In most cases, couples got married within six months of the woman getting pregnant. As for the husband, as a proverb from the south of France put it, "Nobody can blame a man who washes a bowl after he soiled it."[62]

As it happens, the south of France is the setting for the most famous contemporary dramatization of exactly this situation. Marcel Pagnol's play *Marius* was a huge success in Paris when it opened in 1929, and generations of filmgoers know it from its classic 1931 movie version. Marius is the handsome son of César, who runs a café at the old port in Marseille. Regulars in the bar include the widowed fish-seller Honorine and her attractive daughter Fanny, who has loved Marius since childhood. Despite Marius's ambivalence about marriage, he sleeps with Fanny, and the pair is discovered by her mother. Honorine reacts like the mothers of Aline and Pierrot, weeping and screaming as she confronts Marius's father: "She's eighteen, César! Eighteen!" César is unfazed and rather amused: "Come on, better this should happen than a broken leg." When Honorine threatens histrionically to take a stick to her daughter, César happily turns the tables on her: "Oh, *that* would be helpful. If your mother had killed you with a club when you were engaged to poor Curly . . ." "Not the same thing," snaps Honorine. "We lived on the same landing and there was only a hallway to cross!" César is the mouthpiece of sympathetic conventional wisdom ("That's youth, Norine. It's gone in a flash."), and his is the obvious conclusion: "We'll marry them off in a fortnight, and that's the end of it."[63]

For French working-class girls in the early twentieth century, the rules about sex amounted to this: any romantic goings-on with boys were disapproved of for girls under eighteen. Chastity until marriage was the official norm, which it fell to mothers rather than fathers to enforce, but many young men expected to be intimate with their steady girls or fiancées and pressured them accordingly. Young women knew the risks—abandonment, pregnancy, disease—and reported giving in under pressure, though surely some of them were more easy to convince. As César said of the love-struck Fanny, "Come on, I bet she didn't scream all that loud."[64] The only acceptable standard and goal, however, was married monogamy, and girls who had more than one lover or whose behavior suggested promiscuity were denounced as "not serious" (a strong euphemism) or "vicious."

Violette, who dated boys starting at sixteen and was known to have gone with several young men before her late teens, was quickly singled out for opprobrium in her neighborhood. Disapproval of her behavior extended to her parents, who were deemed to have failed to control her. Although it would not do to blame the victims, in the days after the crime many tacitly agreed with what a newspaper editorial awkwardly suggested: "For having left her free, as they did, to come and go, to receive letters, the Nozière parents might give the impression that their daughter could have much to blame them for."[65]

At age seventeen Violette's life had two interlocking problems. One was her own sexual misbehavior, the other her parents' ambition. After the crime, neighbors and other Parisians commented that it was ridiculous for people of Baptiste and Germaine's class to keep their daughter out of the workforce. A neighbor commented to a newspaper reporter, "You see, Monsieur, that big girl did nothing with her ten fingers, and idleness brings bad counsel."[66] The concierge of the Nozières' building had heard the neighborhood gossip that Violette was "not serious": "She went out and came home late. She had no job. . . . I can't see how the father could stand for that kind of behavior."[67] An anonymous woman wrote to the judge, laying the blame on Germaine: "You will agree that a mother, instead of letting her go without working and giving her delusions of grandeur by saying they had one hundred and fifty thousand francs, would have done better to get her on track for a job."[68]

Germaine and Baptiste's stubborn pursuit of more and better schooling for their daughter was to prove increasingly disastrous. In the fall of 1932 Violette began classes at the Lycée Fénelon, where she belonged neither socially nor academically. Perhaps because she dreaded the humiliation of being in over her head, she had developed at the end of the summer yet another spate of illnesses, including "a beginning of typhoid fever," and started the school year late. Once she was better, Violette rode the metro into the heart of Paris; Germaine, worried about possible misconduct, came at the end of the day to wait for her at the school gate and escort her back home. After a couple of weeks, Violette began cutting classes, and the headmistress wrote to her parents alerting them to their daughter's truancy. The young girl had stopped going to the lycée, but since she had to remain in the Latin Quarter, she had taken to whiling away her time in a nearby establishment, the Café de la Sorbonne, slipping back into the crowd of students when school was let out. Baptiste took the train into Paris to investigate, and a nasty scene ensued when he ran into his daughter in the company of a young man. "Imagine what [her father] said to her," Germaine Nozière later wrote, "and I too said everything that the heart of a decent mother could suggest. I even begged her on my knees to return to the straight and narrow." It was not the last time that Germaine Nozière would inflict such aggressive melodrama on her errant daughter.[69]

By December 1932 Violette's life was on a downward spiral. She was caught stealing a book from an outside stall at the Librairie Gibert on Boulevard Saint-Michel, and only her parents' entreaties and financial compensation saved her from being reported to the police. There was row after row at home, as the teenager pleaded for freedom and her parents tightened their surveillance. Her mother scolded her every time she came home late, and Violette hotly retorted that other girls were less tightly controlled. "I asked her," Germaine later wrote, "why are you unhappy here? You have everything you want, and your papa and I are making every sacrifice to give you an honorable position so that later on you will be happy."[70]

On December 17, Violette expressed her fury by staging a suicide alert. She fled home, leaving a note explaining that she was going to throw herself into the Seine because she was miserable about her lack of freedom; she specified that by four that afternoon she would be dead. Germaine, who found the note, rushed to her husband's workplace, and the two headed off into the city in a frantic search for their daughter, questioning students in the Latin Quarter establishments she might have frequented. Violette, meanwhile, took the metro into the suburb of Auteuil, then headed back into the Latin Quarter in search of her friend Madeleine. Her parents eventually found her strolling on a quay near Saint-Michel in the company of two students. The ensuing row at home rehearsed every classic exchange between desperate teenagers and their angry parents, with Violette sobbing that she was unhappy, that so many girls were given more freedom, and Germaine flinging the door open: "Leave if you want!" Violette's suicidal gesture may have been a cruel manipulation or a plea for help, although the young girl later claimed that she really did intend to kill herself.[71]

For the little family on the sixth floor of 9 Rue de Madagascar, the leaden January skies of Paris must have seemed particularly bleak as 1933 began. Germaine had decided to enroll her daughter in a correspondence school, the École Universelle, so that Violette could study at home under her mother's supervision. Violette felt utterly trapped. She had many reasons to want to escape from home, including the new, exciting friends she had made in the Latin Quarter. Her parents wanted a better daughter, and she desperately wanted out of her family. She would have to find a way to make her fantasies work with theirs.

# THREE

# Violette's Family Romance

MOST CHILDREN WISH THEIR MOTHER and father were different, and many fantasize about wealthier, more powerful, and more glamorous parents. A century ago, Sigmund Freud noted how common such day-dreams were and gave them a name, "family romances." Freud noted in 1909 that small children worship their parents, but as they grow up they experience inevitable slights just as they become aware of the existence of other—richer, kinder, more beautiful—mothers and fathers. They dream of substituting these for their own. This fantasy often begins before puberty and is especially intense for imaginative, gifted, and neurotic children.[1]

Even after entering puberty, some children are consumed with dreams of freeing themselves from parents they despise and replacing them with others. As they grow older, the revenge motive animating these wishes becomes more conscious and explicit: "It is, as a rule, precisely these neu-rotic children who were punished by their parents for sexual naughtiness and who later revenge themselves on their parents by means of phantasies of this kind." For instance, they may concoct stories about their mother committing adultery with a powerful man, wishing themselves bastards. Freud imagined readers recoiling at the thought of such childish "depravity" and reassured them that what looked like rejection might not be what it seemed, since fantasies about "better" parents often include elements of the real parents' identities: "We find that these new and aristocratic parents are equipped with attributes that are derived entirely from attributes of the actual and humble ones." The dream of new parents who are glamorous versions of the real ones is a way for troubled children to recapture the unqualified love they felt before their parents betrayed them.[2]

Violette had always internalized her parents' ambitions and liked to boast about her status and her future. Had she wanted at a younger age to lie about who she was, she could not have done so in the circumscribed settings—Neuvy, Prades, her Paris neighborhood—where everyone knew her parents. When she was in her parents' orbit, she mostly bragged about her future. She told her first boyfriend, the working-class Raymond, about her plans to be a doctor or a teacher. In her father's village, she tried to impress an older peasant girl, Antoinette, with talk about fashionable Parisian clothes and her plans for a career. She wanted to become a math teacher, Violette told Antoinette, but her health problems might get in the way: "My father is pushing me, but I don't think I will be able to make it."[3]

Telling fibs about her parents close to home was impractical, but there was always the option of inventing glamorous relatives outside the neighborhood. A friend from secondary school in the eleventh, Betty Gajiecky, remembered that Violette intended to become a mathematics teacher— saying this time that it was her mother's wish. Violette seemed to Betty very fond of her mother, and also of her uncle, a police commissioner in the Odéon district of the Latin Quarter. She never spoke of her father but gave such detailed accounts of Sunday rides in her uncle's splendid car that Betty was later astonished to learn that the uncle was a fiction.[4] Who better than a police officer, a wealthy one at that, as a replacement for the undistinguished and submissive Baptiste?

Once Violette moved to the Lycée Fénelon, far from her home turf, and started going to nearby cafés, she began to tell outright lies about who her parents were. Violette's stories about herself and her family were reported by a large number of people the police later interviewed, nearly all of them men she had tried to impress or seduce.

There were variations in Violette's self-inventions, but they revolved around the set of themes summarized in the court's psychological report on the young girl: "Sometimes she said she had studied in several Paris lycées and was set for a brilliant future as a teacher; sometimes she was a richly paid fashion designer; her father, by her account, was an engineer with the PLM and had a dowry for her in the amount of one hundred eighty thousand francs (this was the exact amount of the Nozière couple's savings), invested in the Paquin couture house of which her mother was an employee, as was she; an uncle on her father's side was a police commissioner in the Panthéon district, and an aunt on her father's side lived as a richly kept woman in the Ambassador Hotel."[5]

Violette's fantasies were out of a Freudian textbook. Her father was still with the PLM but in management, at the very top of the company. Germaine, who had worked as a seamstress in Neuvy and had always made dresses for her daughter, became, with a swoosh of the wand, a prominent figure in one of Paris's leading couture houses, where Violette—unable, after all, really to let go of her mother—also worked. Their life savings were all going to her, the only sum she could imagine as the dowry of a rich girl. The wealthy uncle and aunt served as surrogate parents, and the details that one was in law enforcement and the other a courtesan lend themselves to infinite interpretation. At sixteen, seventeen, eighteen, Violette desperately wanted to love her parents the way she did when she was six.

Violette retold these stories in different combinations before she committed her crime. Who believed her, and how much? A student named Lucien Balmain, who knew her in her early days in the Latin Quarter, told the police: "I noticed that she boasted all the time and liked to tell stories. . . . She was a rather sad character. She told tales about traveling, in particular about a trip to Madagascar."[6] What stories did she tell about visiting the island her street was named after? Men went along when it suited them; what point was there in contradicting an attractive girl from whose company they could benefit in different ways? Did any of them believe her?

From a psychologist's point of view, Violette's fantasies about her parents could not be more suggestive: she wanted to get rid of them and yet also to hold on to them. To a historian, Violette's compulsive lies and self-inventions raise another set of issues. In 1933 could an engine driver's daughter convincingly impersonate an upper-class girl? Violette at the very least believed she could dress and act the part of someone of higher station, and her conviction that this was possible needs to be understood against the background of class cultures and class relations in Paris between the wars.

In the twenty-first century, Paris, like many great western cities, is becoming uniformly wealthy and gentrified, with most of the poorer people who work there forced into dismal suburbs outside the city limits. In the early twentieth century, however, the French capital was a metropolis of many classes, including a substantial population of artisans and factory workers. There were two overlapping patterns of social division in the city's geography, east/west and center/periphery. Most of the city's working-class districts clustered in the east, from the heights of Belleville in the north, where Zola set his tales of nineteenth-century proletarian misery, down through the areas around the huge Père Lachaise Cemetery where revolutionary workers were gunned down in 1871, to the more middling twelfth and thirteenth arrondissements in the southeast. Western Paris, in contrast, was a land of wealth and lineage. Some of France's oldest families lived on the western end of the Boulevard Saint-Germain, where they had settled many generations earlier to escape the court intrigues of Versailles. Old and new money coexisted in splendid apartments and townhouses around the Champs-Élysées and throughout the seventh and eighth districts, where nannies promenaded children through the broad, quiet streets and manicured parks.

A different though not unrelated pattern had power and influence clustered at the center of the city and anonymous masses pushed out around the edges. On the left bank, the Latin Quarter, the heart of old Paris, housed universities, publishing houses, and government buildings; across the river in the first and second arrondissements were the city's centers of finance, commerce, and entertainment, symbolized by the great Paris Opera and the neighboring Stock Exchange. Living on the edges of Paris, modest folks like the people on Violette's street felt far removed geographically and culturally from the heart of the city.

Getting around Paris was not difficult. The first metro line opened in 1900, and by the 1930s most of the grid that exists today—over a dozen lines circling and crisscrossing the city—was in place.[7] But an observer noted in 1930 that most Parisians, rich and poor, led lives circumscribed by their neighborhoods, neither venturing to nor caring much about what lay beyond. "In the midst of this world-metropolis of luxury," wrote Paul Cohen-Portheim, "[the Parisian] leads a modest, circumscribed, contented little life, just as they do in the provinces." Another writer noted of the Vaugirard district on the south end of the city, "There are plenty of twelve-year-olds born in this patch of Paris who have never laid eyes on the Seine." Cohen-Portheim described Paris as a collection of separate provincial towns. The blue-blooded area around the Boulevard Saint-Germain could also be considered "an aristocratic provincial town that ignores the Paris of the boulevards, the Champs-Élysées, the Republic and the foreigners." A few metro stops away, in the neighborhoods near the Eiffel Tower, life was dominated by France's top military academy: "There one is in a garrison town."[8] Even allowing for some literary exaggeration on the author's part, Paris before the Second World War was indeed a constellation of separate social worlds. The very nature of the city made it easier for someone like Violette to reinvent herself as she moved from one neighborhood to another.

In the early 1930s Paris was a city of about three million, of whom three quarters fell into the category of "poor or indigent."[9] While the big modern factories—automobile and aeronautical—were settling in the suburbs, Paris proper was still an industrial city that housed foundries, steel mills, outfitting and building plants, and even one auto manufacturer, all scattered around its inner periphery. The city also included large numbers of craftspeople—woodworkers, bronzeworkers, leathersmiths, tailors, and seamstresses—as well as workers in high-end trades, such as couture and jewelry. In the decades since the turn of the century, the population of the working-class belt around the edges of the city had exploded, more than doubling in most places, while housing, as we have seen, was in short supply. Many of these workers were foreign immigrants, laborers primarily from Mediterranean countries drawn to France by the country's postwar need for manpower, and Jewish refugees from pogroms in Eastern Europe.[10]

In the 1920s a writer named Jacques Valdour chronicled the lives of Parisian workers by attempting to share their experiences, living in their neighborhoods while earning his keep at unskilled jobs. Like many an urban ethnographer, Valdour was hardly unbiased: a member of the conservative Catholic movement Action Française, he loathed the Left and despised Jews, though he also denounced "capitalists" for their greed. If, however, one wants to understand the world of those struggling to get by between the wars on the margins of the City of Light, Valdour's books are a precious source of information.

For one thing, Valdour makes it clear that there was not one working-class culture in Paris but many. In the heart of Paris, in the Marais district, skilled artisans wore suits, and some of them were opera buffs; this put them in a different league from the masses in Popincourt, in the east of the city, whose favorite form of entertainment was to bellow out songs in the cabarets, known as *café-concerts*. In the fifteenth arrondissement, many workers were peasants straight from the provinces; the thirteenth had a large population of Arab laborers; and up north in Belleville, the Jews, he noted with alarm, were everywhere. Nonetheless Valdour observed many constants while eking out a living in Vaugirard in the southwest of Paris, Saint-Ouen and Belleville in the north, and the railway districts of the southeast.

For one thing, housing conditions were disgraceful everywhere. Valdour found lodging—often with great difficulty—in the furnished quarters known as *garnis,* which workers rented by the week. A typical room in Vaugirard measured six by eight feet, was furnished with a bed, chair, table, nightstand, candlestick, and towel, and was unheated in any season. In Saint-Ouen, just outside the city limit, he got a bigger and brighter room, but the floor was stained, the walls and ceiling grungy. You could wash in the small basin that the landlady filled each day or fetch your own water in the courtyard, but heating water was impossibly complicated. Valdour's worst lodging experience was in Popincourt in the eleventh, where the same sort of accommodation (tight quarters barely containing a bed, nightstand, and washstand) came with dingy sheets and an army of bedbugs. The first few nights, he missed sleep while he killed hundreds of them, but then exhaustion got the better of him and he learned to live with the bugs. Many of the buildings that offered furnished rooms included a makeshift tavern on the ground floor, whose presence ramped up the level of noise and inebriation.[11]

Nor was Valdour, a single man, the worst off, since whole families crowded into *garnis.* In Vaugirard his neighbors were invisible families whose drunken fights he heard at night, but in Popincourt the situation was more convivial. One dwelling on his floor housed a group of five, including two rough teenage boys and a mother given to yelling obscenities. Next door were a mother, two children, and a grandmother inclined to noisy drunkenness. The children played on the tiny landing, which became festive one day when their grandma somehow acquired a gramophone and records. Neighbors all opened their doors and belted out the choruses of popular cabaret songs.[12] In 1929, three hundred and fifty thousand Parisians, over 12 percent of the population, lived in *garnis.*[13]

Budgets were tight for unskilled laborers. A metalworker or a welder earned sixteen to twenty francs a day, ninety or a hundred for a six-and-a-half-day week. Housing in *garnis* may have been wretched, but at least it was cheap, two or three francs a day.[14] It was food that depleted budgets at the time—average working-class families spent over 60 percent of their earnings on keeping themselves fed.[15] Since cooking was impossible in a small, barely furnished room, Valdour, like most workers, ate in local restaurants that were more like canteens, watching every centime. In Popincourt a meal with neither meat nor wine (omelet, cheese, bread, and water) cost two francs seventy-five including tip; if you wanted to splurge on a slice of roast with noodles and some applesauce, that would be three sixty. If you added a glass or a small jug of wine—which most workers considered essential—you would be up to four or five francs per meal, plus fifty centimes a day for breakfast. However you figured it, food and lodging wiped out most of what you made, leaving only a few francs a week for clothing, cleaning, and the most modest entertainment. "It is tough to make ends meet," Valdour concluded, "and even the smallest amount of saving is impossible."[16]

Valdour had no sympathy for the Left, but his observation that workers took little, or only sporadic, interest in politics converges with what we know from other sources. During the Belle Époque, the French workforce had become massively unionized, and the years between 1880 and 1914 saw waves of strikes paralyze the country, led by the Confédération Générale du Travail (CGT). By the 1920s, wartime deaths, the split between Socialists and Communists, and the violent repression of a last massive strike in 1920 had sent union membership plummeting.[17] Valdour did note the presence of serious "Bolshevists" in popular neighborhoods, but mostly people just grumbled in general terms, like a metalworker in Popincourt: "It's seven or eight guys with all the dough who run everything. . . . There's Rothschild, Rockefeller, and gosh, I can't remember the others." When vendors set out piles of newspapers in Belleville or Popincourt, the largest stacks were always *Le Petit Parisien, Le Journal,* and *Le Petit Journal,* apolitical dailies with heavy coverage of crime and sports. Piles of the communist *L'Humanité* were much smaller. The working classes, in Valdour's account, showed much more enthusiasm for the cinema—huge movie houses in these districts sold out on weekends— and for the more traditional *café-concerts,* where audiences could enjoy popular plays and belt out the choruses to songs.[18]

Paris, then, was ringed with districts where the poorest of workers lived in their own worlds, struggling to make ends meet, with no time or resources for much beyond basic sustenance and cheap entertainment. Working-class men especially were easily recognizable from the clothes they wore: rumpled, dark, faded jackets and pants, and cloth caps that rarely left their heads. In the crowds at cinemas and theaters, a few people stood out, those who had made it but still lived in the neighborhood: smartly dressed office workers, the haughty shop clerks known as *calicots,* and their girls wearing modish, sexy outfits.[19] The people in Belleville and Popincourt would avidly consume the details of the Nozière affair, shaking their heads in disbelief that people who had it all—a two-room apartment with a kitchen, savings in the bank—had made such a mess of their lives.

At the other end of the Parisian social world stood the upper classes, known as *la bourgeoisie,* whose members lived in the central and western districts of the city. Elements of the old aristocracy survived into the twentieth century, of course, but only as a peculiar subgroup of a broader social elite defined by its distinctive codes of culture. Only the most fastidious of blue bloods kept to themselves. Simone de Beauvoir's family is typical of the matrimonial and social intermingling of the lesser nobility with the larger pool of upper-bourgeois families that had been going on in France for generations.[20] In many ways the French upper middle class had taken on the mantle of the bygone nobility: they typically adhered to Catholic practice and conservative politics, officially scorned commercial values, and worshipped culture and social grace.[21]

Bourgeois attitudes toward the lower classes were still strikingly paternalistic in the twenties and thirties. We have seen that Simone de Beauvoir's mother confiscated a racy novel from one family maid and dismissed another who was going out with men. Given their professed disinterest in money and their fixation on the riches of spirit, the bourgeoisie assumed that the cultural gap between themselves and proletarians mattered more than the financial one, and that some of the most efficacious charitable acts consisted in bringing treasures of learning to the people. As a child, Simone de Beauvoir shared her parents' view that intellectual and spiritual enlightenment came naturally only to the bourgeoisie. When she was taken to visit her grandparents' farmers, she sensed that their filth and bad odor somehow followed from "the crudeness of their souls." They worked the land all day, never noting the beauty of sunsets. "They did not read, they had no ideals; Papa called them 'brutes,' though without animosity."[22]

As for factory workers, she was told that ever since unions had been allowed, they worked less and earned more. In fact, workers were better off than a family like hers, since they did not have to keep up appearances and therefore could gorge themselves on chicken anytime they wanted. She believed her father when he pointed out that workers hated bourgeois people because they knew the latter were superior to them, and that envy was a very ugly sentiment. Young Simone had never really met workers, never set foot in working-class housing until her mother took her to visit their former maid Louise, who had just given birth. The little girl took in with horror the minuscule sixth-floor room and the families jammed into similar dingy quarters down the entire hallway. When Louise later lost the baby, Simone sobbed and sobbed, imagining the mother trapped with her grief in her miserable surroundings. However, Beauvoir wrote, "I ended up drying my tears without having questioned the social order."[23]

As a teenager, Beauvoir felt alienated from her parents' social world but was never drawn to the working classes, whose "materialism" she despised.[24] Like others of her class, however, she engaged in charitable endeavors aimed at bringing intellectual and cultural enlightenment to the working poor. Some members of the bourgeoisie, women especially, embraced cultural charity as a solution to social divisions: in a popular novel of the time, the protagonist's aunt contracts pneumonia while admirably running a library and living in a working-class district, convinced of the importance of bringing "good books" to the poor.[25] Beauvoir herself as a young student signed up with the women's section of an organization called the Équipes Sociales (Social Teams) instigated by her charismatic young philosophy professor, Robert Garric. Garric, a Catholic idealist, had served in the war and explained to his classes that life in the trenches had taught him the value of cross-class friendship, and that the segregation between young bourgeois and workers amounted to a mutilation of the social body. France would be healed only if the bourgeois overcame their selfishness and the workers their ignorance. Class reconciliation could be achieved by sending bourgeois student volunteers into the working-class districts to dispense culture to the poor.[26]

Simone was accordingly dispatched up north to Belleville, where she found herself explaining the masterpieces of French literature to young working women in the evenings. She was genuinely fired up by Garric and his ideology, but this mother-approved initiative also afforded her a first opportunity to get out of the house alone one evening a week. Ironically, the young apprentices she taught came for the same reason: to escape their parents' surveillance and possibly meet boys, who were being force-fed culture in the next room. Simone dragged them though *Old Goriot* and *Les Misérables,* with everyone involved profoundly bored. After a few months without any cross-class friendships developing, Simone, who balked at telling seamstresses, per instructions, about the greatness of the human soul and the value of suffering and had begun to find Garric's blandishments inane, dropped off the team.[27]

Upper-class observers usually wrote as if there were only two social groups in France: a cultivated and refined bourgeoisie, and a deprived and uneducated *peuple* whom one encountered as one's servants or workers. Both conservatives and leftists, from different perspectives, liked to embrace this view of things, and it fueled some of left-Republican Jean Renoir's cinematic masterpieces of the time, such as *Rules of the Game* and *Grand Illusion*.[28] This dichotomy was untrue; as we have seen, Paris was full of middling people like the Nozières, or the capital's legions of office and service workers, with decent resources and some education but whom nobody at the time would describe as bourgeois. Members of the French bourgeoisie knew that their essence as a class lay in their distinction not from the distant and brutish plebs but from the nonbourgeois middling sorts.

In North America status and power have been linked mostly to wealth, and in Britain a class-segregated school system long sorted the population into sharply defined groups. In France neither of these class markers works in the same way, and the distinction between who is in and out of the upper class has been a more nebulous matter, involving culture, customs, and networks. In the twentieth century, prominent French sociologists puzzled over the question of what makes a bourgeois bourgeois.[29] One of the earliest and most enduring such studies was a book entitled *La Barrière et le niveau* (*Barriers and Levels*), published in 1925 by Edmond Goblot.

To Goblot, writing in the early twentieth century, class was not primarily about money; the fact of class distinction was obvious, he noted, its basis elusive. "You recognize a gentleman from a worker just from seeing them in the street. One does not confuse a 'monsieur' with a 'man,' still less a 'lady' with a 'woman.'" The French upper class, he wrote, was not a caste defined by tangible privileges like the aristocracy of old, but an open group that coalesced on the basis of its own customs and manners and the opinion of others; it was better, as he put it, to be "considered" than "considerable."[30] Hence the title and thesis of Goblot's book: bourgeois class formation was a matter of steep escarpments and flat plateaus, vertical "barriers" and horizontal "levels." The bourgeoisie was defined by the fact that it was both hard to get into—that took time, money, sacrifice, and education—and densely connected once you were inside it.

If you took ten bourgeois randomly, he wrote, at least five would be the sons or grandsons of workers. Goblot described the best practical strategies for entering the bourgeoisie, which happen to be exactly those initiated by Baptiste and Germaine Nozière. An aspiring bourgeois had to accumulate some financial resources for two reasons: to keep the mistress of the house out of the workforce and to give the children a lengthy education. The expense of sending a child to school for years was a major reason, he noted, for the small size of upwardly mobile families: "Birth control is endemic at the frontier between classes."[31]

Climbing the *barrière* involved mastering the unspoken rules of bourgeois conduct, which were visible and learnable but subtle enough to make the code hard to crack and keep intruders out.[32] Language was one of the most powerful class markers, as both contemporaries and etiquette books made clear. A real bourgeois spoke precisely, avoiding lazy locutions like "what's-his-name," and forced his children to do the same, teaching them that you don't say "eat" but "lunch" or "dine." Understatement and silence were eloquent: you address someone as "Madame" but not "Madame the Countess," you say "I ride" but not "I ride horses," and to the servants you refer to your husband as "Monsieur," not "Monsieur Durand." The not-really-bourgeois could give themselves away with one excess word—"Isn't it, Madame?" instead of a simple "Isn't it?"—or torpedo themselves socially by gushing about "the advantage of seeing you" (hideously commercial!) instead of "the pleasure" or "the honor." Anyone who had not been groomed in childhood had to practice not lapsing into a phrase considered "shop"- or "concierge"-speak. How much time and attention did it take to realize that the only possible answer to "bonjour" or "au revoir" was a nod of the head and silence, and that you *never* thanked someone for visiting you because it was assumed that you would visit them in return?[33]

Substance mattered as well as style, of course. In good society, *le monde,* material concerns were never mentioned, whether the behavior of servants or the price of food, and while one sometimes heard it said in a salon that the so-and-so's were well off, it was essential to refrain from looking the slightest bit interested in that statement, much less asking for details. Rather one should direct one's attention to more "serene and ideal" matters; not that you actually had to play the piano, draw, or read a novel, but you should take an interest in the arts if only to listen intelligently. Berthe Bernage warned readers of her etiquette book that "the theater is an important part of elegant life. It is difficult to take part in social conversations if one never goes to the theater."[34]

Of course, only those who actually went to social gatherings would worry about the right and wrong things to say at them. The single most distinctive feature of the bourgeoisie was that, unlike any other class except the aristocracy, it had an organized social life. As Goblot argued, the bourgeoisie existed on the one hand because it was hard to get into, and on the other because once you were inside, its social world was both dense and internally egalitarian—that was what he meant by *niveau*. Outside the class was a sheer drop, inside the flattest of levels: the internal equality gave elites their strength, he explained—why else did the ancient Greek nobility refer to themselves as "the equals"? As Goblot smartly put it, "Levels distinguish, distinction levels."[35] As abstract and schematic as this idea may seem—there certainly were important differences within the elite—it does explain, for instance, why a hostess's skill in managing a salon conversation was crucial. Even if there were actual social or other differences between guests, the art of the hostess was to conceal them. You never used anyone's title; you promoted everyone equally in conversation; and you never discussed political, religious, or professional matters, which could reveal fissures in the company. The golden rule, Bernage wrote, was that "the people assembled in a salon must be regarded as all belonging to the same world and equally deserving of consideration."[36]

The postrevolutionary French bourgeoisie had inherited from the old aristocracy the concept of good society as *le monde,* which means "the world" but could be glossed as "our world, the only one that matters"—a social world that was both private, closed to outsiders, and internally very public.[37] Unlike their noble predecessors, the bourgeois usually earned a living, but work was the lesser facet of their daily life. Another interwar French sociologist, Maurice Halbwachs, explained that the essential difference between the lower middle class and the bourgeoisie was that the former had a life organized solely around their job or profession (think of Baptiste Nozière's dedication to the PLM), whereas the latter's identity was forged and sustained primarily in dinners, visits, receptions, and cultural events where the subject of work was taboo.[38] The private and elaborate social life of the bourgeoisie both reinforced connections for practical purposes and sharpened the codes—all those subtle cues inaccessible to outsiders—that gave the group coherence.

The burden of organizing and sustaining social life fell naturally to the women who marched the servants through instructions for elaborate parties. An elegant dinner, Bernage's 1928 manual tells us, would consist of the classic sequence of ten courses: a good lineup might include consommé,

lobster timbale, braised veal, new carrots, roast duckling à l'orange, let-
tuce, green beans in sauce, meringues with whipped cream, fruit, and
pastries, each served with the appropriate wine. For a "simple" dinner you
could get away with less: soup, fish, two meat courses, salad and vegetables, two desserts, and just three different wines.[39]

Evening sociability involved the men, but women bore the brunt of the
endless afternoon ceremonial visiting that was the bourgeoisie's stock in
trade. The rules were elaborate: at least once a year a woman must visit
each woman of a family with whom hers is friendly; if you are invited to
a party you must go see your hostess afterward, unless it was a first invitation, in which case it has to be both before and after. Most women
had a "day," and hours were always three to seven in Paris, two to six in
the provinces. Young girls must visit their hostess after a dance, as well as
their relatives, the mothers of their friends, and their former teachers; they
must always curtsy when shaking hands. Even when Simone de Beauvoir's
family was destitute after the Great War and there were no more treats for
the children, her mother sent out cards to ladies she barely knew announc-
ing her "day" on the first Friday of the month, and paid "visits" to friends
and relatives and ceremonial "calls" to distant acquaintances. The girls
had to serve tea and cookies the family could barely afford, and which they
themselves were not allowed to touch.[40]

Most women seem to have regarded visiting rituals as tedious, but Bernage was blunt, in her etiquette manual, about their practical importance
for anyone who wanted to remain in the game. Young married couples,
she wrote, sometimes want to keep to themselves and shun their parents'
friends. "This attitude," however, "suggests a lack of understanding of the
world and of true sensibility. If we want to remain of a certain world, let
us not turn away from those who are part of it and whose parents and
grandparents helped ours to maintain their place in society. Let us trust
in longstanding friendships; they have proved their value."[41]

Of course you needed money to participate in social life; those ten-
course dinners were expensive, and a lady needed the right outfits to go
visiting. But the difference between the world of the bourgeoisie and that
of a lower-middle-class (or upper-working-class) family like the Nozières
was a lot more complex than a matter of income levels. The Nozières
never entertained, and their social life was minimal and unplanned, consisting of ad hoc friendships at work and among neighbors. They lived in
stifling isolation, saving their money so their daughter could rise in the
world. A true bourgeois family, however, spent money on social life to

maintain the rank at which they had arrived, the connections that were vital to the family's future. And living in *le monde* both necessitated and honed certain skills—ways of speaking, dressing, and behaving. Could an engine driver's daughter really hope to impersonate a girl bred for salon life, who curtsied and spoke precisely, who attended afternoon teas and evening balls?

At the borders between classes, women have always been more socially mobile than men. Some would argue that women are more attentive to manners and customs and to the nuances of people's interactions, and are therefore better equipped than men to adopt the styles of social spheres above them. Beauty and charm, sometimes combined with unusual talent, have long served as passports into the elite for a small category that includes courtesans, models, and actresses.[42] Such was the case, for instance, for Gabrielle Chanel, born in 1883, a contemporary of Violette's parents. The woman the world would come to know as Coco Chanel was born to a wretchedly poor family in the provinces and spent part of her childhood in an orphanage. Though she showed real creativity as a seamstress and milliner early on, it was only because her beauty snagged her a succession of wealthy lovers that she was able to launch her career as a Parisian designer. In the early years of her ascent, she was sometimes snubbed by the well-born for being "in trade," but Chanel eventually mingled with the highest society in France and abroad. She was for a time the lover—by some accounts nearly the wife—of the Duke of Westminster, becoming friendly with the likes of Winston Churchill. It is difficult to imagine a man of that era from a similarly grim background rising so dramatically in the world.[43]

Even ordinary women crossed class boundaries more easily than men in early-twentieth-century Paris. A study of marriage contracts in the working-class eighteenth arrondissement in 1936 shows that many female office workers had upper-class men as their witnesses: engineers, doctors, lawyers and judges, even a deputy. Men, by contrast, usually had colleagues serve as their witnesses.[44] White-collar work, for which women often traveled outside of the neighborhood, put working-class women in contact with professional men. So did that more traditional means of breaking class barriers, sex. Violette, as we have seen, first dated a working-class boy but moved on to a medical student of good bourgeois lineage.

The novelist Romain Rolland, writing of Paris in the early thirties, described the city as a palm furrowed by criss-crossing lines. The line of wealth ran down its middle, shifting left or right over the years, blurred by the movement of "neutrals and refugees": it divided Paris into a western "pole of wealth" and an eastern "pole of poverty." The city's center was defined by a "line of business," which formed a shape like a sac or a stomach, where "the forces of trade and speculation came to pile up, to warm and ferment each other." Finally, there was the line of physical passion, which did not divide the city into halves or fold parts of it into cocoons: "It was more like a constellation, marking the phosphorescent path of carnal love through Paris, with ramifications here or there like aigrettes and stagnant pools. It resembled a sort of Milky Way."[45] Violette followed her own "phosphorescent path" though different neighborhoods of the capital, in search of love, glamour, and escape.

Violette's home base in the year before her crime was the Latin Quarter, where her parents had ill-advisedly sent her to study. Across the Seine from Notre Dame, the Latin Quarter, the oldest heart of the city, clusters around the hill named for Saint Genevieve, the fifth-century nun and patron saint of Paris whose prayers are said to have saved her fellow citizens from the Huns. For centuries it was a realm of churches, schools, and universities—hence "Latin"—and home to generations of intellectuals. The two most famous boys' lycées in France, Louis-le-Grand and Henri IV, were in the Latin Quarter, along with their more recent sister institution, the Lycée Fénelon. The Sorbonne presided as the intellectual heart of the area, along with two even more prestigious institutions, the highly selective École Normale Supérieure on Rue d'Ulm and that studentless showcase for academic luminaries, the Collège de France.

Twenty to thirty thousand students attended these and other institutions, and while Paul Cohen-Portheim touted the Latin Quarter as "one of the holy places of civilization for the white races," he went on to note, as did everyone else, how international and multiracial the student population was: "The quarter swarms with Europeans of every nationality, besides Americans, Chinese, Japanese, Annamites and Siamese, Arabs and negroes." Boulevard Saint-Michel formed the central axis of the quarter, lined with businesses aimed at students—bookstores, banks, and cheap cafés, restaurants and hotels.[46]

East of the boulevard were the schools and universities, to the west, around Place de l'Odéon, the Latin Quarter's informal intellectual center. The arcades around the Odéon Theater housed stall-lined galleries owned by the bookseller Flammarion, where you could stand and read the latest books and magazines without being bothered, as long as you did not cut the pages. The same went on around the corner at Picard's, where "rows of silent readers took in contemporary literature uncut, by casting a practiced and baleful eye between the pages." On nearby Rue de l'Odéon, literary talent flourished, contacts were made, and books sold, lent, and debated in the celebrated bookstores of those two friends, rivals, and lovers, Sylvia Beach and Adrienne Monnier.[47]

In the nineteenth century, the Latin Quarter students had been central to the great upheavals of 1830s, 1840s, and 1850s and to the Paris Commune, building barricades alongside workers.[48] In the depressed, disillusioned years after World War I, politics were at a low ebb here as in other parts of the city. Although the École Normale Supérieure tilted left, students looking for a cause were more likely between the wars to get inspiration from the neomonarchist Action Française, which consciously courted middle- and upper-middle-class youth. The movement's student league, the Camelots du Roi ("King's Hawkers"), had come together in 1908, when right-wing youths galvanized by the Dreyfus case took the lead in hawking the *Action Française* newspaper, then turned to disrupting the courses of pro-Dreyfus professors. Decades later, in 1931, the case still rankled: in February of that year, the Camelots interrupted a play sympathetic to Dreyfus with cries of "Long live the army! Down with the Jews!" before taking their violence to the streets. Although the Camelots never numbered more than one thousand five hundred in Paris, their energy, discipline, and easy recourse to physical brutality made them seem more numerous. They considered the Latin Quarter their turf and promised a thrashing to groups that made their Republican or leftist sympathies too prominent.[49]

Higher and even secondary education was, as we have seen, limited to a small elite between the wars, and the Latin Quarter student population was in consequence made up of ambitious scholars from upper-class backgrounds, along with a handful of bright and hardworking scholarship students and foreigners from wealthy families. It was the kind of environment that made for solidarity and nostalgia. Jean-Edouard Goby, a student in the early thirties, looked back fondly from 1945 on the "utterly pure intellectual joys" of those days and the brilliance of his professors at the engineering *grande école,* Polytechnique: "Even when teaching the most exact and academic technicalities, they were guided by that high spirituality that is the mark of French genius." Between stretches of hard work, students attended cheap theater performances and strolled in the Luxembourg Gardens. At the end of a final grueling week of exams, they formed a procession, wearing bright ties and skull caps, and ceremonially dumped the plaster busts of antique figures, from which they had learned to draw, into the Seine.[50]

French higher education was public and meritocratic, but the Latin Quarter in the 1920s and 1930s resembled Oxbridge or the Ivy League much more than a public university today. Observers commented—and this was to become a leitmotif after the Nozière affair gave the quarter a bad name—that since the war and with the onset of the economic downturn, students worked hard and had little money to spend on partying. It was understood, at any rate, that the Latin Quarter was where the bourgeoisie educated its own and a few highly deserving escapees from the lower classes. According to a 1931 guidebook, the area trained "the elite of engineers, officers, lawyers, doctors, writers and scientists . . . whose education is one of Paris's proudest titles of nobility." When Goby wrote that the schoolboys, students, and professors "were recognizable not so much by the books and satchels they carried as from their bearing," he was clearly suggesting that they looked upper-class.[51]

The Latin Quarter, however, was not a campus but a big-city district with a resident population of tradespeople and service workers, open to all comers. The area's youthfulness and cheapness, as well as its central location and prestige, attracted many young people who were not in the schools but might just about pass, former and quasi-students, would-be bourgeois, as well as total interlopers. Violette fell into those categories, as did most of the people she befriended in the neighborhood that was to become her new home.

Violette started seeing men in the Latin Quarter before she even began school at Fénelon. Pierre Camus introduced her to a friend there, a design student named Aimé Tessier, and in May 1932 she began an affair with Tessier's friend Jean Leblanc, who was taking design courses while serving in the army. Tessier said that Violette and Leblanc met in the afternoons—probably in a hotel room—since the sixteen-year-old girl was not allowed out in the evening. Rounding out the group of friends were a third design student, Georges Legrand, known as Willy, Roger Endewell, an architecture student, and Bernard Piebourg, a part-time employee of the state tax administration. These young men, ranging in age from nineteen to twenty-one, met daily for a couple of years at the Palais du Café on the Boulevard Saint-Michel.[52] None them was of very high status: they studied design rather than law or medicine, and their families mostly lived in the cheap and bland suburbs just outside the city. Piebourg, who dropped his studies to take a job, had a father who worked as a chauffeur. After the crime, Violette's crowd was derided as effete and inauthentic. *Paris-Soir* described them as young men who wore "Spanish-style sideburns, wide-open collars with ties knotted fat as a fist. Lips curled in contempt, a smug grin on their face, they believe in their own superiority."[53] Pierre Camus, an authentic bourgeois, told the police he stopped seeing Violette because, even though he had brokered the first introduction, he disapproved of the group she was frequenting.

Violette's friends at the Palais du Café evidently knew that she was not who she pretended to be. Like Lucien Balmain, Jean Leblanc said none of them believed her because they knew her as a "bizarre girl who mostly needed to brag and spin unbelievable yarns." Endewell reported that she misleadingly announced that her father was "in the railways," and went on to elaborate boasts about being a model for the Paquin design house and owning a Bugatti. (Endewell later described her as volatile but a "good egg" who stood him many a beer; asked if she was pretty, he exclaimed, "Stunning!")[54] Just by taking up daily residence in the café, Violette undermined her story about being an engineer's daughter, since, as contemporaries noted, a well-bred girl would stop for refreshment in a patisserie and never dream of lolling in a café like a demimondaine.[55]

The young men gave differing accounts of how promiscuous Violette actually was. Tessier said that in those days she only slept with Leblanc, though she flirted a lot with others, while Piebourg claimed that she "had lovers" and seemed always flush with money. The Latin Quarter population had for centuries included women who catered to the needs of students and artists, some of them actual prostitutes, others working girls known as *lorettes, grisettes,* or *midinettes,* who sometimes became the steady mistresses of bourgeois bohemians.[56] Violette kept a careful distance from the "little women" of the Latin Quarter. One of them, who insisted that they had "worked Montparnasse" together when Violette was barely sixteen, told a newspaper that the latter pretended not to recognize her on the street: "Violette needed to protect her reputation as an upper-class 'good girl' with her Latin Quarter friends."[57]

At seventeen, Violette led two lives in different parts of Paris, even though she may have been less than convincing in either role: in the twelfth arrondissement she was a schoolgirl, the closely watched daughter of Baptiste and Germaine; in the fifth she became an emancipated young bourgeoise, the companion of dapper students. At some point—it is unclear when exactly it started—Violette acquired yet another persona in another part of the city: that of an elegant, sexually available woman of mystery in the wealthy commercial districts on the right bank of the Seine.

If you cross the Seine from the Latin Quarter and travel northwest, you will find yourself in the newer, prosperous area due north of the Louvre. The first and second arrondissements are the heart of Haussmann's vision for the nineteenth-century city: wide boulevards, elegant stores, the stock exchange, an opera house that wants to be Versailles, expensive hotels. This is an area of work and play, building after building full of offices, cafés and restaurants lining the streets, and at the northern edge those most modern of diversions, the great department stores. Cohen-Portheim's description of the Avenue de l'Opéra could apply to most of the area: "It is an artery of traffic . . . broad, long and straight, with excellent if rather undistinguished shops, but no soul and no feeling of period about it."[58] Parisians never lived in the first and second arrondissements; they commuted in and out of these areas following the rhythms of the work day. Whereas the cafés of the Latin Quarter and Montparnasse hosted circles of regular patrons who spent hours each day in them, on the right-bank boulevards, "the characteristic thing is the rapidly changing relay of customers."[59] With no neighbors or "regulars" looking into your business, this was probably the easiest part of the city in which to be anonymous and reinvent yourself.

Two famous episodes in the cultural history of interwar Paris suggest that it was not unusual for men to pick up young women—girls who were not prostitutes but might be looking for a little romance, adventure, or extra cash—in the area of boulevards and department stores behind the Paris Opera. In 1926 the Surrealist poet André Breton, aged thirty, approached an intriguing, waifish young woman on Rue La Fayette. He became infatuated with the girl, and although their affair was brief and ended badly, the encounter became the subject of Breton's most famous book, *Nadja:* "Without a moment's hesitation, I spoke to this unknown woman, though I must admit that I expected the worst. She smiled, but quite mysteriously and somehow *knowingly*. . . . She mentioned the financial difficulties she was having, even insisted on them, but apparently as a way of explaining the wretchedness of her appearance."[60] The following year, the forty-six-year-old restlessly married Pablo Picasso noticed a striking blonde seventeen-year-old window-shopping in front of the Galeries Lafayette. She was Marie-Thérèse Walter, a middle-class teenager, and she was for the next nine years to remain Picasso's mistress and muse, the object of his erotic obsession.[61]

It is not clear exactly when Violette's incursions onto the right bank began, but on May 11, 1933, her Latin Quarter acquaintance Lucien Balmain ran into her at the Opéra metro stop. She was well dressed and told him she had a job designing models for a couture house in the area.[62] By early summer 1933, Violette was practicing a form of "genteel" prostitution with right-bank businessmen, in the course of which she spun yarns about her life. Significantly, these included not just lies about her social origins but also narratives that prefigured her father's death.

In July 1933 she was introduced—by whom is not known—to an electrical engineer named Mahmoud Adari, from Sousse in Tunisia, who was in Paris for business and pleasure. Violette may not have slept with Adari, but at the very least she used him to get some practice in the art of seductive manipulation. By Adari's own account, he met her first briefly at a café, where she made an excellent impression on him. She told him that her father, a PLM engineer, had recently suffered from a skull fracture and needed her care; then she left to pick up her brother, a law student. Adari concluded that this was a well-educated, devoted young girl from a good family. A few days later they met again, and she informed him that her father was dead; she needed clothes for the upcoming funeral, and her family could not help right now. She dragged him to Saint-Anne Hospital and had him wait while she went in to borrow five hundred francs from a friend who was a medical intern; she came out reporting problems and asked Adari to lend her one hundred, which he did. At their third meeting, Violette appeared in elegant "half-mourning" clothes—a black suit and a white hat. She burst into tears and explained that her father had a mistress and that the latter had run up a three-thousand-franc bill for a fur stole, which remained unpaid. If Violette's mother found out, she would die of grief, so could Adari please help her out? The Tunisian finally understood that he was being scammed. When he ran into her some time later and demanded his hundred francs, she shook her head and said, "Please don't think ill of me. Goodbye."[63]

Jacques Fellous, who met her in early August, had a better idea of what he was getting into. The forty-five-year-old Fellous was also of Tunisian origin but had earned French nationality by serving in the war. He lived in Paris in a prosperous right-bank area, working as a croupier and "in business." One evening as he was walking near Place de la Madeleine, he noticed a tall, slim, elegant young woman, who was "waiting for a friend" and seemed amenable to being approached. They had a drink and made a date for a few days later, when after a stroll she came up to his apartment and immediately tried to set terms: she had debts, needed to pay off a fur stole, had lost the two thousand francs her mother gave her. Would he help out? He refused, but they had sex anyway, and he gave her a mere twenty francs. He later ungallantly commented that she "bargained like a carpet seller."[64]

Thirty-year-old Robert Isaac Atlan, a small-time businessman who met her on August 2, gave her no money at all. She smiled at him on Boulevard des Capucines and accepted to come for a drive with him and his friend. When they arrived at the hotel where he lived, she made no difficulties about coming upstairs and immediately undressed. They conversed little, and no money was exchanged. On their next date, she confided to him that although her father was an engineer and had settled a large dowry on her, she was troubled by personal debts she had no way of paying off. Her father had had a recent stroke, and in any event might leave his money to a young orphaned cousin her parents had recently adopted. Atlan later claimed, though Violette strenuously denied it, that she added, "Perhaps my father won't recover from his stroke. That would certainly help me out." He wriggled out of the relationship, fearing financial demands.[65]

Several features of these encounters are notable, beyond the unexplained coincidence that all three men had North African origins (Atlan was an Algerian Jew). Violette told her right-bank suitors the same fairy tale about her glamorous identity that she had devised to impress her friends in the Latin Quarter: the bourgeois background, the engineer father, the dowry. Her right-bank story, however, aimed at wheedling money, involved Violette falling on hard times: her father was sick, he had died, she had debts, her mother was fragile. Violette's inventions are psychologically revealing. Her father was indeed, in the summer of 1933, recovering from an accident he had suffered at work, although he was nowhere near dying. As for Baptiste's alleged mistress, the case would later reveal how loaded an invention this was. And what fears lurked beneath Violette's fabrication of an orphaned cousin threatening to usurp her parents' money and affection?

After the crime, the newspapers made much of Violette's manipulation of different identities in various parts of the city. "This perverse gamine who posed as a student only ventured into the boulevards and the Madeleine area the better to impersonate a rich heiress in the Latin Quarter." *Le Petit Parisien* quoted her as remarking that if one of her student friends had surprised her walking the boulevards, she would have "died of shame."

"What a paradox! She degraded herself on one side of the river the better to shine on the other."[66] In truth, though, Violette lied as badly north of the Seine as south of it, and the evidence suggests that she made little money in her right-bank adventures—twenty francs here, a hundred francs there, sometimes nothing at all. Her lack of financial acumen as a courtesan raises questions as to where she secured the money she spent on and with her Latin Quarter friends. And her eagerness to rush into bed with the men she encountered on the right bank suggests that something other than the need for cash was driving her: the same demons that pushed her to give herself so easily to schoolboys and students.

Violette assumed that she could pass for a bourgeoise, and some men believed her—Adari, for instance—while others at least pretended to. Education undoubtedly helped with the role-playing. During Violette's brief time at the Lycée Fénelon, students were asked to write an essay, modeled on the Romantic writer Chateaubriand's reaction to a famous funeral oration, in which they described their own strong response to a work of art or literature or another object of admiration. Violette, whose exposure to art and literature was minimal at best, produced a conventional but perfectly literate account of her reaction to a seascape at Belle-Isle-en-Mer, off the coast of Brittany: "Never will my eyes forget the tableau that appeared before them. . . . Waves three or four meters high crashed against the slabs of rock. The resulting foam rose in the air like snowflakes. A cave glittered to our eyes like silver, thanks to the mica and schist in the rocks that composed it." The essay, written in a strong and elegant hand, earned an average grade.[67] Its author had likely caught on to the message that gratuitous aesthetic delight was part of being upper-class.

The easiest part of playing a role, however, is acquiring the right costume, and clothes were central to Violette's self-invention, as they were, indeed, to her life. Germaine had been a seamstress before she married and made dresses for her daughter as the latter grew up. Their neighbor Simone Mayeul, who did not much care for either mother or daughter, remembered that when Germaine finished a dress she would parade "mademoiselle" out on the landing for everyone to admire: "Isn't my daughter beautiful?"[68] Moving away from her parents' world, Violette remained deeply invested in fashion and clothes shopping, and the stories she concocted about herself and her family nearly always involved the world of couture. She usually said that her mother worked as a *première,* a top saleswoman, for the house of Paquin, and often added that she herself was a designer or a model for that same house. In the summer of 1933, she often mentioned that she was going off to model the newest styles on the beaches of Normandy. Where clothes are concerned, Violette's story is very much of her generation. Before the Great War, it would have been near impossible for a lower-class girl—unless she were a courtesan or an actress—to dress like a lady. By the 1930s, simpler and more readily available fashions allowed someone like Violette to lie convincingly about her status.

At the turn of the century, working-class women typically owned one or two sets of workaday clothes and a better outfit for Sundays and holidays. Before World War I, urban working women wore a shapeless bundle of clothes: a shirt, a layering of petticoats, skirt, and apron, a shawl thrown over their shoulders. For Sundays and outings, they changed into a black merino full-length dress, white cotton stockings, ankle boots, and a brimmed hat. Working-class women typically did not buy ready-to-wear clothing: budgets were tight and devoted mostly to food, credit hard to come by, thrift both a habit and a necessity. They sewed their own, and endlessly altered and refashioned clothes they already owned or bought second-hand.[69] It was unlikely that around 1900 anyone would confuse the lumpy silhouette of a working woman with that of a bourgeois matron dressed in finely tailored clothes, an ornate hat crowning her elaborately swept-up hair. By the 1920s, things had changed dramatically. The writer Pierre MacOrlan described the young women in the working-class neighborhood he lived in before the Great War as "hair pulled back, shoulders covered by a shawl of indeterminate color, the rest of their costume similarly indistinct." When he ventured back there after the war, the women seemed entirely different, younger and fresher, wearing shorter skirts with neatly stretched stockings, bobbed hair, and cloche hats. He surmised that department stores like Le Printemps were behind this transformation.[70]

In the 1920s and 1930s, the consumer market for clothes took off in France: a growing immigrant labor force provided cheap ready-to-wear clothing, department stores and catalogs expanded their range and appeal, and the young women who poured into service jobs felt that they needed and could afford stylish clothes. Couture designs had been protected by law, but by the 1930s the sheer extent of copying and pirating made such protection useless. Catalogs offered the same styles as couturiers for a third of the price, and home sewers could achieve the look for even less. For the first time in France, fashion crossed class barriers.[71]

Hairstyles were part of this transformation too. In the Belle Époque only wealthy ladies could afford the hairpieces and domestic assistance it took to achieve an elegant updo. Whether or not the postwar short hairstyles were liberating, they were certainly democratic: as the number of hairdressing salons in Paris exploded, any woman with a bit of cash could have her hair bobbed and marcelled. In 1933 a popular fashion magazine assured readers that in difficult economic times "even if a woman cannot treat herself to a new outfit she need not neglect the elegance of a hairdo she can manage on her own."[72] High fashion also played a part in blurring the lines between classes. To be sure, Coco Chanel did not aim her radical "deluxe poverty" style—the long sweaters, sailor pants, and simple dark dresses—at women of modest means, and anyone who came near her clothes knew that they were expensive. But she did start a trend toward simplicity and understatement that was soon widely imitated. Anticipating Diana Vreeland's famous pronouncement that "elegance is refusal," the designer Maggy Rouff wrote at the time that "taste is made up of a thousand distastes." In the thirties it was fashionable to look as if you did not care excessively about clothes, and pared-down elegance came within the reach of any woman with a good eye for style.[73]

Violette was tall and slender, and both acquaintances and strangers commented on her stylishness. On the evening of the crime, she was wearing a blue dress and a brown coat with a matching brown beret. Her style formed a sharp contrast with that of her parents: at home Germaine had on a burgundy sweater, blue skirt, white pinafore, and something she described as beach slippers; Baptiste was wearing blue serge pants, a blue jersey shirt, gray suspenders, and bedroom slippers. In the wake of her crime, Violette went on a shopping spree: she may have thought of her new clothes as an alibi ("Look, I was clearly out on the town"), but most likely she sought comfort in shopping. At Galeries Lafayette she purchased an expensive and elegant black evening dress for four hundred and fifty francs—a month's wages for the poorest of workers—and a black beret for twenty. At a nearby store on Boulevard Haussmann she accessorized the dress with a gray bolero jacket and gloves, went on to spend sixty francs on shoes, and rounded off her purchases with a set of silver bracelets and two costume-jewelry rings, one of which she planned to give to her friend Madeleine.[74] After her arrest, her public appearances had her

Figure 5. Fashion ideal: Parisian couture circa 1930.
(Photograph by Roger-Viollet, courtesy of Image Works.)

looking every bit the elegant film noir heroine, in a dark belted coat with
a fur collar and a beret (figs. 5 and 6).

Violette had a predilection for Galeries Lafayette, the most "modern" of
the great Parisian department stores. The first of them, Le Bon Marché,
opened in 1852, Le Printemps in 1865, and Galeries Lafayette in 1881—though
the interior as it exists now, with its huge, ornate glass cupola and open upper
floors with wrought-iron balconies, dates from 1912.[75] Though department
stores represented a dramatic departure from previous commercial practices,
their impact on social life is equally important: their existence promoted the

Figure 6. Fashion reality: Violette Nozière in custody, September 1933. (Photograph by Roger-Viollet, courtesy of Image Works.)

blurring of social classes, while also allowing women to shop anonymously. The very location of the most famous department stores is significant: Printemps, Galeries Lafayette, and other lesser emporia were located along the northern Boulevard Haussmann, at the juncture between the prosperous business districts to the south and some of the city's poorest working-class neighborhoods to the north. If you were a working-class woman from Belleville, this would be the place you were magically transformed before heading south to your office job in the first or second arrondissement. Shopping in a department store also freed women from the stifling relationships and obligations that came with every transaction in a neighborhood store. They could enter freely, know the price in advance, and best of all shop without husband, parents, or neighbors knowing what they were up to.[76]

Galeries Lafayette offered a range of merchandise at an array of prices, aimed at clients of different classes. The mass-market daily *Le Petit Parisien*, widely read among the working classes, carried advertisements for the Galeries several times a week. In September 1933, full-page spreads showed wool coats and dresses starting at a modest ninety-nine francs, hats for ten to twenty, blouses for fifteen. The well-to-do as well as the upwardly mobile shopped in the Boulevard Haussmann department stores. Thérèse and Louise Bonney, authors of an English-language guidebook for wealthy Americans—the sort of women who bought from couturiers—steered their readers through Paris department store merchandise. They advised against buying dresses there, since New Yorkers would find "an appalling lack of originality in the neck and waist lines." But you could pick up a good-looking hat, a smart wool sport costume, or a well-tailored coat for a song. "In looking for clothes," they concluded, "you will find that the Galeries Lafayette and the Printemps have the smartest, the balance shifting from one season to another."[77] A woman dressed in a Galeries Lafayette outfit in 1933—high waist, long slim skirt, small hat tilted forward—could be an engine driver's daughter from the twelfth arrondissement or an heiress from Chicago.

Women, and the fashions they wore, were meant to be seen from a distance—at least that is what one might conclude from the sharp focus, in fashion magazines and other writings of the time, on *silhouette*. To Pierre MacOrlan, the line of women's clothing expressed something fundamental about the aesthetic of an age: "Young girls and young women have been able, by their very silhouette, to popularize the very principles of contemporary design. As expert conduits for secret forces, they have emerged as the messengers of the new aesthetic, which is that of geometric lines barely softened for our viewing pleasure."[78] Indeed, nothing brings to mind the bold strokes of Cubist painting so much as the stark, black vertical forms of women punctuating the pages of early 1930s French fashion magazines like so many exclamation points (fig. 7; see also fig. 8). In the early twentieth century, art and fashion traveled the same road, from the three-dimensional aesthetic inherited from the Renaissance to the two-dimensional experiments of Cubists. In previous generations, fashion designers for women relied on the elaborate creation of volume to expand or constrict body parts dramatically through such devices as bustles,

Figure 7. Long dark lines, crimped hair, small hats: Paris fashion, August 1934. (Photograph by Roger-Viollet, courtesy of Image Works.)

crinolines, corsets, and dramatically puffed sleeves. Even before World War I, however, fashion as sculpture gave way to clothing that looked like the bold, irregular patterns of Cubist collage.[79]

The specific shapes shifted every few years. The flapper silhouette had been instantly recognizable, but as the twenties ended, the *garçonne* dress, which billowed out over a dropped waist, and its accompanying pear-shaped coats and cloche hats gave way to the skinniest of lines. Projecting what the *Petit Écho de la Mode* called "a juvenile silhouette of seduction" became the goal of the new fashions: pared-down clothing over a long, slim body. When the more upscale *Jardin des Modes* reviewed the offerings of the great couture houses in March 1932, the word *silhouette* was there at every turn: Lucien Lelong and Callot both offered a silhouette tucked in at the waist, Mirande a more high-waisted, empire silhouette, Schiaparelli a "new" silhouette with the belt placed high and wider shoulders, Jenny a straight silhouette, and so on.[80] Descriptions of Violette suggest that she managed to approximate the fashion-magazine profile. One witness thus described her walking away from him: "Her dark silhouette stood out, like an elegant blot, from the shops in the background."[81]

Hats and hairdos—carefully calibrated to work together—were a crucial element of the silhouette. In the twenties, women's hats, whether brimmed cloches or severe helmetlike caps, had covered their heads completely, barely showing any hair. In December 1932 *Le Petit Écho* informed women, "We no longer wear hats pushed back; on the contrary, we tip them far forward over the forehead, at least on one side, so that the nape of the neck is uncovered, with curled or crimped hair showing." Hats were now always small and tilted forward, the *Jardin de Modes* concurred. The desired silhouette was supposed to evoke the head of a Louis XV shepherdess.[82] The quintessential look of 1932 was the woman's beret, which took up the trend toward smaller, softer, and more rakish headgear and was soon seen everywhere. "The vogue for the felt beret," *Le Jardin des Modes* observed in April 1932, "is not about to die out, since after having been seen in town during part of winter and in spring it is about to become the preferred hat for sports, car trips, and country weekends." The magazine noted that its popularity owed something to its price, which allowed women to own berets in a range of hues.[83] Violette clearly followed fashion, though by the winter of 1933 she was falling behind. First came the prescriptions to update your beret, for instance by cutting out the crown and sewing in a crocheted circle, and by late summer the diagnosis that berets were on their way out and small Arab-style toques and fezzes coming in.[84] Young women of limited means, however, still sported berets as a practical, inexpensive way to achieve the stylish tilted-forward line.

As fashion historians keep reminding us, there is no automatic correlation between dress style and historical context: the "liberated" short skirts and bobbed hair of the twenties, for instance, coincided in France with women being denied the vote and their reproductive rights being severely curtailed.[85] But history, in the form of the looming economic crisis, did put its mark on women's fashions of the early thirties. Over and over again women were given the same message in fashion magazines: in these penny-pinching times, buy basic black and keep changing the details (fig. 8). Even

**Trois écharpes différentes...**

*...pour poser sur une même robe; l'aspect de
celle-ci en sera ainsi totalement modifié. La robe
reproduite ci-contre, robe type que toute femme
possède dans sa garde-robe, est successivement
représentée avec trois écharpes différentes, dra-
pées sur le corsage et à la taille. Voici (à gauche), deux triangles de crêpe de Chine rouge
vif, triangles semblables, dont une pointe est assez
longue pour entourer la taille et se nouer sur le
côté, tandis que la deuxième est fixée au décol-
leté par un clip et la troisième à la couture de
dessous de bras, par un point. La deuxième
écharpe formant fichu est faite d'un long biais
de romain blanc, double, mesurant environ 1 2 cm.
sur 2 m. 5o. Le troisième modèle est une bande
de fin lainage écossais, terminée par un picot à la
machine et mesurant environ 1 2 cm. sur2 m. 20.*

**Une parure de fourrure...**

*...que vous pourrez porter aussi bien sur votre
manteau d'hiver que sur votre prochain tailleur
ou sur la petite robe-manteau que vous vous
ferez faire pour le printemps. La parure que
nous donnons ici comprend trois pièces. Le col
est fait d'une simple bande rectangulaire de
2 5 cm. sur 85 cm., que trois pinces placées sur un
des grands côtés mettent légèrement en forme
à la nuque; un gros bouton la maintient fermée
on la drapant, mais on peut aussi la laisser
tomber devant comme une écharpe. La cein-
ture mesure 4 cm. de haut, la longueur est pro-
portionnée à la taille. Enfin, le manchon en
forme de barillet mesure 20 cm. sur 25 cm.
Toutes les fourrures plates, à poils ondulés
ou frisés, conviendront pour cette parure, mais
l'astrakan et le caracul plat sont plus élégants.*

Figure 8.   How to change your look on a shoestring: *Le Jardin des Modes,*
January 15, 1932. (Courtesy Bibliothèque Nationale de France.)

an upscale publication like *Le Jardin des Modes* endlessly advised readers on how to update a dress they already owned. The variety of ways in which women were taught in fashion magazines, week after week, to transform a simple dark dress is astonishing: add a white crochet collar, a pair of raspberry-colored sleeves, tie on a bright-colored crepe scarf, run a large white piqué bow through the buttonhole, shrug on a bolero jacket, knot on a fur collar or sew snaps on two circles of silver fox and slide them up your arms, pin on an artificial flower, sew on sequins for evening. You could retailor the sleeves, neckline, and hem, and only after every variation had been exhausted would you finally make your dress into a couple of skirts for your daughter.[86]

The style of the early thirties—stark, youthful fashions adorned on a shoestring—perfectly suited someone like Violette, who had a good sense of style but little money. She was also blessed with a tall and slim body well suited to contemporary fashion, which allowed her to boast about being a model. The circumstances of the moment, high style and low budgets, as well as Violette's knack for dressing, allowed her to pass, at least some of the time, as a woman of a higher class.

Of course Violette's fashion-related aspirations went beyond just dressing well. Most of her tall tales about herself and her family involved the world of haute couture, where she had her mother working as a *première* for the house of Paquin, sometimes adding that she herself was employed there as a designer or model. Violette's fantasy combined her parents' social ambitions, since leading designers achieved both status and wealth, with her own predilection for easy glamour. It was far more appealing to imagine oneself turning, with the help of a well-connected lover, into a version of Coco Chanel than to face the hard work and social obstacles involved in training as a doctor or a teacher. And unlike most other professions at the time, high fashion was a place where a woman could make a big splash.

To be sure, the granddaddy of French couture had been a man, Charles Worth, who built his reputation in the mid-nineteenth century designing gowns for Empress Eugénie, and the years after World War I did see the advent of enduring male designers, such as Paul Poiret, Edward Molyneux, and Jean Patou. But the real rising stars and revolutionaries of the interwar years were women.[87] Madeleine Vionnet made her name creating pleated floor-length evening dresses that draped wearers like Grecian goddesses. Elsa Schiaparelli drew inspiration from her avant-garde artist friends to produce outrageous garments like her famous "shoe" hat. And then there was Coco Chanel, gifted and beautiful, the very icon of modern fashion with her sailor pants, pajamas, jersey dresses, sweaters, and long ropes of pearls: " 'Chanel red,' 'Chanel number 5,' 'Chanel tricolour!' " the Bonneys' 1929 guidebook gushed. "There must be something dramatic and unerring in this woman's personality to produce 'headlines' like this each season."[88] Compared with the years after World War II, when French haute couture was ruled by the likes of Christian Dior and Yves Saint-Laurent, the interwar fashion firmament was heavily female. (And no matter that these female designers generally loathed each other, with Chanel famously dismissing Schiaparelli as "that Italian artist who makes clothes.") Even in fashion houses nominally run by men, the actual dress designing was often done by women, and outside of the owners and business managers, the hierarchy within such establishments was almost entirely female.[89]

The house of Paquin, the object of Violette's fixation, was a case in point, an establishment where a woman had risen to fashion stardom, albeit initially in the shadow of a man. Paquin dated to an earlier generation, that of the Belle Époque, and like so many fashion houses its story is one of movement from the periphery to the center of society. Paquin Frères was originally a modest clothing store in Caen, in Normandy, which in 1840 passed into the hands of a Jewish merchant named Isaac Jacob, who bequeathed it to his enterprising son Isidore. Isidore, now calling himself Paquin, moved to the capital to work as a stockbroker but, unwilling to let go of the family business, found an associate and in 1891 opened a clothing store under the Paquin name on the famed right-bank "fashion street," Rue de la Paix.

By then, Isidore had met a talented and attractive twenty-two-year-old, Jeanne Becker (she "looked Levantine," it was said), whom he hired to design dresses and who soon became his wife. In the span of just a few years, Paquin had toppled Worth off its pedestal to emerge as the leading fashion house in turn-of-the-century Paris, dressing aristocrats and wealthy bourgeoises, leading actresses, famous courtesans, and even foreign royalty. Its fame extended overseas, and Paquin became the first designer to open foreign branches, in London and New York. In recognition of this service to France, Isidore Paquin was awarded the Legion of Honor in 1900, at the height of the Dreyfus affair, over the loud protests of anti-Semites. That same year, the gigantic statue of an elegant Parisienne that towered over the capital's Universal Exposition was wearing an outfit by Paquin. By then, however, it had long been clear that it was to the artistry of Jeanne Paquin's ethereal pastel-colored and fur-trimmed concoctions that the house owed its success. Widowed in her forties, Jeanne kept the business going strong. In 1913 she was also awarded the Legion of Honor, the first woman ever to be granted that distinction. As one fashion historian concludes, "If anyone was Worth's successor it was she."[90]

Violette's predilection for Paquin is interesting, since by the early thirties, more than a decade after Jeanne's retirement, the house had been eclipsed by a new generation of designers. In the postwar decades, Paquin was part of an older fashion establishment less in favor with younger clients, with Jeanne's less talented successors focusing mainly on well-tailored coats and furs. The Bonneys' 1929 shopping guide diplomatically opined that "Paquin at number 3 [Rue de la Paix] has conceded little to the demands of time," and probably discouraged its readers with the comment, "Your mother or grandmother may have been their clients."[91] Why did Violette choose to imagine her mother and herself working for a couturier like Paquin whose star was on the decline? Was it something she had read or heard? Did she believe that a house with an older pedigree would be better suited to her mother, or did the choice reflect her own innate conservatism? Or was she, a worker's daughter from the eastern end of Paris, simply ill informed, unable to grasp the difference between Paquin and Chanel?

Equally intriguing, though more explicable, is her decision to allot to her mother the position of *première*, or first saleswoman. Violette could not, of course, pretend that her mother ran a couture house, since that lie could easily be exposed. Most people, however, were well aware of the power and prestige inherent in the position of *première*. In the hierarchy of the house, *premières,* who ruled over a workshop of twenty to thirty seamstresses, stood just below the designer. They were both fashion specialists and managers.[92] As an American writer explained in 1925, *premières* "are the most expert dressmakers in the establishment. Nearly all of them share in the gift for design, and every now and then one of them will turn out to be a great genius. The designer consults with them freely in working out the season's line. Every great *première* has the ambition to head her own establishment."[93]

The position was socially as well as artistically glamorous, since *premières* personally advised the highest caliber of clients, which in some cases included royalty. Only *premières,* who did fittings, had personal, physical contact with such clients. The departure of a talented *première* could be a blow to a fashion house, as she might take her customers with her. In the leading houses, the *premières* carved up the Western world like conquerors: at Paquin in its heyday, Isidore's cousin Jane Bloch had an empire that included the Spanish and Russian courts as well the queens of Belgium and Portugal.[94] The world of high fashion, in short, promised both glamour and upward mobility. Talented *premières* like Jeanne Paquin and Madeleine Vionnet had come up in the world to run their own businesses and make their mark on fashion. Farther down the hierarchy, such a future was unlikely. According to an American observer, the girls who modeled clothes—as Violette claimed she did—sometimes came to a bad end. The daughter of a bus driver or a postman, a model got used to her own image wearing beautiful clothes: "But how can she get them? By making a rich marriage? In France marriages of that sort are arranged, and the husband of means goes to the girl whose family can settle a large [dowry] upon her."[95] Almost inevitably, they became courtesans. In Violette's version of her life, however, there was no fear of that happening: her father was an engineer, rich and well-connected.

For years before she tried to kill her parents, Violette had begun to annihilate them in her mind, constructing a fantasy about both their identity and her own. Unevenly successful as they were, her lies reveal a great deal about which class boundaries could be crossed in Paris between the wars, and how. Violette lived in a world that was still sharply divided between an upper class that was aristocratic in spirit if not in fact—a tight nexus of families who had money, worshipped culture, and observed intricate social rituals—and a working class mostly deprived of material and cultural resources and heavily patronized by their "superiors." It took time and patience to scale the steep "barrier" between classes, and Baptiste and Germaine, with their carefully constructed nest egg and cosseted only child, were doing their best. But interwar Paris also allowed for some fluidity, especially for women. With a smattering of the right education and carefully chosen ready-to-wear clothes, a girl could just about pass— but how convincingly?—as the person she wanted to be.

What makes a person shift from fantasizing a crime to committing it? Violette kept trying to obliterate her parents, going so far as to tell strangers that her father was dead. Yet without them, she had nothing but an occasional lover and a posse of unreliable friends in a Latin Quarter café. So she held on to them in her fantasy life, recasting her father as an engineer and her mother as a style maven, heedless of the fact that the kind of man who graduated with a degree from Polytechnique would never be married to a woman who worked, much less in fashion. As long as she had no other option, Violette could not dispense with the only people who cared about her. But she fell in love, and when she did everything changed.

# FOUR

# A Crime in Late Summer

ONE OF THE REMARKABLE FEATURES of Violette Nozière's crime was that she committed it twice, making a first attempt on her parents' lives in March 1933. In January, Violette had turned eighteen, the legal age of emancipation, but she must have felt anything but free. She had withdrawn from Lycée Fénelon, and her parents had enrolled her in a Paris correspondence school, École Universelle, so that they could keep an eye on her while she worked at home. In those early winter weeks, she had no excuse to get out of the house, and her depression and anger at being cut off from her Latin Quarter friends translated as usual into a series of physical ailments. Her only opportunities to venture into the city were trips to visit Dr. Henri Deron, who saw patients at Hôpital Bichat, located at the northwestern end of Paris. On March 16, Violette went in for blood tests, and she again saw the doctor on March 22. Germaine worried that her daughter might have tuberculosis, but Violette may well have known what her symptoms suggested.[1]

Was it fear of the diagnosis that precipitated Violette's first attempt on her parents' lives? During the subsequent investigation, the young girl stated that in March 1933 she was suicidal, and her intention had been for the whole family to die together. On March 23, in a dress rehearsal of her August crime, Violette went to a pharmacy and purchased a tube of the medication Véronal, a barbiturate commonly used as a sleeping aid and available without a prescription. She ground the pills into a powder, which she wrapped into three packages. At home, she explained to Germaine and Baptiste that the doctor had suggested they join their daughter in taking these medications so as to "avoid contagion." The Nozière parents complied and later fell into a deep sleep, only to wake up suffocated by the smoke from a fire that was consuming the curtain in front of their bedroom door. The next-door neighbor, an electrician named Ernest Mayeul, wakened by the commotion, called an ambulance and a fire truck, and the blaze, which Violette said she had set accidentally, was put out. Violette herself was apparently unscathed, but Baptiste remained ill for a while and Germaine even stayed briefly in the hospital. Their malaise was attributed to the smoke, and no investigation was carried out.

Less than a week later, Violette was informed by Dr. Deron that she had syphilis. She was furious, and one of her friends later heard her blame Pierre Camus for infecting her. Dr. Deron knew the probable cause, but he took pity on a young woman with a drama-prone, overbearing mother, a girl he later described as sweet-tempered if somewhat remote and "insensitive."[2] He had undoubtedly run into this sort of family crisis before and offered to lie for her: he would tell her parents, who expected to be informed of the diagnosis, that she was still a virgin, and explain that this sort of illness could be hereditary, often skipping a generation or two. On April 10, Baptiste Nozière went to visit the physician, who gave him the news. According to Germaine, he said, " 'Tell me the whole truth, M. Deron—my daughter is no longer a *jeune fille;* she got this illness from a man. . . .' Monsieur Deron said to my husband that Violette was a *jeune fille* and her illness was hereditary. My husband answered, 'I can't believe that.' "[3] Did Baptiste and Germaine will themselves to believe the doctor's lie, in the face of all they knew about Violette? Just to be sure, they both got tests, the results of which were negative. For the sake of family honor, it was necessary to espouse the view that some wanton great-grandparent in Neuvy or Prades was responsible for this disaster.

Dr. Deron was to become, to his dismay, an unwitting accomplice in Violette's crime, since it was a forged letter in his name that induced her parents to imbibe the drugs in August. Before that, however, Violette had successfully pressed him into service as a character in the fantasies of social promotion that she shared with her parents. Henri Deron was clearly a member of the upper classes, with a home and private practice on Rue de Passy, in the wealthy western sixteenth arrondissement. Given his class and status, he was not subject, during the investigation, to the same scrutiny as other witnesses, and when he gave his one deposition, the tone that came through was that of a man used to being treated with deference by everyone, including policemen and judges: "Need I say that I am not the author of the letter that she showed her parents," he began; as for her illness, he peremptorily concluded, "you will allow me to retreat behind professional confidentiality."[4]

Later in April, the Nozière parents made a formal visit to Deron to thank him for treating their daughter. "He is a highly considered doctor, and we would never question anything he said or recommended," Germaine later explained.[5] The fact that Henri Deron was exactly the kind of man to impress and intimidate her parents was a point not lost on Violette. She informed them around this time that during her frequent visits to Deron, she had met his sister Janine, who had taken an interest in her and suggested an outing. Soon telegrams began arriving from the entirely fictional Janine asking Violette out for an afternoon in town or an evening at the theater. Violette had found a means of escaping home that her parents encouraged, thrilled that the sister of a doctor from the sixteenth would patronize Violette and might possibly sneak her into the inaccessible world of the bourgeoisie.[6] Violette would make sure that her parents had no further direct contact with the doctor, and they all understood that she could not possibly invite someone like Janine Deron to the unglamorous Rue de Madagascar. "Janine Deron" served as a convenient alibi, but she also became part of Violette's fantasy life. The concierge at 9 Rue de Madagascar, Angèle Bourdon, sourly remembered that "the Nozière girl barely talked to me except to ask for her mail, but she did tell me that she was going off to be a companion to Dr. Deron's sister." Violette also boasted to her good friend Madeleine that the doctor gave her money and that his sister took an interest in her.[7]

For the next few weeks, Violette followed a medical treatment for her venereal disease and resumed her social life in the Latin Quarter. Madeleine Feydit, the intern who treated her twice a week at Hôpital Bichat, described Violette as remote and narcissistic: she talked a lot about both herself and her parents, of whom she seemed fond, and claimed that they were going to adopt the son of a recently deceased cousin. She gave as her address an apartment on the elegant Boulevard Saint-Germain in the center of the city.[8]

In May, Germaine decided, no doubt to Violette's chagrin, that it would be a good idea to get her daughter out of the city, and she opted to visit her husband's family in Prades. Violette had no formal classes to keep her in Paris, the weather was warming up, and travel was heavily discounted for railway families. Baptiste himself never stayed more than two or three days in Prades; he invoked work as a pretext, but in truth his relationship with the authoritarian Félix had long been fraught. Violette remained in the village from May 20 to June 26, while Germaine traveled back and forth, tending to husband and daughter in two different locations.[9]

The spring in Prades was uneventful. Violette, as usual, cut quite a figure in the village, where "her elegance and tall tales caused a sensation." She boasted a lot but on a scale appropriate to a rural hamlet where her parents were known, giving herself a position as a mathematics teacher. Germaine asked a young girl named Antoinette if Violette could spend time with her, and so they did. Violette came out to the fields and read a lot, once informing her companion that her book was in English. "And I did see," recalled Antoinette, "that the book was not in the French language." Rumors flew that Violette was dissolute, that she climbed out of her window at night to go with local boys. Though the mayor stated that he saw nothing of the sort going on, lads in nearby Langeac later said that they always rejoiced at the arrival of *la parisienne* in the area. Certainly when Germaine was around she kept her daughter on a short leash: Madame Vigouroux, who owned a local café where a dance took place on June 4, remembered that Violette's mother came to fetch her around 7:30 and slapped her right there at the ball, angry that her daughter had not shown up for dinner.[10]

Violette returned from Prades on Monday, June 26, and by the end of that week had met a man who changed her life. On Friday the 30th, at an outside table of the café La Capoulade, her friend Willy introduced her to the twenty-year-old Jean Dabin. Only one letter separated his name from that of the era's most famous male movie star, Jean Gabin, but the young man's looks could not have been more different from that of the robust, earthy Gabin. Jean's appearance was soon to become famous, reproduced in many photographs, lampooned in cartoons. He was handsome in an effete way, tall and thin with elegant long fingers. As one paper put it, "He does not lack for a special kind of appeal," a reference to possible bisexuality. He dressed a little too well, in the style of dapper young men of the day: a dark wide-lapelled jacket broad through the shoulders and narrow at the waist, wide trousers, an extra fat striped tie and matching pocket handkerchief, carefully slicked-down hair, and large, round tortoiseshell

Figure 9. Jean Dabin. (Courtesy Archives de Paris,
D2 U8 379 and 380.)

glasses (fig. 9). His pale, narrow face and myopic eyes probably made him
look dreamy and vulnerable; in any event, Violette was smitten and soon
fell in love. When asked during her trial if Jean was the only man she had
ever loved, she answered, "The only one."[11] She picked up the tab and
made it clear that she wanted to see him again; he invited her to meet him
for a movie on the following Monday. He was flattered, he later said,
proud of his "powers of seduction."[12]

The relationship between Jean and Violette was later described by many
journalists as a cross-class affair: he was a law student, she a worker's

daughter, modern and corrupt avatars of *La Bohème*'s Rodolphe and Mimi. In reality, the fact that they had a lot in common must have been part of the attraction. Jean's family was very similar to Violette's, although socially a notch above hers. His father, Émile, worked for the railways like Baptiste but as the stationmaster for the freight depot in the suburb of Ivry, just southeast of the city, on the Orléans line: with a managerial job, even a modest one, he could legitimately be considered bourgeois. What is more, the Dabins lived not far from the Nozières, on Quai de la Gare, which ran along the Seine in the thirteenth, across from the Bercy wine depots. This was hardly a glamorous location, but then the Dabins had an actual villa, fronted by an ivy-covered iron gate bearing a brass plaque that read: "E. Dabin, Stationmaster."[13] They had gotten their only child, Jean, into university to study law, and Émile Dabin's description of the family's struggle exactly mirrors attitudes in Violette's family and milieu: "I have worked for the company for over twenty years, having gained my position through hard work and persistence, and I raised my family honorably. . . . I gave my son a solid education at the price of great sacrifices."[14] Jean undoubtedly seemed to Violette like her dream come true, because his family embodied the aspirations of her own parents.

Jean's achievements were in fact very slight. He later proudly told a journalist that at age seventeen he had published "a book that met with some success among the initiated."[15] *Remarks on the Spirit of Contradiction* can hardly be called a book: a fifteen-page collection (in very large print) of extremely banal aphorisms, the pamphlet aims for urbane wit and delivers teenage wisdom: "The contradictor cannot live in isolation. He needs Society"; "The history of philosophy cannot be explained without this critical factor: the spirit of contradiction"; "The real contradictor replies, 'That is not true' to the woman who says she loves him."[16] A first-year law student, Dabin had not taken the June examination because he was on a "study trip" in Rome. According to his friend Willy, he was rarely seen in class and spent most of his time in cafés.[17] Jean may have cut classes for the same reason Violette did during her time at Fénelon—for fear of failing if he, a stationmaster's child, tried to compete with the sons of academics and politicians. He had initially sought comradeship in the Latin Quarter by joining Action Française as a student "hawker." Membership in the right-wing student movement probably offered him the sense of belonging he lacked at the university, as well as an outlet for his frustrations. The party's racist nationalism held particular appeal to the lower end of the bourgeoisie, among people who felt insecure about their social status.[18] Jean, however, was not even to excel at right-wing thuggery: he was expelled for stealing from the Camelots' cash box, as he later explained with much embarrassment: "I left because I appropriated a certain sum of money. It's a complicated story, and in any case I reimbursed the funds."[19] According to one newspaper, Dabin was arrested the previous year along with a friend, the son of a high official of the Paris-Orléans, for a politically motivated assault. A fellow law student recalled that Jean, like Violette, lied about his background: "Mostly he pretended that his father was a high official in the Paris-Orléans railways, when he was just a simple stationmaster for that company."[20]

Like his paramour, Jean had tastes beyond his means and was unscrupulous about making up the difference. One can see why he would seem a quintessential bourgeois to a worker reading about the case: living at home with his needs taken care of, he got one hundred and fifty to two hundred francs a month from his father for his expenses, and his mother discreetly slipped him another hundred to make ends meet. Most of the time he could manage on his allowance, but once he met Violette his needs changed.

At their first meeting, Violette gave Jean a detailed version of her fairytale background: she had studied at various lycées in Paris, including Fénelon, and had just left school to design clothes for Paquin. Her mother had been a *première* there, and her father, an engineer for the PLM, had invested one hundred and eighty thousand francs, Violette's future dowry, in the couture house. Her father's brother was a police commissioner in the Panthéon district of the Latin Quarter. The aunt with a wealthy protector also made an appearance, with Jean once having to wait near a fancy hotel while Violette "took tea with her aunt and her mother." Did Jean believe her? He emphatically asserted that he completely bought into her "stories about millionaire aunts and uncles with inheritances." It is possible that his own lack of true bourgeois pedigree made him oblivious to subtler social cues, but he surely heard the men in his circle dismiss her as a phony. He said that he never accompanied her home—she took taxis a lot—but she eventually admitted that her home was on Rue de Madagascar.[21] Jean lived close enough to that area, and would be sufficiently aware of the world of railways, to know that management-level personnel of the PLM did not live on that sort of street.

Almost immediately, however, Violette's high social and financial status became a necessary fiction between them. Violette and Jean met again the following week and on Saturday became lovers. According to Jean, over the course of the next six weeks, until he left Paris on August 17 for a holiday, they had seven or eight sexual encounters in a cheap hotel on Rue Victor Cousin, in the afternoons or evenings. They once spent a night together, Violette having told her parents "that she was going to Grandville to visit a friend named Madeleine, a medical doctor." Jean had initially sometimes picked up the tab in cafés and restaurants, but he quickly confessed to her that he was *raide,* broke. It was always Violette who took care of the hotel room, and she soon fell into a pattern of giving Jean small amounts of money—one hundred francs every few days, he said—so that he could make a show of paying. Witnesses, who later professed shock on the subject, said that they sometimes saw him delving into her purse for money. Jean was surprised, he said, that she was so flush, but she told him that her father gave her three thousand francs a month, her wealthy aunt one thousand more. Violette once showed Jean fifteen hundred francs, which she said were from her grandmother in Neuvy. As for family dynamics, Jean said that Violette expressed a strong dislike for her father and once confided that he hit her mother and even herself on occasion when she tried to intervene. She never said anything negative about her mother.

Jean and Violette's idyll went on through July, but by early August she was complaining of financial problems. She disappeared for five or six days early in the month, saying that she had to go to a funeral in Neuvy. This was the period when she was seeing Atlan and Fellous on the right bank, but as we know, her ventures into quasi-prostitution did not prove especially lucrative. When she returned, she explained that money was tight because her father had contracted gambling debts and as a result his bank safe had been sealed. This was bad news for Jean, who was due to leave on August 17 for a vacation in Brittany with his parents and had planned to borrow some money from his girlfriend. He ended up cadging three hundred and fifty francs from Willy, which Violette promised to repay.

Meanwhile, Violette was contemplating a large expense. She told Jean to start looking for a used car, and eventually he and Willy located a secondhand Bugatti for sale. Jean, who knew how to drive, was due back from vacation on September 1, and the plan was for the four of them, Violette, Jean, Willy, and Violette's friend Madeleine, to take off on holiday in the car after his return, headed for the fashionable resort town of Les Sables d'Olonne on the Atlantic coast. Violette was confident that her aunt would come through with the money but also talked about visiting a family friend on Rue de Sèze—the address of Jacques Fellous—who was arranging for the sale of twenty thousand francs' worth of stocks belonging to her mother. As the time for Jean's departure approached, prospects for the Bugatti and seaside holiday were not looking very good. Violette may have been, as she later insisted, madly in love with Jean, but she apparently understood him well enough to assume that only the money she lavished on him could keep him by her side.

Back on Rue de Madagascar, the summer had not been easy.[22] There were no reports of big family fights—Violette, in love, must have been in excellent spirits—but Germaine did remember that in early July her daughter got up and uncharacteristically brought them coffee in bed. The coffee tasted bitter, and Violette was instructed to throw it out. Her mother was later to see great significance in this small event, insisting that coffee she made right afterward from the same package tasted fine. More dramatic at the time was an accident that occurred on July 14th, France's national holiday, when Baptiste, ever the model employee, was working on his locomotive at the station. He slipped and fell off his engine, landing hard on the platform. Just how much harm he suffered from the fall is unclear, but it kept him at home until July 30. Baptiste tried to go back to work, but complications from the fall sent him back to the hospital from August 5th until the 17th (on the day he came back, Germaine remembered, they had sex for what was to be the last time). He was assigned rest at home for another two weeks after that. Baptiste's medical problems would have given Violette more freedom to conduct her romance that summer, with her father in and out of the hospital and her mother visiting and tending to him. Baptiste's accident seems also to have spurred her to think about ways in which the demise of her father, or maybe of both parents, would make her life easier: it was in the wake of Baptiste's fall and health troubles that she began telling her right-bank lovers that her father was ailing or dead.

Those late-summer weeks in the sixth-floor apartment must have been hot and frustrating for everyone—the ailing Baptiste, the worried Germaine, the increasingly restless Violette. On August 12, Germaine, who had been at the hospital, returned to find a telegram, prominently displayed on the table, from Janine Deron inviting Violette out. When she went to get something in the bedroom closet, however, she found the door jammed shut and, after she pried it open, four hundred francs she had hidden there missing. This may have been the time, a few days before Jean's departure, when the lovers spent a whole night together with Janine as an alibi. Violette had previously stolen thirty francs from her father's wallet, but when she returned and her mother confronted her, she denied having taken the money. The following day, Germaine found a photograph of Dabin in Violette's wallet and demanded, to no avail, to know who he was.

Adding to the tension was a crisis involving extended family. With Baptiste in poor shape and Germaine having to tend to him, it had become clear that there would be no family vacation to visit relatives. Still concerned about Violette's health, and undoubtedly her morals, Baptiste wrote to his father asking if the young woman could return to Prades. Félix Nozière did not answer, later protesting a bit too much as to why: he did not know how to write, and besides his son and daughter-in-law had always freely sent the child to him, so why bother with the formality? Ancient bitterness between father and son, with the old man's daughter-in-law Marie as a flashpoint, must have resurfaced in the spring. Baptiste, bored and brooding in his hospital bed, decided he had had enough. He composed and sent a classic instance of those letters better left unsent. In the missive, dated August 13 and preserved in the archives of the case, Baptiste wrote in long, poorly spelled and punctuated sentences, addressing his father in the formal mode, as *vous* rather than *tu:*

> After the silence following the previous letter we wrote I am writing my last letter to you, I am not so stupid as to not understand why you did not write back. It is obvious that you did not answer the letter that my wife wrote to give news of my daughter and tell you that she needed to go back to the country, not wanting to have her in the way again. But either way you can rest easy, I did not want to send her back since I understood too well that she was a big hindrance to your little comforts. You will excuse my handwriting since I am writing from my hospital bed, I fell off my machine on July 14 and am not yet better, not that you care, I know perfectly well that you have no affection at all for us. It has been fifteen years that agreement between us has been hanging by a thread, all because of my sister in law, a gossip [whose tongue] could kill a whole brigade, well she got what she wanted. As far as I'm concerned it's over, you will never see me again back home, love your sweetheart since people in Prades have not been shy about telling me lots about what goes on between the two of you. Nozière, Baptiste.[23]

On August 17, Baptiste came home from hospital, and Jean left on vacation as planned. The city was hot and empty. There was no escape for anybody.

Violette readily admitted that her crime was carefully planned. In the week before she acted, she had bought rat poison, but she changed her mind about using it after learning that it caused horrible suffering when ingested.[24] On Sunday, August 20, a pharmacy student named André Malbois sold tubes of S_oménal, a new barbiturate-based sleeping drug, to a tall and elegant young woman aged, he thought, about twenty, who entered his pharmacy on Avenue Daumesnil between five and six in the evening. She wanted two tubes of twelve tablets each of the drug, which did not require a prescription. Why so many? Malbois asked, probably less out of professional concern than because things would be slow on a Sunday in August, and asking about sleeping pills would be a good way to get an attractive woman around his own age into intimate conversation. The young lady showed no inclination to linger, however, after explaining that she suffered from insomnia, was going on vacation, and was afraid of not finding this type of drug at her destination.[25] Violette later bought a third tube of Soménal in another pharmacy on Place Daumesnil, as well as an innocuous all-purpose drug, a heavily advertised magnesium sulfate marketed as Kruschen Salts. She had thought it all out carefully, she explained. In a nearby café she made up three small paper packages, identical in size but folded differently so that each looked distinct. In one she put the contents of two tubes of Soménal, ground up; in a second, half a tube and enough Kruschen salts to make it equal to the first; the third package of equal size, which she marked with a cross in pencil, contained only salts.[26]

On August 21, a Monday, Jean was very much on her mind. After eating an early lunch with her parents—veal brain in oil sauce—Violette left home around two thirty, allegedly to an appointment with Dr. Deron. As she crossed the courtyard, her mother waved to her, noting with pride that Violette had dressed up to see the doctor in clothes she had made for her—a blue skirt, bolero jacket, and gray hat.[27] Violette went in reality to the Latin Quarter, where she wrote her lover a passionate note on the letterhead of their favorite meeting place, the Palais du Café. The letter begins bizarrely with a lie: she had been unable to write because she had hemorrhaged after being hit by a motorcycle on Place de la République. She may have felt the need for an excuse for not yet having paid Willy the money "they" owed him, which she promised to do the next day. The rest is a love letter, conventional but no doubt heartfelt: "Darling, I am so terribly blue, time is so long when we are apart. . . . Oh, soon my love, let us be together, away from you life seems so dull, everything annoys and exasperates me, I am in an awful mood. . . . If I were ever to lose your love I think my life would be over, without you I feel no happiness. I love you as I never have loved, madly and passionately." She promised to be in Les Sables d'Olonne "on Thursday morning," by which she probably meant the last day in August, ending with "long and tender kisses" from "your beloved little woman."[28] Either before or after writing to Jean, Violette penned another letter, this one to her parents from Dr. Deron.

Violette and Germaine both told the authorities what happened later in the day of August 21, and the accounts are quite similar, although Germaine's contained details consonant with her desire to emphasize a financial motive for the crime.[29] For instance, Germaine reported that she had planned at some point in the day to take three thousand francs to the bank, but Violette found various excuses to delay her until after the bank had closed. In any event, Violette returned home that afternoon to a family uproar. While she was out, her parents had combed through her possessions, searching for evidence that she was seeing someone. It was difficult to hide anything in the family's tiny lodgings, and the couple found what they were looking for concealed between the pages and under the covers of Violette's schoolbooks: letters and telegrams from Bernard and Jean, including a particularly troubling note from the latter, dated August 9: "Your crazy lover waited for you until the midnight train, but your spies must have kept you in," followed by words in English they could not understand. They also found a photograph of a fashionably dressed young man with round tortoiseshell glasses. Germaine was distraught, but Baptiste pleaded that she not "cause a scandal" and insisted that they calm down by taking a stroll in the Bois de Vincennes.

When Violette came home, the storm erupted nonetheless, with both parents demanding to know who this Jean was, screaming their outrage and shame at their daughter. Germaine recounted the scene in the written account she provided a month after the crime, no doubt embellished and inflected for her own purposes: "'Who are those letters from?' her father asked. 'Your mother and I have been too patient, you will leave the house tomorrow.' Then she started crying and said to both of us, 'So you're throwing me out?' Her father said, 'We are sorry to have to do it, I always had hopes for you, Violette, but you always lied to us and you always will.'"[30] When they pressed her for details, Violette sobbed that Jean was the man from the photograph, that he was pursuing her, and that even when she stood him up, he would insist on seeing her again. He had tried several times to come to the house and meet her parents, but she did not want him to. Baptiste pressed on: what did this young man do?

"He is twenty-three, doing his legal internship," Violette replied. "His father is a stationmaster."

Those details appeared to stop Violette's parents in their tracks. A lawyer in training, really? Pursuing their daughter, wanting to meet them? Suddenly the agenda changed to proving to this prospective suitor that Violette was no dissolute creature but a well-bred girl whose parents worried about her morals and prospects. They told Violette that if she wanted anything further to do with this young man, she should write him a formal letter asking that he write back stating his intentions. After providing a sheet of their best pale blue notepaper, they watched as Violette carefully penned the following: "Jean, my parents, having just discovered the correspondence between us, would be pleased to know of your sentiments where I am concerned. I am therefore counting upon you to write to them. Please accept the expression of my sincere friendship, Violette."

By the time the letter was done, the atmosphere had changed completely. Germaine volunteered that if the response was acceptable, they would not stand in the way of two young people in love. In fact, they had always talked about using some of their savings to set up their daughter, and maybe they could come up with fifty or sixty thousand francs as a dowry. Baptiste agreed but added that it would be important to be honest with the young man's family: they would have to inform the prospective in-laws of Violette's illness.

The possible links between the domestic drama that played out on Monday afternoon and Violette's murderous action constitute, as we shall see, one of the central mysteries of the case. It is clear that she had on the very eve purchased and planned to give them both barbiturates, as most likely she had done five months before. Was it just a coincidence that her parents found out about her affair the very day she was planning to act? Or did the scene provoke her action? With the promise of both money and the man she loved, why go through with it?

The evening proceeded normally, with the family eating a supper of soup, salad, cheese, and grapes, and Violette playing cards, as she often did, with her father. As bedtime approached, Violette sat her parents down and produced the three paper packages, along with a letter signed by Dr. Deron. Although Violette said she threw the note away later that night, versions of it, similar but not identical, appear in both Germaine's memorandum to the judge and the court-ordered psychiatric evaluation of Violette. Germaine had evidently written to Deron about the headaches her husband was suffering since his fall, as well as her own migraines. "Dr. Deron" begins by apologizing for having lost their address and having to send home his response through Violette. He adds that he has consulted one Dr. Lacazée, a specialist in "cephalogy" from Lille, that the latter happened to be coming to Paris and would drop by, along with Deron's sister, to examine them the next afternoon, Tuesday. "Dr. Lacazée" believed that their headaches were linked to their smoke inhalation the previous March, but for him to confirm his diagnosis they must take the powders in the packages he was sending with Violette. The young girl was to take the contents of the packet marked with a cross, which would help with her sinus problems. In both versions of the letter, a final sentence assured Mme Nozière that the doctor stood ready to intervene with the PLM if Baptiste needed to take early retirement for health reasons.

If Violette penned the letter herself, she must have had to disguise her handwriting. Its style in the transcriptions was direct and rather clunky, with at least one major grammatical mistake, not at all the fluid and commanding style one would expect from a man like the real Deron.[31] The court psychiatrists commented on the matter, noting: "As simple, uneducated, and trusting people, Violette's parents were surprised neither by the sending of the packages nor by the style of the letter."[32]

Violette and her parents sat at the family's massive dining room table with the glasses and the little paper packages. It was just before their bedtime, and Violette's folding cot had already been set up nearby. In Germaine's first account, she remembered that Violette had just winced at her own medicine, saying, "Taste this, Maman, my powder is awful." In later descriptions the story became darker. When she and her husband hesitated to drink the medication, Violette egged them on with irony: "Come on, you're not very brave. Are you afraid I'm trying to poison you?" Germaine went on: "I was there, holding my glass, and there she was taunting me, and she never moved when I put the glass to my lips." Germaine said that the drink tasted so terrible she ingested only half of it. The last thing she remembered was her husband collapsing, herself crying, "Papa, what's wrong?" then falling toward him and blacking out. To contemporaries this was the pivotal scene in the case, evoked in the crime magazine *Détective* by a photomontage of Violette, Baptiste, and an eerily large hand pouring powder into a glass (fig. 10).

We have only Germaine's account of the chilling detail that Violette pressed her parents to drink by daring them to suspect her of poisoning them. Violette herself neither confirmed nor denied the matter on the record, but the story made its way into every newspaper account of the crime, greatly contributing to the general perception of the young woman

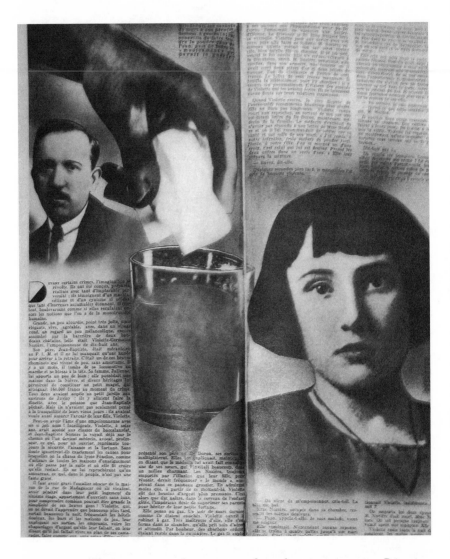

Figure 10. An August 31, 1933, photomontage from the crime magazine *Détective* with images of Baptiste and Violette Nozière. (Courtesy Éditions Gallimard and Bibliothèque des Littératures Policières, Paris.)

as a "monster." The gestures certainly took place, and one can only wonder what was going through Violette's mind as she watched the man and woman who had raised her drain their glasses and collapse.

Only one witness remained to recount in detail what happened after the "medications" had been downed.[33] According to Violette, "My father had prepared my cot for bedtime and went to sit at the end of it. That is where he fell. My mother came to his aid, undressed him, and lay down alongside him on the folding bed. Meanwhile, I went and lay on my parents' bed. My parents did not call me. I stayed two hours, maybe a bit more, on their bed. I went out around midnight. I went to see my parents before leaving; they were not moaning." Medical reports at the scene of the crime specified that Germaine had a gash four centimeters long and not very deep on her head, the probable result of falling from the bed, and that Baptiste had suffered severe internal hemorrhaging as a consequence of absorbing a toxic substance.[34]

Violette said she had stolen one thousand francs that morning from her mother's "corset" in the cupboard; Germaine later insisted that Violette took the cash off her body, from a belt in which she always hid larger sums of money. Violette found a further two thousand in the cupboard and left the apartment, wandering for several hours around the Bois de Vincennes. As morning approached, she went into the city and checked into a hotel on Rue Victor Cousin, possibly the same one where she and Jean had gone to make love. She went to her room but was unable to sleep and finally left the hotel at seven in the morning, returning to the twelfth to arrive early at the home of her friend Madeleine Debize.

Violette told Madeleine she was eager to see her before going off to meet Jean at Les Sables d'Olonne and informed her that she had lots of money, five thousand from her mother and one thousand from her aunt. Violette treated Madeleine, who had to work, to a taxi up to the area around the Opéra, and they conversed cheerfully about clothes and popular singers. As they parted, Violette said, "I don't know if I will see you again, you never know what the future holds, find a way to go out this evening." Violette would arrange things with her parents if Madeleine got hers to agree as well. Madeleine pointed out that Violette could not go out that evening in the clothes she had on, a blue dress and a "sport coat." Violette answered that she would borrow clothes from a girlfriend.[35] As we know, Violette proceeded to go on a shopping spree, purchasing a glamorous and expensive evening gown and various accessories at Galeries Lafayette and other stores on and near Boulevard Haussmann. Around six that evening, Violette sent her parents a cable to let them know that she would not be home before one in the morning.[36]

On Tuesday, August 22, Zoé Tesseydre, age fifty-five, was lunching with her husband in the hotel they ran on Rue Victor Cousin. The same young woman who had stayed there the previous night and left early reappeared and asked to rent a room again. She was wearing the same brown coat and blue dress, but this time she carried two boxes from clothing stores and one from a shoe emporium. The next day, after she left, the Tesseydres forced open the closet she had left locked and found the boxes with the coat, dress, and shoes the woman had been wearing. There was a handbag as well, and in it a tin box containing rat poison.[37]

Violette appeared at Madeleine's house at eight thirty that evening. She emerged from a taxi like Cinderella from her coach, wearing a black evening dress, short gray jacket, black gloves, and black beret. She was so elegant, Madeleine later told a journalist, "that I looked like her chambermaid."[38] She and Madeleine first made a stop at the Palais du Café, chatting with Willy as Violette paid back his loan to Jean, then proceeded south to Montparnasse. They had a drink—chocolate, since Violette had no taste for alcohol—at La Coupole, the huge café on Boulevard du Montparnasse that was becoming in those years the favorite haunt of intellectuals like Hemingway, Sartre, and Beauvoir. Around ten, the young girls met two young men, Raoul Terrey, age twenty-five, and Stéphan Aram, thirty-three, who were cruising the boulevard in a car. Terrey described himself as a diplomat. Madeleine remembered that they said they were Egyptian and spoke part of the time in English. They reported driving the girls, a blonde and a brunette, first to the Bois de Boulogne, then to Terrey's place near the Arc de Triomphe, where he offered cognac, then to dance at the famous Montmartre nightclub, the Bal Tabarin. Around one o'clock, the brunette said she had to get home because she was preparing for a trip, and Terrey drove her home.[39]

Violette climbed up to the apartment alone and opened the door but did not turn on the light. She went straight to the kitchen and opened the gas main and the cook-top burners, then waited on the landing until the smell was strong enough—though not too long, she later insisted. She then went to alert the same neighbor, Mayeul, whom she had roused the previous March: she was just back, she gasped; her parents seemed to have committed suicide. Soon the whole building was awake and crawling with firemen, police, and gawking neighbors. Germaine and Baptiste were rushed to Hôpital Saint-Antoine, on the western edge of the twelfth, where the latter was declared dead on arrival. It says a lot about the Nozières' relationship with their neighbors that their daughter was not taken in that night by any sympathetic family but ex officio, as it were, by the concierge, in whose lodge Violette spent the remainder of a fretful night.[40]

The next day District Superintendent Le Guillou de Penanros visited the apartment in the company of Violette. He noted that both beds were undone, the cot's sheets soaked in blood. In a sideboard drawer, he found the couple's log of daily expenses, with entries for August 21 but none for August 22, and on the hallway table Violette's letter to Jean Dabin, whom she called her fiancé. She mentioned to Penanros that she had been due to leave that day for a vacation in Les Sables d'Olonne with the sister of Dr. Deron from the sixteenth arrondissement. Penanros also checked in with the eyes and ears of the building in the person of the concierge, Mme Bourdon. The latter distilled for him the neighborhood wisdom where the family was concerned. The couple was harmonious—no drinking, loud fights, or infidelity, it seemed—but the girl was "not serious," coming home late and lacking employment. She seemed to get on well with her mother, but "I don't see how the father could appreciate her behavior." As for the mother, she seemed a bit "abnormal" and "unbalanced," sometimes friendly but other times completely mute.[41]

Reporters were also on the scene by Wednesday, putting together the stories that would break in the morning newspapers. The August 24 dailies ran first- or second-page stories on what became known in the next few days as the mystery or crime of the Rue de Madagascar. Before Violette's villainy made her famous, the event, like other unsolved puzzles (the Mystery of the Rue Morgue, the Whitechapel Murders) was identified and evoked in the minds of readers through allusion to a locale. Blood always sells, and that was where reporters first directed their attention: did the gash on Germaine's brow and the pool of blood in which Baptiste was found—his body carried no wound—suggest foul play? *Le Petit Parisien* reported that Mme Nozière was moaning, "Blood, blood!" as they took her away. Violette spoke to the journalists, explaining that she had been away and had sent a telegram—but why had her parents locked the door and failed to answer when it was delivered? She pointed out that her father had recently suffered a severe accident and that all of them had been sick from a previous asphyxiation. One paper surmised that the man had suffered a hemorrhage, and that his distraught wife had attempted suicide with sleeping pills and gas.[42]

In the papers, the initial emplotment of the case was falling into place. *Le Journal* subtitled its article "A Happy Family": here was a model couple, a husband earning enough for his family to live comfortably, a family doing so well that their child went to a lycée. The concierge chimed in that they were a loving pair, and frugal too, "much appreciated by their neighbors and tradesmen." The only hint of trouble was their daughter, whom the newspapers described euphemistically—out of respect for the dead—as having leanings toward "independence," which caused some trouble.[43]

By the next day, the euphemisms disappeared after the case took the first of several astonishing turns: the Nozières' daughter vanished from right under the nose of the police. On Wednesday afternoon, Inspector Guedet brought Violette—whom the police must have considered at the least a "person of interest"—to Hôpital Saint-Antoine to see her mother, who was regaining consciousness. He left her in an antechamber, where a nurse was working behind a desk, and went in to prepare Germaine for the visit. Certainly the last person Violette wanted to see at that moment was her mother. After a few moments, she got up and turned to the nurse. "I'm leaving," she said. "I can leave, can't I?"[44] Guedet was astonished to find her gone but imagined she had returned home or to her relatives, the Desbouis. By the following morning, it was clear that Violette was a fugitive hiding somewhere in the city.

Violette's flight resolved the initial mystery of what had happened on Rue de Madagascar, as did the unfolding account by Germaine of the events on the night of the crime. The latter incriminated her daughter, lacing her story with self-dramatizing flourishes, which the newspapers seized upon eagerly: "I no longer have a husband, I no longer have a daughter. Leave me to die!" While the major newspapers tried for some restraint, the popular press began to sink its teeth into the horror of it all: "A singular girl, this Violette Nozière. Precociously vice-prone, a liar, she had long been the despair of her parents, excellent people who had bled themselves dry trying to make her into someone they would be proud of"; instead their daughter had become "gangrened by a life of easy pleasures."[45] Very quickly a drumbeat of suggestion was heard that maybe the parricide had gone off to kill herself, as well she should: "Some investigators believe that the young criminal committed suicide by throwing herself in the Seine or the Marne," said one paper, while another chimed in that "perhaps she would rather put an end to an existence that has already been condemned." But maybe not, sneered *Paris-Soir:* "It takes a certain nerve to do justice to oneself, and this weak and cowardly girl probably can't manage it."[46] One can only wonder whether journalists and editors assumed that the young girl would be reading the papers and thought to send her a message. Even after she was arrested, *Paris-Midi* expressed disappointment: there was relief, the paper commented, but "one might perhaps have preferred that this criminal girl had avoided the most odious court case by doing justice to herself."[47]

But Violette refused to follow the script that the media were writing for her, to expiate her crime by jumping into the Seine. For the next five days, from Thursday, August 24, to Monday, August 28, she remained defiantly alive and at large in the city, while her face and story were emblazoned on the front page of every newspaper in the country. "Police Forces All over France Looking for Violette Nozière," titled *Le Journal* on August 27, above the photo that appeared in every newspaper, a recent shot of Violette half-smiling, a white beret tilted rakishly sideways over her bobbed hair. "Where is Violette Nozière, Who Poisoned Her Parents, Hiding?" echoed the front page of *Le Petit Parisien*.

Readers were told what she looked like—one meter sixty-six, sixty-five kilos, brown hair—and what she was wearing. On Wednesday morning, before the visit to her mother in hospital, Violette had found time to outfit herself for her new role as a bereaved daughter. In the shopping district around Galeries Lafayette, she bought a set of mourning clothes: black skirt, sweater, fur-trimmed coat, and beret.[48] Paris was, however, full of elegant young women dressed in fashionably dark clothes, and over the days after she went missing, Violette sightings multiplied: she was seen in the Luxembourg Gardens, on Place de la Nation; she was the woman who tried to throw herself into the Seine from the Hôtel de Ville bridge, or the mourning-clad one on a train headed out of Paris toward Saint-Étienne who described herself as an orphan. An alert went out Saturday morning on Rue Ordener in the eighteenth, around a young housewife going to market. The public's active involvement in the case was already evident in those early days, as calls and notes poured into the Paris police headquarters and the local Picpus station near her home.[49]

Violette was neither headed out of the city nor, apparently, contemplating suicide. She was hiding in plain sight, in hotels and with lovers in different parts of the city. On Wednesday evening, she made her way to a nightclub in Montmartre, on the lookout for a onetime lover. Jean-François Pierre, a black jazz musician from the French Caribbean, had met Violette at the end of June, when they had engaged in a one-off fling in a hotel. (Pierre never knew her real name.) He gave her no money at the time, just cab fare home, though she later tried to get a loan from him and even asked to move in with him for a month. On the night of August 23, she came to the Montmartre club where he was playing, Melody's, and settled near the orchestra until his sets were over. She asked to come home with him, but he put her off—he lived with a woman—and around six in the morning took her to a hotel a block from Pigalle. He left three hours later.[50]

The hotel clerk remembered her coming in with "a tall, strong negro" who paid the twenty francs for the room. Violette stayed there two more nights. The second day she ran out of money but went out and returned with more. Pierre ran into her on Friday. He said she looked bedraggled and asked him for one hundred fifty francs to buy a dress. He gave her fifteen and told her to go get something to eat. During the two or three days she spent in the hotel, she sent the chambermaid out on errands, giving her twenty- and then fifty-franc bills to buy tweezers, sanitary napkins, and two days in a row *Le Petit Parisien* and *Le Journal*. Violette read about her story in the newspapers day by day, improvising her next move. Was it utter lack of imagination or indifference to her own fate that led her to register at the hotel under the name of her friend Madeleine Debize?[51]

Violette's last weekend as a free woman was also the last act of her self-invention: she moved to an entirely new part of the city, taking on another name and persona. On Saturday night, August 26, a thirty-five-year-old civil servant named Alfred Rolland struck up a conversation with a young woman in Café La Motte Picquet, located in western Paris near the metro stop of the same name, not far from the Eiffel Tower. Her invitation was symbolically suggestive: she asked him to help her clean out her handbag, in which a tube of cream had burst. Nonetheless, he said, "at first she seemed so sweet and such an ingénue that I hesitated to proposition her." The stranger introduced herself as Christiane d'Arfeuil, a resident of the upscale Rue de Bassano near the Champs-Élysées. When she complained that the woman friend she lived with was not home to open up for her, he took the hint and offered her "hospitality" in his room a few blocks away. The next day he bought her lunch and she began bargaining for a loan, but she failed to show up for their next date. On Sunday the 27th, Raphael Cohen, a twenty-six-year-old salesman of Turkish origin who also lived near the Eiffel Tower, offered a drink and shelter for the night to a young woman who explained that she had had a falling out with her mother: the latter was remarried and "Christiane"'s stepfather kept propositioning her.[52]

Violette's odyssey through the neighborhoods and classes of the capital ended at the top, with the aristocracy. Before it became a public garden and the site of Paris's most famous monument, the Champ de Mars was what its name suggests: a martial field, an open space for practicing military maneuvers. It owed its existence to the nearby École Militaire, the prestigious institution built by Louis XV in the mid-eighteenth century to train the sons of the nobility in the art of war. The Eiffel Tower, the 1889 monument to modern Republican France, thus loomed over an area traditionally dominated by the old aristocracy, for whom the military was a quintessential vocation. Violette had begun to visit the Champ de Mars in the days after her flight, possibly as early as Wednesday afternoon. This was as far as she could get, during daylight hours, from where people might recognize her.

Pierre Gourcerol was a cavalry officer in his early twenties, a student at the school in Saumur in the Loire Valley that for centuries had trained France's equestrian elite. On leave in Paris at the end of August, he made a habit of meeting young men of his acquaintance at the Champ de Mars.[53] One afternoon that week, as a group of them were chatting, a young woman took a chair nearby. Since she was pretty, they engaged her in conversation. Her name was Christiane d'Arfeuil, she revealed, domiciled on Rue de Bassano and a science student at the university. Her mother was a *première* at Paquin; her father, an engineer for the PLM, had died nine months previously. They played cards and tossed tennis balls, and Gourcerol asked if she was allowed out in the evenings. Not after the shows end at eleven, she answered. "I'm closely watched over at home." With these men, Violette kept up her act as a well-bred young heiress, rushing off at the end of the afternoon: "I am expected to eat at my aunt's."

Gourcerol noticed that the young woman always had two or three dailies with her, and as he himself was staring at a photograph of the fugitive in *Le Journal* of Sunday the 27th, he became convinced that Christiane was Violette. That evening he mentioned the matter to a friend of his, a nobleman in his late twenties, Count André de Pinguet. Pinguet was only too happy to play amateur detective. The young men decided to spring the newspapers on her, hoping to startle her into a confession. They had underestimated Violette's astonishing sangfroid, a possible effect of her investment in her own fibs. When they met, Gourcerol showed her a picture of Violette Nozière, commenting on the resemblance. She studied it carefully: "Indeed, we have the same chin." Pinguet was more direct. Pointing to a picture of the criminal, he asked, "Aren't you Violette Nozière?" "Luckily for me, I'm not!" she shot back. Pinguet offered that the resemblance was unfortunate for her, she might get bothered, to which she breezily responded that she would have no problems, since her papers were all in order, and in any case she was the niece of M. Lasard, the police superintendent for the Odéon district. The next day, the young men made a date with Violette for that evening at eight in a café near the military school. Pinguet spent the day amateur-sleuthing by looking into all her stories—Rue de Bassano, Paquin, the policeman uncle. None of it checked out, and by Monday afternoon he made a final call, to Paris police headquarters.[54]

The final scene of Violette's escapade was right out of a movie. Indeed, *Le Journal* carefully set the scene for its readers: "An illuminated café terrace on Avenue de la Motte Picquet, on the corner of the Place de l'École Militaire, full of women in light-colored outfits and officers in summer uniforms. In the warmth of the evening, an orchestra behind the potted palms was resurrecting the euphoria of the Viennese waltz." At eight fifteen a group of young men was waiting anxiously. "Suddenly, she appeared. Slender and delicate in her simple black outfit, she hurried toward the brasserie. Entering the red halo outlined on the sidewalk by the metro streetlight, she smiled slightly." Three men emerged from the groups of passersby and walked up to the woman, whose smile froze. Offering no resistance, not even looking back at the café, she climbed with them into the yellow limousine parked at the sidewalk.[55]

We can only guess how readers really felt about the story unfolding in their daily newspaper. The papers insisted that the only possible reaction was profound shock and horror, though these were surely inseparable from the deep pleasure readers took in this tale of suspense and surprise. *Paris-Soir* nonetheless couched the story, on the day after Violette's arrest, as collective trauma: "Sometimes, at the end of a nightmare, a half-woken sleeper vacillates between dream and reality. That is a feeling we have all had upon reading of the horrific drama of the Rue de Madagascar, which seems to have been lifted from some new tale by Edgar Allan Poe. It sometimes happens that exceptional circumstances tease out of daily, ordinary life a psychological problem we examine with dread. The crime is a sphinx that endlessly asks us the same question: why?"[56] Violette, under arrest, was about to tell them why. The nightmare had only begun.

FIVE

# *The Accusation*

MOST SOCIETIES HAVE CONSIDERED PARRICIDE—and its close analog, regicide—the most heinous crime imaginable. In ancient Rome, father-killers were sewn into a bag with a live monkey, a rooster, and a viper, symbols of unreason and viciousness, and thrown alive into the river Tiber or the sea. The French Revolution abolished all forms of torture and mutilation in the judicial system except for those who killed their parents: a parricide approached the guillotine barefoot and wearing only a long shift, his head covered by a black veil, and was executed after having his hand chopped off. Although the hand amputation was dropped in 1832, twentieth-century parricides still walked to their executions barefoot with their heads draped in black, the only modification to the death penalty allowed under French law.[1] And death on the guillotine was, barring any mitigating circumstances, the likely penalty for the premeditated killing of one's parents.

Medical and psychiatric experts in early-twentieth-century France held that parent-killers were both deeply sick and entirely responsible: nothing that a parent did to their child could in any way explain or excuse such a crime. A turn-of-the-century expert wrote that since a child's first moral instincts flowed outward from the experience of their parents' love, the murder of a father or mother self-evidently demonstrated the perpetrator's moral "monstrosity." This was true regardless of anything a parent might have done: "We cannot conceive that even a father's gravest faults, the most sustained provocation and violence, might incite bloody retribution by the being to whom he gave life without assuming in the latter a psychic constitution different from our own, an innate and instinctive cruelty more or less modified and increased by acquired vices."[2]

The leading contemporary expert on the psychopathology of parricides, Dr. Gustave Asselin, drew on prevailing theories of "degeneration," the view that crimes were likely to be committed by individuals whose physical and moral constitution had been severely eroded by a family history of illness—particularly sexual disease—alcohol, and drugs.[3] The "degenerate" exhibited traits we associate today with the psychopath: indifference, lack of affect, and an inability to empathize with the sufferings of others. To kill a parent was automatic proof of degeneracy. Oddly enough, Asselin offered as an example of such degenerates a young man who killed his father because the latter, an alcoholic, savagely beat his mother, with whom the son was apparently able to empathize. Asselin commented, perhaps a tad defensively, "Love for a mother can never excuse the murder of a father. A son can have no rights on his forbear. Only impulsivity and the degenerate's want of mental and moral balance can explain so monstrous a crime."[4]

The degeneracy thesis was still common currency in 1925, when Dr. Élisabeth Cullère wrote her thesis on parricide. Cullère paid more attention to female parricides than did the male doctors who preceded her, but only to conclude that they too suffered from some form of hereditary degeneracy usually combined with that catchall female problem, "hysteria." Cullère ended her thesis with the case study of an eighteen-year-old girl, a rural textile worker, who pushed her inebriated father over the edge of a high embankment and then defended herself incoherently: "As far as I'm concerned he killed himself. . . . Sure I didn't do it, I'd much rather not be the one who did it." The girl was bright, healthy, apparently normal in all ways, although she responded strongly to pressure on her breasts and ovarian areas. Her father had been a brutal drunkard. Cullère concluded that her act was that of a degenerate, a "nevropath with hysterogenic zones."[5] Children who fought back against violent alcoholics were assumed to have been impelled to act not in self-defense but by the degeneracy they inherited from their parents.

"Degeneracy" had strong class connotations, since hereditary blights such as alcohol and venereal disease were presumed to be far more rampant among the poor than among the rich. Specifically, parricide was assumed to be far more frequent in the countryside—experts cited figures to prove it—where hatreds thrived among members of uneducated families residing in tight quarters, generations struggling for scarce resources under the rule of authoritarian patriarchs. This was where one was likely to find the most incomprehensible of parricides, motivated by greed rather than hatred: the old man smothered under a pillow, the verdigris mixed into an evening supper, the impassive son returning from the funeral "relieved no longer to be seeing that old invalid whose inactivity irritated him." Parricide for gain, wrote one expert, is almost exclusively a rural phenomenon.[6]

The standard narratives about peasants getting rid of useless mouths or of young men striking down brutal fathers in anger had done little to prepare contemporaries for the fact of a young girl from a respectable, loving family coldly administering poison to her parents, apparently to get her hands on their savings. Those beings labeled "monsters" are often people who mix categories that should be kept separate—a half-human, half-animal creature—or act in ways that defy nature, as when a parent kills a child. Violette Nozière was immediately labeled a "monster" because she represented something incomprehensible: a cold-blooded parricide driven by greed who was the product of a civilized urban environment and a vice-free family.

In the days leading up to and immediately following Violette's arrest, the motives for her crime were clear to everyone: she tried to kill both her parents out of grasping calculation so as to secure, and spend, their savings. The phrase that came up again and again in the newspapers was that Violette wanted her parents' money in order to *vivre sa vie*—"live her own life." In a society where families worked hard together to achieve or maintain social status, to "live one's life" was a supreme expression of selfishness, an affront to deeply held values of family solidarity. Baptiste and Germaine perfectly embodied those ideals, depriving themselves for the sake of the next generation. They had saved, and she poisoned them in order "to spend in nightclubs the savings amassed for her by the poor old couple."[7] The newspapers may have been accurately mirroring the reactions of many readers when they spoke of horror, of a sense of nightmare in response to Violette's crime: "The girl who wanted to 'live her life' and who, in order sooner to enjoy the one hundred fifty thousand francs or so of her inheritance, did not hesitate to poison those who gave her life, that girl, once unmasked, cornered, lost, did not commit suicide."[8] Self-obliteration was the only imaginable response to so violent an affront to the ideals embodied by a family like the Nozières.

Violette did not kill herself, and she did far worse than stay alive. Shortly after her arrest, the authorities and the public would find out that the case involved an even greater taboo than parricide.

The police official heading the Nozière case was Inspector Marcel Guillaume, the head of the "special brigade" of the Paris police headquarters on Quai des Orfèvres. The special brigade (nicknamed the "ace" brigade) investigated Paris's most high-profile criminal cases. Because of the resulting media exposure, Guillaume was probably the most famous policeman in France.

Marcel Guillaume was sixty-one at the time of the Nozière affair and owed his prominence to many years of hard work.[9] An immigrant from the provinces, he had come to Paris and been rescued from a dead-end job in a grocery store by his father-in-law, a policeman who urged and helped him to join the force. Guillaume put in plenty of time as a district officer in gloomy suburbs like Meudon before finally gaining a promotion to Paris headquarters in his forties. He was evidently smart and ambitious, very good at his job, but it was his human qualities that made his reputation: he was an old-style policeman who knew the city and its people inside out, a patient investigator, and a compassionate man free of self-righteous moralism (he opposed the death penalty). Guillaume had friends in many of Paris's social circles, one of them the young Belgian writer Georges Simenon, whose fictional detective Maigret is in large part modeled on the Parisian policeman. Guillaume was in fact a lot more glamorous than Maigret: tall, thin, and unlike his uxorious fictional counterpart, something of a womanizer. Simenon jokingly complained in 1937 that by obstinately sticking to cigarettes Guillaume was "ruining" his pipe-smoking Maigret.[10] But like Maigret, Guillaume was by all accounts excellent at his job because of his understanding of the human heart.

It was Guillaume who had sent Inspectors Gripois and Verrier to the brasserie in the fifteenth to pick up the young woman, who did indeed turn out to be Violette Nozière, and he was the first official to have an extended conversation with her after her arrest. Three years later, Guillaume was to write a memoir of the most famous cases he worked on, which was published serially in a newspaper in 1937. Although the memoir was touched up by a literary collaborator, it probably constitutes a reasonably good account of the tenor of the conversation that took place in Guillaume's office on Quai des Orfèvres late in the evening of August 28.[11]

As soon as Violette was brought in, Guillaume sent for the investigating judge, the *juge d'instruction*, in the case, Edmond Lanoire. Under French

Figure 11. Violette Nozière shortly after her arrest, September 1933. (Photograph by Roger-Viollet, courtesy of Image Works.)

law, once an arrest warrant had been issued, the police's job stopped and the judge's began: only he and his associates could formally question the suspect. Guillaume was no stickler for procedure, however, and decided that there was no reason he could not have a conversation with the young woman while they waited for Judge Lanoire to arrive. He found her slumped in an armchair in his office, her head buried in the fur collar of her coat. After reading the arrest warrant, he suddenly asked, "Why did you do it?" She shrugged. "What's the point of explaining? I'm guilty, I admit it, leave me alone." He kept after her: did they keep her from what she wanted, was it a fight? Why, he asked, did she poison her father and mother?

That last word caused her to react: "That's not true. I did not want to poison my mother!" Guillaume pushed ahead: "So it was your father you resented?" She burst into tears, and Guillaume moved into full good cop mode: "Talk to me frankly, like an old friend. Try to tell the truth, I'll help you. You'll see, kid, it feels good to confide in someone." More sobbing ensued. "You wouldn't believe me," she protested. "I assure you that I believe at this moment you are incapable of lying." "Oh, no," she replied, "I swear I am going to tell you the truth."

That was when it all came out: once, when her mother was away on a trip, her father had sexually abused her. When her mother returned, Violette had been too scared to say anything. For months and years this had gone on, and she came to feel only hatred and contempt for her father, until one day she met a man she loved and tried to refuse her father's advances, only to realize there was just one way out. Only death could rid her of Baptiste, and that was why she began to think of poisoning him. Suddenly Judge Lanoire burst into the office: "M. Guillaume, you are not to question this person; that could be grounds for a mistrial." Not only was Guillaume encroaching on Lanoire's turf, but the judge already had strong opinions about the case.[12]

Violette never denied that she had given her parents poison, nor did she ever deviate from any of the details of her account and explanation. On September 9, questioned at length by Lanoire, she filled in the troubling details of her accusation. Here was how she said it began:

It was when I was twelve, when my mother was off at the market, that he started touching me with his finger. At that point I was very ignorant of those things. He took me the first time one morning when I went to his bed to say good morning. The beds were placed then as they are now. I was surprised and did not resist. At the start and for about a year, I gave in. But when I became a woman I realized the horror of my situation. The reason I said nothing to my mother is that my father had convinced me I was as guilty as he was. At that time I was in school on Rue de Wattignies. There was no teacher who took any special interest in me, and I had no intimate friend. I had no close relatives in Paris. The encounters continued at home when my mother went out shopping, for instance to get food for my father's [work] basket, or in the shed in the garden we used to have. We had relations sometimes on a chair and sometimes on the ground. The shed was about one meter fifty by two fifty, it was torn down less than three years ago. . . . My mother did not know what was going on, but she could have noticed. She saw Papa kiss me on the mouth several times, and he was constantly stroking me. Sometimes when she came up from fetching the milk she found me lying beside Papa. But she did not say anything. I was in my nightgown. She never said anything to my father in front of me, and I don't know if she ever said anything to him in private.[13]

Violette had previously indicated that the encounters took place irregularly but on average about once a week, and that her father had told her that if she told her mother he would kill her and then kill himself.[14]

Violette's explanation to Guillaume, which she repeated to Lanoire on Tuesday, made the newspapers on the morning of Wednesday, August 30. With very few exceptions, the papers expressed not only disbelief in her story but shrill outrage at her allegations. The mass-circulation Paris dailies, which catered to a large working- and lower-middle-class readership, all took the same position: since it was obvious that Violette was a cold-hearted liar, she had surely cooked up this story about her father to lay the groundwork for her defense. *Le Petit Parisien* (circulation over one million) bore the front-page headline "The Poisoner Violette Nozière Accuses, in Her Own Defense, the Father She Murdered." Its competitor *Le Journal* phrased it thus: "The Parricide Violette Nozière Already Prepares Her Defense by Making Odious Accusations." *Le Matin* weighed in with the wordiest and most ham-fisted entry: "Violette Nozières, No Doubt Elaborating an Abominable Lie in the Service of a Desperate Defense, Claims That She Murdered Her Father Because He Abused Her." Only the smaller-circulation and more avowedly political papers showed some hesitation in rushing to judgment. The left-Republican *L'Œuvre* titled its article simply "Violette Nozière Accuses Her Father" and buried the revelation a few paragraphs into its article, and the Communist *L'Humanité*, while not suggesting she should be believed, scoffed at all the show of "virtuous indignation." The right-wing *Action Française* pulled its punches: "Does she want in her own defense to dishonor the father she killed? Or might she be telling the truth?"

The political extremes were less interested in defending Violette than in casting aspersion on the mainstream press for its sensationalizing of trivial stories when the real issues of the day were so much more important. They certainly had a point: even as the Nozière case unfolded in September 1933, the newspapers printed parallel accounts of the Nazi Party's huge victory rally in Nuremberg. The mainstream mass-market dailies, however, had a combined circulation of over four million—one copy for every ten French citizens—and they were not inclined to withhold judgment on Violette's account of her motives.[15] *Paris-Midi*'s gloss on the matter, which invoked a famous aristocratic murderess, is representative: "Not satisfied with having murdered her father, she soils his memory. Lacking the courage to do justice to herself, showing none of the remorse that might humanize this bargain-basement Brinvilliers, she is already building her defense upon the most cowardly accusation." If Violette's accusation had not already damned her in the eyes of readers, her lack of affect and refusal to act out remorse would have done the job: *Le Matin* noted her frightening "calm, insensitivity, indifference," *Paris-Midi* the disconcerting "cold-blooded cynicism" behind her "odious but cleverly reasoned defense."[16]

By all accounts, Violette's contemporaries reacted with shock and outrage to her allegations about her father. But incest and the sexual abuse of underage girls were matters most people knew about in early-twentieth-century France. The sexual molestation of little girls had been an extremely common offense for most of the Third Republic: it was the single most frequent crime against persons between 1871 and 1940, a full third of such felonies. The victims were overwhelmingly—nine out of ten—girl children under the age of fifteen. Such crimes did, however, decline dramatically over the course of this period, from about six hundred reported cases a year in the 1880s and 1890s to under two hundred a year between the wars, an evolution linked to changing social conditions. Victims of molestation were most often very young girls whose schooling was cut short by the need for family income and who were sent out to work in unsupervised and isolated settings—watching animals out in a field, for instance. Rapes of young girls were most commonly perpetrated by young working men, often impoverished and marginal laborers, such as farmhands. Historians have argued that both the decrease of child labor and the loosening of sexual mores after World War I—which made grown women more available—likely played a significant role in making sexual attacks on girls less common.[17]

Although sexual attacks on girls were known to happen frequently, tolerance for pedophiles was no greater then than it is nowadays. One of the most sensational crimes of the early years of the century in France was that of "the monster Albert Soleilland"—admittedly, a murderer as well as a child molester. In January 1907, Soleilland, a married working-class man living in the eleventh arrondissement, invited the eleven-year-old daughter of close friends to accompany him to an afternoon show; he took her instead to his apartment, where he raped and strangled her, later covering up the crime and pretending to help with the investigation before his lies were exposed. The funeral of little Marthe drew fifty thousand to one hundred thousand Parisians, and the case provoked such strong emotions that it derailed a well-supported legislative project to abolish the death penalty.[18] In 1931 in Auxerre, when seventeen-year-old Robert Péchenot confessed to raping and murdering an eight-year-old girl, crowds also screamed for his blood, as reported in a magazine article entitled "The Beast."[19]

Incestuous abuse no doubt accounted for a minority of sexual offenses against young girls, although measuring the extent of so intimate a crime has always been a challenge. One study finds that one fifth of recorded sexual offenses against girls were committed by men from their own family. Of seven hundred such cases of molestation from the 1870s through the 1930s, 102, or 13 percent, concerned abuse of daughters by fathers; in many such cases, the perpetrator was a widowed man, sometimes one who saw nothing wrong with exercising what he deemed a paternal right.[20] Of course, we will never know how much incestuous activity went unreported.

Contemporaries, then, were well aware of the frequent sexual victimization of little girls and knew that such acts included incestuous abuse. Then as now, however, the impact of a crime or an allegation was a function of the social setting, with certain acts deemed more likely among certain kinds of people. Though recent studies demonstrate that incest is not class-specific, middle-class writers long assumed it to be a crime of the underprivileged: social observers in the nineteenth century presumed that unmentionable acts took place at night in the hovels of the wretchedly poor, where entire families were forced to share a single bed.[21] Even in the 1930s, it was common to believe that members of indigent and marginal groups, less civilized and unused to controlling their impulses, would be more likely to engage in this form of deviance.

The tales of incest that surfaced occasionally in the pages of *Détective*, the premier crime magazine of interwar France, always involved poor and uneducated populations. "Forbidden Fruit," a May 1933 article, concerned Polish immigrants in a northern French mining village. Streams of Polish workers had poured into France after the Great War, the article explained, as those French workers who had survived the trenches now refused "the work of termites." The Poles arrived, the men in round hats and the women in headscarves, "with their traditions and manners, their priests, and the inevitable dregs that come with any wave of immigrants." The promiscuity of the mining camps resulted, *Détective* reported, in a steady stream of incest and abortion cases: one man raping his daughter, another all four of his girls, a mother tolerating a stepfather's sexual abuse of her child in exchange for pay, and so on. "Racial" solidarity and a misplaced sense of family honor made it all but impossible for the authorities to intervene.[22]

More typically, however, incest was associated with the peasantry. "Shame in the Home" told a true story worthy, *Détective* commented, "of a collection of peasant tales written by a new Maupassant and Freud together." In the countryside outside of Vesoul in the Alps, an old drunkard of a farmer, Père Didier, was found strangled, a deed traced back to his son-in-law Achille Tribout. The latter had recently found out that Didier, widowed when his wife burned herself alive by lighting the stove the wrong way, had forced his teenage daughter, now Tribout's wife, to sleep with him for five years. Tribout could not tolerate the shame of it, not to mention the expense of supporting his wife's father. To its urban readers, the magazine described old Didier's demands of his thirteen-year-old daughter as both pragmatic and bestial, exactly what one would expect of villagers living in the filth and ignorance of a place like Montcey-lès-Vesoul: "I can't do without a woman forever. You understand that, Constance?" "Yes, Papa." Didier was a primitive, "in thrall only to animal instinct and not given to subtle intelligence. . . . He reasoned, in the way of many peasants accustomed to seeing their animals engage in incest, that doing as they did was just taking nature as a model."[23]

Equally "primitive" was Albert Nouchet, the village baker in Pellouailles-les-Vignes in the Loire wine country, who had seen two wives to their deaths and was left with his daughter, Lucienne. As the magazine explained in its article "The Unripe Fruit," Nouchet's sexual relations with his daughter stopped only when a vindictive recently dismissed worker tipped off the authorities. Even after his arrest, his daughter, dressed in mourning, ran his business with only the tight-lipped comment, "He's my father."[24] Nouchet's status as a baker gave him some authority in the village, and one cannot help but think of old Félix Nozière, also a peasant baker, whose cohabitation with his son's widow had caused scandal in Prades and alienated Baptiste. These isolated communities, with their all-powerful patriarchs and deep secrets and hatreds, were where one might expect to find fathers engaging in unspeakable acts with their daughters. For all that they hailed from such places, the Nozières were civilized city people, an intact model couple with a well-educated, chic daughter: the incest accusation just did not make sense. On top of that, endless numbers of people were ready to vouch for Baptiste's impeccable morality, starting with his wife.

Germaine, still in the hospital, had been told of her daughter's allegations against Baptiste, and she vehemently denied them. Violette was being held in the Paris women's prison, La Petite Roquette, and had not seen her mother since her arrest. Judge Lanoire decided to set up a "confrontation" between the two women. The practice of bringing a suspected or indicted person face-to-face with the accuser was a long-standing feature of continental jurisprudence; until 1950, however, the right to confrontation was not written into French law but rather left to the discretion of the investigating magistrate.[25] Early on Friday, September 1, the judge removed Violette from prison for a visit to Hôpital Saint-Antoine.

Lanoire got to the prison early, but even so there was a crowd assembled outside, waiting to get a glimpse of the murderess. When she did appear, they greeted her with cries of "À mort!" ("Death!"). At the hospital, the judge first met with the women separately. He asked Violette for more details about the night of the murder. His interview with Germaine began with events of the evening of August 21, then he moved on to inquire as to whether she had ever noticed anything suspicious in her husband's attitude toward their daughter, anything that suggested "guilty desires." "No sir, never," she responded with conviction, before going on at some length: they never went out together, he never saw her without her clothes, the garden shack offered no space or privacy, and finally she herself washed all her daughter's clothes and would have detected anything amiss. "Had there been anything suspicious between my husband and my daughter, I certainly would have noticed."

Germaine was sitting in an armchair, and a group of officials was present: Judge Lanoire, who did the questioning; a man named Moser, who stood in for the public prosecutor; the two lawyers who had been assigned to Violette's case, Henri Géraud and René de Vésinne-Larue; and a clinician from Saint-Antoine, Dr. Henri Paul. When Violette was brought into her mother's room, their fraught encounter would take place before a heavily male assembly of forbidding, black-clad professionals. If the audience was expecting drama, the women certainly delivered. The official record is sparse: it seems that Violette was initially seated, and that Germaine began shouting at her about what she had done. She spoke so fast that the scribe could not write down most of what she said, managing only to note a few phrases: "Why did you do it?"; "Why didn't you talk to us?"; "You would have done better to kill yourself"; "I promised these gentlemen that I would live until you are judged"; and "I will never forgive you." It was noted that Violette showed signs of intense despair, sinking to her knees and then collapsing completely in front of her mother before being propped back up to a kneeling position. Dr. Paul finally ended the encounter out of concern for Germaine's health.

Were journalists present as well? Did some of the witnesses talk to the press? The next day the newspapers carried fuller accounts of the lurid scene, including one in the top-selling *Le Petit Parisien* that opened with Germaine screaming, " 'You killed your father, you killed my husband, kill yourself! I'll forgive you after you've been judged, when you're dead.' . . . The 'kid' is there before her, a mound of flesh shaking with sobs, crumpled up, rolling on the ground, escaping those who try to hold her up . . . a terrible, abominable scene." Germaine went on with her histrionics: "Violette, Violette, you killed your father, such a good man! You killed him! No matter about me, but your father, Violette! My husband! Your father! . . . And you're speaking, you're saying . . . You're making accusations, oh, against your father! Kill yourself! I'll never forgive you, never!" Finally Violette melted onto the floor, rivers of tears streaming down her face: "Forgive me, Maman, forgive me!" "No, never!" "I beg you, Maman, forgive me!" If this is too much for the reader, it was evidently too much for the audience as well. This account, and every other one, makes much of the fact that all the witnesses were overwhelmed, with judges, lawyers, doctors, and nurses barely able to keep from weeping, suffocating with the anguish of it all. "The judge, profoundly moved, stopped telling the scribe what to write down; Dr. Paul later said that in forty years he had never been present at so tragic, so melodramatically human, a scene."[26] Of course the scene, truly wrenching as it was, would never have taken place if Lanoire had not decided to stage the confrontation.

A minority of newspapers did protest that the setup was, as *Paris-Midi* put it, "useless and atrocious"—useless because the melodramatic encounter

Figure 12. Germaine Nozière on the cover of the September 14, 1933, issue of *Détective*. (Courtesy Éditions Gallimard and Bibliothèque des Littératures Policières, Paris.)

undermined the dignity of the judicial process, and cruel for the suffering it inflicted on Mme Nozière (nobody ever expressed compassion for Violette). *L'Humanité*, which had its own axe to grind regarding Violette's boyfriend, also denounced the scene as cruel and useless, "ignoble and indecent," aimed at training the ire of readers of the "bourgeois press" on Violette alone and ignoring other possible suspects and broader interests swirling around the case. The Communist newspaper tried to puncture the scene's theatricality: of course Mme Nozière used overheated language, they pointed out; the situation was set up to elicit extreme reactions.[27]

While accounts may have differed in their details, there is no gainsaying the violence of Germaine's response to her daughter: she repeatedly told Violette to kill herself and insisted before assembled witnesses that the only thing keeping her alive was her determination to live long enough to see her daughter judged and executed. Although the press expressed nothing but sympathy for Mme Nozière, the scene opened a first window onto the soul of a troubled woman whose narcissism and lack of maternal empathy for the child she allegedly cherished were equally breathtaking.

Hers was but the first and most shrill voice in the chorus of indignation and denial that greeted Violette's accusation. Baptiste was buried on September 1 in Germaine's village, Neuvy, where the press rushed to gather information on the family. Germaine was still in the hospital, so the principal mourner was her mother, the eighty-three-year-old Philomène. *Le Petit Parisien* drew on high cultural references to evoke for its Parisian readers the rural exoticism of a scene "that might have tempted the pen of a Flaubert, the paintbrush of a Courbet." Indeed the funeral, as described, so closely resembled Gustave Courbet's famous *Burial at Ornans* that one might well wonder if the journalist was really there: old widow Hézard in her black Sunday best, satin apron, and high white headdress; the beadle opening the procession with his floating black and violet surplice, the blond choirboy behind him carrying a tall silver cross, the hearse drawn by a sturdy plow horse.[28] The population of Neuvy reacted with predictable and unanimous indignation to Violette's accusation, though they could not resist indulging in gossipy moralism about the family. "Nothing was too good for that girl, was it? Her parents spoiled her, that was a fact, and she had a big head all right, always going on about having a car and servants up there in Paris. Her mother could not do enough for her, shining her shoes, bringing her breakfast." But as for Baptiste, as one cousin put it, "Never, you hear me, never will I believe such a thing."[29] On September 4, Germaine left the hospital, traveled to Neuvy, and immediately visited her husband's grave, where she collapsed, so weakened by grief she had to be carried to her mother's house.[30]

Since Germaine, locked in her grief and protected by her relatives, refused to say anything more, both the police and the press made their way farther south to Prades, where they recorded the same homilies in praise of Baptiste and expressions of outrage at his daughter. Schoolteachers speaking for their less literate neighbors vouched that both Baptiste and his father enjoyed "universal esteem and consideration." The younger Nozière was a man "of good morality and good conduct, and that's the opinion of the entire population of Prades." The mayor chimed in that the couple seemed to get on well and that nobody ever saw anything suspicious in the family's relations. Closing ranks, none of the villagers mentioned the recent rift between Baptiste and Félix, though the latter did explain the matter to the police, taking care to exonerate his son and cast aspersion on his granddaughter: "I was astonished to get this letter, since we had never had disagreements and he never said an objectionable word to me. I assume that the letter was written on Violette's advice." To a journalist, the old man commented, "When I think—it's awful—that Violette could have poisoned me, and stolen the little money I have!"[31]

Over the course of September, the police spoke to as many as possible of Baptiste's bosses and colleagues in the railways, eliciting a portrait of a model worker and uxorious husband, a helpful and likable fellow. "In our line of business," one of them told a reporter, "we know everyone's good and bad qualities, and there is no way that kid can pull a fast one on the likes of us."[32] Between the lines, however, there are strong hints that Baptiste was thought to be too serious, too puritanical, too family-oriented, and generally not much fun. The praise is formulaic, with the same phrases coming up regularly: "irreproachable morality and conduct," "enjoyed the esteem of all." He was even-tempered and certainly seemed to love his wife, was often seen walking arm in arm with her. As for morality, colleague after colleague reported as a notable fact that Baptiste never ever talked or joked about women. "He never kidded around on the subject of women and never talked about racy matters." Dominique Tomasi, a tanned older man sporting a Basque beret, confided that railwaymen had plenty of opportunities to, as they put it, "slice into the contract" or "put a hole in the moon." There were always women available when they had hours to kill at the hub in Nevers, but Baptiste was never game. In fact he was known to shoo women away from the group of comrades when they were out walking. He was, in the expression used by two of his colleagues, "excessively serious." Where the bottle was concerned, "it was a matter of public notoriety that Nozière never drank."[33] The assumption behind this line of questioning, behind the details spontaneously offered by Baptiste's supporters, was that only an obviously depraved man would sexually abuse his own daughter.

The person to whom it would fall to decide if Violette's allegations contained any truth was the man who took up the case after the arrest, the *juge d'instruction,* or examining magistrate, Edmond Lanoire. In Third Republic criminal procedure, the first stages of a case after the suspect's arrest were in the hands of a *procureur,* who filed charges, and a *juge d'instruction,* who investigated the matter before recommending for or against an indictment. The legal code enacted under Napoleon in 1810 was a compromise between the secret procedures of the old regime, in which fact-finding and the questioning of witnesses took place in private, and the Revolution's commitment to an open English-style procedure. Under the Third Republic, criminal cases were heard in a public assizes court and the verdict rendered by a jury, but the *juge d'instruction* had considerable leeway to shape the case in private before it went to trial. If he concluded that an indictment was warranted, he summarized his case in a written *acte d'accusation.* The judge could look into whatever aspects of the case he pleased, rely on experts if he so chose, select the witnesses, and question them at his own discretion.[34]

Sixty-year-old Edmond Lanoire, who would manage Violette's case, was a quintessential representative of the Third Republic elites. Marie Romain Joseph Edmond Lanoire was born in 1873 in Bordeaux. The son of a landowner, he remained attached to his native province and the land he eventually inherited there, occasionally asking his superiors for a few days' leave to go supervise the grape harvest. His personal fortune was not great, but he increased it in the traditional way, by marrying the daughter of a wealthy industrialist. After successful studies—literary and commercial degrees as well as a *licence* in law—he was posted to a succession of remote towns before becoming, in 1909 at age thirty-three, a prosecutor in Hazebrouck in northern France. Located thirty miles south of Dunkirk, Hazebrouck was soon in the thick of a war zone, and Lanoire courageously chose to remain at his job even as his family was forced to flee and his house was destroyed by enemy artillery. Later transferred to Bordeaux, he reached the apex of the system in his late fifties, becoming a judge in Paris in 1931.[35]

Lanoire's superiors had always sung his praises. The report for his promotion to Paris described him as "an excellent magistrate with an open intelligence, a subtle mind . . . an excellent juridical sense, and experience ranging over multiple domains." Prior memoranda had similarly noted his fine judgment, elegant writing style, fluent speech, and extreme professional conscientiousness. Information in the files also suggests a pleasant disposition: he was variously described as "straightforward," "both energetic and kindly," "tactful and firm," and "even-tempered and courteous." Edmond Lanoire fully fit the criteria of the governing elites. Confidential personnel reports confirmed that he was a good and loyal Republican, that his religious background was Catholic, and that he (prudently, no doubt) had his two children privately educated at home. He spoke German and English and was a "man of the world" with "excellent social habits" and a wide literary and scientific culture.[36]

A typical representative of his class and gender, Lanoire was hardly the sort of man to be sympathetic to Violette's point of view, and it is to his credit that he investigated her allegations as fully as he did. Nonetheless, he made no secret of his skepticism. On September 9, questioning Violette in detail about her accusations, he began thus: "The information thus far collected about the character and conduct of your father renders your charges improbable. Please give us details and cite some facts that can be corroborated." Incest, like rape, is one of those crimes to which there are usually no witnesses, an allegation of the he-said, she-said variety—with the complicating factor that "he," in this case, was dead. Violette first offered details about how and when the incest happened, then told the judge that she had confessed the matter to Pierre Camus, the medical student she was involved with eighteen months previously. He had been sympathetic but offered no advice. She had also confided her secret, but in more ambiguous terms, to friends like Jean Leblanc and Roger Endewell.[37]

Camus did indeed corroborate Violette's story when the judge sat him down for questioning on October 12. A little while after they met, he said, she began talking about her father, and on several occasions she sank into what seemed like despair. "During one of those crises, I pressed her with questions to find out what was causing such deep sadness. It was then that, with great reluctance, she uttered a sentence I remember distinctly because it struck me so much: 'Sometimes my father forgets that I am his daughter.' I pressed her for the exact meaning of this phrase. She told me but without giving any details." Camus did not remember exactly what she said, but he came away with the impression that her father had designs on her but had not acted on them. "I tried several times to find out more, but in vain. She seemed very embarrassed and was extremely reticent when she spoke."[38]

As Violette had told the judge, Camus was not the only one who knew that there was a problem between her and her father. Other testimonials came to revolve around a single syllable. Finding Jean Leblanc was no easy matter, since he was carrying out his military service in Lebanon. Leblanc's friend Aimé Tessier, questioned on September 19, offered ambiguous testimony: Violette said that her father had *violentée* her. The verb Tessier quoted means "used violence," or "abused," and can refer either to sexual or to general physical abuse. When Leblanc was eventually tracked down, however, he was a lot more specific. Questioned in Beirut on October 9, he distinctly remembered that Violette used the word *violée*, "raped." She had said as much to other friends as well, he added, though of course nobody believed her because she was a bizarre girl who told so many tall tales.[39] Leblanc was at the time extremely upset by Violette's confidences. He later told Tessier that Violette had brought up the matter again: "It was not the first time she mentioned it, but this time she was much too specific." Leblanc was so "sickened" that he slapped her and broke up with her on the spot.[40]

During her September 9 interrogation, Violette struck observers as unusually calm and self-assured, especially given that she was discussing such upsetting matters. Even those committed to disbelieving her were rattled into doubt. *Paris-Soir,* a paper not given to treating Violette kindly, commented that "the murderess's responses gave an impression of spontaneity. No exaggeration, no useless details, never a moment's hesitation." The assessment in the more sympathetic *L'Œuvre* was similar. The judge accused Violette of planning her parents' murder for the money: " 'That's not true,' she replied, with a spontaneity that made her statements all the more striking. . . . When asked to specify her accusations, she did so with such a concern for exact detail, such an abundance of particulars that further doubt seems impossible. . . . Violette Nozière did not seek to color her account." She gave Judge Lanoire the details with "a strange sort of objectivity," which seemed to the reporter a matter for psychopathology.[41]

Violette's self-possession was all the more remarkable in that she was asked for, and provided, shockingly graphic details. She described her father's unclad body: he was not generally hirsute but had clumps of hair on his breasts and a hernia on his left side. Then came the most disturbing detail of all: "In order to avoid making me pregnant, my father would withdraw from me and ejaculate in rags that he hid in the corner at the back of his room near a red suitcase, right beside his fishing gear."[42] The particulars were shocking, but so was fact that it was hard to imagine anyone making them up. As one paper put it, "Either the girl is an abominable, shameless liar, and such details are the miserable fruit of a feverish imagination, or else . . ."[43]

With the promise of concrete—all too concrete—evidence, the police went back to the Nozière apartment. Sure enough, they found a blue rag in exactly the place Violette had mentioned. It was a sleeve cut from a man's shirt, bearing stains that forensic analyses later revealed to be semen. In the course of the same search, the police also made some surprising discoveries. In the bedside drawer, they found a log of Baptiste's professional journeys, including his itineraries, expenses, and various incidents; the back of the book was filled with handwritten obscene songs with pictures drawn to illustrate them. On top of the wardrobe lay a roll of pornographic prints and photographs bearing the general title *Le Pinoscope* (*pine* is a vulgar French word for penis), the handiwork of a printer in the tenth who specialized in such materials.[44] At the very least, all of this hardly squared with Baptiste Nozière's puritanical demeanor. In a society unfamiliar with the idea of sexual repression, Baptiste's apparent interest in pornography would have been viewed not as an understandable outlet but as the sign of a sexual depravity that might carry over into other venereal transgressions. Two weeks later, Violette was shown both sets of pictures and testified that when she was younger her father had asked her to fetch the notebook in the nightstand and let her look at it, and that he had shown her some of the racy prints a couple of months back: "I knew the one with the menu on it, but not the one of the naked woman with a sort of mechanical contraption."[45]

The doubts that had begun to surface during and after Violette's September 9 interrogation became stronger after the police discoveries of September 12 in the apartment. In the following days, the story in most of the newspapers was that while matters remained far from clear, the young girl might not have been lying after all. Everyone had thought that Violette's accusation was a desperate defense strategy, said the article in *Le Populaire;* now one hesitated to consider the alternative: "What revolting mystery was hidden behind the apparently peaceful life of the honorable Nozière family? Could the young criminal's psychology be explained by a profaned adolescence, a legitimate and pitiless hatred of one who violated her youth?" *L'Intransigeant* likewise suggested that Violette's accusations had "shed the appearance of being simply a defense strategy and now open up room for doubt." *Paris-Soir* cautiously hid behind a double negative: "Might Violette not have lied on all fronts?" while *La République* boldly titled its article "Violette Nozière's Accusations Appear Increasingly Plausible." *L'Œuvre*, finally, crowed that it had been the first to give her story any credence, and reprinted the about-faces of all its competitors.[46]

It was far from the case, however, that the public now believed Violette's version of events. As we shall see, the case provoked intense and disparate personal reactions, no doubt touching off fraught discussions within families and between neighbors. The newspapers, while publicizing every shred of information about the affair, often commented on the oppressive "anguish" the story evoked in all who followed it. *Le Petit Parisien* probably best summed up the frustration of those who followed the crime: "It is easy to see that everything she asserts is both entirely possible and completely unverifiable."[47]

Only one person could effectively challenge Violette's increasing credibility. Germaine remained secluded in Neuvy at the home of her sister and brother-in-law Desbouis, but even so she could escape neither the breaking news in the case nor the intrusions of the press, since many of the big papers sent reporters to Neuvy. A journalist from *Paris-Midi* was greeted from behind the door with "Go away! I have nothing to say to you and I don't want to talk to you!" He lay in wait and managed to follow Germaine when she went out to the dairy, where he inflicted upon the poor woman all the particulars about the search, the pornographic drawings, and the stained rag. (It is more likely that Germaine emerged to use the outhouse, a detail that would have been changed out of decorum and to underplay the ruthlessness of the newspaperman, who was clearly talking to her through a wall.) "Then the voice of my interlocutor became shriller, almost enraged: 'That is false, and in any case it proves nothing. Violette lied—it can only be a lie. Why are you coming here to tell me stories about some search? Get out! Get out!' "[48]

On September 15, Germaine gave an interview to reporters from *L'Œuvre* and *Le Journal*, for the first time using the press to tell her side of the story. She went through the entire tale of Violette's youthful transgressions, her thefts, her lies, and her two previous alleged poisoning attempts. Then she made her position clear: "The truth is that she wanted to kill us to get money, to 'live her life,' as all the girls put it now." What about the song book? "It belonged to a cousin. You know, in the army you don't worry about the morality of some kinds of songs. My husband used the notebook to record his trips." Violette had said her father showed it to her three years ago. "Impossible!" And the shirt sleeve? "I put it back there, and Violette obviously knew it." Germaine concluded by looking forward to a judgment that would "wash [her] husband of this filth." Down in Prades, Félix declared that he feared only one thing, "that the punishment she gets won't be severe enough," causing the reporter to comment that this whole family seemed to share a terrifying hard-heartedness.[49]

In later depositions, Germaine went into further detail, explaining that the notebook had been given to Baptiste by their cousin Prosper Bernard, since deceased, and that Baptiste used it to keep his pay sheets and the logs for his train routes. Her account of the rag, true or not, evokes all too vividly the family's physical and emotional promiscuity: "The rag came from the sleeve of my husband's blue shirt, and we used it when we had intimate relations. It was used the last time on August 17, when my husband came back from the hospital. I changed the rag every eight days. Sometimes I put it between the mattress and the bedspring, but since Violette found it, I moved it behind the closet by my husband's fishing rods. For sure my daughter found it, since she rummaged everywhere. She'd found it before while making the bed. I still have normal periods. . . . That is why my husband took precautions."[50]

The day before Germaine first broke her silence and spoke to the press, journalists were waiting outside the judge's chambers in the Paris Palais de Justice, hoping for sensational quotes from witnesses as they emerged. The Tunisian Isaac Atlan had come out after questioning and was telling them how relieved he was to have convinced everyone that he was only a bit player in this lurid affair, when a tall woman dressed in mourning strode toward Lanoire's rooms, causing a stir: "Why, it's Mme Nozière!" Germaine had arrived unexpectedly in Paris, driven up in an automobile by the heavy-set man sporting a graying handlebar mustache who accompanied her. As a confused policeman exclaimed, "Who let that woman in this way? It's forbidden!" a startled Lanoire let her into his office. He was even more astonished by what she had to say: Germaine Nozière was officially entering the case as *partie civile* (the term for the plaintiff in a criminal case), prosecuting her own child for an offense that warranted the death penalty. The man with her was her lawyer, Maurice Boitel. Did she understand, Lanoire asked her, that she could no longer testify as a witness? She did. Did she know that she would probably, in order to sue, have to give up guardianship of her daughter, who would now be legally orphaned? She knew that too. Less than half an hour later, Germaine emerged and rushed past the journalists, hiding her face in her gloveless hands.[51]

The first to be astonished were legal professionals, starting with Lanoire. Even though he had made it clear that he had no sympathy for Violette, the judge could not hide his bewilderment: "In my whole career I have never seen anything of the sort." No less surprised were Violette's lawyers. Vésinne-Larue told reporters that he knew of no precedent for a parent seeking to prosecute her own child in this way, and that whether or not it was acceptable to the laws of men, such an action clearly violated the laws of nature. Germaine's decision caused a commotion in legal circles, where it was the object of much commentary and debate. But the legal technicalities, said one journalist, were eclipsed by "the Shakespearean grandeur of this tragedy." Maybe, wrote another, the sobbing mother did not realize "the Aeschylian nature of her action, suggested by overzealous and clumsy friends." Lawyers and journalists were far from the only people debating the matter, as arguments raged among the public at large: "It's an inhuman act, say some people. As abominable as Violette's crimes may be, she's still her daughter, the flesh of her flesh. The poor father has been murdered twice, others say. After she poisoned him, she tried to dishonor him to avoid the worst punishment."[52]

Why did Germaine do it? What would make a mother seek the indictment and possible execution of her only child, after screaming at her that she should kill herself? One can only speculate as to the emotional roots of Germaine's extreme devotion to Baptiste. Nor, at this distance in time, is it safe to pronounce on the psychic complexities of a household where incest may have occurred: if it did and Germaine, like so many women in such situations, tried not to know about it, her fury at Violette may have been a displaced expression of shame, self-hatred, and deep rage toward the man who betrayed them both. If the psychological roots of Germaine's stance must remain obscure, the precipitant for her decision is perfectly clear: there were two agents behind her entry into the judicial fray—herself and the Communist Party.

On September 19, Germaine wrote a letter to Judge Lanoire officially stating the reasons for her decision to enter the case as a *partie civile*. In the aftermath of Violette's declarations and the search of their apartment, she tried to do everything in her power to defend the memory of her beloved husband. "They have now begun to put the victim on trial. I indignantly protest the inferences that are being made from the recent search of my home. I swear that the songs are not in my husband's hand and that the rag was for my personal use." If what her daughter said was true, how come her husband had tested negative for the contagious disease she was carrying? These were predictable statements and questions, but Germaine went on to raise other matters: if she, Germaine, collapsed on the folding bed in the dining room, why was she found undressed in her own bed? Violette certainly would not have had the strength to drag her mother's inert body to the next room and then hoist it onto the elevated bed. Germaine came round with a gash on her head: who had hit her? What had happened to the letters and telegrams that disappeared from the apartment? *Who, in short, had helped Violette commit her crime?* Germaine was bringing her case, she wrote, in part to help justice seek her daughter's accomplice.[53]

From the very beginning of the case, even before her arrest, the press had fanned suggestions that Violette must have had an accomplice, probably one of the venal young men with whom she was involved, most likely Jean Dabin, who stood to gain most financially. Some of this speculation arose from horror at the nature of the crime: "It is difficult to imagine," ran an early article in *Paris-Soir,* "that the young parricide, no matter how depraved, acted entirely on her own initiative."[54] But the desire to exonerate Violette, at least in part, was inextricable from an impulse to belittle her by making the case that on her own she would never have had the energy, intelligence, and nerve to pull off her crime. The fake letter from Deron, for instance, could not have been written by her alone; it was too precise, firm, and skillful, and it was well known that Violette was of mediocre intelligence, thinking and writing in clichés. "Maybe her hand traced the letters, but did her brain think it up?"[55] While Violette firmly maintained in session after session with the judge that she had devised and carried out her plan entirely on her own, the kinds of questions posed by Germaine Nozière surfaced insistently in the press: who hit the mother over the head, who undressed the victims, who dragged the body, what happened to the money? The answer, either implied or clearly stated, was usually Jean Dabin.

While there were broader cultural reasons why Dabin was suspected and reviled by the public, he was also the man through whom politics entered the affair. Although, at the time of the case, there was no sign of his still being politically involved, he had been an active member of Action Française's youth squads, the Camelots du Roi. For that reason, the Communist Party had seen him from the start as a convenient means of scoring points against their right-wing foes. From the earliest days of the case, the party's newspaper, *L'Humanité,* had laid out the script to which it was doggedly to adhere: Violette, the child of "honest workers," is corrupted by a milieu of hedonistic young bourgeois. Turning her back on her parents' class, she begins to crave money, "and perhaps there is someone behind her pushing her to take it." Of course, no accomplice's name will emerge in the "bourgeois press"; would they not want to shield one of their own? The left-wing paper harped on the theme at every turn of the case, arguing, for instance, that the melodramatic confrontation between mother and daughter had been set up as yet another distraction from the *real* issue, the accomplice.[56]

The alliance between Germaine and the party was a natural one: she was isolated and bereaved, they had a tradition of taking care of their own, and despite his lack of any discernible interest in politics, Baptiste had been a paid-up member of his Communist union, the CGTU. Taking advantage of her distress over her daughter's allegations, "the comrades" not only pushed Germaine to enter the case as *partie civile* but bestowed on her their lawyer, Maurice Boitel, a party member specialized in defending union members. Boitel, who had "the physique of a kindly giant," pointedly declared to the press that Mme Nozière's aim "was to continue the search for her daughter's accomplice and defend her husband's memory."[57] From the party's point of view, either Boitel could actually pin the crime in part on Dabin and through him on royalist nationalism, or at least he would continue clamorously to make the point that the effete student-pimp was "not an exception but a representative of his class."[58] And Germaine, for all her rage at her daughter, probably wanted to believe that her child could not have conceived of the dreadful act on her own.

Rumors about a possible accomplice were certainly not limited to the left-wing press: they surfaced in all the newspapers over many weeks and fueled many a dinner table or grocery store debate about the case. Elements allegedly at odds with Violette's account added murder-mystery allure to the story: Why were both parents unclad? Who hit Germaine over the head and moved her? What happened to the three thousand francs Violette took but no longer possessed when she was on the run? Was it not obvious that the crime was committed at someone else's behest and with another person's help?

There turned out, in the long run, to be absolutely no basis for the belief that anyone else had assisted in the crime or inspired it. Some of the "clues" were undoubtedly figments of Germaine's imagination, such as her claim that Violette on the evening of the crime bore traces on her neck, as if someone had tried to strangle her. As for the location of the bodies and their state of undress, Violette explained it all to the police, with increasing weariness: her father collapsed on the dining room cot, and her mother removed his pants and socks. Germaine then told her daughter to go into the bedroom, where she joined her and undressed, though she later got up and went back into the dining room to lie down with her husband.[59] Most likely, Germaine, groggy from the drug, fell out of the cot and injured her head, waking up just enough to make her way back into the bedroom and collapse on the bed. Medical reports confirmed that the gash on her head was small and very superficial, and the doctor who saw her in the early days of the case reported that the wound could "only be the result of a fall."[60] As for the money, Violette explained, she had spent at least a thousand of the twenty-seven hundred francs initially on clothes, taxis, hotels, and the like, and threw away six hundred when she realized she would be suspected. She honestly could not remember, she said, what might have happened to the rest. From her first interrogation on, Violette was adamant: "I never told anyone, not even Jean, of my intention to kill my father. Nobody incited me to do it."[61]

Dabin himself of course vehemently denied any involvement in the crime, and it was his good fortune to have been hundreds of miles away in Brittany at the time it took place. By the time Violette was in custody, it was clear that he should return and face the music. On September 4, Judge Lanoire leveled a barrage of questions at him, wanting to find out whether he had put pressure on his girlfriend to provide him with money. How much did she give him each time they met? Was it spontaneous? Witnesses said that he dug in her handbag, that he left her just enough to take the metro. He was very demanding just before the crime, wasn't he? Did he know her father's real occupation? What about the car? Dabin protested that Violette gave him small amounts of money and not every time, that he did not habitually take cash from her purse, that he really did believe she was wealthy. He ended with a bald lie concocted to save face: "Violette and I planned to get married, I did anyway. I considered the subsidies she gave me as a loan rather than a gift. I never knew she was a prostitute."[62] Privately, Dabin said both before and after the crime that Violette meant very little to him.

Rumors about Jean Dabin's role in the case persisted, along with even more far-fetched hypotheses involving various urban underworlds. One story had it that Violette was connected to the spiritualist milieus of Montparnasse and had been hypnotized by Dabin or someone else to commit her crime. The police went so far as to interrogate Paris's most famous hypnotist, Fakir Tahra Bey (*né* Louis Pezinet), a publicity hound who swore he'd worked on her and pompously diagnosed her with an Oedipus complex.[63] The press, which had floated the rumor in the first place, proceeded to dismiss it as absurd: "The crime of Rue de Madagascar includes no hypnotism or witchcraft elements," sniffed *Le Petit Parisien*. "It is complicated enough as it stands."[64] Figures spuriously linked to the case included "the Corsican," an underworld boss alleged to have been Violette's lover and pimp and the real force behind the murder: tall and handsome, with dark features, irresistible to the many women whom he enslaved and forced at gunpoint to work for him, seen in Violette's company around Pigalle, and so on.[65] To many contemporaries, the crime was so much bigger than its perpetrator that someone, a man of course, had to be behind it.

Although none of the wild rumors about accomplices proved true, there was yet another man lurking in the shadows, a final player in the case, whose possible existence became the object of obsessive speculation among the public at large in the latter part of September—a person whose role in Violette's life, if indeed he did exist, would shed a dramatically different light on many aspects of the affair. Right after Germaine announced that she was filing suit against her daughter, Violette's lawyers informed Lanoire that their client had information to give the judge about a man who had been her "protector."

Between September 17 and 19, the major newspapers reported that Violette had informed the authorities that she used to go out regularly with a gentleman she knew only as Monsieur Émile. She had never been told his last name but could describe him exactly: he was an upper-class older man, aged around sixty, tall and slim with graying hair and a mustache, notable for wearing old-fashioned starched collars ten centimeters high. He wore the ribbon of an important decoration on his lapel. Violette sent Lanoire a letter through her lawyers declaring herself ready to tell him everything she knew about Monsieur Émile: he was an industrialist, married with grown children, had an office near the Madeleine, lived in an eastern suburb of Paris, and drove a dark blue fifteen-horsepower Talbot in which he took her for rides. He gave her fifteen hundred to two thousand francs a month and asked for nothing in return: the relationship was, she maintained, platonic.[66] Violette had seen no reason to bring up this gentleman's existence, as he had no place in the drama she had touched off, but her defense counsel convinced her to come forward with the information. Violette's lawyer, Henri Géraud, explained to the newspapers that if her "protector" had been giving her large sums of money, then the financial motive for the murder made far less sense and Violette's accusation of sexual abuse became more plausible. As *La République* put it, if the existence of this man and his largesse were proven, "the hypothesis of murder for money will take quite a hit."[67]

Monsieur Émile was understood to be an important witness for the defense. Newspapers, while retaining some skepticism about his existence, expressed the hope that he would come forward soon or that the police would locate and question him. Maybe it was too much to hope for him to volunteer his identity—an important bourgeois would have "imperative family reasons" to hide his involvement with Violette—but how long could it take to find him? How many men of that description could there be? How difficult would it be to track down the gentleman, especially given the wealth of details Violette had provided?[68] Harder than one might think, it appeared. It took several weeks to determine that there were thirty-three of this brand of Talbot in Paris, only seven of whose owners even remotely fit the profile of Émile, and only one of those a real possibility. Violette, however, did not recognize his photograph.[69]

In a late September interrogation, Violette was very specific. She had met Émile about four months previously in the Café Viel on the right bank and had enjoyed a dozen or more rendezvous with him for meals and special outings, but nothing more intimate. On four or five occasions, they went to a private salon in the restaurant Le Bœuf à la Mode, but they also ate in a secluded room at Prunier near the Madeleine. He put the monthly money in the white bouquet she always carried on such occasions, or else in her purse. She remembered very well what they had for lunch the last time she saw him, on August 17, at Le Bœuf: filet of brill, entrecôte with cress, apples mousseline and matchstick potatoes, peach Melba, a Graves and a red wine. He also took her to the opera, where they watched *Faust* from their own box, and to the movies at the Paramount to see a film about the Great War, *Les Croix de bois*.[70] She described him as kind and compassionate.

While many contemporaries were suspicious of the belated appearance of this conveniently exculpatory character, the case records give good reason to believe that Monsieur Émile did exist. A police inquiry confirmed some of the details Violette gave the judge. Inspectors Goret and Verrières questioned Achille Lemoine, a waiter at Le Bœuf à la Mode, who remembered serving the menu of that day, which another colleague confirmed—brill, entrecôte, peach Melba, and a good bottle of Puligny-Montrachet—to an older gentleman and a younger woman on August 17. Though employees at Prunier did not recognize any of the photographs, the manager at Café Viel recalled an older gentleman in his late fifties with a blue Talbot who came in around eleven in the morning in the summer.[71]

Better still, a letter to Violette signed "Émile" had surfaced in the "hold for pick up" department of the post office at Les Sables d'Olonne, addressing the young girl using the formal *vous:* "Very surprised at not seeing you Rue Tronchet, I wondered what might have happened. Nothing bad, I hope, no doubt you were not able to free yourself as anticipated . . ." The letter concludes with a hope of seeing her in late September, when she would be back from her vacation, and ends rather formally: "In anticipation of that pleasure, please accept my best sentiments."[72] In mid-September Judge Lanoire received an anonymous note from someone identifying himself as a friend of Émile's, offering a deal: Émile would be happy to come and tell the judge what he knew so long as his identity could be kept a secret from the public. Lanoire made it known publicly that he was in no position to accept such an offer. On September 21, yet another letter arrived, written in a firm and elegant hand and signed "E.L." Ironically, those were the judge's initials. The writer said it was useless to search any longer for a six-tyish industrialist in the suburbs, since elements of that description had been made up: "I was for a few months a disinterested benefactor for this young girl who, I believe, suffered a great deal in her family environment." In closing, the writer commented, "I must add that were it not for the facts, I would never have believed that this child, whose sensitivity I often observed, could have committed such an abominable crime," and concluded, "You will understand my firm intention to remain anonymous."[73]

A persistent rumor surfaced in the press to the effect that the police were not doing all they could to locate a man who no doubt had important connections. On September 22, *Le Matin* titled an article "Violette Nozière Seems To Have Told the Truth about the Existence of 'M. Émile'—But There Seems To Be Little Effort To Find Him," and *L'Intransigeant* echoed that "the police seem rather slack in their pursuit of the truth" and that asking the authorities for Émile's real name would be like expecting an attractive woman to tell the truth about her age.[74] Although the police were officially on the lookout for Violette's swain, Lanoire did not seem overly eager to pursue the matter. For one thing, he had committed himself early on to the version of the crime that had a selfish and grasping young woman killing her parents for their savings. That, in his view, was the beginning and end of it.

Perhaps he and the police did know Émile's real identity and were shielding a person with important connections, but it is also plausible that the judge's reaction was determined by class and gender solidarity with this other "E.L." Lanoire too was an upstanding sixty-year-old professional who very likely had enjoyed his own share of amorous encounters with young women of lower status and would do anything to protect his family and reputation. One can easily imagine where his sympathies might lie, whether consciously or not. Violette herself innocently offered an equation between Lanoire and Émile: asked by the judge to describe her "protector," she responded, "He has a small white mustache, just like you."[75] The same solidarities of age, class, and gender come through in a statement that Violette's lawyer, the elderly and patrician Géraud, made to a newspaper in the middle of September: "I do believe that this man behaved generously toward her, with no designs and no demands for a quid pro quo. It would be a shame, were the name of this sixty-year-old to be known, for him to be thrown into the public's maw. So far he is the man who has behaved in the most generous and disinterested way. And he has nothing to do with this case."[76] There is much to suggest that Émile did exist and was known to a few, and that a deal had been struck.

It is easy to understand why the events of August and September 1933 triggered such strong emotions in Violette's contemporaries, offering as they did a succession of surprises and ample opportunity to moralize and speculate. The central and most controversial revelation remains the one Violette made first to Guillaume and then to Lanoire on the evening of August 28: that her father had forced her to have sex with him on a regular basis for the preceding six years. While most of Violette's contemporaries—at least, as we shall see, those who expressed their views in public—were inclined to disbelieve her, in the twenty-first century we tend to give the victim the benefit of the doubt. How did, and does, the evidence for and against her claims stack up?

As contemporaries abundantly pointed out, Violette was a habitual liar, and the fact that she cried wolf one more time does not prove that she faced a real predator. Some expressed disbelief on the grounds that she claimed to have endured abuse without protest for six years: why would she suddenly take action after all that time? Violette failed to live up to the accepted script of "outraged virtue," and her promiscuous behavior further undermined her claim. As Anne-Emmanuelle Demartini has argued, we nowadays tend to look for proof of incest in the soul, where earlier generations sought it in the body. Violette's scandalous sexual past made bodily proof impossible, both materially and symbolically.[77]

More concretely, many people, notably Germaine, argued that given the family's living conditions and habits, the incest could not materially have occurred without her noticing it. The strongest physical evidence adduced at the time against Violette's claims was that Baptiste tested negative for syphilis in March 1933; it would have been almost impossible for him to avoid infection if he had physical relations with his daughter on a regular basis. But did Violette really have syphilis? In 1933 her diagnosis would have been based on the so-called Wasserman Reaction, an antigen test that had been routinely used since the beginning of the century. As early as the mid-1930s, however, medical specialists began to warn that the test was diagnostically unreliable, producing positives for a range of illnesses, including tuberculosis, a disease Violette had suffered from in the past. The Wasserman test was eventually discarded because of its lack of accuracy.[78]

Though Violette's version of events cannot be proven, many circumstantial details suggest that she was likely telling the truth about her father. When she lied about her social status, her falsehoods took the form of bragging: she spontaneously told friends and acquaintances about her glamorous family. Testimonies from her boyfriends and Superintendant Guillaume, on the other hand, show that she revealed the story about her father reluctantly, ambiguously, and with great distress. At the time he published his memoirs, Guillaume insisted that he never doubted she was telling the truth: "There are cries from the heart that cannot be mistaken," he said. "I heard one of those on the evening of August 28."[79] Some of the details she offered are convincing: it is hard to imagine anyone inventing the matter of the stained rag, even if Violette did, as her mother maintained, spy on her parents' lovemaking.

Most of all, many elements of the story coincide with what specialists describe as the psychology of incestuous relationships. Violette's explanation—that she did not inform her mother of what was going on because Baptiste both threatened violence and convinced her that she was just as guilty as he—is entirely typical of the ways perpetrators of incest typically manipulate their victims.[80] Above all, Violette's symptoms and behavior correspond very closely with those of sexually abused girls. As a child, she seems to have been well adjusted—healthy, successful at school—until exactly the age, twelve, at which she said the abuse began. In her early teens, Violette developed constant illnesses and became erratic in her schoolwork. Not much later, she started engaging in promiscuous sex, seeking endless reassurance from men to counter what must have been a dismal sense of herself.[81] Were her social fibs a form of dissociative behavior, a way of escaping into an alternate life? She maintained on several occasions that both in December 1932, when she left her parents the note about jumping into the Seine, and in March 1933, when she first staged what she maintained was a family poisoning, she was genuinely suicidal—again, a common trait of incest victims. Only when the relationship with Jean Dabin gave her a sense, however illusory, of being loved was she able to turn her rage fully outward.

The most sinister clue about Baptiste's behavior was provided, quite unintentionally, by Germaine herself. In a final round of questioning in December 1933, the judge asked Violette why she proceeded with her plan to poison her parents even after they had agreed to a possible marriage with Dabin and offered her a dowry. Why would she have gone ahead with the crime, if not for more gain? Violette explained to Lanoire that her father had discovered Jean's existence in the middle of July, when he found letters from the young man hidden in her possessions. During the ensuing confrontation, she had told Baptiste that she wanted to stop having sex with him because she was in love with Jean. Her father, she said, responded that she could be Dabin's mistress but that he would never give her up by letting her marry. That was when she decided that killing her father was the only way out.[82]

If this seems just too dark to be true, think back to Germaine's account of the evening of the crime, when she and her husband told Violette that if she loved Jean and his intentions were serious, they would be happy to countenance him as a son-in-law. It was Germaine herself who mentioned, on two separate occasions, that Baptiste had added the proviso that they needed to be honest with Jean's family and tell them about Violette's disease. Why would he suggest such a thing? Germaine believed these words to be a glowing testimonial to her husband's honesty, but Violette would have heard a different message: "No family will accept a syphilitic daughter-in-law. I have the power to ruin any engagement. You are mine, forever."

The last days of September added a final, highly speculative twist to the story. On the 24th, a rumor surfaced in the major newspapers that Violette may not have been Baptiste's biological daughter. This gossip was apparently touched off by the recent revelation that Germaine had been five months pregnant when she married Baptiste, and it may have been fueled by Violette's lawyers to cast doubt on the very definition of her crime as "parricide." As *L'Œuvre* commented, if Violette's incest allegations were verified, her act could be seen as "a crime of passion of a curious sort, maybe, but which would earn its perpetrator the greatest indulgence from a Parisian jury."[83] The story may have originated from people who claimed to know the family, at least two of whom sent letters to Lanoire on the subject of paternity. One, unsigned, written on September 9, informed the judge: "Nozière is not Violette's father and all those involved know it; this explains a great deal."[84] The other missive is a longer one, dated September 22. The writer, who signs himself J.H., says that he knew the Nozières many years back and that their daughter was not Baptiste's. Germaine was pregnant by a lover when they married. Baptiste knew this and agreed to recognize the child as his own, for which his wife was forever grateful. The writer says that he had forgotten all of this until the case.[85]

This possibility was the stuff of conjecture, though the filmmaker Claude Chabrol was so taken with it that he made it the key to the story in his movie.[86] If it were true, how would one explain that Émile met his eighteen-year-old daughter apparently by accident in a café, and then knew who she was? If one believes in Émile's existence, is it not more plausible simply to assume that he came into Violette's life as the most successful and lucrative of her ventures into occasional prostitution in the areas around the Madeleine and the Opéra? Of course it is. Except that Monsieur Émile did not ask for sex in exchange for his largesse. Why would a man spend so much on a young woman just for the pleasure of her company? Why would he treat her with such apparent tenderness and compassion and go so far, she claimed, as to offer her the loan of a car for a vacation with Jean?[87]

The hypothesis that Émile did exist and was Violette's biological father is highly speculative, but it offers a glimpse of an alternative story, one worthy of the plots of novelists like Hardy and Dreiser, or of classic film melodrama.[88] Turn the kaleidoscope a little, and the pattern tells the story of a handsome young woman, recently separated from her husband, living in Paris on her own in her early twenties and carrying on an affair with an upper-class man in his forties. She gets pregnant, but because of his status, or maybe just because he is a cad, her lover will not recognize the child. By good fortune, she knows a lonely, serious, quiet fellow who perhaps has already been courting her. He agrees to raise the child as his own if they get married, and she will forever be devoted to him for saving her. She never does forget, however, whose daughter this really is, and wants to raise the child to approach the status of her "real" father: only the best clothes, the best education will do. Her husband goes along with all this on the face of it, but repressed as he is, his anger will come out in the form of inarticulate revenge: if the child is not really his, if he has to work hard and save money for this young princess, well then he might as well get his due.

It is an ugly story perhaps, but like all the stories about Violette and her parents, it gets to the core of what kept contemporaries hypnotized: the complicated patterns of sex and class that both linked and divided the city, its neighborhoods, and its families.

# SIX

# Letters to the Judge

AS SOON AS THE NOZIÈRE affair began to make headlines, men and women of all social classes started writing to Judge Lanoire to offer tips, make suggestions, or simply open their hearts about the ways in which the case had touched them. Most—though not all—of the letters are anonymous. They begin, "The crime of Violette Nozière terrifies me," "The Nozière affair torments me," "Please forgive an unknown woman for writing to you," "I read the *Petit Parisien* every day and could not hold back my tears when I saw what she said about her father," "I changed my handwriting because if my old man knew what I'm about to tell you he'd give me a hiding." High and low are represented here, from the man who signs himself "Little Jesus"—"When I was in the service, I had a young corporal who was smarter than you at getting the goods from folks. You want to find that broad Violette's accomplice? Piece of cake, you don't have to be some genius . . ."—to the one who writes, "I would feel bad, M. le Juge, were I to prolong indefinitely the period through which the law, and a particularly eager public, expect from me a burst of enlightenment next to which the rising of the sun would seem a secondary matter."[1]

Some letters serve merely to vent strong feelings, such as this one, written in a large, angry scrawl: "It's obvious that like all the others you are attracted to your little Violette, men are all so stupid! A whore, a slut that all those students spat on. . . . It's an outrage to all mothers and fathers."[2]

A "group of fathers" demands that the judge assign two lawyers to the protection of Baptiste Nozière's memory: "The slimy press is having a ball destroying him, may you be damned in your heart as a father if you don't do this." The letters advance every hypothesis and point of view. A woman writes in pencil, on cheap notepaper ("Forgive my anonymity, Your Honor") to suggest that Violette was a lesbian whose accomplice must have been female; a good number of men write in for the sheer pleasure of sharing their sexual fantasies about the young woman with the judge. The writers defend or denounce each of the principals in the case, and even the bit players, sometimes appearing to settle personal scores: "The jazzman from the Melodie's [Club] . . . is the most disgusting character, all those of his race detest him, he's a liar, thief and pimp, capable of anything." They use the crime to get at personal enemies: "Go ask Gilbert Heime at 13 Rue de Bisson and his mistress Mathilde Lene what they know of Violette Nozière, who bought sleeping pills on July 28 [sic], you'll find out some fine things all right."

The existence and tone of these letters suggests that the case was not simply amplified by a scandal-hungry press: the Nozière story took on a life of its own because it touched a raw nerve in many contemporaries. How and why? Violette's crime was certainly horrible: it is hard to imagine anyone planning so carefully the cold-blooded murder of a parent, even should they have an understandable motive. Yet the case involved no spectacular bloodshed, nor did it implicate anyone famous. A few months before Violette poisoned her parents, two maids in a provincial bourgeois home savagely butchered their mistress and her grown daughter, crushing bones and gouging eyes with household implements; a few months after her deed, a prominent Paris city council member and nightclub owner was strangled in his office by a gay lover. While the crime of the Papin sisters and the murder of Oscar Dufrenne—both are described in the next chapter—each garnered massive amounts of publicity, in the end neither rivaled the Nozière case in the reactions elicited among the public at large. Even at the time, commentators picked up on this paradox: "Some people are surprised at the extraordinary resonance of this case," wrote one editorialist, "since its tragic and horrific elements have been equaled and surpassed before." Why, he went on, was public opinion so "shaken up"?[3]

Why and how do ordinary people become involved in a "big case" such as this one? A group of French sociologists, anthropologists, and historians recently proposed a model for understanding the effects of major public transgressions in different societies.[4] Most such events, they argue, fall into the category of either a "scandal" or an "affair." Scandal in its purest form is typical of homogeneous or premodern societies, in which most people adhere to collective norms. When a person transgresses those norms—committing a crime like murder, blasphemy, or infanticide, or misbehaving in ways that do not break laws but offend prevailing rules of decency—the entire community unites to condemn and punish the wrongdoer. A scandal is an event whereby a group reasserts its norms, united in its desire to see the wrongdoer punished either judicially (death, prison, banishment) or socially (ostracism, ridicule). Scandal in its purest form endures, of course, to this day.

Modern societies have seen the advent of the "affair," a form of scandal that divides the community instead of uniting it. Affairs are characteristic of pluralistic societies with modern media. A typical affair starts as a classic scandal, in which a villain stands accused of a heinous crime and is punished or facing punishment. The scandal turns into an affair, however, when a "defender" appears on the scene, insists that the accused is innocent, and turns the tables by indicting the accusers. In a diverse society with developed media, affairs can be deeply divisive, with forces lining up on moral, emotional, or other grounds either with the villain/victim or with the forces of authority. Because of the status of its public intellectuals, modern France had a tradition of such *affaires*. In the mid-eighteenth century, Voltaire touched off the Calas affair by rushing to the defense, in print, of an obscure man named Jean Calas, a Protestant wrongfully accused of the murder of his grown son. Calas had already been tortured and executed, but Voltaire got him posthumously pardoned and his family's name cleared by denouncing the anti-Protestant prejudice that had vitiated the original judgment.[5]

A century and a half later, the Dreyfus affair revealed the endurance of religious bigotry in the land of the Rights of Man. In 1898 a Jewish army captain, Alfred Dreyfus, was framed and wrongfully accused of high treason, publicly disgraced, and sentenced to hard labor for life. When evidence of his innocence emerged, the French High Command covered it up, deeming it better to let a Jew rot in prison than to publicly tarnish the honor of the French military. Dreyfus's family, a small group of supporters, and the controversial novelist Émile Zola fought for and obtained a revision of Dreyfus's trial and cleared his name, in the process touching off bitter divisions that lasted for generations, between and within families.[6] Republican France over time made this sort of *affaire*, with the courageous intellectual battling the forces of darkness, into a national heritage. When

Figure 13. Public obsession with the case: a cartoon on the front page of *Le Journal* on September 17, 1933, is captioned "L'Affaire" in allusion to the Dreyfus affair. (Photo ACRPP, Paris.)

police forces threatened to investigate Jean-Paul Sartre for his involvement with Algerian insurgents in 1960, de Gaulle, who personally disliked Sartre, intervened with the solemn pronouncement "One does not imprison Voltaire."[7] The Nozière case was sometimes referred to as "l'Affaire," a reference to the Dreyfus case, as in the cartoon that appeared on the front page of the September 17 issue of *Le Journal* (fig. 13).

Scandals reassert and shore up a society's norms; *affaires* challenge and often change them. The first offer participants and witnesses the reassurance of collective wisdom, the second an occasion for cultural or political change. The Nozière case had elements of both, but in the end it does not fit either of these comfortably. How does one describe a case that should have been a straightforward scandal, never gelled as such, but did not evolve into a classic affair with partisans neatly aligned on either side of a rift between authority and emancipation? The controversy around Violette was constant and wrenching, yet never clearly burst into the open. It was disturbing in an entirely new way.

Certainly, the case began as a classic scandal, uniting France in its horror at the attack of a selfish girl upon the parents who had given her everything: "The Spoiled Child," screamed the front page of France's premier crime magazine, *Détective,* on August 31. Each time she was moved from jail to the courthouse and back, crowds assembled sometimes hours in advance and screamed for her head: "À mort!" ("Kill her!"). Hundreds congregated in front of La Petite Roquette prison, mobbing the windows of all the houses in the vicinity, hoping to catch a glimpse of the "monster," to show their children the face of evil. On September 10, the journalist for *L'Œuvre* professed stupefaction at both the size and composition of the crowd. "There were children in the crowd, little girls mostly. They were seven, seven and a half, eight years old. A fair-haired tot of five was saying proudly to another little girl beside her: 'I've seen her three times!'—'Who?' we asked—'Why, Violette!' A mother was inconsolable: 'If I'd had my Dédé with me, I'd have put him up front.'" Other housewives in the crowd were chattering away between calls for Violette's death: "'Ah, those students!'—'You know, I take Véronal every day.'"[8] Some accounts suggest that the crowds may have been mostly made up of women, whom this domestic tragedy touched in a special way. As late as November 23, when Violette was brought to the Rue de Madagascar for the reconstitution of the crime, she faced an enormous booing crowd: "The people of Paris, representing in this instance the people of France with its brutal love of justice, its universal common sense, and its disdain for psychological complications and for half-measures, shouted its vindictive blame at the poisoner-girl."[9]

In many forms of popular culture, the line between villain and hero is easily blurred, and Violette's notoriety made her into fodder for one of the most ancient of forms, the ballad. In the fall of 1933, verses about her crime, bearing the title of a well-known tune one could sing them to, were printed on individual sheets for sale. Before the spread of radio and the arrival of television, songs were central to the lives of ordinary French people, especially in the lower classes: you would hear them and sing along with the choruses in the cabarets known as *café-concerts,* sing along to an accordion or a phonograph—later in the thirties, perhaps a radio—in your boarding house or café, sing solo or in a group at work or at a wine-lubricated dinner.[10]

The type of performance most evocative of the bygone world of prewar France was street singing, endemic in the popular districts of Paris. That was how the career of the *grande dame* of twentieth-century French song, Édith Piaf, began—as a nine-year-old urchin helping out her shiftless father, a contortionist. Édith's childhood friend Simone Berteaut wrote of the experience of singing in the streets when both girls were in their teens: moving from one neighborhood to the next, applauded by bystanders, chased away by angry concierges, having slops or coins thrown down on them from courtyard windows, arrested and released by sympathetic policemen, and making up to a hundred francs for a day's work in 1930. Crowds would assemble, and stay, and pay for another song. The girls bought sheets to look more professional. Even in the poorest neighborhoods, they gave money "for pleasure, because they were happy, not just to be charitable."[11] This was undoubtedly the kind of audience at which the Violette songs were pitched.

For centuries in France popular booklets known as *canards* had detailed the evil acts and well-deserved punishments of famous criminals, while the many who could not read heard of the misdeeds of assassins and bandits from songs called *complaintes.* One journalist remarked on the archaism of the form, the songs' "fake innocence combined with great solemnity." Composed and sung in twentieth-century Paris, their form evoked remote cottages where you sat by the fire cracking nuts, waiting for the peddler to come by with his stock of string, matches, tobacco, and new *complaintes* adorned with engraved portraits. The new "Violette" versions of these songs, the reporter went on, were not all that different:

A double crime, abominable
Was the act of a youthful girly
But the monster, imperturbable
Will say naught of this mystery
To every query, she says merely
I alone have done this deed.[12]

Violette ballads follow the oldest of forms: verses that narrate the crime, a judgmental chorus, an ending that anticipates punishment and draws lessons for the listeners. "Violette Nozières, Her Parents' Killer," to be sung to the tune of "When You Are in Love," begins:

Behold that sweet little girl
Babbling gently by their side
On her head with charming curls
Rests her parents' hope and pride.

Its couplets are punctuated with the refrain

She poisoned her parents
Wicked Violette Nozières
Did it all for the money
Did it without a care.

Verses have the wicked ingrate partying and racking up boyfriends, the last one ending, "And now the whole world awaits / Her awful and well-deserved fate."[13] "The Assassin Violette Nozières" (tune: "A Song in the Night") begins,

A hideous crime begets indignation
In families through the land
With its horror and its passion
Taxing our imagination.

The refrain evokes Violette's compounding of her own scandal:

By good chance the poison
Left her mother live and clear
So that she could rise and rescue
Her dead husband from the smears.

The concluding lines are an admonition to young women:

O young girls behold this crime
Think about it every day
Guard your virtue whatever men say
Your old parents keep in mind.[14]

In the early days after the crime, the universal perception of the case fit into the melodramatic parameters of these songs: a promiscuous, grasping, cold-hearted child had poisoned, in one case fatally, parents of unmatched devotion and generosity. This was the stuff of classic scandal: who could imagine another side to the story, or any reason to excuse her act? Her own explanation of her deed was further proof of her villainy, and reprobation was universal: "The entire city," *Paris-Soir* reported, "shares in the emotion that has gripped the Picpus neighborhood."[15]

As the investigation proceeded, however, it soon became clear that "public opinion" was not going to settle down into straightforward denunciation of Violette. At first, as we saw, the papers expressed the hope that Violette would kill herself and make the whole wretched business go away. But she didn't and it didn't. When Violette was arrested, many papers evoked a general sense of relief: "Some crimes are so horrible, so upsetting to everyone's feelings and provoke such reprobation that they demand a clear solution, and there is no sense of justice until the criminal is captured."[16] Capture, as we have seen, solved nothing.

People in Paris gossiped and argued about the Nozière affair for weeks on end: "It has been a very long time since any case has caused people to react as passionately as they have to the odious parricide of Violette Nozières," reported *Paris-Midi*. "In the street, in the metro, in cafés, everywhere there is commentary on the twists and turns and dreadful details of this crime. . . . It's all there: premeditation, as shown by her previous attempts, the setup, the attempted cover-up, her flight—not away from guilt but to prolong her wretched existence in a life of pleasure—and finally the cowardly attack on her father's memory."[17] The impact of the case extended throughout France, even outside cities and towns. The writer Jean-Louis Bory, fourteen at the time, later recalled how his classmates spoke of the crime in his rural school. His own family tried to avoid mentioning the affair in his presence, but at recess it was clear that his friends' parents showed no such restraint. "They echoed their families' opinions. Violette Nozière was a low tart, a sicko, had a heart of stone. . . . That was the general view in this *collège* in rural Beauce, where peasants have a strong sense of family (family is land) and a passion for savings. The fact that the 'miserable' Violette pinched the paternal nest egg to support a vulgar little pimp who dreamt of Bugattis and gold signet rings seemed to them as unforgivable as the murder itself."[18]

A great deal of what kept tongues wagging was the element of mystery in the case. Judge Lanoire's assumption (she did it for the money) and

Violette's counternarrative of sexual abuse were both straightforward and coherent, but people could not shake the sense that *there was more to it than that*. Talk was most intense, of course, among those who had known Violette, like neighbors in the building: "Ever since her parents had to take her out of the Lycée Fénelon because she was running around the Latin Quarter with men, she wasn't the same girl," one housewife declared. "She was proud and acted like some fancy lady."[19] Interest was just as passionate on Violette's other home turf, the bars around Saint-Michel: "Who didn't know her in the Latin Quarter? Every conversation yesterday was about her adventure."[20]

They talked everywhere: at home, in cafés, at work, in stores. Several cartoons related to the case are set in a prime location for the exchange of news and opinion, a building's entrance hall just outside the concierge's loge. (The concierge, who chatted with everyone going in and out of the building, served as a sort of human gossip and information switchboard.) In all these places, judgments and theories flourished. "Yesterday by chance I ran into one of my suppliers," a man wrote to Judge Lanoire. "Now, this supplier told me that the previous day he had taken a taxi whose driver lived in the same building as the Nozières, and that man declared to him that he thought Violette was an innocent victim because her parents were 'not much to speak of.'" According to this man, Germaine, who was especially "not much to speak of," slept with everyone on the street. A woman was equally negative about Mme Nozière: "Yesterday my landlords, who are wealthy jewelers, were saying that woman is a mother only in name. She dishonors those of us who are good mothers and really love our children." A shopkeeper ("Since I am in business, forgive me for withholding my name") wrote that she felt she had to contact Lanoire "because I need to tell you what I hear in my store about Violette Nozière." One of her customers, she went on, "who is a person of some consequence, was saying to my husband and me that Jean Dabin is her accomplice, it's obvious. . . . If he was in Hennebont on the day of the crime, it was to escape trouble and give himself an alibi."[21]

Newspapers offer an occasional glimpse into the arguments that erupted around aspects of the affair. One hotly debated item was whether young André de Pinguet acted honorably in turning Violette in to the police. Despite the reportedly universal relief at her capture, there were plenty of voices to express dismay at Pinguet's lack of gallantry: loathing of Violette was pitted against deep-seated standards of chivalry. Many, *Paris-Midi* reported, say about Pinguet, "Shame on him! A man does not do that to a lady, not even to *that* one. As soon as you have flirted, exchanged smiles and compliments, she becomes sacred. Your duty is to walk away in a hurry." That's too easy, say others. What about the World War I spy Mata Hari? Her lovers refused to turn her in, but she was a menace to the country: "We need to be done with all this fake romantic chivalry!" But Violette was hardly a menace to society, "nothing suggests that she had any other parents left to poison." Nonsense! A criminal who goes unpunished is always a danger, if only because of the bad example she sets. So? The police would have caught her one way or another—that's their job! "We offer shelter from the law to family members; we don't ask a husband to turn in his wife, a father his daughter, or a brother his sister." Fine, do you want to extend that protection to any woman you've just met?[22] The debates raged on and on.

Journalists and ordinary people fastened onto two sets of issues: who was *technically* guilty of the crime, and who should bear *moral* responsibility for what happened on August 21, 1933, at 9 Rue de Madagascar. The death of Baptiste Nozière was perceived both as a murder mystery and as a psychological puzzle involving a range of characters, soon erected into icons of different aspects of contemporary society.

As a whodunit, the case generated a series of possible narratives, almost always involving men who were *really* behind the crime. Some were unnamed and unknown: underworld bosses, Corsican gangsters, hypnotists. For a long time, suspicions focused heavily on Jean Dabin, since it seemed to contemporaries a small step from accepting money from a woman to pushing her into a crime of lucre. A twenty-seven-year-old named Gustave Lautel, an accountant living in the eighteenth who himself had been in trouble with the law, wrote to Lanoire: "I am revolted at the thought that her accomplice, Jean Dabin, is getting away with it, since he is by his own admission an actual procurer. Your honor, how can you allow this man to remain free? Here is a man who pushed a minor, Violette Nozière, to commit prostitution . . . and then got her to poison her father to get his hands on the couple's money."[23] But no matter how much people wanted to believe in Dabin's guilt, no matter how often the judge cross-examined him, the case against him never stood up to scrutiny: on August 21 he had been in Hennebont in Brittany for five days in the company of his parents. Violette was adamant that she had never mentioned her plans to him, much less acted on his instructions. Jean might have been wildly unpopular, but no case against him ever stuck.

More remarkable was the public's obsession with Monsieur Émile as a possible key to the case. As soon as the name and tale of the distinguished but elusive industrialist emerged, Parisians jumped eagerly into the business of finding him; the case records contain more letters about Émile than any other protagonist of the affair. Nobody suggested that the wealthy sexagenarian, if he did exist, was a culprit or accomplice to the murder, though the occasional correspondent might assign him his share of blame. "An indignant female reader" of the daily *Le Matin* wrote to Lanoire that she was appalled to learn that the judge had promised "discretion" in his handling of Émile. Why should he get special treatment, when the names of all the youths who had been her lovers had been splashed all over the papers? "Isn't this Monsieur E., who is said to have given one thousand francs a month to that kid, more responsible than anyone else for her misconduct?"[24]

The Émile letters in the judge's file fall into two general categories: those that appear to be good faith tips and those designed to get an enemy in trouble, although in some cases the writer's wishful thinking blurs the line between the two. Émile-spotting was something of a sport in the fall of 1933, to judge from the number of missives that came in over the judge's transom. "Monsieur Émile owns a car with plate number 4906 RF5; he is convalescing near Châteauroux," "Monsieur Émile is Émile Aubon, a hotel manager in Breteuil, well known to run around with the women," "You might want to look and see if a man named Émile living 7 Rue Vollon is not the one you are after. . . . He's always after the young ones; he says he is a former businessman." "Another Émile, you will say, but if you don't look into this one you will be sorry. . . . He is a merchant from Nantes who comes to Paris once a week. . . . This is not a joke," "M. Émile Bokend, a businessman in Les Lilas, has a car and a dicey reputation," "M. Ernest Favre, a manager at the Printemps stores."

Some notes offer very long shots, probably from people desperate to get involved: ask Jeanne Recurt, a dancer at the Folies Bergère, wrote one eager correspondent, about the wealthy and distinguished Émile she dated twelve years ago. And then there are many, no doubt from nasty neighbors or bitter ex-lovers, designed to drag the authorities and a dose of scandal into someone's life. An illiterate, scrawled note on a scrap of paper informed the judge that "Mlle Buzy, a teacher at the elementary school on Rue de Buffon knows Monsieur Émile *intimately*." Another urged, "Try Ferdinand Delforterie, from the Thaon Laundry, 23 Rue de Merignan in Paris. And do inquire about the child he had with his secretary back when he was in Thaon—you will learn things that will surprise you. You are dealing with one lousy individual." Émile is no businessman, another writer insisted. "He is a crooked doctor who lives at 32 Rue Saint-Paul. . . . He says he is good at hypnotizing, and people say behind closed doors that there aren't four like him in Paris who can do what he did. . . . I was one of his many victims and would be in danger if I signed this."

Parisians saw Monsieur Émile everywhere because he *was* everywhere. The capital was full of older men with money and influence who enjoyed the favors of younger women. Sometimes the police followed up on tips about these aging Lotharios. A young man who signed himself "Martin" wrote, he said, to help with the investigation and get some things off his chest. He offered that he knew Violette a couple of years back in the Latin Quarter, where her "serious friend" was the head of the company that produced the famous Kalmine tablets. "Papa Kalmin," as they called him, had moved on to a nursing student, the daughter of the concierge at 7 Rue Boileau. The police found the concierge's daughter, who happened to have once worked in the same office as Violette's friend Madeleine Debize. "Papa Kalmin," now living with yet another nineteen-year-old, was Pierre Métadier, a fifty-year-old former judge in the colonies, now a sales representative for his brother's pharmaceutical business, which did indeed produce the famous tablets. Métadier was not Émile—different car, different girlfriend—but he could well have been.[25]

Jacob Wulf Guirschovitz was not Émile either, nor did his description match that of Violette's friend in the least: he was short, walked with great difficulty, and spoke with a foreign accent. None of his six cars was a Talbot. He was known as Jacques—not Émile, as the tipster insisted—but, as a wealthy Jewish furrier, was likely to attract the authorities' attention, or at least not warrant their willful inattention. The police went in on a long shot: the masseur of the wife of the tipster had worked on Guirschovitz, and had seen a young girl with him whom the old man *might* have called Violette. The driver who picked up the masseur said (and then denied, fearing for his job) that he went in to Paris often from their suburb of Asnières to pick up "the boss's chick."[26] The police were infinitely more careful with Pierre Perret, a fifty-six-year-old high civil servant and officer of the Legion of Honor. A typewritten anonymous letter had informed them that Violette had served as a "beard" for Perret, whose tastes ran to young men. She went out with him to the cafés in Montparnasse and used her local contacts to find out the names and addresses of the men who struck his fancy, and whether they were "game." Lanoire wrote a note in pencil on the tipster's letter, underlined three times: "Proceed with *extreme* discretion." Perret denied everything, of course, and the report by Inspector Verrier ended stiffly: "In light of M. Perret's attitude and of the information given, it appears that said letter presents nothing of interest in the matter of the case against the woman Violette Nozière."[27] Though none of the leads apparently checked out, it is clear that some Émiles were much more interesting to the police than others.

Émile was the only character in the case besides Violette to warrant a song: "Where Are You, Émile?" to the tune of "Rosalie." Violette's disappearing swain had instantly become something between a joke and a game, represented in cartoons as a barrel-bellied old lecher with mustache, waistcoat, and pocket watch. A verse of the song has every street urchin in Paris chanting: "M. Emile hides away / Wearing a suit of checkered gray / Yellow gloves, fancy cane / Squinting hard at every dame." Want to find him? No problem, another verse taunts, take a tour of the Administration, the Ministry, the Chamber, or the Senate, and do check in your wife's bed: he changes names all the time![28]

The randy old bourgeois was a stock in trade of French boulevard comedy in a tradition stretching back to Molière, which is one reason Monsieur Émile became a favorite character in the case: he was reassuring in a way that the depraved Violette, the ambiguous Jean, and the hard-hearted Germaine were not. He also provided an occasion for easy cynicism about the authorities and social establishment, since most people were inclined to believe that the police could easily find him if they wanted to.

But there was more, no doubt, to the public's obsession with Émile than the thrill of the chase and the fun of jokes about old codgers and their young mistresses; the missing man was imagined as the key to the case. The fantasy endured that if he were found, all would become clear: whether or not Violette needed money, who this gentleman was to her, whether the incest, if it happened, was really incest and the murder really parricide. "Émile" embodied the hope that the story's troubling opacity could be neatly dispelled.

The hypothesis that anyone else was involved in the crime proved hard to sustain in the face of Violette's unflagging insistence that she alone was the perpetrator. Her endorsement of full responsibility did not prevent people from writing in to the judge about her. Some offered clues and hypotheses: she would have had occasion to plant the famous cloth and obscene photos in the apartment; and if she was syphilitic, how come her father was not? Most just wrote to spew venom. Letters rolled in from friends of Baptiste, alleged acquaintances, railwaymen, fathers outraged at a daughter's act: "She is a lazy slut. . . . She deserves severe punishment"; "Violette told me that if she could steal all of her parents' lolly, she would"; "She is smart, ingenious, and vicious enough to have set it all up in advance"; "Shame on murderous young girls who soil their fathers' memory when they are not there to defend themselves. . . . We need a great reckoning for such a monstrous crime"; "Send that creature to the guillotine; neither the workers nor the bourgeois want to keep feeding that bitch." Rare was the letter, or indeed any public or private expression, like that of a woman who wrote around the end of the case: "If there is anyone I pity in this whole affair, it's that poor girl; I speak to you with a mother's heart."[29]

Could Violette be exonerated, at least in part, if she suffered from a psychological affliction? Were her coldness and apparent lack of remorse, her very "monstrosity," not signs of such a condition? Nothing suggests that the general public thought anything of the sort, but medical and psychiatric experts were asked to weigh in from the first days of the case. As early as the first week of September, journalists were making the rounds of famous doctors and psychiatric experts, and on the fourteenth of that month, Violette's lawyer, René de Vésinne-Larue, wrote to the judge requesting that his client be examined by a team of forensic medical specialists, including a neurologist. He pointed out that his client had been constantly sick for the last six years with sinusitis, migraines, hemorrhaging, and other ailments, which, along with her vengeance obsession and suicidal thoughts, suggested a cerebral malfunction.

Vésinne-Larue was probably trying to place Violette's patterns of promiscuity and lies, and her incest accusation, within the context of an established tradition of diagnosing women like her as "hysterical" or "mythomaniacal." Hysteria had been the catchall diagnosis at the turn of the century for women, especially those with overly developed sexual appetites. A 1903 article by Dr. Paul Garnier, "Female Hysterical Accusers," argued that the female hysteric presents a "deep instinctive perversity that makes her by nature dangerous to the safety and honor of persons." Attention-hungry hysterics would do anything, even mutilate or accuse themselves, out of craving for attention. A case in point was twenty-two-year-old Camille D., whose hysteria could be traced back to an alcoholic grandfather. Camille first accused a priest of impregnating her and, when this proved baseless, moved on to accusing her father of incestuous designs and then threatening suicide. Acting on her "auto-suggestions," she engaged in dramatic behavior, entering her father's room at night half-clad, carrying a stick and a lamp.[30]

No diagnosis was applied to Violette Nozière, both formally and informally, more frequently than that of *mythomanie,* the contemporary label for a form of mental illness in which the subject lies compulsively for the sake of self-aggrandizement, in the process sometimes subjecting others to calumny. At the beginning of the century, Dr. Ernest Dupré devoted a whole unit of study to this disorder in his courses in forensic and psychiatric medicine, explaining to students that *mythomanes,* compulsive liars, remained blocked at the stage of children, who fib for pleasure or out of vanity before the normal progress of adult intelligence and discernment curbs their self-serving fantasies.

Of all of the variables governing mythomania, none was more significant than gender, since "little girls have more precocious, pronounced, and abundant tendencies toward falsehood than boys." All normal children lie, but abnormal children, those touched by "degeneracy," do so out of "moral idiocy," acting on malicious instincts: "Thus do many little girls of weak intelligence accuse their father of raping them, their mother of beating them, and so on. These are malevolent little liars who become *fake child-martyrs* and draw sympathy from public gullibility." Manifestations of mythomania were class- as well as sex-specific. Vanity is typical of "unbalanced mental retardation," Dupré offered. "The simple retarded individual who does not suffer from unbalance usually stays in his place and remains in his rank"; "unbalanced" specimens will have delusions of social grandeur.[31]

A colleague of Dr. Dupré's, René Charpentier, drew on Dupré's work in a study of female poisoners published in 1906. Women who poisoned family members were typically "hysterical degenerates" impelled by "pathological selfishness" and vanity. Their altered sense of morality often expressed itself as *mythomanie:* "Their fertile imagination in the service of morbid selfishness is expressed in a need for fairy tales, for the extraordinary, a craving for attention, a bent toward performance that is utterly typical of hysterical degenerates."[32] Dupré and Charpentier were writing at the turn of the century, but their ideas were still common among specialists in Violette's day. In 1929 a young student of forensic medicine published a psychiatric study of a trumped-up rape charge that drew heavily on Dupré's assumptions and diagnostic categories: such accusations were often the work of attention-cravers, the author argued, "pathological mythomaniacs" of the "vain" or "malicious" sort, most of them prone to sexual overdrive. He concluded that it was vital for judges and magistrates to be aware of mythomania when dealing with women or girls who made accusations of sexual assault.[33] In mid-September 1933, *Paris-Soir* carried a front-page article in which two different medical specialists diagnosed Violette as a *mythomane*. One surmised that Violette, a girl of premature sexual instincts, was unconsciously attracted to her father and accused him of acts that he did not commit but that she wished for in the depths of her being.[34]

He was not the only contemporary to put forth the "wishful thinking" hypothesis, and many an editorialist or casual commentator threw around the expression "Oedipal complex" when musing about the crime. They were wrong, of course, since what they meant was "Electra complex," the correct Freudian terminology for a young girl's romantic attraction to her father. Freudian diagnoses were mostly invoked, however, for the purpose of ridiculing them. French translations of Sigmund Freud's works had begun to appear a decade earlier, starting in 1923, but both the medical establishment and the general public were hostile to what they knew of psychoanalysis. The French only opened up to Freud's ideas in the 1960s, half a century after Americans did. Historians have suggested that American society, rootless, socially and geographically mobile, was fertile ground for approaches that focused on the deep self as the locus of both problems and possible solutions. French psychiatrists were far more likely to look to theories like that of "degeneration," which emphasized neurology, heredity, and social environment. In the early twentieth century, French doctors may have cavorted with their mistresses after hours, but they expressed deep shock at a foreign theory that posited the existence of dark sexual impulses and secrets within the bourgeois family.[35] Professor Henri Claude, head of psychiatric services at the prominent Saint-Anne Hospital in Paris—and thus institutional gatekeeper for the psychiatric profession—once lost his temper in public during a consultation alongside the Freudian analyst Marie Bonaparte: when Bonaparte suggested that a young girl's phobias about a bar of soap had to do with fantasies about her father's testicles, Claude shouted that *his* daughters would never think of such a thing.[36] Freud's name came up occasionally in editorials about Violette, nearly always in the context of churlish populist dismissal of the Viennese doctor. Thus *Détective,* on September 28, reported that after fakirs and hypnotists, psychiatrists and "sexologists" had been consulted—the defense was that desperate—to establish whether the young girl was deranged. But keep in mind, the editorial continued, that she is a *mythomane* who lies every time she opens her mouth. "We at *Détective* believe that there has been too much Freudianism and mystification around this affair already."[37]

Journalists made the rounds of medical specialists, trolling for authoritative insights about the case. The professional authorities, who knew nothing more than what they had read in the newspapers like everyone else, offered little but speculation and platitudes. Dr. Gilbert Robin, the country's leading specialist on family and youth psychiatry, pointed out that society as a whole and parents in particular should be alert to the symptoms of disturbed youth, concluding provocatively that "innocent people get killed because they bring it on themselves."[38] Dr. Henri Toulouse, an advocate for criminal prophylaxy, also spoke of "preexisting morbid dispositions" in young delinquents. On the subject of incest, he was dismissive: "It's quite possible, such cases are frequent. But what does that mean? She put up with this assault on her privacy for six years. I would have understood a reaction of immediate revolt, whereas here the habit was established. And when she's eighteen, giving herself to every which one, she gets upset? It might be true, but it's not likely, and in any case it justifies nothing."[39]

That was also the opinion of the most famous sexologist in Europe, the German Magnus Hirschfeld, who was on hand to comment, having recently fled the rise of the Nazis in his homeland. Interviewed by the weekly *Vu,* Hirschfeld delivered a surprisingly moralistic assessment of both Violette and the society that produced her. Hirschfeld believed that only candid sexual education would counter the problem of half-knowledge, but in the meantime contemporary semiemancipation bred "venomous flowers" like Violette. The sixty-five-year-old professor deplored the contemporary "malaise of youth," the semiliberation that produced corrupt types, gigolos instead of Don Juans, " demivirgins" and "demipimps." Hirschfeld concluded, like all of his eminent French colleagues, that "it would be dangerous to give credence to Violette Nozières' claims," since such accusations are frequently the fruit of the "erotico-hysterical imagination" of adolescent girls, and that even were there a psychosexual motive to the crime, that would in no way excuse it.[40] Thirty years after Sigmund Freud backed away from his "seduction theory" because the notion that fathers in middle-class households could really be having sex with their daughters was too disturbing to his colleagues, the French medical establishment echoed their discomfort: it did not happen the way Violette said it had, and even if it were true, it would not matter.[41] The only groups of people who believed Violette were, as we shall see, women and poets.

On November 6, the panel of three experts who had been assigned the task of evaluating Violette Nozière's mental health produced an eighty-one-page typewritten report. Its authors were among the most distinguished specialists in France: the panel was headed by the very same Dr. Henri Claude, professor in the Medical School of the University of Paris and head of psychiatric services at Saint-Anne, who so forcefully objected to psychoanalysis. Assisting him were the head of neurological medicine at Paris's famous Salpêtrière Hospital, Dr. Oscar Crouzon, and Claude's colleague at Saint-Anne, the psychiatric expert Dr. Victor Truelle. That so distinguished a trio had been set the task of evaluating a working-class teenager suggests the importance taken on by the Nozière case. Eyebrows were raised, however, at the presence of Truelle on the panel: that doctor had been the lead expert at the trial of the Papin sisters, and his evaluation a few months earlier that the wild-eyed, inarticulate sisters were perfectly sane and competent to stand trial had been greeted with much scorn and derision.[42]

Judge Lanoire assigned these three specialists to address three questions: did the accused offer evidence of insanity such as would warrant a defense as established by article 64 of France's penal code? Were the illnesses she suffered of a nature to affect her nervous system in a way that would notably alter her responsibility for her crime? Could the syphilis and sinus problems she suffered have occasioned brain damage?[43]

To all three questions the eminent doctors responded no, not just clearly and forcefully, but with judgmental venom. Their report reads less like a sober professional evaluation than like a vengeful indictment of the young woman. The first sections describe Violette's background, life, and education before August 1933, followed by the crime and its aftermath. The authors make no effort to conceal their bias, repeating the most damning comments of teachers and peers, scorning her suicidal gestures ("Far from contemplating suicide, she plunged back into her life of pleasure"), writing off any exculpatory evidence (her father's stash of pornography "was discovered under circumstances that do not exclude foul play.")[44] They went on to dismiss most of her reported illnesses as imaginary or exaggerated—except, of course, for the syphilis.

When the doctors reported on their questioning of Violette in person, their level of prejudice verged on the comically absurd: "When asked to explain how and why, instead of leading the quiet, studious, and honest life appropriate to a girl of her age and social station, she indulged in the life of pleasures and vices that led to this tragedy," she refused to respond.[45] How on earth, one wonders, might she have answered such a question?

Violette's nonresponses to a series of extremely loaded questions of this sort were cited in the report's section on the subject's "psychology and mentality." Her silence bespoke a "devious and dishonest" personality, though her dissimulation was calculated rather than pathological. Neither did these experts accept the label of *mythomanie*, since that too implied pathology: her lies were not the fruit of an "overflowing, constantly changing and inventive, whimsical imagination," not poetic and self-defeating in the style of the true mythomaniac. Violette's falsehoods and inventions were calculated and utilitarian. They served the ends of cold, rational malice.[46] Was she a pervert? Not, the good doctors opined, "one of those real perverts well known to psychopathology," but more of an opportunistic pervert, not a slave to sex but a careful planner of her own pleasure. Her calm and self-mastery excluded the possibility of her being "unbalanced, impulsive or excited"; they bespoke, rather, "the mediocrity of her affect and sensibility." The conclusion to the report was inevitable: no evidence indicated the slightest trace of psychopathology in this "devious, calculating and selfish girl devoid of moral sense and of filial affection."[47]

Not until page 75 of the eighty-one-page text do the authors address Violette's explanation of why she committed her crime. The matter is rapidly conflated with Freudian nonsense before being dismissed in a particularly convoluted passage: "It is possible to think that one might be in presence of a parent hatred resulting from one of those long-repressed psychosexual traumas that causes a more or less obscure psychic trouble and which results by way of compensation either in suicide or in murder, the latter being less a form of revenge than of self-punishment. Unless that hatred was but the visible mask of a very different feeling toward her father, repressed within the unconscious and hence obscured. These are fine matters for dissertations in the Freudian mode."[48] In other words, Dr. Henri Claude, he of the pure daughters, did not want to think about it.

According to these experts, then, Violette was to blame and that was the end of it. But in a society where children had few rights, responsibility naturally fell to parents, and it was hence difficult to keep the blame from drifting back to those who raised her. People were loath to criticize the deceased victim, Baptiste, but it was also understood at the time that while fathers might lay down general principles for the household, the day-to-day supervision of daughters was the mother's responsibility.[49] Mme

Nozière was unpopular among her neighbors, who found her cold, snobbish, and volatile. Even when she was in the hospital on the day after the crime, the building's concierge described her as "abnormal" and "unbalanced": "Sometimes she spoke to people she met, and sometimes she just walled herself in silence, for no reason."[50] As Germaine's personality—her aloofness, vindictiveness, and penchant for histrionics—came publicly into focus, tongues and pens loosened up. It was not just that *any* mother should have done a better job of keeping her daughter off the streets, but that even more should be expected of a woman with a single child, a well-paid husband, and the luxury of staying home. Hostility to Germaine intensified—at least for some people—when she publicly turned her back on her daughter and wished her dead, and then launched the civil suit against her.

Some of the letters to the judge denouncing Germaine accuse her of specific faults or felonies. "Please give this letter to the Nozière woman" begins one. "Ask her about her relations with Henri, and other men." Baptiste was not the girl's father, and he knew it: "You heartless woman, sending your daughter to the scaffold. . . . She was beautiful and he took her and you're dying of jealousy, that's why you're getting back at her." Who do you think stood to profit from the crime? asked another. Look no further for Violette's accomplice, it's all a setup. Yes, chimed in another, the two women got Baptiste to write the grandfather that letter in order to stage his suicide.[51] Crime novels and movies evidently fired up some people's imaginations.

The largest group of letters about Germaine, however, is from women who denounce her for failing at her job as a mother: "A good mother keeps an eye on her daughter, down to the smallest details," wrote one M.G. from Neuchâtel in Switzerland. "If her daughter went so far as to commit a crime, I am sorry for [the girl], but her mother is responsible. She is reaping what she sowed." A "wife and mother" explained that she had been following the case with considerable anguish, feeling pity rather than reprehension toward Violette: "If her mother had kept an eye on her, would she be in this pass, if her father had asserted his authority too, they had only her as a child, they have no excuse." A letter from an obviously well-educated woman suggests that instead of cursing her daughter Germaine should have asked her to forgive her mother for doing such a poor job of raising her: "When a little girl of twelve or thirteen becomes perverse, lies and steals, you get professional advice, get her medical help and even take her to hospital." "An Old Mother" agreed, in another letter addressed to Germaine: it was your duty to find a neurologist or a psychiatrist. "How do you dare blame her for vices that developed before your very eyes as an educator?" That mother had her priorities wrong, another woman wrote to Lanoire; she "loved her husband too much and not enough her daughter, whom she neglected for the sake of her conjugal happiness."[52]

Criticism of Germaine was not confined to these private letters. The newspapers published similar pronouncements, as for instance in *Détective*'s interview of a "typical family woman": "Of course Violette Nozière is a sad little creature. But what about that mother, letting her go in and out as she pleases and then complaining when she finds she's corrupted?" And, this "average mother" went on, "Do you think a *real* mother could say to her daughter 'I will forgive you when you're dead'? . . . [Mme Nozière] seems well outside the norm, and maybe that's the explanation of the Nozière case."[53] The feminist magazine *La Française* also came down hard on Germaine Nozière's "cry against nature." Since she had entered the legal process as a plaintiff against her daughter, initial sympathy for the histrionic widow had been crumbling fast: "The kaleidoscope now shows a diabolic image, that of a twisted, vindictive creature looking for help from society. . . . All of her sentimental appeal is gone."[54]

Censure of Germaine as a mother was often mixed with resentment of her as a creature of privilege, at least compared to most among the legions of working-class and lower-middle-class Parisians who followed the case. Women who put in long days in factories and offices, some raising more than one child, came down hard on a full-time mother who could not even pull off that job, displaying their jealousy of the couple's financial success. "[The mother] should have been strict and even, since her husband earned fifty thousand francs a year and they had one hundred sixty-five thousand saved up, it was her duty to say to her daughter you will no longer go out alone, only with me, and if you protest we will put you in a home until you are twenty-one," one R.C. wrote to the judge, expressing compassion for Violette. The fact that the young girl did not work was a bone of contention among neighbors who could not afford to keep their teenage children out of the workforce. For the concierge at 9 Rue de Madagascar, Angèle Bourdon, Violette's sexual misbehavior was linked to the fact that she did not have a job. Another neighbor agreed: "That big girl did nothing with her ten fingers, and idleness brings bad counsel."[55]

It was as if Germaine and Baptiste had failed their daughter as much by earning and saving too much and by giving her too much schooling as by letting her run around with men. A letter to the judge railed against Germaine ("That mother's putting on an act. . . . She was dying and now she wakes up?") and even Baptiste for their inability to control their girl and give her direction: "You will agree that a mother, instead of letting her go without working and giving her delusions of grandeur by saying that they had one hundred fifty thousand francs would have done better to set her straight by having her work."[56] "The Spoiled Child" was the headline splashed across the first issue devoted to the case by *Détective*, France's premier crime magazine. The lead article introduced the family with reference to Baptiste's considerable savings ("He was one of those railwaymen who live off very little, with no bitterness") and to the couple's devotion to their daughter, blinded as they were by social ambition. The magazine was more pointedly critical in an editorial that ran a couple of weeks later: "It may be that, as we have intimated, the unfortunate parents can be blamed for their excessive kindness, indulgences, and treats, the effects of which are now damningly clear."[57]

*Détective* was echoing the sentiments of the Nozières' neighbors and of people of modest standing all over the city. Envy of Germaine and Baptiste, whose six-figure savings came up repeatedly, was laced with a strong shot of *schadenfreude:* they thought they were so high and mighty, with their money in the bank and their pampered child in the lycée, and look what happened. One woman of obviously higher status who wrote to the judge explicitly alluded to the social jealousies that ran through reactions to the case: "I do not mean to look down on the concierge and the neighbors, but they are small fry and are not very keen on people of their milieu rising in the world. I am not saying, please note, that Violette Nozière was really rising socially, but since people did not know what she was really up to and just seeing her clothes and attitude, they must have found her too stuck-up. And the father going to market with the mother, and adoring her."[58] With their financial success and their apparently happy marriage, the Nozière couple embodied an achievement that people around them both envied and resented. Deep in their hearts, many looked upon Violette's behavior as punishment for the couple's hubris. It was all somehow their fault for doing too well.

The sharp ambivalence with which peers regarded Baptiste and Germaine Nozière is a reminder of how deeply people around them identified with their experience and ambitions. The Nozières stood as quintessential representatives of the new interwar middle classes, a group that one contemporary sociologist evaluated at one quarter of the nation's forty million inhabitants.[59] Only after 1918, with the rise of white-collar work and the extension of education to large segments of the population, did it come to be generally understood that French society was made up of not just two classes, bourgeoisie and manual workers, but three. The *classes moyennes,* wrote Lucien de Chilly in 1924, could be thought of as a crossroads for people on the move. In the upper classes, capital and investments made it possible to live without working, and the maintenance of rank made it necessary to spend. The life of the middle classes, by contrast, revolved around two principles, hard work and saving. The tangible sign of that saving was what was known as a family's patrimony, *patrimoine*—the small hoard of money that was a talisman for future success: "Each generation leaves after itself more than it received, son following upon father; the patrimony is to be kept and increased."[60]

The shock caused by Violette's act must be understood in the context of the middle classes' new importance, and within their culture, of the centrality of saving to amass a *patrimoine*. Germaine and Baptiste had done this, perhaps too successfully for the taste of their peers. Violette's parricide was appalling, but so was her attack on financial patrimony: she poisoned her parents but also spent their money, shopping away the sacrosanct *patrimoine*. The phrase newspapers endlessly repeated, although there is no indication Violette ever actually uttered it, was that like many young people of her generation she wanted to "live her life," *vivre sa vie:* "This arrogant girl," went one typical entry, "unhappy with the modest station of the honest and simple workers who gave her life, simply decided to get rid of them in order to 'live her life' and squander in nightclubs the savings of her poor old parents."[61]

Every generation has fears and worries about its youth, and the interwar years in France were no exception. Children born, like Violette, during the Great War came of age at a time when educational opportunities were expanding dramatically, while a faltering economy limited the number of available jobs. In October 1932, the newspaper *L'Intransigeant* ran a series of ten articles about the problems created by the oversupply of students and the scarcity of good jobs awaiting them. "Latin Quarter 1932" surveyed the lives of the thirty-five thousand or so students jostling for survival in the Paris university system, living in cheap hotel rooms, desperate for a seat in the overcrowded Bibliothèque Sainte-Geneviève, perennially overworked and tense about the competition.[62] The Paris universities were already experiencing the stresses that would later affect the elite institutions of Oxbridge and the Ivy League: those brought on by the shift from socially limited finishing institutions mainly for the upper classes to more open, highly competitive meritocracies. *L'Intransigeant* noted the change in language that went with this shift: previously you simply "prepared" the baccalaureate, your undergraduate degree, your doctorate, now you "push" yourself, you need to "break out"—like a rash![63] The head of the university system, Rector Charléty, told the newspaper that ambitious parents had brought about this "tragic bottleneck." They crowed over their children's cribs, "My son will be a lawyer" or "My daughter will be a pharmacist," when the kids had one chance in a thousand of making it and would be more fulfilled as a carpenter, a grocer, or a seamstress.[64]

The question of who did and did not belong in the universities and the Latin Quarter was clearly in the air, and the Nozière case raised it with renewed urgency. The case, wrote one journalist, "has shone a spotlight on the ideas and habits of university youth. . . . That is no doubt one of the indirect reasons for its extraordinary resonance."[65] Violette was an interloper in the quarter, a failed exemplar of those lower-middle-class children pushed too far by their parents. Jean Dabin did little more than pose as a student, cutting classes and spending his parents' and girlfriend's money in cafés and hotels: he was the perfect emblem of the social decay of the universities. Articles and editorials about student life ran in most of the major newspapers in connection with the case. Some of them portrayed the Latin Quarter as a louche environment peopled with ambiguous figures like Violette and Jean, while others hotly insisted that a vast majority of students were *not* like those two but, on the contrary, serious and hardworking.

The editorial in the September 3 issue of *Le Journal* had it that these two unsavory youths were typical: "There are [in the Latin Quarter] too many little adventuresses who say they are students but are not; too many 'emancipated' girls who have much in common with prostitutes, too many young men with jackets of extremely narrow waist and coat-hanger shoulders, with Mexican-style trousers, too many gigolos who follow the 'course' only of their bad instincts."[66] The journalist for *Paris-Midi* reached for overheated prose to conclude: "Violette Nozières will remain in our memories a sad and lovely ode to perversity. She is the inverted muse of youth, the scarlet idol of a capsized world, the flower of evil of our age."[67] The left-wing press was quick to react to the implicit charge that lower-class students were responsible for all this decay. *Le Peuple, L'Intransigeant,* and *L'Ère Nouvelle* ran articles explaining that the most serious, determined, and hard-working young scholars around Saint-Michel were the scholarship students.[68] For all the blandishments about the studious youths in "the other Latin Quarter," it was clear that the case had dredged up plenty of anxieties about the fates and behavior of parasitical, aimless young people in an era of constricted economic opportunity.

Some inhabitants of the Latin Quarter were alarming because they did not fit accepted and acceptable categories: they were not bourgeois students headed for their allotted slot in the elite, or legitimate hardworking scholarship students, or even "real" men or women. Anxieties about youth, class, and masculinity converged upon Jean Dabin, the single most reviled character in the affair outside of Violette herself. As one commentator put it on September 4, "It is no longer Violette Nozière who is on trial before public opinion but the young man with the tortoiseshell glasses." L'Œuvre introduced him thus: "The most perfect specimen of this underwater fauna is a dried fruit, a student who has not managed in three years to pass the examinations for his law degree. His physique is of the sort that makes young women swivel around in the street. He is elegant like a gigolo."[69] Dabin's physique and dress were the object of endless description and caricature: all a cartoonist had to do was sketch a figure in a fitted suit with flared pants, sporting a wide tie, pocket handkerchief, and round glasses, for readers to know who this was.

It quickly appeared that Dabin could not have been in any way directly implicated in the crime. All he had done was to have a brief affair with a sexually available young woman: why then was he so universally despised? The left-wing papers singled him out as their target of choice because of his past connection with the ultranationalist Action Française. For the Communist L'Humanité, Dabin was no exception but one of those "boys from good families who look like they have forgotten their hanger in their jacket . . . [a] member of the Latin Quarter bohemia, which will spawn highly decorated judges and doctors."[70] For Le Populaire, the political violence in Dabin's background went hand in hand with his compromised sexual morality. In defense of God and king, "he loved to wield a club—ten to one, of course—against 'kraut-loving pacifists' or 'judeo-masonic Marxists' as much as he enjoyed receiving discreetly under the table from a lovely hand a sweetly scented banknote with which to pay the bill."[71] Le Peuple commented, as did others, on the irony of this unscrupulous creature being, at least officially, a law student. Occasionally one of his kind would actually make it and end up "as a judge whose strictness will be legendary." *L'Œuvre* echoed the sentiment: you could imagine the station-master's son as a future prosecutor with a penchant for cases involving young adventuresses of the sort he exploited in the past.[72]

People disliked Dabin for his social ambiguity: the Left tried to make him into a typical representative of overprivileged bourgeois youth, but everybody knew that as the son of a station master he hardly qualified as upper-crust: like Violette and her parents, he was socially neither here nor there. And like Violette, he was undermining his parents' social ambitions by failing at his studies: he too came from "an honorable family that spared nothing to give him, thanks to education, the means to attain a higher station."[73] The single greatest sin he committed, however, was to break the rules of middle-class masculinity by accepting money from his lover. Soon after the affair came into the open, Jean was expelled from the university for misconduct, and while specific reasons were not given, his tarnished sexual reputation was clearly the issue.

Technically nobody could pin anything on the young man, but letters to the judge, as well as articles in all the papers, made it clear that he was considered morally implicated in Violette's crime.[74] Some people believed that Jean had encouraged Violette to get rid of her parents, while others pointed out that as a law student he would have known that she could not inherit the money until she was twenty-one. Jean's unquestioned transgression in everyone's eyes was that in taking Violette's money he behaved exactly like a pimp. Contemporaries saw little difference between sending a woman out on the street to work for you and paying for meals with your girlfriend's money. The reference in *L'Œuvre* to "underwater fauna" was a pointed one: French slang for a pimp is *maquereau* (mackerel) or by extension *poisson,* and fish references and jokes proliferated around the unfortunate Dabin. Since the term *écailles* means both tortoiseshell and fish scales, many a wit commented, like the writer in *Le Populaire,* that "the scales are not all on his glasses."[75] The legal term for procuring was *vagabondage spécial,* a particular form of homeless parasitism a man could be charged with for living off the proceeds of a woman's work; the expression was applied constantly to Dabin. As *L'Ère Nouvelle* explained, "It is the very same business, whether in a dive in the slums where you play cards while waiting for the streetwalkers to get back, or in a Latin Quarter café where you are slipped a hundred-franc note, earned in a hotel, under the tablecloth from purse to wallet. A man who lowers himself in this way is always to be despised and punished."[76]

In some contexts, pimps are considered ultravirile because they control, often violently, both the work and the sexual services of one or more women. In Jean's case, the opposite was true, and this applied to his friends as well: these foppish, idle middle-class students, who saw nothing wrong with accepting a woman's money, were wanting in masculinity and probably gay: "ambiguous youths," *Paris-Soir* called them.[77] Descriptions of Jean Dabin often included telling references to his "special beauty," his long and elegant fingers, the smoothness of his clean-shaven face. One of Lanoire's correspondents went on at some length about "those young gentlemen of the Latin Quarter . . . who make such a show of being gallant with the ladies in order to hide all their vices: a woman looks so good on the arm of a pretty boy."

In a city where specific populations were expected to remain in their own districts, the presence of alleged pimps and homosexuals among the intellectual elites of the Latin Quarter amounted to a violation of social turf. An editorialist in *L'Œuvre* evoked an earlier generation, the 1880s and 1890s, when gangsters from the northern districts set up brasseries in the Latin Quarter that were staffed by prostitutes. The university wanted this population out of the neighborhood, and when the police declined to intervene, students launched a ten-month guerrilla war against the pimps, beating them up and throwing them in the fountains of the Luxembourg Gardens, until they finally moved out of the area. Another writer in the same paper remembered that in his youth students had dealt in the same way with sexual transgressors: "When we learned of the presence of a homosexual or an 'Alphonse' in our midst, we seized the unwelcome fellow and dunked him in the Luxembourg fountain. After this, we ceremonially escorted the comrade to the Saint-Michel Bridge and asked him to cross over for good to the Right Bank, where society was a bit more mixed. Thus did we excommunicate those heretics in love who made the mistake of preferring men to women, or of accepting money from the ladies."[78] Anthropologists have long noted that ambiguous figures—such as pimps, prostitutes, and homosexuals—are usually perceived as carriers of pollution; hence Parisian students a century ago "cleaned up" their neighborhood by ceremonially washing and expelling the unclean. A generation had passed since then, but someone like Jean Dabin, a man of indistinct social class, sexuality, and educational status, could still be cast as the perfect scapegoat for the anxieties generated by the case.[79] The endless censure and mockery directed at Dabin can be connected to a substantial body of writings in the 1920s and 1930s which claimed that male homosexuals (in the language of the time inverts, *invertis*), once confined to specific milieus at the very top and bottom of society, were now covertly present in all social circles. A writer claimed in 1938 that, in contrast to the nineteenth century, "pederasts flourish in all milieux and there are more of them than ever."[80]

Dabin was not the only man in the case to be heavily censured. This story about a woman was also, as contemporaries increasingly noted, a story about men. A cartoon in the September 9 edition of *Paris-Midi* made this clear. It is framed as an elongated frieze, like a rolling film, of male figures in the case (fig. 14). From left to right are Judge Lanoire searching for Émile with a lantern; Émile himself, a short, fat man in a three-piece suit; Dabin wearing high-heeled shoes and idly strumming his long fingers; the musician Pierre as a grinning Sambo, hands clenched in front of his crotch; an Arab carpet-seller, standing for the likes of Atlan and Fellous; Count de Pinguet with brow furrowed, wearing a crown around his bowler hat; and finally an everyman as "poet," fantasizing about Violette. *L'Humanité* made the same point in class terms: "What the Nozière affair reveals is the decay of the bourgeoisie, with its cavalry officers, its high civil servants, and its little pimps, all of them good patriots in the manner of Jean Dabin."[81] Violette's lovers and associates were treated differently by the authorities and the press. Pierre Camus, her early medical-student boy-friend, was generally held to be a decent sort: he had not had any recent contact with the young girl and so could not be held in any way responsible, but also this son and grandson of doctors probably radiated the kind of affability that is often bred of social self-confidence.

More surprisingly, despite the racist caricatures in *Paris-Midi,* neither the public nor the newspapers expressed any hostility toward Violette's black and Arab lovers, nor is there any evidence that the police treated them any differently from anyone else. The *Petit Parisien* described the black musician Pierre as "a decent fellow," an "athletic negro" elegantly dressed in a blue suit and light-colored hat, and sympathized with the Tunisian Fellous when he joked that "some people win a million in the lottery and I have to meet Violette Nozière and give her my address!" *L'Œuvre* concurred in describing Pierre as both attractive and likeable and the Algerian Atlan as an elegant businessman whose affairs seemed to be going well.[82] Male elegance was damning for some, it seems, but redemptive for others. Nor did Violette herself come in for censure for engaging specifically in cross-racial affairs: her behavior in this respect was surprisingly but clearly not an issue.[83] One of the few references to the matter, in

A la recherche de l'amant inconnu.

— Si je lui donnais de de l'argent ?... Oh ! ça, je jure que j'étais aimé pour moi-même !

— Ah ! monsieur le juge, le budget d'un jeune homme est mince... et. l'é- caille est hors de prix !

— Ouâ ! Ouâ ! Ouâ ! Ouâ !

Figure 14. The men in the case: cartoon from *Paris-Midi,* September 9, 1933. (Photo ACRPP, Paris.)

the conservative *Le Matin,* remained in the mode of light irony: "There is one thing one cannot blame Violette Nozière for, namely harboring racial prejudices."[84]

On the other hand, the man who, after Dabin, attracted the most scorn and censure was a scion of the traditional elites, Count André de Pinguet. One might expect hostility from a left-wing newspaper like *Le Populaire,* which declared that Pinguet was "the most sickening" of all her suitors. "He sees Violette, recognizes her, trifles with her for hours, giving her a gallant rendezvous, then sends in the police inspectors in his stead, with that typically French gallantry that was always the privilege of our aristocracy."[85] But the mainstream press similarly disparaged him, both for doing the police's work and for flouting widely accepted norms of gallantry. *Détective* dismissed Pinguet as an "operetta-style Sherlock Holmes" and a publicity hound. As we have seen, his role in handing Violette over to the authorities proved extremely controversial. Some people, reported *Marianne,* believed that he did his duty in turning her in, while others, even though they considered Violette a monster, were revolted by his duplicity and astonished at his "mentality."[86] True, Pinguet had not done much for his image by trying to peddle his story to several newspapers. But, as an aristocratic snitch, he also disturbed categories in the same way as Dabin: turning in a fugitive violated widely held norms of antipolice solidarity, doubly

# "L'AFFAIRE"

## par H.-P. GASSIER

—ji ti vends di beaux tapis...
veux zoli collier ?...

Plus fort que Sherlock
Holmès : le vicomte de la
Tour Pointue.

Un poète.
— Etre Jean Dabin... et mou-
rir d'épuisement !

so if the criminal was female and had been approached flirtatiously. The fact that the count, a bona fide aristocrat, had acted like a vulgar police informer, gave rise to a telling pun: the joke went around that Pinguet was an *homme donneur*—a "man of honor" *(homme d'honneur)* but really, since *donneur* or "giver" meant snitch, the most dishonorable of creatures. An aristocratic snitch, a middle-class pimp, a teenage female parricide, a mother with a death wish for her child: all these oxymoronic characters were deeply disturbing because they upended people's expectations about gender- and class-appropriate behavior.

These were the issues and characters debated in public. The central and most explosive matter was one that newspapers approached only tentatively, obliquely, using roundabout phrases like "odious accusation." As we have seen, the initial certainty that Violette was lying about her father's incestuous activities to minimize her crime was dented when the elements of proof she offered—her boyfriends' testimony, the stained rag—proved reasonably convincing, if not necessarily conclusive. But after a flurry of speculation in mid-September, around the time the Nozières' apartment was searched, the matter died down. An editorialist in *Gringoire* wrote a commentary on September 22 to the effect that anything was possible in this world and that "those who are ravaged by these sorts of passions don't shout it out over the rooftops or confide in their colleagues." He carefully protested that he had no opinion of the Nozière case specifically.[87] The column was an exception: the silence in the press on the subject of incest was deafening.

One wonders whether people talked about it among themselves, at home or among neighbors and friends. Judging from the sheaf of letters Lanoire received on the subject, there is no question that the issue of sexual abuse in the family had deep resonance for many people, reluctant as they might be to raise the matter in public. Some people wrote in to disprove the incest: a few letter-writers believed that Baptiste was not Violette's father, several pointed out that her father was not infected with syphilis, and one woman, "a mother," ventured that a woman who did all her family's laundry would have noticed if something like that had been going on when her daughter was young. A couple of others confirmed Violette's allegations. A gentleman from Normandy said he had met her near the Printemps department store and that in the hotel they went to she had confided to him about the abuse. A barely literate writer sent a letter to Violette's lawyer, Henri Géraud, from Germaine's village, Neuvy: "One day going to work I was seized by the call of nature and went on the other side of the hedge and found Nozière with his daughter. Nozière begged me for his wife and his family to say nothing ever. Since 1929 I think I said nothing, but Mme Nozière's denial of her daughter forces me to tell the truth." We cannot know, of course, whether the man from Normandy really met Violette or if the correspondent from Neuvy had actually seen what he described.

Violette's claims triggered the strongest response from one category of letter writers: women who reported that they had themselves been abused, either by their fathers or by other relatives, and who wrote to the judge begging him to believe her, or to Germaine asking for her pity and understanding. In the process, the writers pour out their own stories, often mentioning that they have never told a soul before. Trust me, many of them wrote, a man can do this and still be considered a paragon by everyone who knows him. A highly literate lady explained, "As for the neighbors, how would they know anything? All of this is hidden, nobody knows about these sorts of family dramas." Let me tell you a story I know from close up, she continued: it is about a bourgeois family in which the father keeps trying to attack the eighty-year-old grandmother, "yet this man is a ministerial officer and legal professional, held in the highest esteem."[88] "My father was highly esteemed among his acquaintances, his workers, the entire town," wrote F.R., "Oh, Mr. X is such a good man, but he acted badly with me." The writer, aged sixty, had been raped by her father when she was fifteen and never told her mother for fear of forcing a parental separation. "I have known the same thing," confided another, hiding behind the third person. "When the child was older she went in for the worst debauchery thanks to the bad example of the man who had been abusing her since she was nine. She dared not say anything to her mother, and the whole thing was only discovered much later. . . . So do you really think, Your Honor, that you will know anything about Nozière's honesty by asking his friends and relatives? Do you think that these individuals are going to boast about their vice to their colleagues? They pose as real patriarchs, setting themselves up as examples."

Some letters are long, pathetic autobiographies. One is even signed, by a Mme Party Hochstrasse in Saint-Dizier. The facts are spelled out in detail: she was fourteen, in bed with her sister, and felt a hand touching her; she grabbed the hand and stared at her father. "It caused profound disgust in me, and I understood things I should not have known until much later. And in spite of my decision to tell my mother everything, I did not dare, I was ashamed, and was seized with such self-disgust that I wanted to kill myself, but I loved my poor mother too much." Later, when her father exposed himself to her, she did tell her mother but was not believed: "She cursed me out to the whole family, and since that time I was known as a little pervert and liar. My poor mother wished me dead. I wept to her to give me back her love, but my tears and entreaties had the opposite effect— what a Calvary it was for my whole life. I am now fifty-eight and I remember this as if it were yesterday."

There are letters written to Mme Nozière, like the one with the cover note that comments, "She is so so cruel to her child I need to let her know what I suffered and what her child might be suffering." This letter is handwritten in pencil on a huge sheet of something that might be wrapping paper, with spelling that is nearly phonetic. "Madame, do not believe that it is impossible, a father can be a good man but weak." The writer grew up in the country in a family of six children, and when her father asked her to share his bed, it made her happy because she was so fond of him. When it happened, she could not believe it and did not say anything. When she was older and there was company, she had to share his bed again "and in the night it was the same thing such a horror from a father especially since my sister and her husband were in the room and I was terrified that they would hear something. I resented my father as since he knew his own passion he should have slept on a mattress on the ground." The letter ends with an appeal to Germaine: "Madame, if really your child went through this torture it is horrible, forgive her, protect her, she has suffered enough, this is an unhappy mother and grandmother begging you."

At the other end of the social scale, a woman "from the best society" pleaded with to Lanoire to believe "that poor little Violette" because her own youth was ruined by her father's abuse and by the hostility of a mother who refused to believe her and wanted to lock her up. "I beg you with all my heart, Sir, to believe that poor child who is hated by all of Paris, and I hope that my courage will bring her good luck. For I am fifty years old, and still ashamed to have had such a father. . . . I ask you to publish this letter in the newspapers, and I beg women who have gone through what I have to do as I am doing. I beseech you to take pity on that child, if she fainted in front of her mother she must really love her." Of course, no such appeals were ever published.

A case that prompted a dozen women to write to a man they did not know and tell him intimate stories they may not have told anyone else in the world does not fit neatly into the categories of "scandal" or "affair." The Nozière story never settled into a classic scandal because the objects of indignation it offered were unstable: the unquestioned villain was Violette at first, but then maybe not entirely, and then other villains emerged to compete with her: the mother who raised her so badly and then wished for her death, the boyfriend who exploited her, the upper-class snitch who turned her in, even the father who at best should have looked out for her virtue and at worst may have done the unspeakable. If the function of scandal in society is to generate "indignation that unites," the Nozière case hardly fits the bill. But then neither was it an affair, since nobody—except, as we shall see, a group of avant-garde poets in a foreign publication—emerged in public to take Violette's defense. Women's groups in the 1930s were preoccupied with reproductive rights and the suffrage that Frenchwomen would achieve only in 1945. Sexual abuse in the family would not gain public recognition as an issue for decades, and in any event Violette, a promiscuous spendthrift and cold-blooded parent-killer, was hardly a good poster child for any cause.

The Nozière case did resonate strongly with contemporaries, however, because it involved matters that got to the heart of everyday experience for many thousands: the perils of upward mobility, the ingratitude of children, the responsibility of parents, and the proper behavior of young men and women. And the truth of it was always just beyond reach. Could anyone ever know what went on behind the closed doors of a "good" family any more than they could know what went on in the mind of a beautiful but opaque young woman?

All of this explains the universal fascination with a story that generated thousands of pages of print but also impelled women and men of all social classes in Paris and beyond to share their anger, anxiety, or excitement with the Judge Lanoire. In early September the novelist Pierre Drieu La Rochelle attempted to explain in a magazine article the hold of the case over contemporaries.[89] Most people, he surmised, think sometimes about high politics, sometimes worry about the 1924 election or the rise of Hitler. Most of the time, though, "they think about the three or four themes that govern their individual fates: family, love, money and death. . . . It is because they think so much about family that little Violette hit them so hard." When the Nozière case broke out, people's first reaction was: "She killed. This is no 'affair.'" Then the questions started: how many people did she want to kill? Who helped her? Whom in fact did she kill, who *was* her father? And then people took positions and started arguing, and the case became a sort of "political" case, Drieu argued, not in the sense that we usually understand the word, but rather a politics that does not divide people according to their interests, their class, or their culture. "Women especially read to find out about what they need to know, right now, about the way things go for other people; compare this with what goes on for them; and then fit what seems so particular, so strange and solitary, into the general rhythm of breathing." The story made members of the public stake out positions, defend them, and change them, caused them to think over and revise the matters that touched them most closely.

A whole constellation of contemporary experience was packed into the story of Violette and her parents, Drieu observed, and as a result much was projected onto the elusive antiheroine of the crime: "Every time Violette Nozière makes a move, something shifts, sending out waves, and in the circles expanding from one face to the next we discover a hundred of the secrets we all keep." Some famous crimes are given meaning by the commanding voice of a Voltaire, a Zola, or a Darrow; others, more quietly, by the buzz of a thousand anonymous conversations.

# SEVEN

# A Culture of Crime

IT IS EASY TO IMAGINE Violette Nozière as a film noir heroine, as she was indeed portrayed by the great French actress Isabelle Huppert in Claude Chabrol's 1978 movie about the case: long, dark silhouette, tilted hat, fur stole, pale skin, and scarlet lips. Indeed, as a character, she fits a classic description of the film noir woman as a "*femme fatale* who is fatal to herself": "Frustrated and deviant, half predator, half prey, detached yet ensnared, she falls victim to her own traps."[1] On the one hand, the Nozière case was, in its particulars, intensely real to contemporaries: brain in oil sauce for lunch and soup for supper, card games and dirty rags, cheap hotels and department store shopping. From another angle, however, Violette's story fit into a rolling succession of crime narratives and a cultural environment in which dark, inexplicable deeds were given pride of place in both literary and mass culture. This was the age of the first hugely successful French crime weeklies, of the literary birth of Inspector Maigret, of killers like Henri Landru and the Papin sisters, whose names still resonate in France. High literary culture fully partook in the cult of the bizarrely violent. André Gide, arguably the most admired and influential writer of the years after World War I, produced novels in which characters committed unexplained killings and suicides, and the dominant avant-garde movement of the time, Surrealism, drew much of its creative energy from fantasies of sadistic transgression.

It would be absurd, of course, to label any historical period "the age of crime"; fascination with tales of violence is inevitably present in all times because acts of evil delineate the outer limits of every generation's moral and social landscape. What matters in historical terms is the specific nature and shape of that fascination: What sorts of crime and which criminal populations draw attention in a given period? How are murder and mayhem "sold" and "consumed"? In Germany between the wars, for instance, both the general public and the literary and artistic communities were intensely preoccupied with what was known as *Lustmord*—sexual murders by serial killers—a phenomenon that echoes the late-nineteenth-century British obsession with Jack the Ripper but has no real French equivalent.[2]

Beginning in the later nineteenth century, crime as a commodity in France had a new format, the *fait divers.* The term, which has no real counterpart in English, comes from journalistic practice. Newspapers carried items of substance, such as political and economic news, as well as reporting on more entertaining fare, such as culture and sports. As the newspaper press developed, editors were at pains to find a designation for items of great interest that had no obvious relevance to the public world, such as sordid private criminality. These were corralled into a section labeled *faits divers,* "diverse" or "miscellaneous" happenings. It is tempting to equate *faits divers* with what we call the crime rubric, but the category is more capacious and includes bizarre or tragic coincidences: a person killed by a suicide's jump from a tall building, a man who "killed after his own death" (the coffin fell on the priest), an executioner who dies on the way to carrying out his function.[3]

By the 1930s squalid private crime had been an item in the newspapers for many decades. The term and concept of the *fait divers* goes back at least to 1869, when reports of the foul deeds of Jean-Baptiste Troppmann, cold-blooded killer of an angelic family of six, increased tenfold the circulation of *Le Petit Journal* and made it into the capital's leading daily.[4] Stories of "everyday crime" were not new, but the 1920s and '30s in France could be called the "age of the *fait divers*" because of the intense interest in and coverage of these kinds of crimes. Before the mid-nineteenth century, crime reporting was embedded in the practices of an oral culture: crime narratives were broadcast by street criers and singers, or printed on one-sided handbills called *canards,* which were posted where people could congregate and discuss their contents.[5] The stories retailed in these archaic modes were often those of larger-than-life criminal figures, such as the outlaws Mandrin and Cartouche or the would-be regicide Damiens in the eighteenth century, or in the early nineteenth the intellectual dandy and murderer Pierre Lacenaire, who entertained the cream of Parisian society in his prison cell and cultivated his image as a doomed poet onto the very steps of the guillotine.[6] In the nineteenth-century city, crime also became a sociological rather than individual category. With increasing migration from the countryside and separation of classes in the city, workers appeared strange and alarming to the middle classes.[7] During the Belle Époque, the good bourgeois shivered as they read of the violent acts of Parisian street gangs. These youths pouring into the center of the city were dubbed Apaches by a sensation-hungry journalist. Around 1900, reports of "Apache" violence for years fueled readers' paranoia that an "army of crime" controlled the city, even as stories about the Apache "queen" Casque d'Or ("Golden Helmet") stoked their fantasies.[8]

In the wake of World War I, this preoccupation with dangerous classes and armies of crime was displaced by fascination with offenses committed by "people just like us." Fears of the unknown gave way to fears of the known, of the violence that might be committed by the normal-seeming person next door or even an intimate. To put it another way, the cultural framework of crime moved from the melodramatic to the "noir" mode. A 1936 article in the crime magazine Détective evoked the melodramatic romance of Belle Époque Parisian crime, at once titillating and reassuring, since criminals clearly came from elsewhere: the piece evoked the era when bad boys from the northern districts and their molls with hair piled high on their heads came down to the center city to settle scores at knifepoint and eat snails at L'Ange Gabriel, the "Maxim's of the Apaches." "It is hard for us, remembering the prewar underworld, to separate our memories from the images in the popular pageantry of successful melodramas, or of songs in the style of [Aristide] Bruant." Before the war, there were crimes of passion, of course, but no "improvised criminals." Felons belonged to a certain milieu and had rules and codes of honor. They might be violent, but they did not cheat. Now, the journalist continued, with social mobility and the influx of foreigners, all that is gone and you can hardly tell who is a criminal: "You see boys from good families, like Gaucher, like Dabin, become would-be pimps and would-be gangsters."[9] Evil could be right beside you, and you would not know it.

Melodrama as a genre was born in the eighteenth century and flourished in the nineteenth. Displacing older religious traditions, it located the struggle between good and evil in the social world, making morality easily legible to the larger, socially mixed audiences of plays and early movies, or to readers of cheap popular fare.[10] It took little sophistication to figure out what the mustache-twirling villain, gothic monster, or white-clad virgin was up to; but melodrama was also morally comforting, since evil was depicted as external and radically "other." The aesthetic that has come to be known as "noir," by contrast, locates evil within or beside us. The literary critic Jonathan Eburne observes: "Could not the standard noir plot twist be described as the uncanny realization that an evil 'out there' against which the protagonists so gallantly attempt to safeguard themselves, is suddenly revealed to have been in their midst all along?"[11]

Although melodramatic and noir conventions and sensibilities often coexist, it is the latter that typically informed crime reporting during the interwar years in France. The Nozière story is emblematic of the 1930s *fait divers:* not only did it happen to "people just like us," not only was the evil it portrayed chillingly intimate, but, hatred of Violette notwithstanding, it became increasingly difficult as the case proceeded to identify an entirely guilty party or an entirely innocent one.

Melodramatic conventions are easily pressed into the service of the us-against-them spirit of political ideologies: good French against evil Germans, pure proletarians versus wicked capitalists, and so on.[12] What is striking about the *fait divers* is its detachment from broad ideological and political patterns: the significance of these bizarre, morally opaque stories lay precisely in their *lack* of obvious meaning. And this in turn must be understood in relation to the political vacuum of the time. The horrific absurdity of the First World War—millions killed for reasons nobody could, in the end, quite fathom—combined with the violence of the Russian Revolution left a generation disillusioned with grand systems of belief, such as nationalism and socialism. The cronyism and graft rampant among the Third Republic leadership alienated ordinary French people from the political process: the big battles against the Church and for universal education had been won in previous generations, leaving in their wake only complacent mediocrity. Little wonder that so many sought diversion and meaning in sensational, fragmentary, ambiguous tales of private tragedy.[13]

In 1928, France got a new magazine devoted entirely to crime, *Détective,* subtitled "The Great *Fait-Divers* Weekly." The periodical's genealogy is interesting, since *Détective*'s origins were in the world of high literary publishing. The person who brought the magazine into being was one of

France's legendary publishers, Gaston Gallimard, whose name adorns what is still today the country's most prestigious literary imprint. Born in 1881, Gallimard, the son of a book-loving Parisian architect, was a brilliant and charming man of the world who did not do much of anything until age thirty, when he was recruited by the rarefied group of intellectuals around André Gide to launch a press as a spin-off of their successful literary periodical, the *Nouvelle Revue Française*. The choice was a stroke of either luck or genius, since Gallimard turned out to possess both an excellent business sense and an extraordinary flair for literary quality. The upshot—the NRF Press—was a collaboration between the period's best writers and its best editor that, while it made literary history, was also famously rocky. Tensions erupted at regular intervals between Gallimard, a pillar of the social scene who loved comely actresses, flashy cars, and long lunches and did not despise money, and the group around Gide, high-minded intellectuals, several of Protestant or Jewish descent, whom Parisians sometimes mocked as the "Calvin Follies."[14] One contemporary later marveled that Gide and Gallimard had been able to work together for thirty years: "Gaston is weak and irascible, Gide is oblique and treacherous." In 1919 Gallimard went on to create his own publishing house. He was to discover and promote such canonical French writers as Louis Aragon, Pierre Drieu la Rochelle, and Albert Cohen, snap up the journalist-turned-crime writer Georges Simenon, and publish Dos Passos, Faulkner, Hemingway, and Steinbeck in translation. He continued to work closely with the *Nouvelle Revue Française* group, publish their works, and help them out. When Gide committed the epic literary mistake of turning down Marcel Proust's *Remembrance of Things Past* ("Too many duchesses, not our style"), it was Gallimard who pulled the chestnuts out of the fire for him, eventually wooing Proust back from the competition.[15]

By the late 1920s, Gallimard had the most prestigious list in France but was facing severe financial difficulties linked to the incipient international economic crisis. Since he scorned neither the profit motive nor middlebrow culture, Gallimard was receptive when the brothers Kessel came to him in 1928 with an intriguing proposition. Joseph and Georges were two of the three sons of a Russian Jewish doctor, Samuel Kessel, who had immigrated to France via Argentina. The eldest Kessel brother, Lazare, one of France's most promising young actors, committed suicide in 1920. Joseph was both a highly successful novelist (later elected to the Académie Française) and an international adventurer-journalist who became a cult figure between the wars, flying his own plane to exotic places and shaping his travels into tales of virile adventure. He and Georges shared burly good looks and a taste for high living, drugs, and women. Georges, twenty-four years old in 1928, was a well-dressed and witty dilettante with a rich wife but whose weakness for horse races and poker left him in chronic need of cash.[16]

Joseph and Georges came to Gallimard with a proposal: since readers obviously hungered for the *faits divers* section of newspapers, why not bypass the "serious" news and devote a whole magazine to crime? Gallimard recognized the idea's potential. Georges, the prime mover for the initiative, recruited two journalist friends of his, Marius Larique and Marcel Montarron, between horse races at the Saint-Cloud track where he was gambling away most of Gallimard's start-up money.[17] Somehow the first issue of *Détective* got produced under the wire and on borrowed money. Dated November 1, 1928, and with a cover story on "Chicago, Capital of Crime," it was a huge success, reportedly selling three hundred and fifty thousand copies. Two years later, the editors claimed that they produced six hundred thousand copies of each weekly issue and had a readership of about one million, or one in every forty French people.[18] Though these figures were probably exaggerated, there is no question that the magazine had a huge audience, which it retained well into the 1930s. The magazine's success produced a rash of imitators over the next few years: *Police Magazine, Faits Divers, Police et Reportages,* and *Scandales,* none of which, however, seriously dented *Détective*'s sales or threatened its status as the iconic publication in the genre.[19] Gallimard was later to remark that *Détective* was his greatest commercial success, its heyday the only time his publishing house made serious profits.[20]

The magazine's staff was made up of reporter-journalists with serious credentials, most of whom moonlighted for *Détective* while keeping their jobs at established dailies like *Le Journal.* The 1930s in France were the heyday of the romanticized danger-courting reporter, a figure soon to be immortalized in the comic-strip character Tintin. Some of the newsmen who worked for *Détective*—Larique, Montarron, Paul Bringuier, Henri Danjou, and Georges Simenon—were skittish about being associated with the pointy-headed intellectuals at the *Nouvelle Revue Française* and Gallimard. They liked to think of themselves in the tradition of the great Albert Londres, who had achieved glory by exposing the abuses of France's overseas penal colonies in the 1920s, and they carefully cultivated a reputation as the *enfants terribles* of the Gallimard house. The magazine's reporters held shooting practice sessions in the warehouse they were given for an office, and even faked a William Tell scene once when the Gallimard brass came for a visit: Bringuier pulled a bottle off his head with an invisible string when a colleague fired a blank at him, while the others shot real bullets into luxury editions of the works of the highbrow Catholic writers Charles Péguy and Paul Claudel.[21] At first the enterprise was very much seat-of-the-pants. At the beginning, before the magazine had its own photographers, the journalists purloined whatever shots they could from other agencies and archives and tried to fit them to their stories: "We were the ragpickers of the *fait divers*," Montarron later reminisced.[22]

*Détective* covered "crime" in the broadest possible sense, not just criminal acts but also criminal and dangerous milieus. Especially in the early years, pride of place was given to exotic overseas locales, allowing the editors to make claims about the educational value of their publication. Cover stories often dealt with foreign crime and especially punishment: torture and chastisement in Afghanistan, the Antipodes, the Philippines, or China, where, decapitations and crucifixions notwithstanding, the article reported, "death is the least feared of punishments." A January 1929 article on foot-flogging and ceremonial strangulation in Afghanistan piously concluded a report destined for armchair voyeurism: "Barbaric customs, rituals one might believe long abandoned, that is what I believed it my duty to reveal to the readers of this great magazine."[23] Nor was all this exotic cruelty third-world based. American legal and extralegal brutality got plenty of coverage too, in features about the police techniques known as *le grilling* and vigilante violence or *la loi de Lynch*.[24]

Most of the reporting naturally focused on France, much of it dealing with criminal or carceral underworlds. Prisons, especially women's prisons, and France's harsh penal colonies in Guyana and elsewhere got plenty of attention. So did the Parisian underworld, the *milieu*, whose argot, score-settling, and crime bosses were evoked in rich detail: you could almost hear the strains of the accordion and make out through the cigarette smoke the gangsters known as *marlous*, in their striped jerseys and wide pants, keeping an eye on their heavily made-up venal girlfriends, the *pierreuses*. Since some of the readership was provincial, the underworlds of other cities in France were awarded their own articles, sometimes plausibly (Marseille), other times less so (Dijon?).[25]

The magazine's readers probably covered a wide swath of society. For most of the 1930s, *Détective* cost one franc fifty, a small luxury for an unskilled worker making one hundred francs a week and a very affordable indulgence for office workers making twice or three times that amount. The magazine also appealed to middle-class intellectuals seeking ammunition for their fiction: André Gide, the novelist Paul Nizan, the philosophers Jean-Paul Sartre and Simone de Beauvoir, the playwright Jean Genet, and poets from the Surrealist group all looked at it at least occasionally.[26] The best clues as to who read the magazine are offered by the one or two pages of advertising in each issue. Ads for the books of literary figures like Gide, Drieu la Rochelle, or Erich Maria Remarque pointed to the publication's origins in the Gallimard high culture world and flattered readers' cultural ambitions. Beside these, notices appeared weekly for astrologers, tarot readers, and private eyes. The biggest ads in *Détective* were for the sort of newly available consumer goods that would be particularly appealing to families rising in the world: furniture for art deco bedrooms or faux-Renaissance dining rooms, purchasable on credit from department stores; traditional household goods like linens and pan sets; and the spoils of modernity, cameras, radio consoles, phonographs and bicycles.

Most revealing are the frequent ads for educational and vocational self-improvement. The issue of May 15, 1930, for instance, included half a page touting a new "autodidactic encyclopedia" and reminding readers: "It is known that the best positions go to those who have acquired in their schooling the components of the literary, scientific and practical baggage of the 'Great Schools' . . . TO KNOW is already TO SUCCEED." Other issues carried publicity for the Écoles Pigier, which offered training for white-collar jobs, illustrated with vignettes of well-dressed young men and women seated at desks. "You are young! You are ambitious! Succeed!" trumpeted an October 1930 advertisement for a private vocational school. To succeed one might have to transform one's appearance—or so one might surmise from the frequent ads for diet products, facial treatments, bespoke clothing, and tattoo removal services that also graced *Détective's* pages.

Judging from the advertisements it carried, then, *Détective* was pitched at families exactly like the Nozières: lower-middle-class urban households with some educational background and a strong desire to better themselves. The editorial in the very first issue evokes the isolation of new urban families eager to experience the world vicariously. *Détective,* the editors announced, would be the readers' eyes and ears. *Partout, pour tous* was the magazine's motto: everywhere for everyone. Like a private eye, *Détective* "will spy, stalk criminals, follow the police. Sometimes wearing canvas shoes, sometimes elegant pumps, he will wield a blow-torch if need be to force open secrets. . . . With him you will be at the world's center, at the heart of life's great dramas: the nights of Chicago, the slums of Singapore, the Whitechapel ghettos, the secrets of the North Pole. . . . You will have your weekly film at home." All of this was promised in the name of "a team of ten, twenty, maybe one hundred young and experienced men, ready for any adventure"; half a dozen was closer to the truth, at least initially.[27] *Détective* proposed to its readers something like what television was to offer a few decades later: a "film at home" made up of sensationalized information, a mixture of the exotic and the familiar available for consumption right in one's own living room. To the housewives, civil servants, and office workers who read it, *Détective* trumpeted its literary respectability as a scion of the house of Gallimard, while offering thrills and a sense of connection within an increasingly atomized world.

*Détective* reassured readers about who they were not. They could read, as their nineteenth-century forebears did, about the capital's dangerous classes, the frightening population of slum dwellers in *la zone* on the edges of the city. Depictions of life in this no-man's-land of the wretchedly poor were horrible in a conventionally Zolaesque way, a catalogue of brawls, knifings, prostitution, family violence, alcohol, and incest.[28] More innovative was the sensationalizing of rural crime for the benefit of urban readers. An overview in April 1932 entitled "Villages of Crime" explained that rural folk, living close to nature, had primitive instincts and their limited horizons made them grasping and self-interested. An article later that year recounted the murder of an ancient farmer by a young woman who may have been his mistress. The old man's widow hisses at the reporter, "You don't know! You can't know! It's infernal here! This place is the village of hatred!"[29] Men burn down their enemies' farms and shoot their families; a farmer beats both of his girlfriends and has them wear metal chastity belts; the dissolute Louisette bludgeons her married paramour to death under what the article's title labels "The Apple Tree of Passion."[30] Many urban workers spent their summer vacations, as did the Nozières, in these villages of "hatred," "fear," and "passion," but this apparently did not blunt their interest in the sordid goings-on in someone else's grandmother's village. The articles in *Détective* probably reminded them of why they were right to have left such claustrophobic and impoverished places.

The bread-and-butter of the magazine, as of the *faits divers* of the big daily papers, was the reporting of day-to-day urban crime. In 1931 Paul Bringuier contributed to *Détective* an article in the form of a memoir explaining how he learned the trade of a *fait divers* reporter. As a young man, he applied for a position on the crime beat at a leading newspaper, whose editor-in-chief delivered his usual discouraging speech: "You need an overpowering vocation, the energy of a brute to stay in the game. Talent? Doesn't matter. . . . You know how to write? Don't answer, I'm telling you that you don't. You got university degrees? Actually I don't give a damn, I only ask because of spelling. There, I got had again, another clumsy rube we have to train. Jeez. Here, guys, you show him the ropes, I'm dying here." His new colleagues toss him a cigarette and explain that Paris is divided for the job into eight sections, each assigned to one reporter. His task is to make the rounds of a dozen police stations, trawling for news. Young Bringuier makes his way to a first police station, where he's told that nothing's going on. As he starts to leave, a gendarme stops him: "Nothing. It's a manner of speaking. You want an eighty-year-old man who shot himself seven times in the head? Didn't die, by the way. Yes? The report's over there on the desk, that one there, you can copy it out. Do you play poker, by the way?" Bringuier tells of autopsies in village cemeteries, of provincial train stations in the dead of night, of crowding into a Montmartre crime scene with the police, blood on everyone's shoes, of articles scribbled on cardboard or butcher's paper in the back of a taxi. He makes the job sound frenetic and also romantic.[31]

*Détective*'s tone of obligatory high seriousness—pathos, indignation, something verging on hucksterism for the foreign articles—sometimes broke down when the story warranted it. In 1936, for instance, Marcel Montarron reported on the trial of a pudgy fiftyish grocer in the dreary suburb of Vauréal-sur-Oise who tried to supplement the faltering income from his small business by operating a salon for sadomasochistic practices on the side. The trial of the grocer and his equally dowdy wife ("Madame Rod" for professional purposes) was a local sensation even though, Montarron regretfully reported, there was no reconstitution of the offense. Best of all, some clients were dragged into court to testify. A stammering Monsieur K. explained that he became a client because "I was curious about the underside of Parisian life." The prosecutor exploded: "You call this Parisian life? Vauréal-sur-Oise?"[32]

*Faits divers* magazines lived for the "big crimes" that would provide a sustained run of news. "Monsters" like the family-slaying Troppmann or the pedophile Soleilland could boost sales for weeks at a time. In the early 1920s all of France was in thrall to the deeds of Henri Landru, the "Bluebeard of Gambais." Landru was a middle-aged engineer with a heavy black beard and a sideline in stolen goods who between 1915 and 1919 lured ten women out to his country house on the outskirts of Paris. His newspaper ad indicated an interest in marriage, an effective bait at a time when most young men were at the front (he kept the letters of over two hundred others who had written in). All ten women, and the teenage son of one of them, simply disappeared, though some of their effects were found in the villa. Landru, who had probably incinerated their bodies, dared the prosecutors to prove him a killer. Complicating matters further were the existence of Landru's estranged but respectable wife and four children, and his longtime and tenderly devoted mistress. Landru insisted he was innocent right up to his execution in February 1922.[33]

After a series of smaller cases in the 1920s, in 1933 an extraordinary run of "big crimes" began, their importance magnified by the *fait divers* press. The novelty of this later period was how much importance was invested in the crimes of apparently ordinary folks. Just six months before the Nozière affair, French readers were shocked by one of the most grisly and inexplicable murders in modern French history. The crime of the Papin sisters can be considered the archetypal *fait divers* because the sisters' exceptionally violent act could never be made to fit any of the contexts invoked to contain it. No case better evokes the essence of the interwar *fait divers:* the mysterious power vested in an obscure and ultimately inexplicable private event.

Christine and Léa Papin were respectively twenty-eight and twenty-two when they committed their crime in February 1933.[34] They worked as cook and housemaid for an archetypal family of the provincial bourgeoisie in the western French town of Le Mans. Their employers were the Lancelins—a retired lawyer, his wife, and their twenty-one-year-old daughter Geneviève. Christine and Léa's existence had been grim, consisting mostly of poverty and neglect. Their parents, Gustave and Clémence Papin, uneducated small-town laborers, had three daughters and a wretched marriage that ended when the children were young amid rumors that Gustave, a violent alcoholic, had sexually abused the eldest daughter, Émilia. Clémence, in charge of the girls after her divorce, showed a distinct lack of maternal affection: she placed the two eldest ones in an orphanage and sent Léa, then two, to live with a brother. Émilia eventually entered a convent, and Clémence placed the two younger girls as servants as soon as they were of age, always demanding a large cut from their wages. At first they worked in separate households, but eventually they managed to get hired together. Christine and Léa, alone in the world (they broke off relations with their mother in 1929), developed an intense symbiotic relationship in which the older girl acted as the younger one's mother. They showed no interest in the outside world and communicated only with each other. The Lancelins hired them in 1927.

Relations between masters and servants in the Lancelin household were fairly typical of the time and place, chilly but not abnormally fraught. The Lancelins were formally "good masters": they paid their servants a decent wage and a half month extra at Christmas, fed them well, and did not make unusual demands. Much was later made of an episode in which Madame pinched Léa's shoulder and forced her to go on her knees and pick up a scrap of paper from the carpet, but the maids never described their treatment by the Lancelins as harsh or unfair. The interactions between servants and masters can hardly have been called warm: M. Lancelin never addressed the maids directly, and Geneviève barely talked to them at all. The household seems to have been a universe of smug propriety in which Madame gave orders and everyone knew their place. The Lancelins were actually very satisfied with their household help, even bragging about the sisters to their acquaintances. Christine and Léa also insisted, after the fact, that they had no complaints about their employers. Certainly, master-servant relationships in the house involved their share of tensions and oddities: there had been an incident a few months earlier in which the sisters wandered into the town hall looking somewhat deranged and complained about persecution by their employers; they sometimes called their mistress "Maman" and their mother, while they still spoke to her, "Madame." But what lives, what relationships, would not offer up some element of the bizarre when subjected to the kind of scrutiny that follows an act of extraordinary violence?

In the early evening of February 3, 1933, a fuse blew in the Lancelin house. The electric iron had recently come back from the repair shop, its breakdown attributed to the maids' carelessness. When Mme Lancelin and Geneviève came home from visiting at the end of the afternoon, the ironing was still not done and the house was plunged in darkness because the iron had short-circuited and blown a fuse. Mme Lancelin reprimanded the maids, who reacted with crazed savagery: with Christine taking the lead, they threw themselves on the two women and tore out their eyeballs with their naked fingers, then fetched household implements—a pewter jug, hammer, and knife—with which they battered and cut their mistresses to death. Some of the cuts, on the victim's naked buttocks and thighs, seemed sadistically sexual in nature. Surveying the bloody damage,

Christine dryly commented, "Eh bien, c'est du propre"—"Well, this is a fine mess." Christine and Léa locked the front door, went upstairs to their bedroom, washed and put on their dressing gowns, then waited huddled together in bed, by the light of a candle, for the arrival of the police. They immediately confessed to the crime, describing it in detail but giving no explanation.

Predictably, many commentators and contemporaries rushed to embrace a narrative of class exploitation: it would have been reassuring to believe the murders were just an uncommonly feral response to years of abuse by harsh masters and a cruel social order. The Communist *L'Humanité* naturally promoted this view of the matter, titling its summary at the time of the sisters' trial "Seven Years of Slavery": "The true reasons for this murder can be found in the hell these two servants lived through with this bourgeois family. . . . It is not the Papin sisters who should be on trial, but the sacrosanct bourgeois family, which nurtures not only the most shameful secrets but cruelty and contempt for those who earn their keep serving it."[35] The left-leaning *Marianne* echoed the sentiment: "Let's not forget that for bourgeoises like the women who were murdered, a servant is less than an animal . . . a creature of another species, marginal to society, basement-dwellers to those honorable social strata that give birth to lawyers, notaries, the salt of the earth."[36] Intellectuals like the young Beauvoir and Sartre, exiled to entry-level teaching positions in dull provincial towns, took sides in a flash: "In Rouen, as in Le Mans, perhaps among the mothers of my students," wrote Beauvoir, "there were certainly women like that, who deducted the price of a broken plate from their maid's wages and pulled on white gloves to discover traces of dust on the furniture: in our view, they were the ones deserving death a hundred times over."[37]

Some journalists sought to "tame" the case by means of the fear and contempt of rural folk felt by many city dwellers. *L'Intransigeant* went straight for the clichés: "Christine and Léa Papin are country girls, stubborn, limited, jealous, vindictive, but normal and responsible for all that." *Vu* tagged them the "bad sheep" of the Bon Pasteur (Good Shepherd) Orphanage; *Détective* headlined "The Rabid Sheep" (fig. 15). *Le Journal* revealed the unfamiliar expressions they used to describe their acts of violence, the language of the slaughterhouse and the butcher shop: "Je l'ai alourdie" ("I weighed her down") for the skull fracturing, "Je lui ai fait des enciselures" ("I cross-hatched her") for the knifing.[38] George Imam in *Candide* shared with readers the "peasant brutality" of Christine's first declarations to the police: "When Madame came in, I reported to her that

Figure 15. Christine and Léa Papin in a *Détective* photomontage of February 9, 1933, with objects like the ones they used for their crime. (Courtesy Éditions Gallimard and Bibliothèque des Littératures Policières, Paris.)

the iron was broken. She wanted to attack me, and that is when I jumped at her and ripped out her eyes with my fingers."[39]

However much journalists and commentators tried to press the case into a familiar mold—cruelly exploited workers, bestial country people—these efforts were insufficient. Pent-up anger at a demanding employer, even coupled with a particularly wretched background and life story, came far short of explaining why one would tear out eyeballs, bash in skulls, slice flesh to ribbons, and then barely seem to register the carnage. The obvious explanation was that the women were severely deranged, a diagnosis that Christine's behavior seemed to confirm: in prison the older sister babbled incoherently, licked the ground and walls as if in penance, experienced a monthlong fit during which she threatened to tear out her own eyes, and finally had to be placed in solitary confinement in a straight-jacket. The rages were apparently triggered by separation from Léa—the latter remained mute and catatonic—whom Christine on at least one occasion called "my husband." After a seizure, she hallucinated that she saw Léa hanging from a tree with her legs cut off.[40]

A panel of specialists, composed of two local experts and the same Dr. Victor Truelle from Saint-Anne who later weighed in on Violette's mental capacities, was convened to evaluate the sisters' sanity. There is no telling what caused the medical experts to deliver their astonishing verdict, though it is easy to surmise that the shock at so hideous a violation of quasi-familial relations made the pressure for retribution overwhelming. It was not that long ago, in prerevolutionary France, that the penalty just for stealing from one's master had been death.[41] The three specialists concluded that there was nothing in the women's physical state, heredity, or mental competence of a nature to diminish their responsibility. "The Papin girls are not sick," the prosecutor argued, following their lead. "They are not mad dogs, just bad dogs."[42] Despite a rebuttal by another specialist called in by the defense, the prosecution's case prevailed. It took a jury of middle-aged local men forty minutes to judge the sisters guilty on all counts, with mitigating circumstances allowed to Léa Papin, who was clearly not the prime instigator of the violence. Christine Papin was condemned to death—though her life was eventually spared—and Léa to ten years of hard labor.[43] When she heard the verdict, Christine fell to her knees, apparently in gratitude.

The experts' diagnosis caused considerable skepticism and debate. Some newspapers commented that the sisters' impassive behavior and clinical description of their crime did indeed suggest complete sanity. Spectators at the trial, however, were heard complaining that the report was biased, based on two half-hour interviews. Sartre and Beauvoir were disgusted, having come to believe that the sisters were clinically paranoid. Janet Flanner, writing for the *New Yorker*, pointed out that the Papins' father was a "dipsomaniac rapist," their mother a money-grubbing hysteric, and that various cousins had hanged themselves or died in mental asylums: "In other words, heredity O.K., legal responsibility one hundred percent."[44]

The Papin case caused a big stir both around the time the murders were committed, in February 1933, and then at the time of the trial in late September, when it overlapped with the Nozière affair. The crime of the "savage sheep" of Le Mans received less coverage and evidently affected contemporaries less, however, than the case of the teenage parricide. Christine and Léa's act was grotesquely violent, but the issues and characters involved fell within a narrow range: were the women crazy or, as the prosecution put it, angry souls who gave in to their worst impulses against people who had treated them decently, and then faked madness to escape punishment? Were the Lancelins good masters or cold bourgeois prigs? The story did not offer a vast amount of fodder for debate.

What the Papin case did generate was a rich intellectual and literary legacy. Both the Surrealist group and the psychiatrist Jacques Lacan would draw inspiration from its most sensational features. The case later served as the basis for at least two major plays, Jean Genet's 1947 masterpiece *The Maids (Les Bonnes)* and Wendy Kesselman's 1982 *My Sister in This House*. Since 1963, at least four movies have depicted the case either explicitly or in modified form. The story of two troubled female servants caught in a possibly homosexual and incestuous fantasy world of their own and violently killing a mistress both hated and revered has all the elements of a primal allegory. It evokes other disturbing stories, such as the 1954 case of the New Zealand teenagers Juliet Hulme and Pauline Parker, who, absorbed in mutual passion and the shared fantasy worlds they had created, planned and carried out the gruesome bludgeoning death of Parker's mother.[45]

The Papin case was full of "mirrors, fusions, and splittings": Christine and Léa, conjoined in their *folie à deux,* violently attacked two other women.[46] The sisters may have been lovers, and their mistress merged with their hated and longed-for mother. Their cruelty seemed both gratuitous and laden with symbolism and ceremony: eyes were torn out so that the all-seeing mistress/mother and her favored daughter would not contemplate the desecration, and the crime was followed by careful washing (the murder weapons were cleaned and put back in their places) and the expectation of punishment. Both Beauvoir and Flanner picked up on the unsettling nature of the sisters' bond: "The newspapers informed us that they were in love," Beauvoir remembered, "and we imagined the nights of caresses and hatred they shared up in the desert of their attic." Flanner got it in a nutshell: "The Papins' was the pain of being two where some mysterious unity had been originally intended."[47] The maids' twisted pathway of desire—for each other and their absent mother—led through a bloodbath.

The Nozière and Papin cases fascinated contemporaries for some of the same reasons: the two crimes were committed in utterly mundane settings by women whose motivations remained controversial or opaque to the end. Both stories were quintessential *faits divers* because neither fit any known, reassuring plot line. By contrast, the early thirties offered plenty of more familiar criminal cases—stories that, while sometimes very lurid, did have obvious precedents.

Writing in the *New Yorker,* Janet Flanner coupled Violette Nozière's crime with that of Germaine d'Anglemont, the better to draw a sharp contrast between the "mediocre murder" committed by Violette and the "stylish assassination" carried out by Germaine. Mme d'Anglemont was forty-five when she killed her paramour, and Flanner wrote tongue-in-cheek about the "decline in the younger generation. Mme d'Anglemont shot her lover like a lady, because she was jealous; Violette Nozière killed her father like a cannibal, because she wanted to eat and drink up the savings that were his French life and blood." Our grandmothers might be right, Flanner ironized—there looked to be a sharp drop in standards among female murderesses.[48]

Flanner's sarcasm hinted at the fact that Germaine d'Anglemont's story was as classically French as the Hall of Mirrors or truffled foie gras.[49] Armande Huot (such was her real name) was born in 1888 to a working-class single mother in a poor district of central Paris. Shunted off, like the Papin sisters, to a religious orphanage, she was returned at age thirteen to her neglectful mother and soon took a predictable turn toward prostitution. By seventeen, she was living a script straight out of Zola, down to her "professional" name, Nini. Pretty, ambitious, and fond of reading, Nini Huot believed that she deserved better than the men she picked up in smoky accordion bars. An author of popular novels with whom she slept suggested that she change her name to something aristocratic-sounding, and together they came up with Germaine d'Anglemont. The fake nobility of a courtesan did not fool anyone, nor was it meant to: it was a convention going back centuries—Louis XV's mistress Mme du Barry had also been a high-end prostitute—that merely signaled that one was on one's way up. And up she went like a rocket, first snagging a wealthy Dutch merchant, then casting him aside for bigger fry. She became a fixture of the Belle Époque establishment, was almost engaged to Prince Franz Josef of Bavaria, dated the president of Mexico, and reportedly received ten million francs from a Polish count. Her early life was similar to that of her contemporary Coco Chanel, but without the talent and business acumen.

Many luxury apartments, townhouses, furs, and jewels later, Germaine settled down, more modestly, with a French politician, Jean Causeret, the prefect of Bouches-du-Rhône. It was a perfect, and perfectly normal, arrangement that went on for years: he was married, and on his frequent trips to the capital from Marseille, he stayed in her luxurious apartment. The letters between them suggest there was love on both sides of this classic French "second marriage." But eventually, when Germaine was in her midforties, it all became too much like a proper marriage; Jean began to stray, and Germaine hired a woman to tail him. On March 7, 1933, Causeret told his lover he was going off to work at the ministry, but a phone call from the spy reported that he was in fact picking out luxury gifts of a silken variety, clearly not intended for his middle-aged companion, at the Printemps department store. When he returned, there was an argument, one of the guns Germaine kept for protection went off, and Causeret was dead. D'Anglemont insisted, implausibly, that the shooting was a complete accident unconnected to any domestic discord.

The trial in April 1935 resulted in a mere two-year prison sentence for the woman once again known as Armande Huot. Flanner, who admired d'Anglemont's style, believed that a light sentence was inevitable because the jury "saw, all around the court, the visiting politicos who would demand and obtain her pardon."[50] That is likely, and so is the possibility that the prosecution antagonized the jury by repeatedly describing Germaine as Causeret's overly clingy "old mistress": a wife had social status and the law to protect her, but only an utter cad would threaten to abandon a vulnerable longtime mistress.[51] Mostly, though, Germaine's crime fell within the classic parameters of the female "crime of passion," for which the courts often found excuses. In 1914, a jury had acquitted Henriette Caillaux, wife of the former prime minister Joseph Caillaux, for the shooting death of the editor of *Le Figaro*. The latter had published intimate letters between Henriette and Joseph before their marriage, and her crime was in the end deemed an understandable female emotional response to a humiliating invasion of privacy.[52] The leniency of juries in the Caillaux and d'Anglemont cases stemmed from a long-standing French tradition of going easy on those who killed while in the grip of romantic turmoil—a husband, for instance, was always let off if he committed murder upon the discovery of his wife with another man.[53]

The story of Germaine d'Anglemont, unlike those of Violette Nozière and the Papin sisters, had plenty of precedents and models, both in the universal tale of a courtesan's ascent and decline (as in William Hogarth's "Harlot's Progress") and in the more specifically French narrative of the crime of passion. Looking back from the 1950s on the courtroom culture of the interwar years, the prominent lawyer Maurice Garçon deplored the leniency of Parisian juries toward crimes of passion, which he viewed as the result of confusion between life and fiction. The theater was mostly to blame, especially the advent of nineteenth-century romantic drama by the likes of Alexandre Dumas, but the movies did not help correct the jury's misapprehension that a crime of passion was a good cathartic story, which deserved applause rather than retribution. They forget, chided Garçon, that on stage the victim can get up and take a bow, while in real life he cannot. Juries went easy or acquitted when murders conformed to a well-worn narrative: the murderer acted impulsively, then called the police and wept over the victim. If there was any evidence of premeditation or even of ex post facto calculation, all leniency would evaporate from the courtroom.[54]

Another big case came at the end of September, hard on the heels of the Nozière affair, in a remarkable autumn of *fait divers* news. It might have been a crime of passion but was more likely what is known in France as a *crime crapuleux,* a crime for gain. A prominent man killed and robbed in his office by a prostitute: such a tale would have warranted attention in any case, but in this instance the victim was not any man, and the killer no ordinary streetwalker. Oscar Dufrenne, the victim, had a remarkable biography.[55] He was born forty-eight years earlier to a modest family of artisans specialized in carpets and upholstery in the northern city of Lille. Working occasionally on theater sets with his parents, young Oscar soon caught the acting bug, which sent him off to Paris. He played on small, then bigger stages, made some money, started directing. He and an associate made a small fortune with a "realist" melodrama that they took out on tour, *Flower of the Sidewalks.* A combination of skill and charm eventually landed him the successive directorship of major Parisian theatres—Château d'Eau, Mayol, and Ambassadeurs. In 1923 he founded his own music-hall-cum-cinema, the Palace, and the following year the aptly named Empire.

There was more to Dufrenne than his growing entertainment empire. Close to the ruling Radical Republican Party, he won a place on the Paris City Council representing the tenth arrondissement, belonged to various of the capital's boards for the arts, and in 1932 ran unsuccessfully for a seat in the National Assembly. Dufrenne was, in short, a prominent personality. He was also gay, and his friend and business associate of twenty years, Henri Varna, chief mourner at the funeral along with Dufrenne's sister, may have been his companion in private life, though Dufrenne also had a charged relationship with his secretary, Serge Nicolesco, who quarreled loudly with him and had recently attempted suicide.[56] Burly and gregarious, Dufrenne was liked, even loved, by his employees and associates, and was known for helping people when they were in trouble.[57] The chorus of praise in the newspapers after his death seems heartfelt, and many thousands of people, ordinary Parisians as well as dignitaries from the worlds of politics and the arts, attended his September 27 funeral.

Whatever the nature of Dufrenne's relationships with Varna and Nicolesco, his death was certainly the result of a gay assignation. During the penultimate week of September, Dufrenne boasted to a friend that he had "met a handsome sailor."[58] On the evening of Sunday, September 24, he ate dinner and played cards in his apartment with his sister and Nicolesco, then returned to his office at the Palace around nine thirty, saying he was going to work. Around ten Dufrenne came down to the theater gallery, where a young man in his mid-twenties dressed in a sailor suit was watching the movie with other patrons, having gained admission thanks to a complimentary pass signed by Dufrenne himself. The two men went up to Dufrenne's office together. At half past midnight an employee found Dufrenne's body rolled in a carpet under a mattress. It bore traces of strangulation and seventeen stab wounds; Dufrenne's expensive watch and a great deal of cash were missing. The perpetrator had fled, and over the next few weeks the sailor became as iconic a cartoon figure as Jean Dabin (wide pants, narrow waist), and as elusive but repeatedly sighted as Monsieur Émile. It was as if one case bled into the next one.

Dufrenne's friends and colleagues may have grieved, but for all of its sensationalism the murder was not of a sort to deeply touch or disturb most readers: what did they have in common with the sleaze and glamour of the "inverted" denizens of the world of show business? The gay nightlife scene was a recurrent topic for features in *Détective*, as exotic as foreign lands and penal colonies. Reporting on the cross-dressed carnival ball at the Magic Palace in 1932, Marcel Montarron fully indulged his readers' voyeurism: "With laughter that sounded like women being tickled, the troubling revelers hailed each other by their female names, pelting each other not with confetti but with the flowers from their corsets: 'Look at Susie, she's so nervous tonight. . . .' "[59] A few years later, in early April 1936, the Dufrenne assassination was echoed by the similarly sordid murder of another gay show business personality, Louis Leplée, the impresario who discovered Edith Piaf and had the genius to preserve and market her street urchin persona. *Détective* noted that it was Dufrenne who had given Leplée his first big break in the business. Leplée certainly had talent, the magazine noted, sometimes sharing a stage with Maurice Chevalier; but his appetite for young men ("which others called his vice, but he called his taste") also served him well, gaining him access to "that strange milieu of homosexuals and snobs, which is a hermetic freemasonry."[60]

The only mystery in the Dufrenne case concerned the identity and whereabouts of the sailor, though the press did its best to play up other possible angles. *Le Populaire* mused darkly about pressure and blackmail on the part of the fraternity of men, some in very high places in government and business, who went in for "the love that nowadays dare perfectly well speak its name."[61] The judicial authorities charged down a predictable series of blind alleys, while the newspapers solemnly explained to readers—many of them surely chuckling out loud—that there were sailors and then there were *sailors. L'Intransigeant* reported that the police were investigating in two directions because sailors could be (1) members of the national fleet, or (2) "those who wear the blue collar and headgear with a pompom out of a concern for refinement and elegance that is hard to explain but has nothing whatsoever to do with our national fleet."[62] The Dufrenne case illustrates the complex status of male homosexuality in Parisian culture at this time. On the one hand, with sodomy decriminalized since the French Revolution (as long as it did not involve minors or disturb the public order), gay nightlife was licit and more open in France than elsewhere in Europe. On the other hand, Gallic cultural universalism dictated that gays should blend in with the dominant French heterosexual culture and exposed them to ridicule or worse if they did not. Throughout the Dufrenne affair, the press maintained a tone of joking complicity with readers who were always presumed straight.[63]

After many months, a young male prostitute named Paul Laborie was arrested and charged with Dufrenne's murder, though the trial resulted in an acquittal for lack of sufficient evidence. (As the proceedings started, the judge warned the packed courtroom that the case was rife with obscene details, and advised women and minors to leave. Nobody moved.)[64] The Dufrenne murder happened just in time to feed an appetite among the public for crime whetted by the Papin and Nozière affairs. Cases overlapped, so that at the end of September 1933 a cartoon in a daily newspaper showed a concierge declaring to a housewife, "I'll tell you something, Mme Michu, all of this business at the Palace is a setup so that there will be no more discussion of Monsieur Émile and the Nozière affair."[65] But the Dufrenne case, like the crime of Mme d'Anglemont, was ultimately more sensational but less disturbing than the Nozière affair. The script was already in place for Oscar Dufrenne, as it was later for Leplée, about whom *Détective* commented: "Louis Leplée was vulnerable, as are all aging and notorious pederasts, who as time go on demand pleasure from ever more lowly types."[66] As for Germaine d'Anglemont, her story had been written many times before, most notably by Balzac, Zola, and Dumas. Whatever real sympathy people might feel for Oscar Dufrenne or the former Nini Huot, there was something inevitable and implicitly right about the downfall of an ambitious and successful sexual outlaw. They led glamorous, dangerous lives and paid the price, affording readers a glimpse of worlds very different from their own.

Why so many "big crimes" at this particular moment? The extraordinary convergence of 1933 was probably coincidental, but the period between about 1930 and 1936 as a whole saw the flowering of a particular interest in crime, notable because it bridged the worlds of high culture and mass culture. The journal *Détective* remains the most potent symbol, as both a cause and a symptom, of the cross-class appeal of the *fait divers.*

Since the nineteenth century, practitioners of what is known as "realist" fiction—novelists who depict ordinary people in richly detailed everyday settings—have looked to the daily papers for their material. Stendhal's 1830 *The Red and the Black,* for instance, follows closely the real story of one Antoine Berthet, a young seminarian from a poor background sentenced to death in 1828 for shooting in church a woman who was his former employer and lover. Balzac, Zola, and Proust all drew on contemporary crime stories, and the tradition is of course not unique to France, since famous instances of such borrowing can be found in the works of novelists as diverse as Fyodor Dostoyevsky, Theodore Dreiser, and Joyce Carol

Oates.[67] Writers between the wars in France, many of them readers of *Détective,* used contemporary crime as the basis of their fiction. But they also departed radically from the conventions of plot and motivation that have been at the heart of realist fiction since its beginnings.

André Gide was probably the most admired writer in France in the twenties and thirties. His novels about rebellious young men broke all the rules of fiction, earning him a passionate following among the educated youth of his day, and as the founder and guiding spirit of the *Nouvelle Revue Française,* he was the unofficial arbiter of "serious" literature in France.[68] Gide, the son of a law professor and grandson of a judge, had a sustained interest in tales from the courtroom. He collected and asked friends to send him clippings of *faits divers* from the newspapers and from 1926 to 1928 published these snippets along with correspondence from readers about them in the NRF. His two most famous novels, *Lafcadio's Adventures* (1914) and *The Counterfeiters* (1927), draw on actual crimes and incidents and include self-conscious references to the genre. In the former novel, when the hero sets out to rescue a family from a fire, the narrator comments: "Lafcadio, my friend, you are going in for the *fait divers* and my pen must take leave of you."[69] The plot of *The Counterfeiters* grew out of two separate *faits divers,* one in which the children of a good family were caught circulating counterfeit gold coins, and another in which a group of lycée students formed a secret society and convinced one of their members to commit suicide after they all drew lots.[70]

In 1912 Gide took notes on his experiences serving as juror for two weeks at the Assize Court in Rouen, and he later published accounts of two famous cases from early in the century: the Redureau affair, in which, in a prefiguring of the Papin murder, a fifteen-year-old farm servant slaughtered seven members of the family he served, apparently in response to a routine scolding by his master; and the case of Blanche Monnier, sequestered in a filthy unlit room for decades by her well-to-do provincial family in the town of Poitiers. In 1930 Gide published his notes on the Assize cases, the Redureau and Monnier affairs, and other fragments about *faits divers* in a volume whose title was taken from the words of Christ: *Ne jugez pas (Judge Not).*[71]

The title says it all: the more he sat in the courtroom, the more Gide was struck by the opacity of the motivations that lead people to act. He became acutely aware of the ways in which judges, lawyers, and juries imposed motives on criminals who might themselves be unaware of the meaning of their act. Young Redureau was not mad but could not explain, any more than the Papins, what caused his bloodletting rampage; and though the press at the time of the Poitiers case had explained the sequestration as an instance of provincial meanness visited on a vulnerable soul, the closer the courtroom honed in on the matter the less those stereotypes stood up to scrutiny. Who could explain the reasons behind any crime, or even if every crime had to have a motive? The possibility of an unmotivated *acte gratuit* long obsessed Gide and became the most memorable event in *Lafcadio's Adventures:* the free spirit Lafcadio dares himself on the spur of the moment to push a man to his death from a train, and does so. "What seems to me so interesting about this affair," Gide wrote of the Poitiers sequestration case, "is that the more we know of the circumstances, the deeper the mystery becomes, taking leave of the facts to settle in the personalities, that of the victim, in fact, as much as that of the accused."[72] Stories that took place on farms and in bourgeois provincial homes seemed at first entirely recognizable, but the more you stared at them the less they revealed beyond their own familiarity magnified into weirdness. As Gide's friend Jean Paulhan put it, in these matters the end does not justify the means, "it stifles and swallows [them]."[73]

Paulhan, who edited the *Nouvelle Revue Française* from 1925 to 1940, wrote an essay in the form of a dialogue, published in 1930, which explored the reasons why contemporary writers and philosophers saw in the *fait divers* the key to a new way of writing. *Faits divers,* bizarre happenings whose meaning may not be obvious, provide anecdotes around which readers are impelled to construct wider contexts, Paulhan observed. Because the *fait* is isolated—*faits divers* are by definition segregated in the newspaper from grand ideological and political narratives—any number of contexts can be made to fit it, but a plurality of contexts and explanations will eventually cancel each other out, revealing the mysterious irreducibility of the perfectly mundane. *Faits divers* expose what Paulhan calls "the illusion of totality," the tendency to generalize from a fragment, as when an Englishman, first setting foot on French soil, sees a redhead and concludes that all Frenchwomen have red hair. The headlines of tabloids like *Détective*—which Paulhan cites—offer one instance after another of the fallacies of common emplotments. "He killed for a [mere] hundred francs!" screams one title, implying that only a truly depraved murderer would take a life for so little. The headline imposes an intention on the murderer, Paulhan points out, that was probably not his own: he only found a hundred francs in the home of the woman he strangled; had he found a million, would his guilt be any less?[74] Quoting the poet Paul Valéry, Paulhan observes that the more shapeless the object of our passion—a god, a lover, a doll—the more we invest in it, and the more we expect the life we project onto it to nourish us in return.[75] *Faits divers,* fragments of other peoples' lives, act as a goad to our fantasies and fallacies, only to confront us with their adamantine resistance to our understanding.

In 1927 the writer François Mauriac published a short masterpiece of a novel that explicitly refers to the sequestration case that obsessed Gide and in certain ways prefigures the crime of Violette Nozière: *Thérèse Desqueyroux* evokes Violette because it too is the story of a troubled young woman, straining against a claustrophobic family environment, who resorts to poison. The book is set among the prosperous bourgeoisie of landowners on the southwestern coast of France near Bordeaux, where the wild beauty of pine forests and sand dunes serves as a backdrop for the scheming materialism of the social elites. When we meet Thérèse at the start of the book, she has recently been freed from police custody. Her husband, Bernard, to whom she administered poison, albeit without fatal results, has declined to press charges for fear of scandal, and now on the train back home to him Thérèse faces a prison of guilt and ostracism far worse than any penal institution.

From the start, Thérèse has no control over her own story. In the opening pages of the novel, she stands on the sidelines while her father and her lawyer discuss how to "spin" the affair in the local press. Go on the offensive in the daily, advises the lawyer, "or would you rather I did it? We need a title like 'The Scurrilous Rumor.'" Thank goodness, her father ruminates, we have nothing to fear from the publisher of the conservative newspaper, we have a hold on him because of "that business with the little girls." They discuss, within earshot from her, the explanations she gave of how and why she acted, her father carping, "How many times did I say to her, 'Find something else, you miserable creature, find something else.'"[76]

Revisiting the past on her train ride, Thérèse tries to reconstruct the events that led to the poisoning, but she comes up with a train of contingencies rather than causes. She had acquiesced, for the sake of family property, to an arranged marriage to smug, narrow-minded Bernard. Shortly after their marriage, Bernard's sister and Thérèse's close friend Anne forms an inappropriate attachment to a pimply, intense young man, a Jewish would-be intellectual bound for Paris. Thérèse helps mediate an end to the love affair, perhaps because she is jealous of the passion Anne feels for her Jean. The unsettling effect of this episode is compounded by depression after the birth of her daughter. Bernard is taking medicine for anemia that contains arsenic, and one day in distraction he takes twice the pre-scribed dose and falls ill. Thérèse observes this but fails to intervene or tell anyone, then begins experimenting with the dosage out of "curiosity." Eventually, like Violette, she fakes a prescription. Why? *Find something else . . .*

After the fact, those around her try to fit the events into a sense-making framework. Thérèse muses that her husband believes she fell in love with Anne's boyfriend Jean: "Like all beings profoundly ignorant of love, he be-lieves that the act I am accused of can only be a crime of passion." Bernard then changes his mind and accuses her of greed for the land. Next, she would have poisoned the child. Thérèse is incensed: "Among the thousand secret sources of her act, that imbecile has not been able to find a single one, so he invents the lowest motive."[77] Bernard can think no further than the conventional dichotomy in French criminal law between the crime of pas-sion and the crime of lucre. Finally the family falls back on the nonexplana-tion that she is a monster, a verdict that Thérèse takes on with aggressive irony: "Thérèse has read that desperate people take their children with them in death; decent folk will put down their newspapers: 'How is something like that possible?' Because she is a monster, Thérèse has a deep understand-ing that this is possible, that it would take very little . . ."[78]

Forever swathed in the smoke of the cigarettes she consumes nonstop, Thérèse is every bit as much as Violette the opaque heroine of a film noir. Eventually, though, Thérèse's depression threatens to evoke another kind of story, which could damage her family's sacrosanct reputation, espe-cially now that Anne has agreed to a possible engagement with the son of a prominent family. Bernard consigns his wife to her room in their coun-try house while he lives in town; the family spreads the rumor that she is a neurasthenic recluse. Falling in with the script, Thérèse stops getting up and washing. She barely touches food, and the servants mostly abandon her. When Bernard returns weeks later, accompanied by Anne's desirable prospective fiancé, he is panicked by the sight of his emaciated, filthy wife: "In a flash that colored image from *Le Petit Parisien* came back to him. . . . [H]e stared, as he had done as a child, at the red and green drawing that showed *The Sequestered Woman of Poitiers*." He realizes that Thérèse could be seen as the heroine of another story, in which she would be not the perpetrator but the victim, a helpless woman locked up by her own fam-ily. "Thérèse was a source of drama—worse than a drama, a *fait divers*."[79] Because a *fait divers* can be more damaging to a family's good name than a tragedy, the relatives soon dispatch her, with her consent, to live alone in

Paris. Thérèse Desqueyroux has much in common with a later and even more famous fictional character, Albert Camus's Meursault, who in *The Stranger* (1942) commits a random murder for too many reasons and no reason at all, and fails to recognize his own life story when it is narrated in the courtroom.

*Faits divers* fired the imagination of novelists in the twenties and thirties and, as we shall see in the next chapter, of poets as well. French intellectuals both before and after the Second World War were mesmerized by bizarre and violent events that seemed to resist the logic of conventional causality, itself under assault from the avant-garde since the aftermath of the Great War: Gide, Paulhan, Jacques Lacan, Maurice Merleau-Ponty, Georges Auclair, Roland Barthes, and many others found in these private crimes a means of coming to terms with what one critic calls "the elusive laws of chance and obsession."[80] Classic Western notions of rationality, widely accepted before 1914, had it that actions could be explained by discoverable patterns of causality, and that effects were commensurate with causes. But what happens to that logic when millions of men die because a teenage fanatic murders a head of state in a remote corner of Europe?[81]

What fascinated thinkers about the *fait divers* was the autonomy conferred on it by its form: a newspaper will present a fragment of reality that departs strikingly from the social norm either because of its violence or because of its bizarre nature: "A man spared the death penalty commits suicide," "A bishop ordains his own father."[82] Such shreds of life disrupt the common order of things; they are both meaningless because ripped out of context and overcharged with meaning because they force our attention and invite an abyss of explanation. Our focus on them invests them with a hyperreality that makes them less understandable the more we stare. They are, in short, the written equivalent of the surrealist object: a thing that at once demands and resists our gaze.

Discrete and shocking events also reintroduced an element of myth and the sacred into modern lives devoid of wonder. *Faits divers* often acquire their salience because of a strong element of fate, which harks back to archaic forms of understanding. "Modern" thought could not explain why a person gets killed by a suicide's jump or a burglar unknowingly kills a member of his own family, any more than it could truly make sense of why an unremarkable comment about a blown fuse or a boy's laziness should lead to carnage. Only destiny can cause such intersections and, as in the case of Oedipus unknowingly killing his own father, elevate them to the status of myth. An avatar of chance and fate that invested ordinary reality with extraordinary resonance, the *fait divers* was the means whereby the sacred re-entered the disenchanted realms of modern life.

The year 1933 marked the apogee of a distinctive form of "crime culture" in France, one that bridged the worlds of the urban masses and of the intellectual elites. Like the *fait divers* itself, this culture was born of a coincidence. Between a lackluster Republican establishment and left-wing parties and unions in disarray, politics were at a low ebb in France in the late twenties and early thirties. Though Hitler's name appeared almost daily in the press, few in France could yet imagine what his growing power portended. "In January 1933 we saw Hitler become chancellor, and on February 27 the Reichstag fire paved the way for the destruction of the Communist Party," Simone de Beauvoir reminisced. They read about all of it, the book burnings, the growing anti-Semitic persecution, not unmoved but without alarm. "Writing today, I am astounded that we witnessed these events with relative serenity." She and her friends were indignant, of course, but everyone concurred that there was no way this madman could succeed and that another war was out of the question.[83] In those years, she and Sartre found more significance in crime news, which they read with great care. They believed, following the surrealist André Breton, that each soul harbors an "unbreakable kernel of night," buried under layers of social routine and conversational commonplace, which only an explosive act of violence could bring into view. Obscurely worried about Sartre's growing influence over her, Beauvoir fantasized, while poring over the *fait divers* rubric, about committing a violent crime that would ensure her separate identity. Sartre himself found in the Papin case evidence of "prelogical thought" and of a "magical mentality" in the modern world.[84]

The preoccupations of intellectuals came together with the culture of the urban masses—the factory hands disenchanted with the unions, the new ranks of office and service workers for most of whom politics meant, at that juncture, very little. For these readers too, crime was what moved newspapers; isolated in their small city dwellings among their new consumer goods, they found in *faits divers* a titillating entrée into another world (as in the Dufrenne case), a shock of recognition (as in the Nozière case), and fodder for debating right and wrong with the concierge and the neighbors. A publication like *Détective,* rooted in the world of the Gidean literary elites but most obviously aimed at modest households, was the perfect bridge between those realms and the quintessential expression of its time.

At the very height of the Nozière affair, the end of this era came abruptly into view. In the late fall of 1933, newspapers began carrying reports of the deeds of Serge Stavisky, a con artist of Russian Jewish origin specializing in financial deals, who had close connections with many members of the center-left Republican establishment.[85] Stavisky, a handsome man-about-town with a wife who once modeled for Chanel, had been indicted for fraud more than once, but the cases always somehow vanished from the docket. This time, the scandal was a big one: Stavisky had worked with local republican politicians to set up a municipal credit institution in the provincial town of Bayonne. Millions of francs' worth of bonds accepted by banks turned out to have no backing. There were many powerful people, it seems, who had an interest in keeping "handsome Serge" from testifying, and when he fled to the Alps in December and the police "found him dead," few believed the official story of a suicide: "he shot himself from a distance of twenty meters" was how Parisian wags put it.

Efforts to squelch the affair did not work. Political parties on the left and right pilloried the government, but it was the right wing that reacted violently when Prime Minister Camille Chautemps dismissed one of their own, the police chief of Paris, Jean Chiappe. The actions of the corrupt republic and its foreign Jewish allies were deemed intolerable. On Saturday, February 6, 1934, right-wing activists, including veterans' organizations and paramilitary leagues, took to the street outside the National Assembly in a long night of rioting that left fourteen dead. Chautemps resigned but the Republic survived, though many had feared it would not. The Stavisky affair was no *fait divers:* an explosively political episode, it strengthened both the Left and the Right, prompting Communists and Socialists to bury their differences in the face of what they saw as a homegrown fascist threat. Both the Popular Front of 1936 and the Vichy regime were to trace at least some of their roots to the riots of February 1934.

With the Stavisky affair, political ideologies came to the fore in ways not seen since the height of the Dreyfus case. The heyday of the *fait divers* was over, but its intellectual and artistic legacy would be considerable.

# EIGHT

# A Water Lily on a Heap of Coal

BY EARLY OCTOBER 1933, coverage of the Nozière case was dwindling, displaced in the newspapers by the salacious details of Oscar Dufrenne's murder and the search for his sailor-assassin. Readers knew to expect a hiatus of many months before Violette's trial. When something did happen, the case still made for front-page news. Hopeful rumors surfaced now and then of an "Émile" discovery, none of which amounted to anything, and Violette's scheduled judicial "confrontation" with Jean Dabin on October 18 provided a small jolt of excitement. This time fully anticipating "nervous breakdowns," the judge had medical personnel on hand. The principals behaved with restraint, however, until the reliably dramatic Germaine Nozière, who was also present, spotted on Dabin's finger a signet ring decorated with a cheap gemstone: "That's my poor husband's ring, I looked for it everywhere!" she gasped. Violette quickly intervened to say she had given the ring to Jean as a love token, and the young man eagerly offered that he had brought it that day intending to return it, but the ring incident satisfied the many who believed in a Dabin-as-mastermind version of the crime.[1]

Before the end of the year, a writer named Jacques Niger had churned out an opportunistic pamphlet, *Le Secret de l'empoisonneuse* (*The Secret of the Girl-Poisoner*), which revealed no secrets whatsoever. Instead, it directed equal parts moralism and prurience at the young woman, described as "a brunette with eyes both hard and inviting, sensual lips, thick nostrils that bespeak her fiery temperament, the slim but fetching body of a twenty-four-year-old." At the end of thirty pages of muckraking and insinuation, the author piously fretted that "perhaps no case has ever churned up this much filth."[2] Not all commentators pilloried Violette. That fall she found champions in two Communist writers, Jean Pidault and Maurice-Ivan Sicard, whose short book on the affair bravely concluded that she was telling the truth about her father. Pidault and Sicard exactly pegged the Nozières' social class as "bourgeois proletarians" and, while accepting Violette's incest charges, otherwise espoused the party's analysis: those to blame were the young "pederasts" and "pimps" of the Latin Quarter, "members of the ruling-class youth, whose most mendacious and delinquent ways are explained away as an overly generous temperament that will disappear once they are in possession of the judicial, medical, or industrial positions awaiting them." Meanwhile, the authors pointed out, Violette had been entrusted to a lawyer, Henri Géraud, whose last celebrity client, the presidential assassin Gorguloff, had gone straight to the guillotine despite his blatant madness.[3]

As these various writers tried to convince readers or to make money, Violette began a yearlong wait in La Petite Roquette for her case to come to trial. Located northeast of the Place de la Bastille, in the heart of dense popular neighborhoods, the prison had been part of a larger penitentiary complex of sinister renown, La Roquette, where prisoners awaiting deportation or execution were held and in front of which the guillotine did its violent business. La Grande Roquette was dismantled in 1899, and its smaller remaining annex became in 1920 a jail for women awaiting trial. At first some of Violette's fellow prisoners attacked her, hitting, cursing, or spitting, but as the ferment over the affair subsided, she became just another among the seventy or so women dressed in burlap and shod in clogs who silently hemmed sheets under the supervision of nuns.[4]

Unbeknownst to her, prisoner 46 at La Petite Roquette was about to enter French literary history. Over the course of its unfolding, Violette's story had attracted the attention and sympathy of France's most prominent group of avant-garde artists and thinkers, the Surrealists. Their leader, the writer André Breton, was viscerally affected by the case, convinced of Baptiste Nozière's guilt and of the shameful connivance of the judicial and medical authorities in silencing Violette's claims.[5] Twenty years later, Breton was to write: "In human memory no criminal case will have dragged out of the wings such a fine collection of bastards."[6] Breton convinced fifteen prominent Surrealists in his orbit to contribute poems and artwork to a collective tribute to Violette, which was published on December 1, 1933.

In the early 1930s, literary and artistic Surrealism was in full swing in Paris. Several of the self-defined Surrealists who coalesced as a group in Paris in the early 1920s, most notably Breton himself, had previously been part of the movement known as Dada, whose heyday extended from 1916 to 1923. Dada was international rather than French, born initially among the avant-garde in Zurich, with adherents soon forming groups in New York, Cologne, and Berlin, though many of them eventually converged in Paris. Gleefully anarchic, Dada was devoted to the destruction of all existing social and cultural norms. Its most famous icon remains the urinal labeled *Fountain,* which Marcel Duchamp presented as a work of art at a New York show in 1917. Followers of Dada were the first self-conscious performance artists, organizing public events at which spontaneity, provocation, and audience participation were the rule—spectators pelted performers with whatever came to hand, and Dada events often turned into brawls. Their manifestoes were strings of nonsensical words and syllables, including the movement's very name, which evoked a drooling baby's first stammer. Formed exclusively around principles of negation and derision, Dada went into decline within a few years.[7]

Though the Dada movement did not last long, its cultural impact was considerable, not least in that it set the stage for Surrealism. In Paris a tight-knit group of friends, including Breton, Philippe Soupault, and Louis Aragon, started taking Dada in a new direction, beginning with the 1919 publication of a text by Breton and Soupault, *Magnetic Fields,* an exercise in dreamlike "automatic" writing supposedly untainted by the control of reason or consciousness. In 1924 Breton issued an initial explanation of the new movement's aims, the *Manifesto of Surrealism.* Surrealism, as shaped over the years by Breton and his shifting band of acolytes, represented a sharp departure from Dada. Where the latter was nihilistic and angrily or merrily destructive, Surrealism aimed to build a whole new program for Western thought, no less than a bridge between the conscious and unconscious realms of the mind. Its founders conceived of Surrealism as a movement that simultaneously furthered both scientific and literary experimentation.

The scientific strain in Surrealism owed a great deal to the professional background of André Breton, the self-proclaimed "pope of Surrealism."[8]

Breton's social origins were not that different from Violette Nozière's: he was born in 1896 in a small town in Normandy, the only child of a former seamstress and a policeman. When André was four, the family moved to Pantin, a suburb of Paris, where his father eventually became the assistant manager of a small glassworks factory. Breton's childhood was materially secure but emotionally bleak. His good-natured but passive father could not stand up to his wife, an angry and domineering, deeply religious and conservative woman devoid of maternal affection for her son. Breton had personal knowledge of what it felt like to be the only child of petit-bourgeois strivers in a household fraught with tension.

Like the Nozières, the Bretons focused their social ambitions on their child, sending him to a Parisian secondary school, Collège Chaptal, where he followed a scientific track. After his baccalaureate, Breton resisted the family plan to make an engineer of him but placated his parents by enrolling in medical school. Along with like-minded school friends, he had fallen under the spell of literature, devouring Symbolist poetry and writing his own. He hoped that a medical career would leave him some time to pursue those interests on the side. Called up during the Great War, he treated shell-shock victims in a neuropsychiatric center in northeastern France, where he discovered, in 1916, the work of Sigmund Freud. After being transferred back to Paris, he attended patients in Val-de-Grâce Hospital. Breton eventually abandoned his medical studies as he became increasingly immersed in the avant-garde literary movements of the capital. Surrealism would be shaped, however, by Breton's early embrace of Freudianism, his experiences as a wartime psychiatrist, and his insistence that he and his colleagues were engaged in an enterprise that was in equal parts scientific and literary.

In group pictures of the French Surrealists, there is never any doubt as to who is André Breton. He either stands in the center of the image or draws the viewer's eyes. With his beefy, handsome face, full lips, abundant dark hair swept back from his wide forehead, and erect posture, he always seems larger than the others. Even in frivolous or mischievous photographs—the Surrealists staged plenty of those—Breton retains an aura of high seriousness, as if ever aware that he is posing for posterity. His moniker as "pope" of the movement may have been conceived in a spirit of blasphemy, but it stuck to him for good reason. As his early collaborator Philippe Soupault put it, Breton did not charm people, he "petrified" them.[9] Breton was a famously difficult man, moody, authoritarian, judgmental, and thin-skinned. His friends teased him about being the son of a policeman, but it was more the case that he had inherited some of his mother's unpleasant traits. His life reads as a series of breakups, some temporary and others permanent, with collaborators, friends, and lovers. Breton's domineering personality was, however, the condition for his remarkable achievement: perhaps never has a person single-handedly done so much to shape and coordinate an important cultural movement over several decades, pushing it constantly in new directions.

Breton's closest collaborator, starting in 1919, was the poet Paul Éluard, one year his senior. Éluard's early family life was less fraught than Breton's, though it may be significant that he changed his name from the less euphonious Eugène Grindel, distancing himself from his parents. He too was an only child from a modest family, with a seamstress mother and accountant father, though the latter went on to start a real-estate business that earned him a lot of money and conveniently passed away when Paul was in his twenties. Although Éluard became a husband and father at a young age, marrying a beautiful Russian girl nicknamed Gala whom he met in a sanatorium when in his teens, he eschewed conventional family life. In 1921 Gala fell in love with the German artist Max Ernst, and for a while the three of them lived and worked together while the Éluards' daughter was raised mostly by her grandmother. When Gala eventually left Éluard for Salvador Dalí, Éluard continued to see her and write her love letters even as he set up house with his new companion, Nusch.[10]

Éluard's collaboration with Breton endured longer than anyone else's, from their initial meeting in 1919 to their first major falling-out in 1936; dreamy, mercurial, and sometimes depressive, Éluard had a knack for avoiding conflict by disappearing at regular intervals.[11] He was at Breton's side in 1929, when the latter signaled a purge and renewal of the movement with his *Second Manifesto of Surrealism*. Heads rolled (the poet Robert Desnos, the brilliant experimental writer Raymond Queneau), while new members were brought into the fold, including the Spaniards Dalí and Luis Buñuel and the Belgian René Magritte. It was in collaboration with Éluard that Breton recast the group's journal in 1930, changing its name from *The Surrealist Revolution* to a title that ratcheted up the movement's commitment to social change: *Surrealism in the Service of the Revolution*.[12]

The relationship between Surrealism and revolutionary politics, specifically those of the French Communist Party, had always been complicated. Breton had thought of joining the party at its creation in 1920 but was discouraged when a representative cheerfully informed him that he would have to "go down into the crowd, crush in elbow to elbow, and sweat together"; equally "repellent" were the bureaucratic procedures involved in signing up. Five years later, however, the newly formed Surrealist group joined forces with the party in protesting the bloody repression by French forces, under the leadership of Marshal Philippe Pétain, of the so-called Rif Rebellion in Morocco. Nineteen Surrealists signed a petition of left-wing intellectuals published in *L'Humanité* supporting the rebellion's leader, Abd el-Krim, and denouncing France's involvement—a highly unpopular position at the time.[13]

From their support for the Rif Rebellion in 1925 to their call to boycott the Colonial Exposition in 1931, the Surrealists espoused anticolonial causes more easily than they did the domestic policies and internal discipline of the party. Their project ran parallel to the concrete social and political aims of Communism, though on a different plane. Where the political Left struggled against material exploitation and injustice, the Surrealists waged war on the tyranny of reason. They wanted to discover those realms of the self hidden from waking consciousness and shackled by conventional reason—dreams, repressed desires, the absurd associations that float through the mind—and bring them to bear on "normal," mundane consciousness. The title of Breton's 1932 book *The Communicating Vessels* aptly telegraphs the group's aim in its early years: as with those scientific experiments in which a liquid or gas travels back and forth between joined recipients and eventually reaches equilibrium, their quest was for a point at which dream and waking life, interior and exterior worlds, could inhabit the mind together in dynamic tension. "Everything tends to make us believe," Breton wrote in his *Second Manifesto,* "that there exists a certain point of the mind at which life and death, the real and the imagined, past and future, the communicable and the incommunicable, cease to be perceived as contradictions."[14] This bringing together of heretofore separate realms of consciousness would open the door to a new form of reality, surreality. The Surrealists clung to the belief that their revolution was a necessary complement to the aims of revolutionary socialism.

The Surrealists' debt to the work of Sigmund Freud is obvious, and indeed, thanks to Breton's early interest in Freud's theories, they were the first group of thinkers in France to engage seriously with psychoanalysis. As early as 1921, Breton traveled to Vienna expressly to talk to the great man, but their meeting was a disaster, at least for the Frenchman. Breton was initially kept waiting for hours, along with several patients, and when he was at last ushered into Freud's presence, the differences in age, culture, and especially purpose between the young French poet and the venerable Austrian doctor made for extreme awkwardness.[15] Breton was so upset he refused even to discuss the event with his new wife, and the failure of the encounter between the father of psychoanalysis and the future pope of Surrealism is emblematic. Freud was a rationalist, an heir of the Enlightenment who explored the unconscious in search of a cure for neurosis. Breton, in revolt against Western rationalist teleology, looked to the repressed as the main source of a revolutionary new form of consciousness.

The Surrealists' investment in the darker, buried realms of consciousness naturally included an interest in crime. On the simplest level, they shared with previous generations of Romantic artists a defiant affinity for those who transgressed the laws of bourgeois society—the more violently, the better. In their articles, poems, and artwork, they claimed the Marquis de Sade as one of their own.[16] In 1923 Louis Aragon—closely associated with Breton at the time—had written of the ways in which art can spearhead moral revolutions, as if anticipating the Nozière case: "A hundred years ago, crimes of passion were punished with death; under the influence of Romanticism, they are no longer dangerous for their perpetrators. In fifty years, under the influence of DADA, parricides will be acquitted with the congratulations of the jury."[17] But the Surrealists were interested in more than just dark impulses and transgressive actions: they were fascinated by the ways in which criminal acts leave traces that blur conventional patterns of representation.

Photographs of crime scenes, for instance, held a particular fascination for them. Photography had upended the Western artistic tradition: if a machine could make a picture randomly, what happened to the respective positions, hallowed since the Renaissance, of the artist and the viewer? Crime-scene shots were especially rich with subversive meaning when stacked against conventions of artistic representation. A photograph of a blood-spattered bed in a locked room purported to document a terrible act but could not in reality be deciphered, because every detail it contained might be pregnant with meaning or entirely meaningless. Only an arbitrary act of will—in its own way an act of violence—could impose a story, a judgment, on a resistant jumble of signs.[18]

Breton and his acolytes lionized great criminals of the distant and recent past—the sex-offending Marquis de Sade, the serial murderer Landru, the Dillinger-like gangster Jules Bonnot.[19] The contemporary criminals they championed were all female. The birth of Surrealism in 1923–24 coincided with the group's celebration of the political assassin Germaine Berton, whose portrait appeared in the first issue of *La Révolution Surréaliste* in December 1924, surrounded by smaller head shots of twenty-eight Surrealists. The page's caption was a quote from Baudelaire: "Woman is the being who casts the greatest shadow, or the strongest light, in our dreams." Berton, a twenty-year-old anarchist, had in January 1923 shot and killed Marius Plateau, a staff member of the right-wing newspaper *Action Française,* in his office. She claimed that her act was a delayed revenge upon the political Right for their role in the assassination of the revered French Socialist statesman Jean Jaurès in 1914. The press portrayed Berton as a homicidal femme fatale, and a bizarre twist of events further accentuated her mystery-woman allure. Ten months after her crime, sixteen-year-old Philippe Daudet, son of Léon Daudet, the general editor of *Action Française,* fatally shot himself in a taxi in the vicinity of Berton's prison; he had recently sought to join the anarchist movement and was said to be infatuated with Germaine. (The Left believed Philippe's suicide was a gesture of Oedipal anger, while the Right maintained that he had really been murdered by anarchists.) Astonishingly, when Berton's case came to trial in December 1923, she was acquitted: the jury, evidently swayed by her eroticized image, chose to label her act of political revenge a crime of passion. After the verdict, Breton, Aragon, and a few others sent her a bouquet of roses and carnations.[20]

The Surrealists' brief but intense investment in Germaine Berton and the gallery of male portraits surrounding an idealized, eroticized woman evoke long-standing questions about the role of women in the Surrealist movement. Feminists have decried the sexual and sentimental objectification of women by the male coterie of Surrealists, their traffic in wives and girlfriends, and the images of dismembered and tortured female bodies they produced. Man Ray's 1930 photographic portrait of his mistress, the artist Lee Miller, in the nude with her head jammed into what looks like a mesh cage comes to mind as an image that, while stunning, does not exactly bespeak female empowerment: it is entitled "The Surrealist Woman." Other scholars point to the presence and artistic activity of women in the movement—Leonora Carrington, Dora Maar, Valentine Hugo, Méret Oppenheim, Claude Cahun, Miller—though most were initially brought into the fold as sexual partners to the men, and all remained secondary figures.[21]

Whatever the status of actual women in their midst, the feminine principle, understood as darkness and danger, was crucial to the Surrealists' creative process. Breton's obsession with femmes fatales can be traced back to his first intense artistic experience, his teenage infatuation with the paintings of Gustave Moreau. Active in the last decades of the nineteenth century, Moreau was famous for his gauzy representations of the great evil beauties of history and legend—Salome, Delilah, Sappho, Helen of Troy. His work belonged to a larger transnational craze for images of feminine evil in the fin de siècle, a gallery of harpies, medusas, sphinxes, and assorted serpent-tailed nightmares of womanhood, visions that even inflected the work of canonical artists, such as Gustav Klimt and the English Pre-Raphaelites.[22] Breton and his colleagues were far from the first group of artists to seize upon the feminine as the principle of night, death, the subjective, and the unconscious. Femininity understood as the instinctive, nonrational dimension of human nature was central to Surrealist endeavors like automatic writing—Breton even claimed that the letter *l* ("elle" or "she") could unlock the writing flow. As Beauvoir tartly put it in *The Second Sex,* woman in Surrealism was "everything but herself."[23]

While the view of womanhood as death, night, the irrational, and the unconscious was conventional, the surrealists innovated by introducing into that tradition metaphors of science and technology, and especially the principle of shock. The most famous sentence in Breton's oeuvre is the one that closes his 1928 *Nadja:* "Beauty will be CONVULSIVE or will not be at all." On the previous page, Breton, struggling to describe beauty in terms that are "neither dynamic nor static," offers this image: "Beauty is like a train that ceaselessly roars out of the Gare de Lyon and which I know will never leave, which has not left. It consists of jolts and shocks, many of which do not have much importance, but which we know are destined to produce one *Shock,* which does."[24] Katharine Conley has described the Surrealist muse as an "Automatic Woman"—not an automaton but a creature whose function is to deliver an electric shock, including the shudder of scandal.[25] In Surrealism, the erotic charge of female beauty is powered by science and technology, in images of writhing hysteria patients, nudes entwined with objects and machines, bodies sliced into fetishistic components. Woman is both central and indispensable to the (male) Surrealist enterprise, and utterly terrifying. In 1929 *La Révolution Surréaliste* carried a full-page group portrait reminiscent of the image of Germaine Berton. This time the mug shots of male Surrealists surrounded an image by Magritte of a nude woman emblazoned with the caption: "I do not see the woman hidden in the forest." The men's eyes are all closed, as if protecting themselves from the Medusalike power of Woman to freeze them in their tracks.[26]

Craving intellectual and emotional shock, the Surrealists, Breton in particular, sought out as muses and heroines women who were some combination of beautiful, dangerous, and demented. Near the beginning of *Nadja*, Breton tells of being deeply affected by a play, *Les Détraquées (Wild Women)* and especially its main character, Solange. The play is set in a girls' boarding school, and Solange, a teacher, appears to be the lover of the school's female principal. When Solange appears onstage, Breton describes her in terms that might well apply to Violette Nozière: "Dark, with brown hair, I don't recall. Young. Magnificent eyes that mingle languor with subtlety, cruelty, despair. Slender, dressed in dark colors, black silk stockings. And something *déclassé* about her that is sympathetic. There is no explanation of her presence, though she apologizes for being delayed. Her apparent coldness is in extreme contrast with the welcome given her."[27] Solange turns out to be a drug addict, lesbian sexual predator, and child murderer. Breton was briefly obsessed with the actress, Blanche Derval, who played her onstage.[28]

Breton's investment in Violette Nozière seems in retrospect almost inevitable: he had been drawn to women like her throughout his life, in particular the real Nadja. In October 1926 Breton was wandering in the rather unsavory part of the tenth arrondissement north of the grands boulevards and the department stores when he spotted a young woman whose demeanor intrigued him: she looked poor and wore strangely accentuated makeup, but had a strikingly "delicate" gait and proud manner. In conversation she told him she had chosen to call herself Nadja. She was actually Léona D., a refugee from the provinces who was subsisting on menial jobs and hoping for employment in the theater. Breton was unnerved and mesmerized by her manner, especially her seeming ability to guess at the precise details of his own life. The encounter, and other chance meetings and sightings over the next few days, seemed an instance of the sort of magic that, according to the Surrealists, could arise from random happenings on city streets: such coincidences revealed a deep causal logic at odds with conventional reason.

Breton rapidly became infatuated with Nadja, started an affair with her, and gave her money, but in less than two weeks his fascination turned to disappointment and alarm: Nadja's rambling monologues began to bore him, accounts of violence and drug trafficking in her past eventually sounded more seedy than romantic. The final straw was her literal attempt at a "kiss of death" when, as they were driving on a country road, she put her hand over Breton's eyes and kissed him as she slammed her foot onto his, pushing down the gas pedal. They were unhurt, but Breton, whose interest in danger turned out to be more theoretical than empirical, pulled away from the relationship, though Nadja continued to pursue him for several months. By March, Nadja had become paranoid and subject to hallucinations. She was interned in a psychiatric hospital south of Paris for over a year, then moved back to the provinces.[29]

Breton never visited Nadja in the hospital nor ever saw her again. In 1928, however, he published his enduringly popular *Nadja,* a book that defies categories. A meditative diary of his affair with the young woman, it includes names and places, photographs of Paris streets and of real people, including the author himself, and Nadja's mysterious drawings. Its text combines documentary facts with prose poetry and invention. Lyrical and romantic, the book illustrates, through the story of a mysterious and blighted love affair, core Surrealist preoccupations with the weight of coincidence or "objective chance" in human life, the ways in which the outside world is symptomatic of the inner life, and the enigmatic power of objects. It evokes with great precision the boulevards and squares of Paris where the affair played out. *Nadja* sold out half its press run in the first week, was warmly received by critics, and remains to this day Breton's most widely read work.[30]

The script was written in advance for Breton's interest in Violette Nozière. Violette was young, stylish, and sexy, had killed in cold blood, and might be slightly mad. Like Nadja, she roamed the city streets—the realm of infinite, magical possibility—and, like Nadja, she was evasive or untruthful about her real identity. Beyond its central femme fatale, however, the Nozière affair offered Breton and his friends targets for some long-standing resentments. Violette's family life, amply documented in the newspapers, must have reminded men like Breton and Éluard of the claustrophobic experience of being the only child of strict and ambitious lower-middle-class parents. If Violette was a heroine, then the men who arrested and prosecuted her, policemen, lawyers, and judges, must be black-hatted representatives of an oppressive state. Most strikingly, perhaps because of their long-standing interest in sexual deviance, the Surrealists chose to believe unequivocally what Violette said about her father. Some newspapers had allowed that the young girl might not have been lying—though that suggestion was most often followed by the comment that even if her allegations were true, her crime would still have been heinous and deserving of severe punishment. Defenders like Pidault and Sicard supported her claim but drowned it in invectives against her various bourgeois swains. Alone among contemporary commentators, the Surrealists laid the blame fully, unambiguously, on Baptiste Nozière. Unfortunately for Violette, they did not enjoy much of an audience.

Breton, deeply affected by the Nozière affair, was as usual the prime mover, and he convinced fifteen colleagues to contribute to a collective volume. The resulting publication was made up of eight poems and eight illustrations, with an uncredited cover image by Man Ray.[31] Anticipating trouble, the group chose to bring out the volume abroad: it was produced by the Belgian poet and publisher Édouard Mesens, a close friend of Magritte, who created a special imprint for the occasion, the Éditions Nicolas Flamel. (Flamel was a fourteenth-century bookseller and alchemist. The Surrealists had long been interested in traditions of the occult and viewed the forays into banned knowledge by medieval alchemists as models for their own enterprise.) The work was published in December 1933, and on January 13, 1934, Éluard wrote to Mesens that copies had been delivered to their friend the bookseller José Corti in Paris. Four days later, however, he sent a worried note to Mesens to let him know that French customs had examined the shipment before sending it to Corti and decided to dispatch a copy to the French Ministry of the Interior. Given what the volume had to say, even in poetic form, about the state, policemen, judges, fatherhood, and family life, this was not good news. Éluard suggested that Mesens send multiple copies directly to the contributors for press release in case the ones in France were seized. That was indeed what happened, and in March Breton mentioned in a letter to Mesens that the book was being prosecuted. At the end of March 1934, Éluard was begging Mesens for copies of the book to send to reviewers. What happened to the case against *Violette Nozières* is not known, but the volume was effectively banned and failed to make an impact until many years later.[32]

*Violette Nozières*—the Surrealists spelled her last name with an *s*—is a work of ferocious beauty, the most vehement contemporary statement about a case that aroused widespread passion. In text and image, its authors intoned again and again the word inscribed in Violette's very name, which nobody before them dared to pronounce: *viol*, rape.[33] They hammered away at a message nobody wanted to hear: families can be evil, maybe most of them are; "happy" families, with their "good" mothers and fathers, can be the worst of all. "There are few of us / Violette," wrote

Mesens, "But we will walk hand in hand with our own ghosts / To terrify the men who judge you."[34]

The most explicit poems in the collection are a howl of anger not just at the family in general, but specifically at the sort of family the Nozières embodied and over which the dailies had shed their crocodile tears: hard-working, money-saving paragons like Baptiste and Germaine, people with new dining room sets and money stashed away in the hems of their clothes. The pinched snobbery with which Breton dismissed Germaine ("The excellent woman had read Corneille in her daughter's schoolbook") suggests how closely what he knew of the Nozière family hit home.[35] The Surrealists celebrated Violette as a heroine for daring to sunder the shackles of kin. Breton sounded the theme in his opening poem, honoring the young girl for her journey out of family and into myth:

> All the curtains of the world drawn across your eyes
> Try as they may
> Breathlessly before their mirror
> To draw the arc of forebears and descendants
> You look like nobody dead or alive
> Mythological to the tip of your fingernails.

César Moro echoed him in more belligerent tones:

> How many good mothers
> And how many bad fathers
> And how many good fathers
> And bad mothers
> Gathered in the name of bourgeois morality
> Will call you slut and whore
> Violette.[36]

The most famous piece in the volume is by Éluard. It invokes the very "mythomania" for which Violette was excoriated as an act of imaginative courage, while conjuring up, with remarkable insight for the time, the psychology of an incest victim:

> Violette dreamt of milky baths
> Of gorgeous gowns of fresh bread
> Of gorgeous gowns of pure blood
> One day there will be no more fathers

In the gardens of youth
There will be strangers
All the strangers
Men for whom you are always brand new
And the very first
Men for whom you can escape from yourself
Men for whom you are nobody's daughter
Violette dreamt of undoing
And undid
The hideous vipers' knot of blood connections.[37]

Popular coverage of the affair had centered on Violette, her mother, and Jean Dabin. Recentering the narrative, the Surrealists made Baptiste into the main character of the story. Breton and his colleagues had in the past suggested that words can play a role in determining events: *soleil* ("the sun") in the name of the child-murderer Soleilland, for instance.[38] They invoked this belief here again, awarding Baptiste the gift of foresight and agency: "History will record," wrote Breton, that Nozières was a farsighted man not just because he saved many thousands of francs, but because he gave his daughter a name whose first syllable was his subconscious "program."[39] The poets wrote, bluntly and repeatedly, the word that everyone else had danced around:

Daddy
Little Daddy you are hurting me
she said
But the daddy feeling the heat of his locomotive
a little south of his belly button
raped
Violette
in the garden bower
amid the shovel handles that fired him up.[40]

Baptiste's connection with trains recurs as a leitmotif in the collection: as the shuddering locomotive at the end of *Nadja* suggests, such machines could embody a quintessential surrealist fusion of eros and technology, though in this case the sexual symbolism was purely evil. Moro was again to put it most bluntly, in the first line of his poem: "You don't drive your daughter like a train," while Péret has the father "feeling the heat of his locomotive" during the rape.[41] Mesens described Violette as "the daughter of a civil suit and of a train." But the association that comes up most frequently is that between trains and state power, as if the poets had in mind the famous 1932 poster of a huge foreshortened black locomotive emblazoned with the words *Exactitude, État* (Punctuality. The State).[42] In the poems, Baptiste is not just an engine driver, but specifically the man who drove the president: "Mechanic it is said of presidential trains," wrote Breton, "In a land of breakdowns where the supreme Head of State / When he does not travel on foot is afraid of bicycles"; "Father Nozières / In the best of all republics / drove the trains of many a president," echoed Moro.[43] The repeated conflation of fathers, trains, presidents, and the state culminates in Péret's indictment of an entire system of patriarchal complicity: "All the fathers dressed in red to indict / or in black to pretend to defend / have been set upon her . . . / because they are the fathers / they who rape / beside the mothers / who defend their memory."[44] The message is underscored by the most explicit illustration in the volume, a drawing by Magritte of a man fondling a very young girl who sits on his lap, while a black top-hatted figure with his back to the viewer looks on (fig. 16). Violette was not just violated by her father, said the Surrealists; she was gang-raped.

Breton, Éluard, and the rest deserve credit for courageously advancing a point of view that went against the consensus of the time: even regardless of the truth of her claims about her father, they insisted, Violette had been sexually exploited by a range of men, and with Germaine's angry defection was left alone to face a phalanx of male authorities, judges, lawyers, doctors, policemen, and journalists, whose gut sympathy clearly lay with her dead father. In taking her claims seriously and exposing the patriarchal bias that infected her case, the Surrealists deserve some plaudits for protofeminist awareness. At the same time, they never met Violette nor did they help her concretely—any more than Breton had helped Nadja—and in the volume the real young woman is reduced to a collection of signs and symbols, including many literally florid images. There are flowers in Man Ray's cover photograph of N-shaped bricks (the father's name?) crushing a bank of violets, and violets again in Max Ernst's illustration, which involves a pelican and some scary dive-bombing birds. Breton wrote that Violette's sex was "winged like a flower of the catacombs," Péret that the young girl was "as beautiful as a water lily on a heap of coal."[45]

As Jonathan Eburne has pointed out, no realistic depiction of Violette appeared in the volume. Though photographs of Germaine Berton and of

*L'impromptu de Versailles*

Figure 16. Illustration by René Magritte for *Violette Nozières*. (© 2010 C. Herscovici, London / Artists Rights Society [ARS], New York.)

the Papin sisters had been reproduced in Surrealist publications, the one murderess to whom Breton and company devoted an entire volume was present mostly as a scattering of clues, "a set of signifiers."[46] Several of the contributions take the form of verbal or visual collages. Breton's poem, for instance, includes a hodgepodge of quotes from the newspapers: Baptiste and Germaine are conjured up in the maudlin stereotypes of the press, *le brave homme* and *l'excellente femme,* model parents who "once more bleed themselves dry for their child." Violette's words about her father sometimes forgetting that she was his daughter appear verbatim.[47] Concrete details of the case, as reported in the newspapers, weave their way through the poems: grim hotel rooms, family pictures on the apartment walls, the tool shack in the garden, the stained rag behind the curtain.

While the poems lift quotes and details from the press with mostly ironic intent, the illustrations reduce Violette to a series of abstract propositions. Those by Yves Tanguy, Max Ernst, Victor Brauner, and Marcel Jean include variations on voluptuous generic female nudes; Hans Arp explodes Violette's body into a series of cell-like blobs. Salvador Dalí contributed the most jarring image, labeled "Paranoid Portrait of Violette Nazière (Nozière)" (fig. 17). It shows a skeletal female figure in profile, composed of phallic, bonelike objects. Jutting from what looks like the skull of a prehistoric bird is a grossly elongated penis of a nose, topped by a fried egg and supported at the tip by a crutch. In the caption, Dalí builds upon the image with a series of nose-related puns and associations: Nazière, nose *(nez),* Nazi, Dinazos (a Belgian fascist group), and a quote from Violette about her parents' gentle snoring as she left the house after her crime. The previous year, Dalí had produced a similar "paranoid metamorphosis" of his mistress Gala, though it is telling that the 1932 drawing, unlike the Violette version, includes a realistic portrait of Gala's head alongside the two "paranoid" (skeletal and phallic) variations. In the early 1930s, Dalí was experimenting, under the influence of early writings by the psychoanalyst Jacques Lacan, with the interpretive possibilities of paranoid delirium, suggesting that obsessions which distort and destabilize normal perception are valuable tools for a revolutionary access to the psyche.[48]

The Spanish artist was also at the time deeply alienating his comrades-in-surrealism by claiming that Hitlerism was a good thing because it too undermined bourgeois moral and aesthetic certainties.[49] Although he insisted that his interest in Hitler was completely apolitical, Dalí probably annoyed them all the more with his Nazière/nose/Nazi contribution in

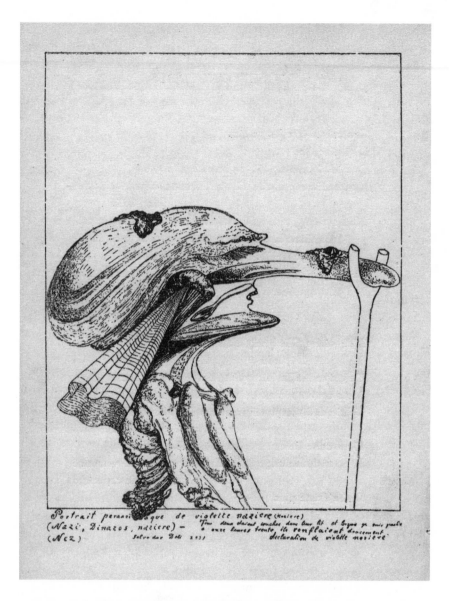

Figure 17. Salvador Dalí's "Paranoid Portrait of Violette Nazière [Nozière]." (© 2010 Salvador Dalí, Gala-Salvador Dalí Foundation / Artists Rights Society [ARS], New York.)

that the period leading up to the fall of 1933 was especially fraught for the group where politics were concerned.

The Surrealists had from the start set great store by their ideological alliance with revolutionary movements. As we saw, they joined the Communist Party in protesting the Rif War in 1925, and in subsequent years they signed many other appeals in *L'Humanité*. Several among them were party members, and all believed in a political solidarity with the Far Left, symbolized by the title of their early 1930s periodical, *Surrealism in the Service of the Revolution*. Despite professed common goals and the Surrealists' participation in the Communist-led boycott of the 1931 Colonial Exposition, tensions were present as early as the 1920s and would cause most of the Surrealists to abandon their formal affiliation with the party by the following decade. At issue, most fundamentally, was the French Communist Party's inclination to define and control "revolutionary" art and literature, and more deeply, the party's distrust of what they took to be the Surrealists' self-indulgent "petit-bourgeois" artistic experimentation and their inattention to the bread-and-butter concerns of the proletariat.

At the time, the Soviet Union was issuing calls for proletarian literary works, most notably in the statements of principle that came out of the Second Congress of Revolutionary Writers held in 1930 at Kharkov. The Congress's resolutions, published in France in November 1931, included a call for the French Communist Party to take the lead in developing an authentic proletarian literature and in general to intervene more actively in cultural affairs. For a while the Surrealists tried to walk a fine line, insisting that since their work was experimental and propagandistic in nature, it did not fall under the category of "literature" and hence did not contradict the party's aims. The argument failed to convince anyone, least of all themselves. By January 1932, *L'Humanité* was denouncing Surrealism as a narcissistic bourgeois endeavor, and in March 1932 Louis Aragon, an early and close collaborator of Breton's and the most politically engaged member of the group, broke with the Surrealist movement and redefined himself as a Communist intellectual.[50] But though *Surrealism in the Service of the Revolution* was discontinued and replaced in 1933 by a glossy literary magazine, *Minotaure,* Breton and his group never ceased to think of themselves as committed to the revolutionary project: their quest as they saw it ran parallel to political activism, just as dreams limn waking life.

The growing rift in the early 1930s between the Surrealists and the Communist Party, and the insistence by Breton and others that their program was analogous to but substantially different from that of revolutionary socialism make it difficult to know what to make of the denunciations, in *Violette Nozières*, of the bourgeoisie and the state and its minions. Their howl of anger at both Baptiste and Germaine Nozière, however, put them completely at odds with the party's support of the deceased union member and his widow. A few months earlier, in May 1933, *Surrealism in the Service of the Revolution* had carried a short commentary by Éluard and Péret on the Papin case that generally espoused the views of *L'Humanité*. "For six years," wrote Éluard and Péret, "[the sisters] endured remarks, demands, insults with perfect submission." Fear, exhaustion, and humiliation had built into a hatred that could only explode as violence. "When the day came, Léa and Christine Papin repaid the currency of evil in coins of red-hot iron."[51] This biblical repaying of evil with evil, the taking of a gruesomely literal eye for an eye is hardly the stuff of dialectical materialism. In both the Papin case and the Nozière case, the Surrealists looked beyond class analysis for new ways to express the horror of intimate exploitation.

How can you talk about the violence embedded in everyday life without resorting to sociological abstraction? How can art convey the psychological cruelty that robs the powerless—a young person, a servant—of a position as subject? In the early 1930s the Surrealists had begun working on such questions, pursuing their longtime goal of breaking down the distinction between subject and object by producing eerie, beautiful, threatening, and complicated *things*.

The Dada movement had founded the tradition of displaying mundane or disturbing objects as artworks, a provocation aimed at undermining the Western belief in aesthetics as a separate and privileged category of experience. There was sly humor involved as artists toyed with their viewers' minds. Duchamp ratcheted up the shock value of his 1917 urinal by titling it *Fountain*, reversing the flow of liquid, and in 1921 the young American artist Man Ray, recently arrived in Paris, took an ordinary household iron and affixed sharp tacks to its flat side so that it looked designed to rip what it was smoothing. He called it *Gift* (fig. 18). Sacred, erotic, and funny, the object is deeply personal: it harks back to Man Ray's childhood, when he was Emmanuel Radnitsky working in the family tailoring business in Brooklyn.[52] Dada artists were the first to intuit the ways in which the subconscious can invest ordinary things with disturbing power.

The tradition continued unbroken—Magritte was painting images of frighteningly precise domestic items throughout the later 1920s—but it was in the period from 1931 to 1936 that the French Surrealists became systematically invested in producing and thinking about objects.[53] The

Figure 18. Man Ray, *Gift,* 1921. (© 2010 Man
Ray Trust / Artists Rights Society [ARS], New
York / ADAGP, Paris.)

catalyst was a work by Alberto Giacometti, shown in a Paris gallery in
1930, which caught the eye of Breton and Dalí: a wooden ball marked
with a "feminine concavity" hanging suggestively by a violin string above
a crescent-shaped object that barely touched it.[54] Over the next few years,
much of the group's effort was directed toward both creating objects and
theorizing about their significance.

Many of the early works were *bricolages* of found objects, assembled to
carry an erotic, "convulsive" charge; the purpose was not just to break
down conventional definitions of art, but also to "desublimate" aesthetic
experience by foregrounding its essentially sexual nature.[55] Breton made a
complicated assemblage of a bicycle seat on a bed of foliage, with atop the
seat a receptacle containing two pink candied almonds nestled in a fuzz of
dark tobacco. His lover, Valentine Hugo, created a mysteriously disturbing scene involving a painted red hand sliding one finger under the lip of
the white glove on another hand, the whole thing resting on a gaming

table. Dalí, not to be outdone, put together what he called *Scatological Object with a Symbolic Function,* a none-too-subtle contraption whereby a sugar cube could be lowered into a glass of warm milk that rested in a woman's high-heeled shoe. Many of these objects were reproduced in the December 1931 issue of *Surrealism in the Service of the Revolution.*[56] Later in the decade, the movement became known for objects that, in the tradition of Man Ray's iron, mischievously defeated their own purpose, or that alarmingly combined the animate and the inanimate: Dalí's "aphrodisiac" telephone with a lobster perched on its receiver (1936), Wolfgang Paalen's umbrella made of sponges (1938), a velvet-covered stool by Kurt Seligmann supported by four shapely female legs in high-heeled shoes (1938), and perhaps the most famous, Méret Oppenheim's fur-covered breakfast dishes of 1936.[57]

These objects evoke the aesthetic of cinema, the only medium in which a close and sustained view of an ordinary object—a telephone, for instance— can carry a deep narrative tension and emotional charge. Breton and company deployed their creations as a new means of breaking down the distinction between subject and object, thus superseding their earlier experiments with automatic writing. For Breton, the making of objects was a new way of looking for a direct passage from dream to representation unmediated by the constraints of reason. Where modernist artists had dissolved the material world into abstraction, Surrealists traveled an opposite route, seeking to give concrete form to the inchoate stuff of the unconscious. Things, as created or "framed" by the Surrealist artist, objectify the subjective, giving material form to the realm of dream and desire; conversely, they subjectivize the objective by defying our insistence on drawing lines between "I" and "it." Breton and his brethren saw in such objects the possibility of a dialectical synthesis between the realm of the unconscious and the world of matter. By removing objects from their normal contexts, placing them within boundaries and drawing out their erotic valence, the artists made them into fetishes, sacred embodiments of our ever-frustrated longing for wholeness.[58]

The Surrealist preoccupation with the mysterious quality of ordinary objects is analogous to the more general craze for *faits divers* described in the last chapter; both of these phenomena culminated in Paris in the same years, the early to mid-1930s. If you flip through the pages of *Détective* in those years, objects are everywhere. Staged photographic close-ups of murder weapons illustrate crime narratives—a knife here, a foreshortened hammer there, elsewhere a glass of liquid into which a hand ominously sprinkles powder (figs. 10 and 15). Turn the page and the objects have lost their menace; they appear in advertisements, ready to be stacked in your kitchen or to grace your living room or bedroom. The accessories of everyday life provide the link between French interwar social experience—city life, office work, early mass consumption, crime-paper escapism—and the quests of the avant-garde. In *Nadja,* Breton mentions a trip to the flea market in Saint-Ouen in search of "those objects that can be found nowhere else: old-fashioned, broken, useless, almost incomprehensible, even perverse."[59] Objects are everywhere in *Violette Nozières,* as poetic alchemy transports clues and crime-scene details into the realm of the numinous. In Breton's poem, the famous rag "shines mysteriously"; in Éluard's, family pictures look down from the walls; Péret's ode features shovel handles, the cloth, a screen, and items of clothing, Germaine's skirt with money sewn into the hem, Monsieur Émile's trousers.[60]

The Surrealists drew upon popular culture—crime, consumerism—as well as from experiences in their own backgrounds, often in modest homes: Man Ray's iron is a case in point. But here again Freud is a crucial influence, not so much for anything he may have written on objects as for his theory of the uncanny. In a foreshadowing of what we now call the "noir" aesthetic, Freud identified and explained in a famous 1919 essay how that which is most intimate and familiar to us can also be supremely terrifying: "The uncanny is that species of the frightening which goes back to what was once well known of old and has long been familiar."[61]

Freud's initial insight comes from the oddly contradictory senses of the German word *heimlich,* which, he points out, means "familiar," "intimate," and "friendly," but also "concealed, kept from sight . . . withheld from others."[62] Magic, for instance, is known as the *heimlich* art. One word, then, comprises two very different conjoined meanings, that of familiarity and that of troubling, shameful secrecy. The meaning of *heimlich,* as Freud noted, therefore tugs toward that of its opposite, *unheimlich* ("eerie" or "weird"). Manifestations of the *Unheimlich* evoke terror because they are deeply ambiguous. The quintessential manifestation of the uncanny resides at the juncture between the animate and the inanimate: dolls, for instance, can be horrific, as endless iterations of the "Chucky" motif suggest. Another common source of horror is doubling: infantile narcissism makes us crave a replica of ourselves, but when we move beyond that early stage, the double becomes a thing of terror. Freud's insights into the commingling of intimacy and horror may not have directly influenced Breton and his colleagues, but the program of Surrealist investigation led them to the same point, where the familiar veers into the deeply disturbing. The

Papin sisters were uncanny doubles, and the Surrealists proceeded to double them again by printing two photographs showing them side by side "before" and "after" the crime.[63] Many Surrealist objects combined organic and inorganic matter, or conflated thing and living creature. And what could have been more *heimlich* and yet more deeply *unheimlich* than the Nozière home on Rue de Madagascar?

For all of its bitter denunciations of bourgeoisie and patriarchy, the real political punch of *Violette Nozières* comes from its conjuring up the profound creepiness of a certain kind of family life: "The parents once more bleed themselves dry for their child," "You don't drive your daughter like a train," a fleeting image of Violette studying "between the miserable mechanic / and the mother plotting revenge / her lessons for the next day."[64] On the face of it, the Violette pamphlet seems at odds with the Surrealists' attitude toward political art at the time, since it was precisely their disdain toward using works of imagination to make explicit ideological points that led to the deterioration of their relations with the French Communist Party. In January 1932 Aragon had been indicted by the French authorities for publishing a heavy-handed poem, "Red Front," which called for the murder of policemen in the context of class struggle. Even as Breton defended Aragon and reasserted the commonality of the group's aims with those of Communism, he poured scorn on his friend's retrograde brandishing of political slogans in the form of poetry.[65] "Red Front" was the catalyst for the Surrealists' break with the party. While some poems in the Nozière volume, especially those of René Char and Maurice Henry, are opaque free associations, it is surprising to see Breton, Éluard, Péret, and others taking an explicit position on the Nozière case.

But *Violette Nozières* hardly offers a coherent political take on the affair: its stance is antipatriarchal but hardly feminist, its message closer to inchoate anarchism than to anything resembling a Marxist critique. The authorities seized it, to be sure, but one would love to know what contemporaries, and especially the French Left, would have made of it had publication proceeded uninterrupted. The Surrealists provided their own version of Émile Zola's famous "J'accuse" in the Dreyfus affair, but the sweeping nature of their indictment made their accusations ineffective. They issued a statement and an analysis, not a call for action.

Notwithstanding Mesens's image of a protest march made up of artists and their ghosts, *Violette Nozières* was intended as a cry of outrage rather than an active intervention in the case. At this time of alienation from the organized Left, Breton and the others could not envision their broader project of connecting consciousness to the unconscious fitting into the framework of any organized political group, even as they clung to the position that what they were doing was a necessary complement to sociopolitical revolution. Arguably, though, they were more clear-sighted than others in their diagnosis of the long-term sources of malfeasance in the society around them. The most catastrophic political failure in the years ahead was not to be the collapse of the short-lived left-wing Popular Front in 1938 but the acquiescence of many French people to the unsavory compromises of the Vichy regime. The attitudes that the Surrealists denounced in *Violette Nozières*—smug conformity, familial self-absorption, private ambition, and the patriarchal entitlement of the ruling elites—would prove politically noxious in years to come.

The Surrealist investment in the Nozière affair was brief but revealing. The case evidently touched Breton, Éluard, Péret, and others as deeply as it did less famous contemporaries, and for many of the same reasons, even if the avant-garde drew different inferences from the story of the Nozière family. In both cases, new social conditions and the eclipse of grand political ideologies forced a different set of questions to the fore: what meaning could be found, for isolated urban families and for the country at large, in the texture of everyday life? Why were family privacy and the ambition for status and goods both highly prized and deeply disturbing?

Contemporaries probably hoped that the trial, anticipated for fall 1934, would answer some of the nagging questions left over from the case. The Surrealists and a few fearless journalists had made the argument that Violette was telling the truth about her father. Whether that case would be made at the trial, whether the word *incest* or *rape* would even be mentioned, remained to be seen.

# NINE

# The Trial

IN DECEMBER 1933, the same month the Surrealists published their book of poems and artwork, Judge Lanoire completed his investigation. On December 16, the judge, the accused, and her lawyers met for a final round of questioning, which took the form of a preliminary indictment. Addressing Violette, Lanoire laid out his view of the case. In spite of repeated demands that she tell the truth, the accused had given only the most implausible explanations; if the incest had taken place, why did she say nothing for six years, even to the mother whom she claimed to love? And anyway, at age eighteen, she could have found a job and left home "like other young girls of your condition." Lanoire launched into a long tirade about Violette's loose morals ("despite your frigid nature"), and especially her social ambition: "Your vanity and mythomania had steadily increased. You lived in a milieu somewhat above your condition and wanted to maintain yourself there. . . . You could no longer go back down to the mediocrity of your real situation, of which your parents' presence served as a constant reminder. Their existence could expose your lies; with them gone, you could continue to play the role that flattered your imagination." In response to Lanoire's long expository questions, Violette was allowed only the briefest answers: "My parents left me quite free. And thanks to Monsieur Émile, I did not need money"; "Those are not the motives that made me act."[1] On this occasion, Violette was a mere supporting player: the final indictment was Lanoire's last chance at the spotlight during this case, and he made the most of it.

Eager to keep the presses rolling, newspapers whipped up anticipation of the next act. In December 1933, after the last interrogations, *La République* had expressed hope that the trial might take place early in the new year. The journalist eagerly anticipated the courtroom drama: "Will she speak? . . . Will she dare to repeat in front of twelve jurors accusations that may be odious but which—we cannot but shudder at the thought— also seem unquestionably likely?" Debates would be impassioned, he continued, because passion marked every page of this "formidable dossier": "Incest, adultery, love both venal and 'against nature' make up what one could call a Baudelairean rosary." Monsieur Émile, the "tutelary faun," might finally appear! Who knows what other mysteries might be revealed about this strange family in which the father had for his daughter the eyes of an old lecher?[2] The journalist need not have worked himself into such a sweat. Violette's lawyers were allowed to appeal the indictment, which they did, and it took another seven months before the case came to trial on October 10, 1934.

Political conditions may have played a part in delaying the case's progress to the courtroom. By the time the official writ of indictment against Violette was drawn up at the end of February 1934, much had happened to distract Parisians and the country at large from the previous year's succession of spectacular *faits divers*. The climax of the Stavisky scandal at the end of 1933 fed into public exasperation with the Republican status quo, which increasingly restless groups on the extreme right eagerly exploited to their advantage. Repercussions from the affair had forced the resignation of one cabinet, and in early February the new prime minister, the left-Republican Édouard Daladier, attempted to flex his political muscle by dismissing the popular Paris chief of police, Jean Chiappe, a Corsican strongman with known ties to the Far Right. In response, the leading royalist, paramilitary, and fascist-leaning groups organized a rally denouncing the Chamber of Deputies.[3]

The night of the rally, February 6, witnessed the worst violence in Paris since the Paris Commune half a century earlier. On the Place de la Concorde, thousands of demonstrators faced off with mounted police guarding the Chamber of Deputies: protesters tore up nearby parks and hurled railings and rocks at the police. They slashed the bellies and tendons of horses with razor blades attached to poles, and the police fired back into the crowd while deputies fled the chamber through the back door. The rampage left fifteen dead, over fourteen hundred wounded, and political tensions at their highest ebb since the Dreyfus case. Socialists and Communists managed to put aside the rancor that had divided them since 1920 and unite—albeit at the very last minute—for a common counter-demonstration on February 12. In March, a group of antifascist intellectuals created a committee that laid the foundations for France's first, and short-lived, Socialist government, the Popular Front.[4] The sclerotic Third Republic survived the crisis but was increasingly overtaken by more vital forces on its right and left.

Despite France's increasingly fraught political climate, the Nozière trial, set to begin during calmer days, on October 10, 1934, would be sure to make headline news. In the days before the trial, leading newspapers ran new versions of Violette's story on their front pages in case readers had forgotten the details: "Is She a Monster or a Madwoman? Will Violette Nozière Finally Give Up Her Secret?" screamed one front-page piece. *Le Journal* ran a headline reporting that the famous criminal was picking out an outfit for the big day. *Paris-Soir* sent its reporter to Neuvy, where he failed to secure an interview with Germaine and got angrily shooed away by her in-laws.[5]

Yet another dramatic event, however, blew the trial off the front page at the very last minute. On October 9, the king of Yugoslavia, Alexander I, arrived in Marseille aboard the steamer *Dubrovnik* for an official visit. Eager to shore up alliances in Central Europe, the French government had invited the monarch and dispatched their foreign minister, Louis Barthou, to meet him in Marseille and escort him by train to Paris. As the king's motorcade made its way through Marseille, a Bulgarian nationalist named Vlado Chernozemski broke through the crowd despite heavy police protection, jumped onto the running board of Alexander's car, whipped out a gun, and fired, killing the king, Barthou, and several other people before being gunned down himself. For a day or two, not even the trial of France's most famous young criminal could compete with the ensuing national grief and humiliation.

The political assassination was very much on people's minds when Violette's trial opened as planned on October 10. The presiding judge, Counselor Peyre, began proceedings with a somber speech honoring the victims, several other officials followed suit, and then proceedings were temporarily suspended in deference to the mood of national mourning. There were further delays while two alternate jurors were added to the impaneled group of twelve men, and the audience in the Palais de Justice must have been getting restless. Crowds had begun to assemble before dawn on the square in front of the courthouse, the Place Dauphine, in the medieval heart of Paris. Fifty republican guards were on hand to control the press of spectators, a majority of whom were reportedly female.[6] Those in attendance had read about Violette for many months, but most had never laid eyes upon her. What drew the crowds, wrote the *Paris-Soir* reporter, was the youth and reputed beauty of the star character in the drama: "The public will always take more interest in a beautiful girl than an ugly one, even, as in this case, when the seductive wrapping hides a diseased body and a stupefying amorality."[7] The anticipation was intense.

The penalty for premeditated murder, especially parricide, was automatically death on the guillotine unless the defense could prove the existence of mitigating circumstances. In 1934 the guillotine was still a fixture of the French political and cultural landscape. The early twentieth century had seen a vigorous abolitionist movement, culminating in a raging debate in the Chamber of Deputies in 1908. The bill calling for the abolition of the death penalty ended in defeat, however, and the following years saw a reversal of the abolitionist tide. Whereas at the turn of the century the annual total of executions was in the single digits, by the interwar period some twenty people a year were decapitated. The legendary Anatole Deibler, the Paris executioner who held the position for forty years, had carried out his grim functions close to four hundred times when he retired in 1939. Executions were still public, held on city streets and squares, and sometimes degenerated into mob scenes.[8]

Ostensibly, Violette did not have to fear going under the blade. The French Third Republic authorities balked at the idea of executing a woman, and though women were still sentenced to the guillotine, since the 1870s that punishment was routinely commuted by presidential pardon to life in prison. (Pétain's reactionary regime was to bring back the death penalty for women, half a dozen of whom were guillotined in the early 1940s, mostly for providing illegal abortions.) The paradoxical upshot of gender-determined clemency was that juries felt free to sentence women to death as a gesture, knowing that they would not have to live with the gruesome consequence of their decision. Violette and her defenders were well aware of all this but must still have been fearful: over the last fourteen months many voices had called for the custom of sparing women to be suspended in the case of the "monster" Nozière.

The French system of criminal justice is technically known as "inquisitorial," in contrast to the Anglo-American "accusatory" approach. In the English tradition, the accused is presumed innocent, and the facts of the case are established in an open court. The modern French system, as first established in 1808, took shape as a Napoleonic compromise between the Old Regime tradition of top-down secrecy and the Revolution's principles of openness and democracy. In the system that prevailed under the Third Republic, many elements of which survive today, considerable power was vested in the *juge d'instruction,* who investigated the case thoroughly and recommended for or against an indictment. Though the case then went before a twelve-man jury in a public courtroom, the private pretrial investigation carried considerable weight, since an indictment amounted to a presumption of guilt for the accused. That bias was reinforced by the status of the public prosecutor, the *avocat général,* within the courtroom. He entered and exited the room alongside the presiding judge, the *président de chambre,* and sat with him on a slightly raised platform; these courtroom mechanics sent a strong signal that the judge and prosecutor were allied against the defense.[9]

Before the trial began, the court impaneled a jury of twelve men. Only enfranchised citizens could serve as jurors, and French women were not granted the vote until 1945. Jurors were chosen by the Ministry of Justice from lists of men of upstanding character supplied by the office of the state's representative, the departmental prefect. In the past, all jurors had been wealthy men, but provisions for lodging and remuneration introduced in 1907 and 1908 made it easier for working-class men to serve on juries.[10] While the exact identities of the jurors who were to decide on Violette's guilt are not known, the list of thirty-six names from which they were randomly drawn has survived in the case records. This master list includes some men of obviously bourgeois status (an architect, a factory manager, an industrialist, an academic inspector, and a "property owner"), but most are of modest but respectable standing: a cobbler, a carpenter, a tailor, a locksmith, a mechanic, several office workers, and many salesmen and shopkeepers. They range in age from thirty-three to sixty-seven, with the largest group, twenty-four of them, in their forties and fifties. The median age is forty-seven.[11] Baptiste Nozière could very easily have been on this list of lower-middle-class worthies; he was forty-eight when he died.

The 1808 Code enjoined jurors to base their decision on "moral proof" rather than technicalities: "The law does not ask the jury to account for the means by which they are convinced. It does not prescribe to them rules on which they must particularly base the fullness and sufficiency of proof. . . . [I]t only asks them this one question, comprising the full measure of their duties: 'Are you thoroughly convinced?'"[12] Juries were asked to evaluate not just a specific crime but a fully documented portrait of the criminal—his or her background, character, and previous activities and possible misdeeds, all of which were detailed in the prosecution's case: hence, for instance, Violette's promiscuity, scholastic failures, rebellion against her parents, and chronic lying could legitimately be brought to bear upon her crime.

While commentators in the late nineteenth and early twentieth centuries railed against jury verdicts as erratic and biased, jurors were doing their task as implicitly defined by the law: bringing social morality to bear upon their decision. Third Republic juries paid close attention to motive and circumstance. They were famously merciful toward crimes of passion, usually deciding, as they did in Germaine d'Anglemont's case, that a betrayed spouse or lover who killed in the heat of the moment should not be severely punished. In general, French juries leaned toward leniency: in the face of a procedure that heavily implied the defendant's guilt, they convicted in only 70 percent of the cases and found mitigating circumstances for eight out of ten crimes. But juries were typically severe in some instances: when criminals killed for money or with premeditation and in cases of multiple murders or the murder of a police officer, a child, or a parent.[13] Three days before the trial, a journalist named Emmanuel Bourcier published in a women's magazine an article entitled "If You Were a Juror in the Nozière Case" that did not bode well for the accused. After reminding readers that they as women could not be in that hypothetical situation, he first surmised that a male jury would side with the male victim, but then added that women jurors would likely show no pity for Violette either. And a good thing too, he concluded: "If I myself were, God forbid, a juror in the Nozière case, I would condemn Violette without a moment's hesitation. Even if she had been the victim of her father. For she could leave him and earn a living instead of killing him, defaming him, and robbing him."[14]

With the jury impaneled and the mood of national mourning acknowledged, proceedings finally began in the trial of Violette Nozière. The appearance of the accused was a moment of high drama in a trial such as this, and Violette finally emerged, wearing the same sort of outfit she had favored at the time of her crime: a black fur-collared coat, and this time a narrow-brimmed black felt hat tilted sideways instead of the beret she had previously worn (fig. 19). She moved quickly to the witness stand, eyes to the ground, her face unreadable. Violette had become such a mythical creature since her crime—the very symbol of glamorous depravity—that in the flesh she could not fail to disappoint, especially since fourteen months in prison had apparently damaged her looks. *Paris Midi* reported on the "great disappointment" the audience felt upon seeing her: "The star of this show may be almost as pretty as predicted, but she walks bent forward, slack, defeated by prison and blemished by illness. No trace of the femme fatale: no cruelty etches the features of Violette Nozière." *L'Œuvre* went for complete demystification: "She's an ordinary little woman like many others, not bad-looking of course, but pretty close to insignificance: a woman friend you could have a beer with."[15]

Proceedings began with the solemn reading of the *acte d'accusation,* the formal writ of indictment filed with the Paris Assizes Court on February 24 after the end of the investigation. The document recorded Judge Lanoire's conclusions and refuted Violette Nozière's defense: it noted her long-standing depravity, recorded the first poisoning incident in March 1933, described her vanity and social fantasies, and made liberal use of the word *prostitution.* It opined that Monsieur Émile never existed, described her incest allegations as an "inane defense," and again harped on Violette's deplorable fibs about her social status. She was formally accused of two crimes, the attempted poisoning in March and its successful repetition in August.[16]

The next procedural step was the questioning of the accused by the presiding judge based on the information in the investigation file. In theory the judge was supposed to act impartially at this stage, since the purpose of the questioning was to inform the jury of the facts of the case, but in practice most *présidents de salle* were so clearly prosecutorial in their interrogation that the Ministry of Justice had occasionally to rein them in.[17] Président Peyre fell right into the pattern; in fact he opened proceedings with a disquisition that, in the form of an address to Violette, warned the jury not to believe a word she said: "Violette Nozière, if I did not fear that my admonition would be for naught, I would exhort you to tell the truth. One of your personality traits is a taste for lying. You lie not only out of self-interest but sometimes for no reason at all. You have lied for a very long time to your parents, your friends, your lovers. Today you stand before those who will judge you. Are you ready to tell the truth?" In response, Violette proffered an almost inaudible "Yes, sir."[18]

Figure 19. Violette Nozière at her trial, October 1934. René de Vésinne-Larue is seated below her. (Photograph by Roger-Viollet, courtesy of Image Works.)

Violette at first gave the same barely audible answer to Peyre's barrage of hostile questions and observations.[19] "You had many lovers?" "Yes, sir"; "Their names were Willy, Bernard, and others?" "Yes, sir"; "You did not hesitate to be intimate with men you had just met?" "Yes, sir." Eventually, though, she began to give fuller answers, explaining her motives and feelings. When the judge pointed out that she cut classes when enrolled at the Lycée Fénelon, she answered that she was discouraged because she felt unable to keep up with the work; when he berated her for her promiscuous behavior over the last year, she simply said, "I was in a depression." As the questioning became more intimate, Violette showed increasing signs of agitation. Asked about her feelings for Jean Dabin, she answered with considerable emotion, "He was the one I loved most, the only one I ever really loved!" The judge commented sardonically, no doubt smirking at his colleagues, "He was a law student," and the prosecutor followed up with an obscure joke in Latin.[20] Peyre also made his skepticism about Monsieur Émile's existence perfectly clear. When Violette protested in response to a question that she had no need of money because of her "protector," the judge responded, "All we know about him is that he had a white mustache and a blue car," with a look on his face that set off laughter in the room.

Eventually questions came around to the issue the audience was most anticipating and Violette was probably dreading. It is one thing to narrate the intimate details of incest with a parent to a sympathetic policeman or even a room full of legal officials, quite another to do so at the bar in front of a large and mostly hostile audience, knowing that your every word will be repeated in the newspapers. Peyre pressed her on the subject: "Come on, tell us all! Explain yourself!" Violette could not do it: "I beg you, M. le Président, don't ask me about that." The reporter for *Le Populaire* showed her no mercy: "So she's prudish now? . . . She doesn't want to talk about it? After all she has done and said?" The judge nonetheless went through all the details, showing the audience the rag and the obscene drawings, getting Violette to admit that her father was free of the venereal disease she carried.

Questioning proceeded to the night of the crime, which Peyre quizzed the defendant about in detail. For the jury's sake, he lingered over the moment when Violette handed her parents the glasses of "medication" and coaxed them to drink: "And nothing moved you to stop them . . ." At this point Violette let out a guttural cry and fell to the ground. When guards approached to help her, she pushed them away, screaming, "Leave me, leave me alone!" and continued to moan for a while "like an animal." *Le*

*Populaire* described this turn of events as a blatantly theatrical ploy: "This was more or less predictable: La Petite Roquette has its traditions, just like the Comédie Française." A doctor appeared and had Violette sniff some ether. She was allowed outside for a few minutes, returning hatless and with her hair in disorder, which, according to the same journalist, "gave her a bit of a wild-child look, which suited her very well."[21]

The judge went on relentlessly through the details of the night, the following day, and her week of hiding in Paris. "Why," he concluded, "this second attempt against your parents' lives? Tell the gentlemen of the jury." In response Violette collapsed again and was once again ministered to by the court physician, Dr. Sicard. The judge asked the doctor whether the accused was in a state to continue the session, and Sicard answered, "Oh, she's talking. She said, 'It's hard.' I answered, 'It's a tough pill to swallow.'" The room broke out in laughter again. Journalists, magistrates, and audience members were convinced that Violette's courtroom collapses were yet another instance of her well-known habits of role-playing and deceit. It does not seem to have occurred to anyone to consider what effect several hours of harsh interrogation in front of a hostile audience might have on a young body and mind weakened by months in prison.

Peyre's questioning finally came to an end. He summed up his conclusion in a question that served as a signal to the jury: "I have searched in vain, in the records of this case, for an element that could be considered a mitigating circumstance in your favor; I searched because I wanted to find one. But it was in vain! If such a circumstance exists, state it here, daughter Nozière." (*Fille Nozière* was Violette's official identity for administrative purposes, but it also underscored her relationship to Baptiste.) In response, Violette delivered a short speech, no doubt carefully prepared: she expressed remorse and asked everyone for forgiveness, especially her mother, whom she invoked twice. The judge's final statement went to the heart of the court case, since the issue was not Violette's actions, which she acknowledged, but the existence of considerations—her health, the deeds of an accomplice, her father's possible guilt—that might spare her a death sentence. Even with Peyre bluntly stating on the opening day what he expected the verdict to be, not a single journalist complained or even commented on a possible bias. In fact, *Le Populaire* went out of its way to describe the judge as "impartial" and "impersonal."

The reporters who covered the event had already decided that the Nozière trial would be a three-act play: day one would feature Violette, day two the other main characters, and day three would be the dramatic climax, when the verdict would be handed down. As if keenly aware of the dramatic pacing of the event, the court spent the rest of the first day hearing the testimonies of various minor players: the neighbor M. Mayeul, Dr. Deron, and the various policemen and firemen called in on the night of the crime. Notably absent from the list of persons questioned was Superintendant Marcel Guillaume, the first person to talk to Violette after her arrest and the one individual among all the officials involved who had most unequivocally stated his belief that the incest took place.

The second day, October 11, began with an expected dramatic highlight: the testimony of Germaine Nozière. Taking a break from mongering conspiracy rumors about the recent political assassination ("Who profits from the crime? Fascism! Beware of provocation!"), the writers for *L'Humanité* had in recent days ratcheted up their ideological reading of the story in anticipation of Mme Nozière's testimony. The objective reality of what went on in this case, *L'Humanité* explained, was that the capitalist baron Émile, whom the police deliberately refused to identify, had used Violette to transfer the money he made from the exploitation of workers into the pockets of young bourgeois like Jean, "the same young men who beat and shoot workers in the name of morality and integrity."[22] The Marxist version of the story—Violette as a sexual pawn in a series of power plays among men—is not without merit, but in the end it was still impossible to make Dabin technically responsible for anything that happened on August 21, 1933. In any case, the French Communist Party was on thin ice waxing moralistic about the manipulation of a vulnerable woman, given their blatant exploitation of Germaine's grief and anger for political ends. While everyone anticipated that Germaine would likely follow the part of her script that involved going after Jean Dabin, her attitude toward her daughter was far less predictable. Would she give a repeat performance of her shocking role as the unnatural mother, wishing death upon her child? Or would the passage of time and the criticism she had weathered cause her to change her tune?

Germaine appeared in court leaning upon the arm of a friend, her face covered, as it had been the previous fall, by a waist-length opaque mourning veil—an archaic sartorial choice that was already excessive right after her husband's death, let alone over a year later (fig. 20).[23] She had been allowed to enter through the magistrates' door to avoid the press of gawkers, thus giving the impression that she was at one with the prosecution. Once she arrived at the witness's bar, the judge asked her to lift her veil, which

Figure 20. Germaine Nozière at the trial with her lawyer, Maurice Boitel. (Photograph by Roger-Viollet, courtesy of Image Works.)

she did, revealing an emaciated face. The judge immediately announced that he had a preliminary question to put to her: "Tell us, why did you, an affectionate mother and faithful wife, choose to file this suit?" He intended to give Germaine a chance at the outset to dispel the hard feelings her vindictive words and actions had created among the public. She came back on cue with a well-rehearsed statement delivered in a monotone: "I chose to become a plaintiff in order to discover accomplices in the crime and to defend my husband's memory. I never sought to condemn my daughter, toward whom I feel no hatred." In the stand Violette dropped her head into her hands and started to sob—although reporters noted caustically that she emitted no convincing sounds.

The judge's questions to Germaine focused on the night of the crime, and Germaine delivered once again the familiar narrative: the argument about Jean, the letter from "Dr. Deron," the powders diluted in glasses of water. Germaine seemed to have forgotten her very recent statement that she had no desire to "condemn" her daughter when, prompted by Peyre, she told a riveted audience about the moment she and Baptiste drank their drafts:

JUDGE PEYRE:     When she asked you to swallow the powder, did your
                 daughter not say to you and your husband: "You don't
                 think I want to poison you?"
MME NOZIÈRE:     Yes, and my husband said: "I don't think you have sunk
                 that low." *(Sensation)*[24]

Amid the gasps and murmurs that followed this exchange, a juror jumped up and asked Germaine if it was not true that she had drunk only half of her glass and thrown away the rest. She answered in the affirmative, then went on to promote the accomplice thesis by reminding the audience and jurors that she had collapsed on the floor and awakened in her bed. The atmosphere became increasingly tense as Violette's lawyer, René de Vésinne-Larue, intervened to question Germaine about the notorious rag. A "storm" of murmured protests erupted, and the judge waded in to interrupt the attorney: "I think that's enough. The gentlemen of the jury understand, and if any one of them does not, let him raise his hand. *(Laughter)*"

Whenever Germaine appeared in public, melodrama seemed to break out, as it did now. Winding down his interrogation, the judge asked Violette if she had any questions for her mother. Violette rose and exclaimed "Maman, Maman, forgive me, Maman!" to which Germaine responded by stretching her arms out toward her daughter and proclaiming, "Violette, I cannot forget that you are my daughter. What you said about your poor father is a lie and an abomination, but you are my daughter! I cannot forget that you are my daughter!" By this time both women were weeping loudly, Violette punctuating her sobs with cries of "Maman, Maman!" while Germaine rounded out the scene by wailing: "Pity for my child!" Germaine evidently assumed that "pity" was someone else's responsibility: she had just spent the last hour recounting details that would likely earn her child a sentence of death or prison for life.

The audience must have been relieved that this lurid scene was followed by medical technicalities. Up next were Dr. Paul, the forensic specialist who examined the victims, Dr. Kohn-Abrest, a leading expert in poisons, and Dr. Henri Claude, head of the panel that had filed the report on Violette's physical and mental health for the investigation a year earlier. The first two delivered the requisite scientific information, including a lecture on poisoning methods by Kohn-Abrest. *Le Populaire* politely commented that "these interesting dissertations gave the jury members a chance to recover from their emotions." Claude repeated the conclusions of his report: where science was concerned, Violette could be considered fully sane and responsible. Vésinne-Larue pounced once again: wasn't one of the panel members Dr. Victor Truelle, the man who had declared the Papin sisters perfectly sane, only to have his conclusions refuted several months later? Attacking the credibility of a prominent medical specialist was a risky move, and it drew fire from the prosecution. Gaudel snapped back that there was no need to retry the Papin case, that he was fully confident in the judgment of the experts, and that at any rate one of the Papin sisters was recognized to be fully sane and had been sentenced to death. The word *death,* wrote one journalist, "landed like a warning, or even a threat."[25] Vésinne-Larue backed down. *L'Œuvre* commented that Violette's lawyer, who had not even called to the bar another medical expert he had recruited, seemed by now to be completely adrift.

For the audience, there was one more treat in the offing for the day: the questioning of Violette's lovers, especially the famous Jean Dabin. The prosecution raised the issue of Violette's many paramours and "indisputable prostitution," and when Vésinne-Larue protested that all this was overstated, Violette was asked to give the names of all the men she had slept with. Gaudel smirked, "This is going to take a while" to appreciative laughter from the room. As the newspapers had done during the investigation, the courtroom was now going to dispense moral judgment on these young men. One of Violette's men friends had already been, as *L'Œuvre* put it, "consigned to oblivion" that day: asked about Monsieur Émile, Police Inspector Gripois had declared on the stand that the older man was just as imaginary as Dr. Deron's sister, a convenient fiction to obscure Violette's gains from venal lovemaking.

Georges Legrand, known as Willy, was called up first. He was now an office worker in an architectural firm, and he squirmed as he admitted that shortly before the crime he had pressed Violette for the return of the three hundred fifty francs that Jean Dabin had lent him. Bernard Piebourg, who came next, sported the same fashionable attire as Willy, the outfit that had been lampooned in countless cartoons of Jean Dabin: jacket with "coat-hanger" shoulders, wide pants, round tortoiseshell spectacles. (Willy's version of the look included a wide bottle-green tie and matching pocket handkerchief.) Newspapers described Piébourg as yet another *éphèbe* (pretty boy), and the judge cracked several jokes at his expense but gained no new information.

Jean Dabin, when he finally appeared, was wearing not the uniform of these Latin Quarter dandies but that of the French Army. By signing up, he had taken the only course of action that would remove him from scrutiny and public shame. Shipped off to Algeria, he was recalled for the trial, to which he would offer nothing beyond himself as an object of scandal and a target for moralism. Dabin was greeted by an "ironic ovation" from the audience, and then proceeded, in response to questions from the judge, to describe once again his liaison with Violette, especially the financial advantage he gained from it. *L'Œuvre* commented on the continuing silence of the defendant's counsel: "One would have liked at this point to have heard something from Maître de Vésinne-Larue, but he seems to have gone forever mute." Nor did the Communist Party try at this stage to push their thesis via Germaine's lawyer, Boitel, although *L'Humanité* speculated that Dabin might have funneled Violette's money to the Camelots du Roi and asked, "How many Dabins were on Place de la Concorde last February 6?"

The judge felt it incumbent upon him to deliver a formal lecture to the young man, telling Dabin that at the very least he was guilty of "thoughtlessness and amorality" in taking Violette's money, that his actions were widely condemned, and that it was to be hoped that the army would straighten him out. When Dabin failed to come up with an appropriate attitude of remorse and instead made a show of ironic indifference, Peyre worked himself up into a lather of moralistic outrage: "Do you not realize what people in this room, including myself, think of you? You have brought shame on your upstanding family. You have lived off this wretched woman here, whose punishment I will be calling for shortly. You yourself are not answerable to formal justice, but to something else. I will tell you this to your face: you are answerable to public contempt." *Paris-Soir* commented that the judge had "relieved people's consciences" by shaking up Dabin, giving some satisfaction to the thousands of people who believed that the young man was morally guilty if legally untouchable.[26]

Peyre's attitude toward the various witnesses mirrored that of his predecessor, Lanoire, most notably in the apparent class bias that led them to privilege the only one of Violette's lovers who belonged to their social world, the medical student and doctor's son, Pierre Camus. Although Camus's testimony—that Violette told him her father sometimes forgot she was his daughter—was the most substantial single piece of evidence in support of Violette's incest allegations, judges and journalists never questioned his memory or integrity and indeed could not stop heaping praise on him. "He is well mannered, precise, and speaks in a measured way," wrote one journalist. Peyre extracted some acknowledgment from Camus that Violette often told lies, then launched into a flurry of praise: "You alone, sir, of all these little young men, have behaved correctly. I need to make this clear."[27] Drawing the line between the real bourgeoisie and lower-middle-class impostors evidently mattered above all else.

The newspapers described the testimonies of Willy, Piébourg, Dabin, and Camus, and mentioned Violette's right-bank lovers Atlan and Fellous. Anyone who was not actually present in the courtroom would not have known that several other men were questioned that day. The testimony of those whose recollections tended to confirm Violette's allegations went unreported in the daily press, but Germaine's lawyer, Maurice Boitel, did mention them, if only to refute them, in the plea he delivered on October 12, which remained unpublished for many months.[28] Jean Leblanc, the man who had slapped Violette when she revealed her secret to him, was now stationed in Syria and deposed in absentia. He repeated that Violette had told him in 1932 that her father had abused *(violentée)* her or raped *(violée)* her, he could not remember which. André Tessier and Roger Endewell did appear in court on October 11, though Boitel dismissed the first as "imprecise" and tried to poke holes in the story told by the second. Camus had mentioned Violette's incest allegations too, he pointed out, but his testimony was "vague." As Germaine's lawyer and a Communist Party member like the late Baptiste, Boitel was every bit as eager as everyone else to discredit Violette's claims, but his published speech unwittingly confirms that the reporters for the major dailies actively colluded in presenting only one side of the story.

For all that, the public interrogation of Violette's lovers had delivered no major surprises, and the parade of secondary characters—Madeleine Debise, Atlan and Fellous, Baptiste's colleagues—that rounded off the day proved similarly anticlimactic. The newspapers concluded that while the play's first act had delivered as expected, the middle section had been a dud. *Le Populaire* complained that this judicial spectacle seemed like a poorly structured show: after the first day's delectable drama, things had gone flat in the second act, with day two ending in a "morose" litany of predictable depositions. Even the morning's histrionic interactions between mother and daughter struck journalists as somehow stilted and overly theatrical, like a play performed by amateurs. The reporter for *L'Œuvre* complained of Germaine that "there was something so mechanical in her attitude that she struck people as not natural." He noted that she spoke "like a legal brief" and shrewdly concluded, "There is a gaucheness in this family, a sort of awkwardness that cancels out pathos and makes everything, on the face of it, seem fake." A family in which a daughter can hand her parents glasses of a lethal mixture and ask, "Do you really think I want to poison you?" is indeed one in which any sense of emotional truth has long been lost. On stage as themselves, the Nozières were not convincing.

The final day of the trial, October 13, could hardly fail to deliver drama. On the one hand, the judge had made it clear that he could see no possible extenuating circumstances, and Vésinne-Larue had so far done a poor job of defending his client. On the other, the defendant was uncommonly young and good-looking, not a hardened woman of the streets but a schoolgirl. Who could predict how much indulgence to expect from the middle-aged men in the jury, many of them probably fathers? Would they use the verdict to express their full outrage at Violette's monstrously ungrateful attack on her devoted parents, or would they think of their own daughters and show some mercy? Did the defense have any aces in the hole? Would Vésinne-Larue finally snap out of his torpor and deliver a convincing plea? Would the sentence be the one that applied in theory to any crime of premeditated parricide—death—or would the jury entertain some possibility that Violette was not entirely or not alone to blame, and spare her the worst?

A verdict and sentence were expected on Friday, October 12, the closing day of the trial.[29] That day the defense was allowed to call "morality witnesses" to the stand, but since the prosecution had already recruited all the major players for their case, Violette's side was left with only her very first boyfriend, Raymond Rierciardelli, who to the audience's delight "could not remember" if he had had sexual relations with her, and a schoolteacher who, instead of creating sympathy, belittled the child she knew long ago. With these last formalities out of the way, pleading by the prosecution and the defense could begin.

Procedure dictated that the opening plea go to the *partie civile* if there was one, with the victim's lawyer speaking first. Maurice Boitel, whose enormous size always triggered in journalists the same clichés ("he looks like a kindly giant") accordingly took the floor. His was a well-defined if somewhat complicated task: he needed all at once to lay to rest for good all of the "calumnies" against the late Baptiste; to salvage something of the party's increasingly quixotic attempt to implicate Dabin in the crime; and at the same time to join his client in requesting mercy for Violette. He acquitted himself competently of his multiple agenda: "Mme Nozière," he intoned, "cannot believe that her daughter carried this out alone; she has always maintained that an accomplice must have counseled, guided, manipulated, and pushed her, and then helped her to dress up the crime as a suicide. In any case, the motive of the crime *is money!* And everything else is a lie!"[30]

Boitel's argument against the incest allegation was lengthy and impassioned, his case for a possible accomplice equally long but considerably less exciting, consisting of twenty-two questions divided into multiple subquestions. Anticipating one of the defense's story lines, Germaine's lawyer insisted that there was nothing wrong with Germaine and Baptiste's ambitions for their daughter. So what if Baptiste dreamed of making his daughter a mathematics teacher? "Let he who has never thought to give his child a better social position than himself cast the first stone!"[31] These were the healthy ambitions of modest folk, but in other quarters the power of money was gnawing away at a corrupt old society. Boitel built up his political-rally-length speech to a peroration in the best Communist tradition: "We are in the midst of a period of transition in which the Old World trembles on its base. . . . Altars and thrones are tottering. . . . We are witnessing, one shudder at a time, the dawning of a New Society in which men will no longer be driven by sordid self-interest, by ferocious self-interest."[32] Stepping back suddenly from the cusp of political apocalypse, Boitel remembered to mention in closing that Germaine had asked the jury to be merciful to her daughter.

Germaine's belated plea for pity for her daughter was a classic case of too little too late, especially delivered in conjunction with her lawyer's lengthy encomia of Baptiste. Merciful dispositions would also likely be challenged by the vehement allocution offered next by the prosecutor Gaudel, who made his intentions clear from the start: "When we have jointly traveled the length of this horrible tragedy, I will ask you, gentlemen of the jury, to return a death penalty against this miserable girl who, not content with killing, has poured upon the grave of her victim, of her own father, a hideous flow of calumnies and lies sprung right from her perverse imagination." Gaudel rehearsed Violette's "life of debauchery," sketching for audience and jury "in a masterful hand the silhouettes of her best-known lovers" except for one, Monsieur Émile, whose existence was now, he noted, proven to have been a complete fiction. There were no accomplices involved, not a single attenuating circumstance. In his concluding remarks, the prosecutor empathized with the jury, explaining that faced with the monstrous crime of this very young girl, he too had had to struggle with the competing demands of "my conscience and my sensibility." But there was a well-established way, he reminded them, of sending a message of ultimate condemnation without having to live with its most dreadful judicial consequence: "Gentlemen of the jury, you know that for fifty years women have no longer gone to the guillotine. Do not hesitate. Do your duty as I did mine."[33]

After a brief recess, the starring role in the proceedings would now devolve to Violette's defense team. How much did the jury know of the political leanings of Violette's lawyers? If the *partie civile* was a mouthpiece for the Communist Party, the defense was made up of lawyers whose sympathies lay on the far right of the political spectrum, although, unlike Boitel, they did not put their political beliefs on display. At the start of the affair, Violette's case had been entrusted by the legal hierarchy to a celebrity of the French bar, Henri Géraud. At sixty-one, Géraud carefully cultivated his image as "the Moses of the bar" by sporting a waist-length split beard; a lifelong bachelor, he never returned home later than six in the evening for fear of causing his mother anxiety. Géraud had initially made his fame in 1919 with his participation in the defense of Raoul Villain, the right-wing nationalist who killed Jean Jaurès; to the disgust of the Left, Villain won acquittal. Géraud was unable to repeat that judicial feat in 1932 when assigned the defense of the presidential assassin Paul Gorguloff, who died on the guillotine. Was it a coincidence that Géraud took on the defense of two men who had murdered prominent Third Republic politicians? After 1940 Géraud collaborated with Pétain's government and faced trial at the end of the war. Although he was acquitted, the stain on his reputation caused him to resign from the Order of Barristers in 1947.[34]

Géraud was at Violette's side for much of the pretrial investigation but withdrew voluntarily from the case in March 1934, for reasons never made clear, leaving the defense in the hands of a much younger colleague, René de Vésinne-Larue.[35] Behind the latter and the other young lawyer who was to join him, Jean Vincey, stood an eminent figure in the legal profession, the sixty-five-year-old Émile de Bruneau de Saint-Auban, who at the time occupied the revolving position of *bâtonnier*, or president, of the order. Saint-Auban's politics were much more conspicuous than Géraud's. Descendant of an ancient aristocratic family, a fervent Catholic nationalist and outspoken anti-Semite, Saint-Auban had first come to prominence at age thirty, when he defended a politician and editor accused of personal attacks on a Jewish government minister, David Raynal. "Yes, he has a burning faith!" Saint-Auban had thundered of his client, "Yes, he is fighting, and will fight, the Jewish moneyed interests!" Saint-Auban later represented France's most famous anti-Semitic writer, Édouard Drumont, voiced virulent opposition to Captain Dreyfus and his supporters, and offered his legal services whenever needed to Catholic orders and organizations, ranting throughout against the evil power of the Jews and Freemasons who had taken over France. Even after World War I, he believed that reconciliation with Germany was possible and desirable because France's hereditary enemy was really Britain. In the years after World War I, Saint-Auban's political activism was less pronounced, though he spoke out frequently against materialism and socialism, became an enthusiastic Wagnerite, and wrote that Hitler was a Christ-like figure, the "German Redeemer."[36]

Émile de Saint-Auban was present in the courtroom throughout Violette's trial but spoke only briefly at the end; mostly, he served as the éminence grise behind the defense team he had set up.[37] Assisting Henri Géraud in the Nozière case was an assignment that could make a beginning lawyer's career, and this plum appointment had been Saint-Auban's to dispense. In early October 1933 the *bâtonnier* entrusted the job of junior counsel in the case to a thirty-year-old lawyer who was serving at the time as his secretary—the equivalent of a law clerk. Naming René de Vésinne-Larue to a coveted role in the cause célèbre of the day reportedly made for a good deal of jealousy among others of his age and stage. The young lawyer made a great show of modesty when questioned by the right-wing weekly *Candide,* explaining that he got the assignment because he happened to be in Paris at the time the case broke in August 1933, while most of his colleagues were on vacation. In cases where nobody else was on hand, it was traditional for the *bâtonnier* to designate a close associate, he said with a smile.[38] That was hardly the whole truth of it, since rivals for the assignment had taken the first train to Paris from their beaches and country homes, only to be crushed with the news that the job was already filled. Vésinne-Larue was not just a close collaborator of the older man but also a distant relative.[39]

Journalists at the trial noted the physical contrast between René de Vésinne-Larue and his opponents in court: Boitel and Gaudel were very big men, whereas Vésinne-Larue, short, slight, and boyish, reportedly looked like a jockey.[40] He spoke loudly in a strange nasal voice, which earned him in the law courts the affectionate nickname "the Duck," and his combination of energy and eccentricity charmed many of his colleagues: "a personality that few will soon forget" was the phrase used in his professional obituary.

Like Géraud, Vésinne-Larue was a lifelong bachelor, except for a marriage that mysteriously ended in midhoneymoon. A brilliant polymath who held advanced degrees in mathematics, economics, and physics and could converse in Latin, he joined the bar in 1931 and was soon singled out by the powerful Saint-Auban. They undoubtedly had a good deal in common, starting with a distant family relationship, aristocratic names, and royalist sympathies: the younger lawyer was obsessed with Marie-Antoinette, as he later would become obsessed with a real-life young, beautiful, and tragic woman. Like Saint-Auban, Vésinne-Larue was a man of the right with strong Catholic leanings; after the war, in which he fought bravely and was wounded, he took pride in his high-profile defense of General Henri Dentz, a Pétainist officer sentenced to death for his collaboration with Axis powers.[41]

The story of Vésinne-Larue's involvement in the Nozière case was to be a remarkable tale of devotion. His family joked that he had a crush on the young woman, and one wonders if he saw himself as a chivalric defender of womanhood in peril, in the mode of the dashing Count Fersen trying to save Marie-Antoinette from the guillotine.[42] In October 1933, Violette wrote a letter to Saint-Auban from prison, asking if she could have permission to give Vésinne-Larue an honorarium to express her gratitude. She was extremely touched by his devotion, particularly the fact that he had recently, despite being extremely ill, made a point of being present to support her during the "confrontation" involving herself, her mother, and Jean Dabin. Even were she allowed to give him money, she wrote, "I will never be able to prove my full gratitude to him, it is so overwhelming."[43] On the eve of the trial, *Paris-Soir* mentioned that Vésinne-Larue had visited her daily in prison throughout her stay.[44]

Vésinne-Larue, only a decade or so older than his client—and younger-looking than his real age—was the mainstay of Violette's defense over fourteen months, with Saint-Auban hovering in the background. At the last minute, he was assigned a colleague, a young man exactly his age, Jean Vincey. Precisely when Vincey was recruited to the case is not clear, but at the trial he told the jurors that he had "entered the affair at the same time as they did."[45] Vincey, one of the original disappointed candidates for the Nozière assignment, also fit the profile of Saint-Auban's young protégés. The son of an agronomist and a lawyer since 1929, Vincey was a young firebrand in the Croix de Feu, an ultranationalist Christian movement with fascist leanings originally made up of World War I veterans. He delivered rousing speeches at rallies, tried with little success to recruit working-class members to the movement, and was put in charge of propaganda by the movement's leader, Colonel de la Rocque.[46] Did Saint-Auban attend a Croix de Feu meeting and hear Vincey speak, or was he merely aware of the young man's reputation as an orator who could hold a crowd of thousands spellbound? Did the older man have doubts about Vésinne-Larue's courtroom abilities? As it turned out, in the contest between these two thirty-year-old lawyers, Vincey did, by all accounts, outshine the man who had devoted much of the last year to Violette Nozière.

During the prosecutor's speech calling for the death penalty, Violette had seemed understandably agitated, and the doctor was once again sent to see to her. The young woman had focused her anxieties on what she called her lucky key, a small rusty object for which she was frantically searching: "It must have fallen under the bench."[47] We are not told whether she found the key, but an ultimate chance for her luck to change was in the offing, since the defense had planned to bring on one last surprise witness before their speeches. The last witness called to the bar was a young man named Paul Ronflard, a student who said he had volunteered to come forward to "free his conscience." His bourgeois pedigree was impeccable, his father serving at the time as the French consul in Warsaw. Ronflard testified that two years earlier, in 1932, Violette had told him explicitly about her father's sexual abuse; he said that other students of his acquaintance knew even more about the matter, and that he was disgusted that they did not have the courage to come forth and testify. Gaudel immediately cast doubt on Ronflard's account—why did he wait so long to share this information?—and the room was soon abuzz with different reactions, audience members arguing among themselves and shouting comments at the officials. The judge called for order so that the defense speeches could start.[48]

It was difficult to predict what tack the defense would take. Since Violette had admitted to murder with premeditation, there was no chance of an acquittal. As the judge's opening remarks made clear, the argument between prosecution and defense would center on the presence of attenuating circumstances. When Violette first made her accusation against her father, hostile journalists had claimed that she was "already preparing her defense." But even proven incest—proven how, one wonders?—would not have outweighed her crime: the French penal code did not officially recognize incest as a crime, and comments about the case in the newspapers mostly inclined to the view that even if were it true, her father's wrongdoing would explain but not excuse her act.[49] Violette's lawyers might argue for the likelihood of the incest claim to establish a strong attenuating circumstance, though blaming the victim would be a high-risk strategy; or they might focus their defense on the defendant's physical and mental health.

The themes that surfaced most conspicuously in the defense's arguments turned out to be neither of those, but issues of class and social ambition. That these matters were very much on some people's minds is suggested by the front-page article by a reporter named Alexis Danan in *Paris-Soir* on the eve of the verdict. The key to the whole case, he wrote, could be found in Violette's fantasies "that she was a student and the daughter of bourgeois." As the reporter proceeded, however, he seemed to be pointing the finger at the tasteless mediocrity of her parents' life: "At home, in her real life, there was a sickening affluence of frugal workers who have paid in small monthly installments for their sewing machine and beaded lampshade, for the pitch-pine mirrored armoire, the radio, and the gold-framed copy of Millet's *Angelus,* and her dream placed her one or two floors above this unpleasant bric-a-brac."[50] Violette's lawyers would evoke her social world as well, looking to free her of some of the blame by pointing beyond her to the background and the parents that made her what she was.

Vésinne-Larue's speech was going to be closely watched, *Le Journal* pointed out, by all those members of the lawyerly confraternity whose "vigilant hatred" had been aroused by his appointment to Violette's defense. Rapidly glossing his speech, the paper reported that Vésinne-Larue had "made an effort that commanded esteem," begging the jury to show indulgence to his client on the grounds that she had been driven to her crime by illness and depression.[51] But for the past two days the papers had been reporting that Vésinne-Larue seemed to be flailing, and others did not even grant the young lawyer *Le Journal*'s belittling praise for "effort." According to *Le Populaire,* Vésinne-Larue faced a difficult task and was not up to it. "This exceptional affair was beyond him. He did make a few sound arguments here and there, but they were lost in the whole of his flaccid speech." *L'Œuvre* lamented that Saint-Auban had done the accused a bad turn by appointing a relative for her defense, and mockingly cited a couple of astoundingly gauche sentences from his speech: "She lost her virginity because she was incompetent," or to the prosecutor, "The defendant is not up to the level of your plea."[52] A later account of the trial reported that those who expected to see the lawyer organize his defense around incest and go into lurid details were disappointed. Instead, Vésinne-Larue argued that Violette never wanted to kill her mother, once again attacked Dr. Truelle's expertise, and made the case that Violette's venereal disease could have had deleterious effects on her psyche. Mostly, though, he stigmatized her parents for their incomprehension of a sensitive child, their lack of vigilance, and the ambition that drove them to try to make her into a "bluestocking." She was just a child, he pleaded; she should be forgiven.[53]

By all accounts, Jean Vincey, who spoke next, utterly stole the show from his colleague. The newspapers fell all over themselves praising his oration. Vincey was "a revelation" said one newspaper, while another commented on his excellent phrasing and voice (no doubt in pleasing contrast to "the Duck").[54] According to *Paris-Midi,* Vincey's performance was enough to establish him as "one of the great young hopes of the courtroom."[55] Like his colleague, Vincey cast doubt on the conclusions of the psychological experts. He skirted the issue of incest by emphasizing instead a general "mystery" about the affair: "I do not believe that Violette Nozière now knows exactly why she killed. . . . I do not understand. There is a mystery here that we do not understand." He too pointed an accusing finger at Violette's parents: her "vain" family was to blame because instead of giving her a proper education (by that he meant appropriate to her class), they made of this sickly child "a wreck floating through the Latin Quarter."[56]

Once Vincey had finished his much admired plea, Saint-Auban got up to speak. Instead of focusing on the defendant, he delivered a speech in praise of his two junior colleagues. It was, as *L'Œuvre* noted in disgust, as if he had given an examination topic to his two best students and was now proceeding to hand out prizes. The elder statesman had shown off his young protégés, and Vincey had delivered a career-making performance. The only one of the three lawyers who cared about the defendant, and cared deeply, had apparently fallen down on the job.

Themes of social class had dominated the end of the trial, possibly by default: nobody wanted to get too close to the matter of incest, especially since the judge had made it clear that he thought it an unseemly matter for discussion in open court. It is tempting to read the courtroom dynamic through the prism of ideology. The Left, in the person of Boitel speaking for Germaine, took the position that Violette was the victim of the young bourgeois rakes who had debauched and exploited her, while Violette's upper-class right-wing defenders argued that her parents should be blamed for having ambitions above their station in life, which unbalanced their fragile offspring. Contemporary reactions and commentaries certainly reflect a general view that the crime was somehow linked to Violette's trajectory, triggered by her parents' ambitions, through the neighborhoods and social worlds of Paris.

The journalist for *Le Populaire* reacted angrily to Vincey's criticism of Violette's parents. "What a mistake! It is in fact a matter of pride in working-class environments to be able to give one's children a higher education." The strength of a nation, he continued, comes from recruiting its leaders from the elite of "the people": look at two recently slain and revered political leaders, President Paul Doumer, son of a construction worker from the south, and Louis Barthou, grandson of a skilled artisan. "It was not the legitimate ambition of the Nozières that ruined Violette," he insisted.[57] But it was precisely their ambition that got under the skin of others, especially members of the literary elites. The American writer Janet Flanner, reporting for the *New Yorker,* indulged in particularly egregious snobbery: "Though her doting parents had educated her over their heads and means in a Paris private school, in her brief career Violette Nozière had learned merely how to drink bad cocktails with penniless collegiates . . . and certainly never met any member of the government until, on trial for parricide, she made the acquaintance of her judge." Reporting for her compatriots on the trial, the cosmopolitan and bisexual Flanner showed no mercy to the upstart Violette: "At the trial it was brought out that she was not only a nympho- but also a mythomaniac—or a natural tart and a born liar."[58] It is likely that Flanner was echoing the judgment of members of the French and expatriate cultural elite with whom she habitually consorted.

The French did not read Flanner's appraisal—written months after the trial, in any event—but many did see the controversial editorial penned by another famous bisexual woman writer, an acquaintance of Flanner's, Colette. Aged sixty at the time, Colette had been since the turn of the century a literary celebrity with a personal life as shocking as her scandalous novels (in addition to her several husbands and her affairs with women, she had in the previous decade engaged in a conspicuous liaison with her teenage stepson).[59] Invited by *L'Intransigeant* to comment on the trial, Colette created a brief blast of controversy with a front-page article that began: "These are little people. Mother and daughter do not hail from some dark underworld but from dreadful, narrow lodgings, the sort of Parisian dwelling that dishonors family intimacy. They come from that hell where beside the conjugal bed a little cot is unfolded at night and put away in the morning." She went on to mock Violette's way of speaking, noting that in calling Émile "my protector," the girl was using the language of "a courtesan of yesteryear," and circled back to the theme that this family did not have enough class to star as the heroes of a real criminal drama: "Little people, unfortunately yes. What a difference with the feral glow, the glamour of the underworld! . . . A mediocre world comfortable with lies, compromises, and reticence."[60]

There was something supremely distasteful about a wealthy and famous woman who had made her name flouting propriety—in her youth Colette had danced on stage practically naked—displaying such contempt for "little people" whose tight living quarters forced them into "hypocrisy" about sex. Louis Laloy, writing in the left-wing paper *L'Ère Nouvelle,* pounced on the expression "little people": "So this family blighted by an atrocious crime is disappointing to her because they lived in a confined space with ready-made furniture from a department store, and therefore could not play their roles as expansively as required by the drama in which they were actors? What did they lack that they failed to find words and gestures appropriate to the situation?" Surely, he went on, the home of a railway worker was less impressive than the fancy hotels and studios where some people lounged around with their famous cats, but for "little people," the strenuous saving that produced a clock, an armchair, or a vase invested such objects with a wealth of meaning. And maybe one would voluntarily forgo a larger apartment to give a child the education that ensured access to a decent life.[61] Her snobbery exposed, Colette immediately reversed course, offering a contorted and unconvincing explanation that she had really meant *chetit* rather than *petit,* an expression from the patois of her native province that referred to criminality rather than class.[62]

Themes of class apparently came to the fore, then, at the conclusion of the trial, as various commentators joined Violette's lawyers in decrying the mediocrity of the Nozière household and the family's unseemly ambitions, while others protested that the railway worker and his wife represented all that was decent and admirable in the patterns of social mobility of the time. Arguments about class seemed to have displaced debate about whether or not Baptiste Nozière had violated his daughter, a matter the judge had early on declared unmentionable.

It turns out, however, that newspapers failed to report on what really transpired in the courtroom. The very brief accounts in the press of Vésinne-Larue's unsuccessful defense of his client completely obscured the fact that he actually did mount a detailed argument that Violette was the victim of her father's sexual abuse. The lawyer's speech was published the year after the trial in a legal periodical edited by Saint-Auban himself, which carried the pleas delivered in famous court cases. Like his colleague Vincey, like Flanner and Colette, Vésinne-Larue had sounded themes of misplaced ambition in his speech. What did Violette get from her parents? "Contempt for her own status, honorable as it was, a conceited desire to vault oneself into some kind of bourgeois existence, the focus of their every effort." The three of them lived in a space devoid of privacy, where promiscuity took the place of hygiene, but there was a bookcase full of literature and mathematics textbooks because these people wanted their daughter to be a bluestocking, a *fille savante.* "Nothing," he continued, "would ever daunt her parents' ambition."[63]

But Vésinne-Larue did not just intend, as Vincey and others did, to ask for compassion for a young girl pushed too hard and too far by her parents. He also drew a careful and convincing picture of the psychological dynamics of the household and highlighted all the elements in the case that made the incest charge plausible. Violette's parents, he argued, were hardly the paragons some people described. Germaine, the lawyer pointed out, rarely went out or spoke to anybody, and neighbors described her as a strange, conceited, and volatile woman. As for Baptiste, his own father led a scandalous private life, and he himself was strangely tolerant of his daughter's notorious liaisons with men. Why? Why did he never stop her? What secret made it impossible for him to object to Violette's loose morals? The prosecution had justly praised Pierre Camus as the only decent and trustworthy young man among Violette's acquaintances. Why, then, did they not give credence to what he actually said? Was it not notable that he had extracted her confession about the incest from her with great difficulty, when she was in a state of profound depression and unlikely to be telling tales for her own advantage?

Turning to the eve of the crime, Vésinne-Larue, emulating a mystery-novel writer, assembled all the facts into a new and very plausible explanation of events. Violette insisted that she had told her father in July about her love for Dabin and her plans to marry him, and that Baptiste had responded that he would not let her go. Unfortunately, only she could testify to that conversation. But why not believe her, and accept that it was at this stage that hatred for her monstrous father had turned to murderous intent? Skeptics pointed to the evening of the crime and asked why Violette would have gone through with her criminal plans when her parents had just assented to an engagement. The lawyer laid out his interpretation of what had happened on August 21, 1933. Why, he asked, had the parents suddenly discovered Violette's correspondence with Jean? Baptiste knew she was planning to leave town, knew the real reason why, and wanted to stop her. It was he, no doubt, who instigated the search of her belongings for evidence of a liaison, which duly turned up. Baptiste knew that his wife would either put a stop to the relationship or insist that the young people get engaged and married. But Dabin, only twenty years old and having not yet carried out his military service, would not likely welcome an engagement. (Vésinne-Larue did not even mention, perhaps because he did not know it, the detail that Baptiste had insisted that the Dabins be told of Violette's venereal disease.) The likely outcome of the scene was the end of Violette and Jean's relationship and closer scrutiny by Germaine of her daughter's outside activities—exactly what the possessive incestuous father wanted.[64]

Vésinne-Larue also challenged the financial motive for the crime by reminding the jury of the very plausible case for the existence of a real Monsieur Émile. What about all those who saw the couple—the floor manager at the Hotel Moderne where they met, the waiter who exactly described the menu of their lunch on August 17, just as Violette remembered it? What about the letter signed "Émile" that arrived at Les Sables d'Olonne, where she was supposed to go on vacation? What about Violette's insistence to Jean that she could get money for a car from her "aunt," the same aunt she always met in a hotel? He then tried another angle: was it likely that she would kill her parents for money if she knew that she could not inherit for another three years? The only explanation that made sense of all the facts of the case was the one Violette had offered: that her new love for Jean had made the horror of her situation with her father untenable. The only thing that explained her act was a horrific symmetry: "The excuse for this crime against nature is that it was triggered by a violation of the laws of nature."[65]

None of these arguments were reported in the press, which embraced Vincey's performance and his conclusion that the case would ever be a "mystery" as the far superior defense of the two, and dismissed Vésinne-Larue's speech as rambling and "flaccid" without mentioning its content.[66] Three years later, after Vésinne-Larue's plea was published, a prominent academic who had been present at the trial wrote to L'Œuvre to complain that it, along with all other newspapers, had failed to report on the lawyer's explicit argument about sexual abuse.[67] Throughout the trial, incest was a subject that was not to be mentioned. When it was brought up by

Violette's defender, the issue was expunged from the newspaper coverage, just as the Surrealists' volume had been seized by the police. The consensus in the press was that despite Vincey's fine speech, Violette's defense had been a fiasco, and that behind Vésinne-Larue's failure was the vanity of the old *bâtonnier* Saint-Auban, who cared more about dispensing perks to his young acolytes than he did about the fate of the young defendant.[68]

Once the last speech for the defense was over, things went very fast.[69] Violette, asked if she had anything to say, answered: "I ask for forgiveness, and I thank my mother for forgiving me." The jury withdrew to deliberate and came back after barely one hour with a verdict that they announced to the court in the absence of the accused: they unanimously found the defendant guilty of parricide with premeditation, with no attenuating circumstances. The verdict carried an automatic sentence of death. The judge called Violette back into the room and read the details of her punishment, the death penalty modified by an archaic ceremonial reserved for parricides, following article thirteen of France's penal code: the condemned was to be put to death "in one of the public places of the City of Paris," having been led to the place of execution "in a shift, barefoot, head covered by a black veil" and exposed to the public as a bailiff read the sentence.[70] Violette showed no reaction when she heard the verdict and the sentence. She rose to leave, and Vésinne-Larue approached her with a sheet of paper, asking her to sign the petition for an appeal, which had to be filed within three days.

At that moment, Violette's self-control fell apart. "No!" she shrieked, as her lawyer pressed her to sign. As the tension of the three previous days finally broke, Violette became a fury: "Leave me alone! You're a bunch of bastards, you have no shame! . . . You're without pity! I told the truth! To hell with my father! To hell with my mother!" Suddenly feral, she struggled with the guards, flailing around, until she was finally forced out of the room. A few minutes later, still furious, she regained her composure and shook the guards off: "Do you think I can't walk? And what about my handbag, what did you do with it?" A few minutes later, she had calmed down enough to sign the appeal. Most newspapers commented that she had shown her true face at the end.

Outside the courtroom, Violette was rapidly ushered into a car that was to take her back to La Petite Roquette. Jean Dabin watched her get in and, turning to Willy, remarked, "Well, she always wanted her own car and now she has it." Willy stared at him and said, "You bastard." Still, they went off together to share a drink.[71]

On the face of it, the trial forced the Nozière affair back into the mode of melodrama. Trials are by their very nature melodramatic: they take complicated events with messy motivations and force them into simple, clashing story lines. The dynamics of the courtroom often wring overwrought performances from participants, as this trial did with Violette's and Germaine's histrionics and the judge's paternalistic show of outrage at Jean Dabin. Adding to the coutroom's radical simplification of the case was the fact that the trial was dominated by a prosecution closely allied with both the investigating magistrate, Lanoire, and the presiding courtroom judge, Peyre. On the other side, the two thirty-year-olds assigned to the defense, one of them recruited at the last minute, were hard pressed to stand up to the phalanx of senior professionals who peremptorily declared Monsieur Émile a fiction and ruled the incest allegation unmentionable.

Violette was denied extenuating circumstances by a jury not of her peers but of her father's peers, and judges and prosecutors did their best to declare the matter over and done with. Their very efforts at shaping the story suggest that the case would not so easily come to rest. René Vésinne-Larue gave no ground in a courageous plea that failed to resonate in the courtroom and was glossed over in the press. What people did read about, the defense's argument that the crime could be traced back to the unseemly ambitions of "little people," touched off an ultimate round of debate. The story of Violette in the years after the verdict suggests that for many people the clarity of the death sentence in no way resolved the ambiguities of the Nozière affair.

# TEN

# *Afterlives*

VIOLETTE WAS NOT TO DIE on the scaffold, and neither did the prison doors close on her forever. The October 12 verdict was the prelude to three further decades of a life marked by remarkable ironies. While it was generally assumed that France's most notorious female criminal would not be executed, it is safe to say that in 1934 nobody could have predicted how Violette's story would end.

Back in La Petite Roquette after the trial, alone in her cell, Violette must have been scared. Yes, women sentenced to death had been spared the guillotine for fifty years, but who could be certain that the tradition would hold in every case? Violette had heard crowds baying for her blood, listened to prosecutors telling her that nothing could possibly mitigate the sheer evil of her crime, perhaps even read or heard of the occasional article arguing that in her case the customary mercy toward the fair sex should for once not prevail. And though in many instances presidential decisions to commute a sentence were rendered quickly, in her case it took two and a half agonizing months, from the end of her trial to Christmas eve, for confirmation that she would escape the blade of "the widow" *(la veuve)*, the legendary machine of death.

As soon as the trial concluded, a process of both formal and informal appeals began, not to dispute the guilty verdict but to plead for a commutation of the death sentence. Both Violette's mother and her lawyer petitioned the authorities. Germaine wrote to the president of the Republic, Albert Lebrun, on October 22, obsessing as always about the man she held truly responsible for the crime: "The dossier before your eyes, M. le Président, will shed light on the infamous suggestions that led my daughter to satisfy by any means the monetary demands of *Jean Dabin*." In mid-December, Vésinne-Larue requested a personal audience with the president (there is no indication whether it was granted), and Violette herself wrote a sober note to the man who held her fate in his hands: "I had just turned eighteen when I committed the acts that resulted in my guilty verdict; I was not able to resist bad influences and did not fully understand the evil I was doing." Letters to President Lebrun came in from abroad, either produced spontaneously or perhaps solicited by supporters of Violette who assumed that the president would be especially sensitive to France's reputation in other countries. A young American girl named Markela Smallard, who had seen a newspaper photograph of the trial, wrote from Los Angeles in the name of her fellow students: "If a country like France, many years older than our own country, can go back in a few seconds' time—forty years—to the barbarous process of guillotining a woman, nay, a mere girl of eighteen, what is the rest of the world to think?" A man from Switzerland wrote to France's minister of justice, that he had felt "indignation and shame" upon learning that Violette Nozière had been sentenced to death. "I do not know," he continued, "what is being said in other countries, but here in Switzerland Violette Nozière's judges have very bad press, especially among women." He pointed out that the last two famous French murderesses, Germaine Berton and Germaine d'Anglemont, had both been acquitted.[1]

Even the men who had sought the death penalty for Violette appealed to the relevant authorities to request that the sentence not be carried out. On October 26, the principal judge of the Assizes Court wrote to the minister of justice. He detailed Violette's horrible crime, for which she had offered, he said, only "vague and diverse explanations," but added that there were some "slight excuses" for what she had done, such as bad health and poor parental supervision, and that the jury had convicted her to give an example, while firmly believing that the death sentence would not be carried out. The men of the jury had themselves already appealed in unison to the president three days after the trial, asking that the sentence be commuted. Prosecutor Gaudel addressed his petition to the head of the Court of Appeals, which was due to make a recommendation to the president. He too fulminated against Violette's evil ways and spent part of his letter disproving her incest allegations, but he nonetheless concluded that execution would not be advisable in the case of someone who was "almost a child": "While I energetically pursued the harshest of verdicts, I cannot really demand that [the sentence] be carried out." Although all of these men wanted to see Violette shamed and punished, they also sought to make sure that they would not be responsible for the shocking spectacle of a female execution.[2] After weeks of bureaucratic process, the Ministry of Justice recommended, on December 18, that Violette's sentence be commuted from death to lifelong prison labor. It would fall to the president of the Republic, the same man whose train Violette's father had once driven, to act upon the recommendation.

Granting pardons was, in fact, one of the very few things a French president could do under the set of laws that had reformed government in 1875. If the names of Third Republic presidents are obscure, it is because the function was mostly ceremonial: presidents were elected to a seven-year term, not by the people of France but by the Senate and Chamber, and beyond appointing ministers and having the right to dissolve the Chamber in extreme circumstances, they exercised no real power.[3] As a result, very few people today remember the name of Albert Lebrun even though he presided over a period in French history that included the Stavisky affair and February 6 riots, the Popular Front, the Phony War, and the French defeat of June 1940. A farmer's son with engineering credentials, aged sixty-one when he became president, Lebrun had diligently worked his way up the political ladder since winning election to a district council in his home province at age twenty-seven, and was hastily elevated from his position as president of the Senate in 1932 when the head of state, Paul Doumer, was assassinated. A contemporary English journalist described Lebrun as "an earnest, well-meaning, and highly educated man—a *Polytechnicien*—with a hatred for political intrigues." He had refused to pardon Doumer's obviously insane assassin Gorguloff (even though, as wags remarked, he owed the man his job) and in general resisted clemency in capital cases. Nonetheless, the president was an affable family man who courted popularity in the summer of 1933 by dancing around a maypole with little girls at a local fête and ostentatiously offering money for bike repair to a cyclist who accidentally knocked him down.[4] He was hardly the sort of politician who was likely to invite controversy by sending an attractive young girl to the guillotine. On December 24, 1934, Violette and Vésinne-Larue received telegrams informing them that her death sentence had been commuted by the president's will to life in prison.

There is no record of how Violette reacted to her reprieve from the death penalty. All we know is that shortly thereafter, in the heart of winter, she was sent far away from Paris and everything she knew to the country's largest long-term correctional institution for women, the Maison Centrale of Haguenau in Alsace. The only thing central about the prison was its name: its location was about as far from the center of France as you could get, thirty miles north of Strasbourg and very close to the German border, an area that the French and Germans had been grabbing back and forth in the wake of wars for over two centuries. Whether or not this was intended, the prison's site seemed to send a message to inmates that they no longer belonged in France.

In Haguenau, women from all over France serving life sentences inhabited a large featureless structure built as a hospital in the late eighteenth century and converted to a prison in 1822. The Maison Centrale housed about two hundred of the country's most egregious female criminals, In late December the building must have been both dark and cold. Four years earlier, the writer Francis Carco had evoked the deep gloom of the Haguenau prison in a series on women's jails he wrote for *Détective*. He described a huge central space criss-crossed with iron staircases and gangways along which silent inmates shuffled, dressed in shapeless long gray dresses, shawls, and bonnets. Under the supervision of nuns, they caned chairs, sorted threads, and sewed. Carco visited a seventy-eight-year-old woman, incarcerated for life for killing her abusive husband with an axe and terrified that they would take her to the infirmary to die, and witnessed another woman begging to be let out of the frigid punishment cell in the basement where she had been locked up for talking back to a nun. Even allowing for some journalistic exaggeration, the picture of the cavernous jail with weak "rust-colored light" struggling to get through the few windows is a dismal one.[5]

In response to questions from Violette's legal guardian in January 1935, the director of the Haguenau prison was quick to advise his correspondent not to believe the sensational portrayal of the place in "some articles published in the press like the recent one in *Paris-Soir*." He specified that inmates could be sent both money and articles of clothing as long as these were gray or black, and that visits were allowed once a month from eleven to twelve and three to five on a Sunday. Violette received visits from both her mother and Vésinne-Larue, although these were rare, given the prison's distance from Paris. Prisoners also earned wages for their work, six to fourteen francs a day, half of which was put away for their release, although in most cases some or all of the money would go to paying court costs.[6] Even with a few francs to stave off misery by purchasing extra rations of sugar, coffee, or chocolate, the prospect of spending one's life or even a large chunk of it in this grim institution on the cold northeastern frontier of France must have been a horrible one.

Once the doors of Hagueneau closed on Violette, she should have disappeared from view, her story now concluded—but she did not. Quite aside from the efforts of her few supporters, journalists and editors had discovered over the course of eighteen months that the name Violette Nozière sold newspapers. Mysteries in the case remained unsolved, and every intimation that the key to the affair had finally been discovered could be profitably splashed across a front page. In the early months of 1936, for instance, the staff at Le Journal became convinced that they had finally discovered Monsieur Émile, although he was inconveniently dead. In November 1933, a sixtyish man, a wealthy industrialist from Paris, had apparently committed suicide by leaping off a cliff in a northern seaside town. (In an incongruous Magritte-like gesture, he had jumped holding an open umbrella.) The name of this man was . . . Émile Violette. Suddenly, it all made sense. Germaine and Baptiste had invested a lot of money in a bar right after they got married. Where did they get the funds, and why were there rumors at the time in Neuvy that the couple had a "benefactor"? Why did they call their daughter Violette? Why did the industrialist take his life at this time, even though his business was doing well, if not because of distress over a case that would surely soon implicate him? A journalist traveled to Haguenau to show Violette a picture of the deceased, which she recognized, albeit with some hesitation. In the presence of the prison director and a nun, Violette then went on to explain that Baptiste himself had once, when he was pressing himself upon her, insisted that he could do so because he was not her biological father, informing her that Germaine was several months pregnant when they wed. The prisoner recalled being told by her family that the priest in Neuvy had resisted christening her Violette, not a proper saint's name in his view, and that her mother had insisted, saying that the name had been chosen in honor of "a woman friend she had known in a factory where she had worked."[7] The story of this new Émile caused excitement and then died down, either quashed or disproved.

Sometimes external events rather than journalistic sleuthing caused a flurry of renewed interest in the case. Two such events occurred in 1937. The first was the serialized publication of the memoirs of Superintendent

Marcel Guillaume in *Paris-Soir.* Guillaume's already high profile had been raised further in the wake of the Stavisky case, when he was asked to head the committee that investigated the mysterious death of the magistrate Albert Prince, who believed that Stavisky had been murdered by the police. (Guillaume's August 1934 report had concluded that Prince's death was a suicide, angering many on the right who wanted to believe in a political assassination.)[8] Guillaume, the iconic old-time "good cop," retired from his job in January 1937 amid much fanfare in the newspapers. He explained to *Détective* that over the course of his career of investigating high-profile crime, he had seen a shift from the good old-fashioned bandit, the working-class gangsters who took their chances and took responsibility, to a postwar "more complicated, refined, and diabolical criminal," the middle-class Dabins and Violette Nozières of this world. Following his train of thought, he returned to his conversation with Violette the night she was arrested, when she had asked him whether he had children and could understand. "Yes, said Guillaume, but they are good children— That must be, the poor girl sobbed, because you behave like a good father to them."[9]

Readers whose curiosity had been whetted by this preview could read the full account of Guillaume's conversation with Violette after her arrest when it was published in the March 21, April 1, and April 2 editions of *Paris-Soir.* Since Guillaume's credibility was at its highest, his assertion that he was certain she was not lying that night when she broke down and told him of the incest carried considerable weight. Readers also learned of Guillaume's anomalous exclusion from the courtroom: "During the long days of the trial, I waited in the halls of the Palais de Justice, ready to testify and to share with these men whose sacred duty it was to judge a human being my certainty that Violette was telling the truth."[10] Such was the impact of Guillaume's memoir that *L'Œuvre,* always the newspaper most supportive of Violette's version of events, started running articles which argued that the case should be brought back to trial: "Is it too late to return to this forgotten affair? We do not think so. At Haguenau a girl is locked up for life." Guillaume's testimony, the paper argued, constituted the "new information" that was technically necessary to reopen an adjudicated case. In a clear reference to the Dreyfus case, an editorial posed the question: "Revision? Why not? No injustice must remain without redress."[11]

Nothing came from this first flurry of interest in reopening the case, nor of a second one later that year that followed another development: the return to Paris of Jean Dabin. On September 17, *Le Journal* revealed that Dabin had been shipped back to Paris from Algeria gravely ill, and was being cared for at the Val-de-Grâce military hospital at the southern end of the Latin Quarter. The newspaper published an interview with him under the headline: "Jean Dabin, Burning with Fever, Remembers . . ." The journalist claimed that when he had interviewed Violette in 1936, she uttered the following words, which sound remarkably like a film script: "If by chance in the course of your adventurous life as a journalist you should run into Jean Dabin, tell him that I have thought of him always, that I will never forget him. . . . Promise you will, Monsieur, promise you will!" When he was able to carry out his promise and visited Jean in hospital, the latter, looking aged and racked by fever, also sounded suspiciously scripted: " 'Violette,' murmured Jean Dabin, 'Yes, all that goes far back, so far back. In the army I did all I could to forget her. . . . Well, Monsieur, all my efforts to forget her were useless. I can confess to you that I have never stopped thinking of her." Dabin confirmed that Monsieur Émile did indeed exist. "Then, his eyes closed, large pearls of sweat breaking out on his brow, he murmured, speaking to himself as if I had already left, 'Violette.' "[12] You can almost hear the music and see the credits rolling. But Dabin was indeed terminally ill and died on October 27, 1937, his dismally notorious life cut short in his midtwenties.

In the wake of Dabin's death, *L'Œuvre* again upped its campaign to reopen the case, and *Paris-Soir* reported that a clemency measure might be in the works.[13] In October and November 1937, capitalizing on recent events, Germaine Nozière and René de Vésinne-Larue had begun a series of petitions to the Ministry of Justice and the president himself for a pardon. They produced medical certificates to the effect that Violette's health was declining in prison and pointed out that her conduct there had been exemplary. Germaine wrote to the president in July 1938 explaining that, having spoken at length to her daughter, she was convinced that Violette's guilt was far less than she had believed (though she stopped short of giving details), and begging him to reduce her sentence to ten years in prison. Yet another little girl from Switzerland sent the president a letter begging him as a family man to release Violette to her mother. Germaine claimed, and persistent rumor had it, that Dabin had made revelations before he died, but after an official inquiry into the matter concluded that Dabin did not talk to anyone at Val-de-Grâce, the prosecutor general opined in August 1938 that it was too soon and the crime was too serious for a pardon.[14]

By 1938 international developments were making it increasingly difficult for officials to focus on anything as mundane as the revision of the verdict in a domestic crime. In March of that year Hitler's troops entered Vienna as the French Popular Front collapsed. The new French Premier, Édouard Daladier, oversaw a government intent on conservative revenge that recognized General Franco's fascist regime in Spain even as it cracked down on trade unionists and Communists at home. As Czechoslovakia and then Poland fell to the Nazis, France braced itself for a war that, though officially declared in September 1939, seemed never to come. It was not until May 1940 that Hitler launched his *Blitzkrieg* through northern Europe. On June 14, the Germans were in Paris and on June 17 the new French leader, eighty-four-year-old Marshal Pétain, recognized the French defeat before withdrawing to run his government from the spa town of Vichy in the southern unoccupied zone.

These momentous international developments were to have significant effects on Violette's life, first directly, then indirectly. Their immediate upshot was her departure from Haguenau. The prison was in a war zone, and in the spring of 1940 the female prisoners and staff were evacuated and shipped due west across the country to a jail in Rennes, the ancient capital of Brittany.[15] (The Rennes prison, a large hexagonal structure surrounded by formal gardens, had opened its doors in 1870, the very first building erected in France specifically as a jail for long-term female prisoners.) The other effect of the new situation was less immediate but in the long run even more important: the advent of Pétain's Christian and conservative French State would, oddly enough, prove beneficial to the notorious parricide.

Over her short life, Violette had inhabited several personas: she had been the adored and docile only child, the angry and rebellious teenager, the elegant, enigmatic city woman, the tragic defendant. Once incarcerated, she was reborn as the pious, repentant model prisoner. At the time of her death, a biographical account in a leading magazine dated her transformation from her arrival at Haguenau: "That was the beginning of the miracle—the resurrection! as the prison chaplain was to put it. What exactly happened? It is hard to say because prisons—and nuns—guard their secrets closely. But the demonic girl, the rebel who attacked the wardens, insulted the nuns, and fought with her fellow prisoners suddenly became gentle, obedient, and helpful."[16] Her "rebirth" was certainly apparent at Hagueneau in 1938. In the context of Germaine's campaign for a pardon that year, reports and correspondence about her from prison officials were all extremely positive, peppered with phrases like "exemplary conduct," "excellent morality," "diligent worker," and "gives entire satisfaction." In February 1939 a lawyer named Emmanuel Thiebauld wrote to the prison director asking to pay a personal visit to Violette Nozière: he was going to talk about her in an upcoming lecture and wanted to give his listeners a firsthand account of Violette's "spiritual renewal."[17]

Since many detainees need the comfort of religion in prison and experience religious conversions while incarcerated, it would be rash to suggest that Violette's change of heart was calculated, especially since it took place in an environment where religious figures like nuns and chaplains loomed large and her new disposition endured over the course of many years. Her docility and embrace of religion while behind bars were more likely further instances of her lifelong tendency to imitate those she looked up to.

It was Violette's good fortune, however, that her embrace of the Catholic faith while in prison coincided with the advent of a political regime that prized exactly such dispositions. The defeat of 1940 caused the collapse of the Third Republic and its replacement by the Pétainist French State whose social and cultural program was a "National Revolution" devoted to the rebirth all those values and institutions spurned by Republicans. Central to the ideology of the Vichy regime was the promotion of church and family as a remedy for decades of Republican "degeneration." The French State boosted families by increasing child support, restricting divorce, and making abortion punishable by death: in 1943, for the first time in sixty years the guillotine was used on a woman, for providing abortions. Under Vichy every young man in France had to spend eight months in an austere rural Youth Workshop (*Chantier de Jeunesse*) unlearning decadent city ways. Catholicism regained pride of place in the schools, where children recited a new version of the Lord's Prayer in praise of Marshal Pétain: "Our Father / Who art our leader / Hallowed be thy name." Many in the Catholic hierarchy eagerly embraced a regime more supportive of their aims than any had been in generations.[18]

It might seem that the Vichy authorities, if they even had time to consider such matters, might be far less inclined than their predecessors to show mercy to a depraved city girl who had poisoned her parents and made unspeakable accusations against her father. But in fact a tale of moral decay followed by religious regeneration was the exact equivalent, on a personal level, of the Vichy regime's historical self-understanding. More concretely, it would now be easier for René de Vésinne-Larue, a man of the right with royalist and Catholic leanings, to get a hearing from those in power.

Even prior to the "National Revolution," Violette's supporters had already been trying to get her out of prison with the promise that if freed she would join a religious order. In February 1939, in anticipation of the end of Lebrun's term as president, Germaine wrote to the president's wife as a "poor mamma" asking for mercy for her "poor little girl," explaining that her daughter had been accepted to enter the convent of the Dominican nuns of Béthanie; Germaine would go and live with her there too if the president were to extend a pardon before leaving office.[19]

The Dominican convent had undoubtedly been asked to extend their invitation to the repentant sinner by a man whose influence would be decisive in Violette's life. Either on his own or through Saint-Auban, Vésinne-Larue had made contact with a prominent figure in the world of French Catholicism, Antonin-Dalmace Sertillanges, and interested him in Violette's fate. In his late seventies during the Vichy years, Sertillanges had joined the Dominican Order at age twenty and pursued a career as an intellectual, becoming one of the most prominent Catholic philosophers of his generation. A specialist on Aquinas, Sertillanges, whose works are still read today, became a member of France's most elite learned society, the Academy of Moral and Political Sciences, in 1918. Vésinne-Larue got Germaine to write letters to the eminent churchman and help convince him to throw his weight behind an appeal to reduce Violette's sentence. Sertillanges filed a *recours en grâce* in late 1941, testifying that the young girl had undergone a "radical transformation" and explaining that even though Violette herself was keen to "expiate" her sin in prison, she could do so much more productively in the Béthanie convent.

The prosecutor general initially opposed such a measure in view of the seriousness of the crime, but Sertillanges had a trump card: excellent access to a man far more influential than himself. In his petition he mentioned that the minister of justice was favorable to clemency, "and the Marshal as well": for the past twenty-two years, Philippe Pétain had been a fellow of Sertillanges' at the Academy of Moral and Political Sciences. At the end of 1941, Father Jean Courtois, superior of the Dominican Order, asked authorities for permission to visit Violette Nozière in prison "before going to Vichy." On August 26, 1942, by order of Marshal Pétain, Violette's prison sentence was reduced from life to twelve years. She would be released in 1945.[20] In a mere nine years Violette had traveled from serving as antifamily heroine to the Surrealists to being an object of concern and sympathy to the elite—conservative lawyers, Catholic leaders, the old Marshal himself—of modern France's most reactionary regime.

Violette spent France's "dark years" in prison, her life probably changing less than the lives of most of her fellow citizens. A prison report at the end of 1943 specified that while her health was still poor, her conduct gave entire satisfaction, as did her "docile temperament"—a description that would have astonished anyone who knew her in the early 1930s. By 1943, however, the plan for Violette to enter a Dominican convent had apparently been aborted, having presumably served its purpose in securing her freedom: a prison memorandum, addressing her postrelease means of support, anticipated that she would go and live in Neuvy-sur-Loire with her mother, who had settled there.[21] That plan too was eventually scrapped, since both women must have realized that life in Neuvy, where everyone knew her story, would be untenable for Violette. Her best chance for remaining anonymous would be to reside in a big city, which was exactly what the authorities forbade: a decree of March 30, 1944, established that she would be prohibited for a period of twenty years from living in Paris and the surrounding areas, in Lyon, Bordeaux, Marseille, Lille, Strasbourg, and half a dozen other towns, or even in the larger cities of French Algeria.[22]

France's liberation preceded Violette's by a year. On August 26, 1944, General de Gaulle triumphantly marched down the Champs-Élysées as the head of a newly freed nation. On August 29, 1945, the twelfth anniversary of the day the police had picked her up in the café near the Eiffel Tower, Violette left the prison in Rennes surreptitiously in the middle of the night. Her supporters had been worried that de Gaulle's government would rescind judicial measures taken by Vichy, but Violette's release went ahead on schedule. Germaine had requested a nighttime exit from the prison to avoid publicity but was still unable to dodge an interest in the famous criminal, which even the war years had not extinguished. In early September 1945, Germaine wrote a plaintive letter to Vésinne-Larue, begging him to take steps to have the residency restrictions lifted. Her daughter, she wrote, upon leaving the prison in Rennes, "had to hide for three days to escape the journalists and public curiosity." Germaine wanted to conceal her daughter from the press at the home of a cousin, a concierge in Paris. The faithful Vésinne-Larue acted fast, and by mid-October the restrictions had been suspended. Violette could now once more live in Paris.[23]

The prisoner from Rennes could never be Violette Nozière again. When she moved in with her cousin Mme Soret—a member of the Desbouis clan from Neuvy—on Boulevard Jourdan at the very southern end of Paris, she used her mother's name, Germaine Hézard. (Germaine was Violette's middle name, but her choice of identity hints at the complicated symbiosis that had always connected mother and daughter.) It was under the latter name that she enrolled in Paris's famous Pigier school for secretary-typists on September 10, 1945; the story of her youth repeated itself the following spring, as she fell ill and had to drop the course. But the former Violette had other plans and would soon have no need for her mother's name. In prison she had met the man she was to marry, and she was about to move into her life's final incarnation, as a wife and mother.

In the Rennes prison, Violette had put her strong mathematical skills to use by working as an accountant for the prison bursar, and in the context of her work she had gotten to know her boss's son, a divorced man named Pierre Coquelet. They fell in love and planned to wed after her release. Violette could not have imagined getting married anywhere but Neuvy, but after the engaged couple posted their banns at the town hall there on November 1, 1946, somebody scrawled "Murderer!" across the notice. The marriage still took place in her mother's village, but the ceremony was held in the darkness of a late December afternoon, after which the couple quickly departed in a rental car. The following June, a newspaper caught the Coquelets as they returned to Neuvy with their three-month-old daughter, Michèle (like her mother, the bride was pregnant when she wed), this time encountering no problems. Violette was heavier and wore eyeglasses and bright clothing; her husband, a beefy man, was dressed in black. Germaine took a break from her work doing laundry and mending clothes for a local farmer so as to tend to her granddaughter while Violette bowed her head over her father's pink granite tombstone. Violette at Baptiste's grave? Neuvy had opened its arms again to its errant child. The Desbouis family closed ranks behind uncle Auguste as he shooed away the press: "She's paid for her fault. Now she's a good mother and wife, let her get on with her life in peace. And since her mother has forgiven her, why would you want to be more royalist than the king?"[24]

Violette was not to repeat her parents' single-child strategy. Even by the standards of the postwar baby boom, her zeal for giving birth was remarkable: between 1947 and 1959, she and Pierre had five children. (Violette's ease in producing so many children in quick succession casts further doubt on her 1933 syphilis diagnosis, since women afflicted with that disease frequently miscarry.) The couple lived briefly in the heart of Paris, on Rue Saint-Antoine, in a two-room apartment. Violette worked as a secretary for an organization of Christian students, her husband as a cook. After the birth of their second child, Germaine joined them as they began a series of moves through the drab working-class suburbs around the city: Vitry, Clamart, Pavillons-sous-Bois. The couple, their growing family, and Violette's mother lived in modest villas and managed a grocery store, then a café and hotel. A photograph published in a newspaper from that time shows Violette looking very different from her old self: her face is round, almost plump, and she wears a demure white blouse and heavy-framed glasses, her hair permed and piled high in the fashion of the forties. Between the babies and the demands of running small businesses, life must not have been easy. Then tragedy struck in 1950, when Pierre was hit by a bus and sustained injuries that left him permanently handicapped. With the help of his invalid's pension, the French state's generous allowances for large families, and Germaine's income as a railway widow, the family was able to buy a business in a small town near Rouen, a café and restaurant that catered mainly to truckers. Through all these relocations, Violette's true identity was never known to anyone, neither to the neighbors, with whom she entertained excellent relations, nor to the patrons of her restaurant, who would have been startled to learn that lunches and dinners were being served to them by the most famous poisoner in France.[25]

In 1952, with the help of René de Vésinne-Larue, who had remained a friend of the family, Violette began a campaign for *réhabilitation,* pursuing a legal status that restored full civil rights to a condemned criminal, such that their former juridical status no longer appeared on any official documents. Unlike the "revision" of a sentence, which, as in the case of Alfred Dreyfus, declared the person innocent on the basis of new evidence, juridical rehabilitation acknowledged that former criminals had fulfilled all the conditions for reintegration into society: they had served their time, had been out of prison for at least five years, had paid the court costs, and were leading a responsible life.[26] Violette maintained that she sought this status for the sake of her children. She wanted to keep them ignorant of her past, and for that to be possible all traces of the crime needed to be expunged. Twenty years after her crime, however, Violette's name remained famous, and journalists were on hand when she made her way to the court in Rouen to file her petition. They snapped photos of her, but Violette had carefully concealed her features by wearing a broad-brimmed hat and wrapping a scarf around her face.[27]

Violette's first petition was unsuccessful, but she struggled for another ten years, through yet another tragedy, the death of her husband in 1961.

René de Vésinne-Larue pleaded the case before the Court of Appeals in Rouen. *Le petit Vésinne,* as his colleagues still called him, had made of Violette's fate the central cause of his life, and when rehabilitation came through in 1963 it was a landmark in French judicial history: the first time a person given the death sentence had been restored to full civil rights. "This proves," Vésinne declared, "that as low as a human being might have sunk, one should never give up on him. The life of Violette Nozière is a story of redemption, and that redemption is the best plea ever conceived against the death penalty."[28]

The basis for the decision is not known, but the passage of time and respect for Vésinne-Larue's devotion must have played a part. It is unlikely that the sudden appearance of yet another avatar of Monsieur Émile played any role in the matter. In 1963 *France-Soir* reported that Violette's first petition ten years previously had caused a man to come forward and identify himself to the authorities as Violette's elusive "protector." His name was Émile Cottet, and he was sixty-four, a merchant living in central Paris. He had met Violette in 1931 at a big fair in her neighborhood, bought her a drink, and for a while met up with her every evening. He had not seen her for a year and a half when he was astonished to find her photograph in the newspapers. He had tried to make contact with Vésinne-Larue, but in the course of a long spell in the lawyer's waiting room he got cold feet and walked out. The press seems to have wanted to accept this Émile as the real one: at the time of Violette's death, there were mentions of the fact that Émile "waited twenty years to come forward."[29] Cottet was too young to be plausible, however; he would have been in his forties, not his sixties, when he knew Violette, and the details of his meetings with her in the plebeian east end of Paris—he said he took her to a boxing match—do not match her accounts of opera performances and fine restaurants on the right bank.[30]

In the wake of the rehabilitation, a journalist for *France-Soir* visited the Coquelet family in Rouen. It was a Sunday, and a tall and good-looking girl, Violette's teenage daughter, was working at the till behind the bar. A television was on. A thirteen-year-old boy was serving drinks, his twelve-year-old brother trying to reason with the whining five-year-old. Another boy was away at a military school. The girl spoke of "Maman" in glowing terms; she missed her during the week when she had to stay at the lycée as a boarder. Germaine Nozière was there too, seventy-five years old and stooped, washing glasses and glaring at the stranger who had invaded her home. Violette spoke confidentially in the back room. "I persisted so that my five children would be able to face life with the same chances as everyone else. But they don't know anything about this struggle. And even now as I'm winning, I'm afraid. I am afraid of all the noise they will make about me. I don't want any of them to be curious about the past, I want all of them, my daughter and my four sons, to just concentrate on their future."[31]

Violette had another reason to be scared, another reason she had pushed so hard for the rehabilitation to come through. Talking to the *France-Soir* journalist away from her family, she suddenly undid a button of her shirt to reveal the top of a red scar. They had just removed her breast, she said, and she was going in regularly for radiation. Violette's health problems had never gone away. From the moment she entered the prison in Haguenau until her release in 1945, every report had mentioned her poor physical state, and life on the outside and the support of a family had not cured the ills that had plagued her since adolescence. Just before it became clear that her petition for rehabilitation was going to be successful, she had been diagnosed with malignant cancer.[32]

Violette Nozière Coquelet died at the age of fifty-one, on November 28, 1966. She had shown extraordinary courage, hiding the extent of her sickness from her family for as long as possible and refusing tranquillizers at the end so that she could attend to her children and her affairs. Because of her illness, the family had been obliged to give up the business and, now impoverished, lived in one of those lugubrious public housing towers (the so-called HLM—"moderate-rent housing") that had been hastily constructed in the outskirts of most towns after World War II. Her children and her mother nursed her through the last months; the oldest among them knew the truth about their mother's past but pretended ignorance so as not to upset her. At the end, Germaine, the mother to whom she had given poison and who had demanded that Violette kill herself, held her in her arms and closed her eyes.[33]

Violette's death was reported in all the major dailies, sometimes on the front page. "Violette Nozière . . . Do You Remember?" titled *Paris-Jour*. French men and women in their late forties and older would know who she was, but most papers retold her story for those too young to remember: it was *the* affair of the second quarter of the century, the one that inspired street singers and that people at the time compared to the Dreyfus case. From the vantage of the mid-1960s, when the postwar boom later known as the "thirty glorious years" made things like indoor plumbing, central heating, and television sets quasi-universal in urban France, the world conjured up by memories of the affair seemed like a very distant past. *Paris-Match* evoked the heat of that August night at a time when "poor people, who did not go on vacation, stifled in their airless lodgings," *Paris-Jour* reminded readers that "in 1933 it was mostly the children of bourgeois who went to lycées."[34] References to the incest controversy were fleeting if they appeared at all. Only *Paris-Jour* commented dismissively, "It is of no use to stir up all of this muck thirty-two years later, but it does seem that she told the truth. And that would excuse a great deal, if not the crime itself."[35] What mattered to journalists in the 1960s was what happened to Violette after her trial. In the conservative climate of the pre-1968 Gaullist years, her story was presented as a quasi-religious narrative of redemption. A "beautiful human story," titled *L'Aurore;* the real mystery of the case, ran the article in *Paris-Jour,* was "How did a girl who had sunk so low become the exemplary mother that a whole family mourns today?"[36] Although she did raise five children who seemed genuinely devoted to their mother, Violette's life story after her crime—twelve years in prison, her husband's accident and then demise, too many mouths to feed, then cancer and an agonizing death at an early age—is a grim one. It seemed important in 1966 to suggest that Violette's sufferings, as well as the many children she produced, amounted to the expiation of a terrible crime, which even the truth of incest could not excuse.

In France today, memories of the Nozière affair depend on one's age. People under forty either have never heard of it or can't quite place the name when you mention it. I have spoken to several octogenarians who remember the scandal vividly, usually with a comment like "She was a bad one, wasn't she?" When I mentioned Violette's name to one highly educated woman in her seventies, she rattled off the lines from Paul Éluard's poem about undoing the vipers' knot of blood connections. French men and women of the postwar generation, now in their fifties and sixties, usually know Violette's story from another source: the movie about it made in 1978 by one of France's most famous directors, Claude Chabrol, and the arresting performance of its star, Isabelle Huppert.

Chabrol, active as a director until his death in 2010, was one of the original members of the 1950s French "New Wave," which prominently included Jean-Luc Godard, Éric Rohmer, Jacques Rivette, and François Truffaut. Born in 1930, Chabrol was too young to remember the Nozière affair but old enough to know people for whom it was still indelible. One of these was the versatile and enduring actor Pierre Brasseur, born in the early years of the century, who would have been in his teens at the time of the affair. Brasseur, who according to Chabrol "was a surrealist for some time," told the latter about Violette "with tears in his eyes" in the early 1960s.[37]

Chabrol had considered making a movie about Violette at the time, then shelved the project, but returned to it after the publication of the first and to date only nonfictional book about the case, Jean-Marie Fitère's *Violette Nozière*, published in 1975.[38]

Fitère's account is made up of a series of short, riveting chapters. The book focuses solely on the story of the affair. It is both scrupulously documented and partly invented, drawing extensively from the contemporary press and case records (though it contains no notes or documentation) but also peppered with cleverly fabricated conversations between the characters. Both the story and Fitère's invented dialogue are so vivid that it is easy to see how the book inspired Chabrol to make a movie. Chabrol based his film on Fitère's work, which is prominently acknowledged in the movie's credits.[39] The subject was an obvious one for Chabrol, whose stock in trade is the crime film. A disciple of Alfred Hitchcock, Chabrol gallicized the English master's style by drawing his subjects from the tradition of the French *fait divers,* setting his films in the starchy environment of the French bourgeoisie and petite bourgeoisie. The great crimes of France's interwar years have held especial appeal for him: one of Chabrol's earliest movies was about Landru, and in 1995 he filmed his own version of the Papin sisters' murder, *La Cérémonie,* updated via a story by the British crime novelist Ruth Rendell.

*Violette Nozière* is far from Chabrol's best work. The filmmaker modeled his approach on Fitère's just-the-facts narration, intending, he declared many times, to leave the mystery intact. Only the beginning and the end of the film neatly telegraph the thesis about Violette that Chabrol articulated in more than one interview. The film's opening credits roll over a shot of a carceral-looking gate barring the entrance to the Nozières' courtyard, and it ends with Violette sitting in her prison cell while a voice-over narration tells the story of her "redemption" and release. Chabrol's position, clearly shaped by prevailing antifamily sentiments among contemporary left-wing intellectuals, was that Violette's confined family life amounted to a form of imprisonment and explained most of her problems. The filmmaker enjoyed pointing out provocatively that, as he saw it, only once she was in a real jail was Violette able to regain her normalcy.[40] Chabrol sometimes said that he made the film because he was "in love with" Violette Nozière, but more often he spoke of his cinematic account as a psychological study of the effects of an environment on a vulnerable persona: "I don't excuse the crime, but I try to understand how social constraints can act upon a certain kind of personality and lead to revolt and, in this one case, to murder."[41] The filmmaker mentioned to one journalist that he had consulted the case records, and his scrupulous reconstitution of the Nozières' flat, with its cramped spaces, busy wallpaper, bulky furniture, and primitive kitchen bears out the claim.[42] Most of the reviewers, even those less enthusiastic about the movie, were impressed by the power of Chabrol's reconstitution of a stifling lower-middle-class interior at a specific point in the past.

The movie received mixed reviews, with some critics applauding the film's historical accuracy and noir sensibility, and many decrying its leftist bias, lack of clear judgment on Violette and her crime, and confusing recourse to frequent flashbacks. There was general agreement that this was not Chabrol at his best, but also consensus in the praise that greeted Isabelle Huppert's performance as the film's heroine. Twenty-five at the time, Huppert had broken out only the previous year, in Claude Goretta's *La Dentellière*. She was to win the 1978 award for best actress at the Cannes Film Festival for her portrayal of Violette. Huppert looks considerably different from the real Violette—prettier, smaller, and more childlike, with pale skin, freckles, auburn hair, and huge eyes—but the role played to her acting style and strengths. Huppert is a formidable actress known for her disconcerting opacity and her ability to project a combination of cruelty and vulnerability; the role of the teenage parricide perfectly suited her, and she acquitted herself brilliantly.

Chabrol's movie is scrupulous to a fault in pinning down the details of the affair. Shot on a small budget, it offers no grand panoramas of Paris in the early 1930s, but carefully recreates a small number of interiors—the Rue de Madagascar apartment, a Latin Quarter café and hotel room, and the judge's chambers—in which much of the drama took place. It offers glimpses of the jeering crowds that greeted the murderer and even features a street singer crooning one of the original ballads about the young poisoner. If critics were dissatisfied with the movie's lack of a clear point of view, it is because the filmmaker hews closely to the record, leaving most of the mysteries of the case unsolved.

On the subject of Baptiste's guilt, Chabrol is evasive if not downright dismissive. Violette's father as played by Jean Carmet comes across as a typical slippers-and-undershirt figure of the lower middle class, an attentive parent but something of a milquetoast, who tries and fails to mediate between his high-strung wife and daughter. He is physically affectionate with his daughter and in one scene converses with her as she washes in the nude behind a see-through curtain. The movie has Willy mentioning to Jean before the crime that Violette "tells everyone that her father rapes her" and shows her describing her motives succinctly to the judge. In prison, she explains why she killed her father to a truculent lower-class fellow prisoner, who shoots back: "You were right to do it." Chabrol treats the incest allegation as something that Violette claimed and which may have happened, but certainly not the key to the affair. Attitudes toward sexual abuse in the family changed so fast starting in the 1980s that one can easily forget how taboo the subject was even in 1978. Whereas a decade or two later a filmmaker would probably have made the issue a central one, Chabrol almost entirely elided it.

This is all the more notable in that Chabrol chose to depart from the record in one major respect: his version of the affair asserts not only that Émile did exist and that he was Violette's biological father, but that the young girl was flush with money because she was blackmailing him, a notion that appears nowhere in contemporary records or even speculations. In Chabrol's version, mother and daughter are engaged in a conspiracy to keep the truth from Baptiste, carefully hiding letters and photographs of Émile, which they pull out and examine when they are alone. "You have his elegance," sighs Germaine, who has previously declared that she will "make a lady" of her daughter. Chabrol was unable to resist the lure of this classic melodramatic twist, but by implication the version of the story that has Émile as the biological father technically clears Baptiste of the charge of incest, even if it did occur.

In March 1978 Violette's children hired a lawyer to block the film's distribution. Twenty-nine-year-old Jean-Jacques told the press that to her sons and daughter, "Violette Nozière was born in 1945, when she was freed from prison, and to us she was always just a mother. That is the image we want to preserve."[43] In May of that year, Chabrol said that he had not at the outset contacted the family, out of "consideration," but once the movie was complete, he had agreed to let Violette's children view it before its release. "They were able to see that it did not damage their mother's memory, and made no opposition to its commercial release."[44]

Violette's children may not have been thrilled by the film, but neither were they in any position to comment on its veracity, since their mother never talked about what happened in 1933, having hidden the story of her early life from them for as long as possible. By the time Violette was brought alive again on film, nobody with intimate knowledge of the case was still there to comment. André Breton died two months before Violette, Judge Lanoire in 1944. Germaine survived her daughter by only two years, passing away in 1968, and René de Vésinne-Larue lived until 1976. The truth of what happened in that small apartment on the top floor of 9 Rue de Madagascar in the years, months, and hours leading up to the evening of August 21, 1933, now lies deep in the soil of central France, in the cemetery of Neuvy-sur-Loire, where Violette lies buried alongside her husband, her mother, and her father.

# Conclusion

WHY DID CONTEMPORARIES CARE SO much about Violette Nozière that they referred to her crime as "L'Affaire," wrote dozens of letters to newspapers and poured out their hearts in confidential notes to Judge Lanoire? The answer to that question might not at first seem obvious. The case was a private matter that did not, unlike the Dreyfus or Stavisky affairs, implicate government authorities. A genteel murder by poison, the story people read in their newspapers involved no extreme violence, and its cast of characters included nobody famous. Violette's crime proved inescapably fascinating, however, because it echoed everything from storybook horrors to the familiar details of everyday life.

The Nozière affair was framed by what most societies hold as the two deepest taboos, parricide and incest, and these gave it a mythical resonance that people recognized even at the time: "mythological to the tip of your fingernails" was how André Breton described Violette. When Paul Éluard wrote that she dreamt "of gorgeous gowns of fresh bread / Of gorgeous gowns of pure blood," he was evoking "Donkey-Skin," a disturbing fairy tale known to everyone in France.[1] In that story, a princess tries to escape her father's incestuous desires by demanding fanciful gowns the color of the sun and moon, and finally flees in disguise under the magical skin of an ass. The story is an example of a widespread type of folktale in which young girls ask for impossible-to-make dresses as a ruse to avoid the sexual menace of fathers or unwelcome suitors. In these folktales, a princess in flight from a father who wants to marry her typically changes social stations—becoming a scullery maid or a goose-girl—and resorts to disguise to escape the threat of incest.[2]

Even if they did not believe Violette's incest allegations or link her shopping sprees to the tale of Donkey-Skin, contemporaries knew that the case evoked archetypal horrors. Several newspaper articles at the time of the affair retold the historical story of the parricide Beatrice Cenci, a young noblewoman beheaded in Rome in 1599 for plotting and carrying out, with the help of family members, the murder of her tyrannical and incestuous father.[3] Chronicles from the time record that Count Francesco Cenci was a man of pathological cruelty, an assassin who rejoiced in (and probably ordered) the death of two of his sons and raped his daughter; none of this, however, swayed papal justice. The youngest Cenci, a child, was forced to witness the torture and beheading of his sister, brother, and stepmother. When the poet Percy Bysshe Shelley visited Rome in the early 1800s, he discovered the story, which, he wrote, "was not to be mentioned in Italian society without awakening a deep and breathless interest." Even two centuries after it happened, "all ranks of people knew the outlines of this history." Convinced of the power of a narrative that, he believed, contained elements of both *King Lear* and *Oedipus Rex,* Shelley fashioned the history into his 1819 tragedy *The Cenci.*[4]

Even before Violette's crime, the Cenci story was well known in France.[5] A year after Violette's trial and conviction, Antonin Artaud, the playwright known for inventing the "theater of cruelty" and a former associate of Breton's group, penned his own version, *Les Cenci,* which he introduced with the comment: "In *The Cenci,* the father is destroyer, and in this way the theme may be assimilated to the Great Myths."[6] The Nozière affair was the stuff of myth because it broke not just two but three fundamental laws of kinship: besides the parricide and possible incest, Germaine's violent repudiation of her daughter routinely conjured up in the press adjectives like "Shakespearean" or "Aeschylian." The transgression was not double but triple.

Myths, however, endure because of their clarity, and the story that broke in late August 1933 was anything but clear: the Nozière affair was constantly devolving from mythology into *fait divers.* As the case unfolded, each of its many characters turned out to be different from what they appeared. Violette, the teenage murderer and femme fatale from a good family, wearing smocks at home and garter belts in hotel rooms, was joined by a boyfriend who was not a real student, not really middle class, and not even a "real man"; an allegedly doting mother who publicly wished her child dead and sued her; an elusive gentleman friend whose existence and precise relationship to the murderess were both objects of fervid speculation; and a dead father whose exemplary behavior seemed increasingly sinister. The more people—authorities, journalists, readers—looked into the case, the less clear it became, and therefore the more horribly fascinating.

Ordinary readers at the time looked to *faits divers* to debate and define the parameters of their lives; the novelist Pierre Drieu la Rochelle memorably wrote of the Nozière case that people read about it "to fit what seems so particular, so strange and solitary, into the general rhythm of breathing."[7] French men and women were awakening to the understanding, later popularized by Freudianism, Surrealism, and noir conventions, that evil haunts the most familiar and banal aspects of our lives, that the line between homeliness and horror is a thin one. At the same time, crimes like Violette's offered Parisians and other city dwellers a testimony to the meaning and value of their own existence. As Dominique Kalifa writes, stories of crimes in banal, familiar settings enabled regular people to claim the city as their own: "Day after day *faits divers* and crime serials keep reminding the reader that his daily life is worth recounting, that the ordinary is but the seed of the extraordinary."[8]

But what does the case of a teenage parricide in 1933 have to say to historians looking back from the twenty-first century? The 1920s and 1930s in France are usually labeled the "interwar period," an expression that privileges such matters as organized politics and international concerns. In retrospect, it can seem to us astonishing that in early September 1933 many readers of the popular press in France seem to have been more interested in the travails of an ordinary family than in the huge rally taking place in Nuremberg, where the Nazi party celebrated Adolf Hitler's seizure of power. On September 5, *L'Œuvre* even published a cartoon mocking this state of affairs: it shows an angry Nazi official waving a newspaper at a clearly disgruntled Hitler over a caption that reads: "That Violette! It's all about her!"

But what may seem in retrospect like myopia or frivolity is a reminder that much of social experience in France in the 1920s and 1930s had little to do with the consequences of World War I—as momentous as these certainly were—or the anticipation of another conflict that many people wanted to believe would never take place.[9] The mundane crime stories that became *faits divers,* and the case of the Nozière family in particular, force us to pay attention to aspects of the period not captured by the "interwar" label. Violette's crime shines a spotlight on the experiences of families who migrated to the city from the French countryside; on the nature of life in modest homes with a single child; on the trajectories of young girls who for the first time went to school long enough to get a job as a secretary-typist and cross the city for work. The novelty of this period was that a stationmaster's son could go to law school, an engine driver's daughter attend a lycée and buy the kind of clothes that allowed her to pass for a wealthy woman. The ambiguities at the heart of the Nozière case can be taken as a metaphor for a period in which stark divisions of class were dissolving for the first time. Ordinary French men and women who wrote letters to newspapers and to Judge Lanoire used words like *anxiety* or *anguish* to describe their feelings. Both modest people and legal professionals at the trial were troubled not just by a cold-hearted, murderous daughter, an all-too-saintly father, and a cruelly vindictive mother, but by the larger issues of social ambition and mobility that swirled around these characters.

The story of a specific girl in a particular family matters because when social scientists use expressions like "geographic mobility," "growth of the service sector," or "democratic consolidation," there is a danger not just that we will put down what we are reading but, more importantly, that we will forget that these were experiences that affected the real lives of people in concrete and dramatic ways. The characters in this story, not just the Nozières but the families of Jean Dabin and Madeleine Debize, a concierge's daughter in eastern Paris and the young Simone de Beauvoir in Montparnasse, are reminders of this simple fact.

Violette Nozière's is a story in history, but it is also irreducibly particular, and its specificity too demands respect. What law of history could have anticipated the stained rag, Monsieur Émile, or Count André de Pinguet? Who could have imagined that the most famous poisoner in France would one day run a restaurant, or that the girl who was sentenced to the guillotine for coolly urging both her parents to swallow a deadly drug would die at home in the arms of her mother, surrounded by five loving children? Like other *faits divers,* the case invariably escaped, both at the time and over time, the boxes to which people tried to consign it. The story of Violette, Germaine, and Baptiste is very much emblematic of their time, but in the end it is also, and should remain, theirs alone.

# NOTES

## INTRODUCTION

1. Despite its immense contemporary resonance, very little has been written on the Nozière case. An excellent popular narrative of the affair was published in 1975: Jean-Marie Fitère, *Violette Nozière* (Geneva: Presses de la Cité, 1975). The contents make it plain that Fitère saw the police records and consulted the contemporary press, but his book does not include archival or bibliographic references. It served as the basis for a movie that Claude Chabrol made about the affair in 1978, discussed in chapter 10 below. Véronique Chalmet, *Violette Nozières: La fille aux poisons* (Paris: Flammarion, 2004), is a semifictionalized biography also aimed at a general readership and also well informed but devoid of references. There exist two excellent scholarly articles specifically about the case: Anne-Emmanuelle Demartini and Agnès Fontvieille, "Le Crime du sexe: La justice, l'opinion publique et les Surréalistes, regards croisés sur Violette Nozière," in Christine Bal et al., eds., *Femmes et justice pénale, 19ᵉ–20ᵉ siècles* (Rennes: Presses Universitaires de Rennes, 2002), 244–52; and Anne-Emmanuelle Demartini, "L'Affaire Nozière: La Parole sur l'inceste et sa réception sociale dans la France des années trente," *Revue d'Histoire Moderne et Contemporaine* 54 (October–December 2009): 190–214; and a book in preparation by Prof. Demartini. The case is mentioned or briefly discussed in works on Surrealism or on famous crimes of twentieth-century France but has received nowhere near the attention that has been devoted to the exactly contemporary crime of Christine and Léa Papin, described below

in chapter 7. See most recently Jonathan P. Eburne, *Surrealism and the Art of Crime* (Ithaca, NY: Cornell University Press, 2008), 198–214. Both at the time of the case and as recently as Chalmet's 2004 book, the name Nozière has sometimes been spelled with an *s* at the end, as Nozières. The Surrealists entitled their 1934 tribute (discussed below in chapter 8) *Violette Nozières*. I spell the name without a final *s* because that form appeared on official records and was the one used by Violette and her family.

2. Most general histories of this period focus heavily on the political, emphasizing parliamentary politics, extraparliamentary political groups, foreign affairs, and the worsening economic climate. See, for instance, Henri Dubief, *Le Déclin de la troisième république* (Paris: Seuil, 1976); Olivier Dard, *Les Années 30* (Paris: Librairie Générale Française, 1999); Julian Jackon, *The Politics of Depression in France, 1932–1936* (Cambridge: Cambridge University Press, 1988); or the opening chapters of Jackson's *France: The Dark Years, 1940–44* (Oxford: Oxford University Press, 2001). Only one synthetic work balances political, social, and cultural history: Eugen Weber, *The Hollow Years: France in the 1930s* (New York: Norton, 1994). The most salient historiographical debates in this period have focused on the possible continuity between the 1930s and the Vichy regime, and particularly on whether or not the French Right in this period can be called proto-fascist. See, for instance, Zeev Sternhell, *La Droite révolutionnaire, 1885–1914: Les origines françaises du fascisme* (Paris: Seuil, 1978); and *Ni Droite ni gauche: L'idéologie fasciste en France* (Paris: Seuil, 1983); Robert Soucy, *French Fascism: The First Wave, 1924–1933* (New Haven, CT: Yale University Press, 1986), and *French Fascism: The Second Wave, 1933–1939* (New Haven, CT: Yale University Press, 1995). For a more general, and controversial, argument, see Gérard Noiriel, *Les Origines républicaines de Vichy* (Paris: Hachette, 1999). There exists a vast historical literature on every aspect of the Popular Front, from its political struggles to the social and cultural policies it implemented or sought to implement. Works on many aspects of the social history of this period—on workers, women, and youth movements—are cited especially in chapters 1 through 3. Much of the best new research on this period—works by Siân Reynolds, Laura Frader, Kristin Stomberg Childers, Elsa Camscioli, and others—concerns questions of gender, social policy, and citizenship. But there is still very little work on the nature of class relations and class cultures— outside of organized political movements—in the 1920s and 1930s.

ONE

1. Claude Couraud, *Je me souviens du 12e arrondissement* (Paris: Parigramme, 1997), 11, 68–69.

2. Jacques Valdour, *De la Popinq' à Ménilmuch'* (Paris: Éditions Spes, 1924), pp. 40ff.

3. Jacques Valdour, *Ouvriers parisiens d'après-guerre* (Paris: Arthur Rousseau, 1921), 81.

4. Couraud, *Je me souviens,* 46–54, 70.

5. Ibid., 13; Jean Ferniot, *Pierrot et Aline* (Paris: Grasset, 1973), 31.

6. Ibid., 33, 103.

7. Ferniot, *Pierrot et Aline,* 33–34.

8. Alfred Fierro, *Vie et histoire du XIIème arrondissement* (Paris: Hervas, 1988), 112; Claude Couraud, *C'était hier, le XIIème arrondissement* (Paris: Le Point, 1990), 112.

9. Couraud, *Je me souviens,* 21–25; Couraud, *C'était hier,* 112; Fierro, *Vie et histoire,* 72.

10. Couraud, *Je me souviens,* 19.

11. The 1881 census for Neuvy lists Alcime, 37; Philomène, 33; and young Philomène, 12. By 1891 Germaine is listed as a two-year-old, and her elder sister had moved out. Archives Départementales de la Nièvre (hereafter ADN), 6M 193/2 (1881) and 6M 193/3 (1891).

12. ADN 6M 193/6 and 6M 193/9.

13. Jean Frapat, "Histoire de Neuvy-sur-Loire" (1917), typescript, ADN NIV 6555, 2–3, 18–31.

14. "Les Vignerons de Neuvy-sur-Loire travaillaient dur et buvaient ferme," *Centre-France Dimanche,* August 1, 1976, 4.

15. Yves Fougerat, *Neuvy-sur-Loire: Le commerce et l'industrie aux 19ᵉ et 20ᵉ siècles* (Longué: Lemercier, 1994), 51–129.

16. Details on Germaine's early life from her interrogation by Judge Lanoire in the investigation records, Archives de la Ville de Paris (hereafter AVP), D2U8 379, September 25, 1933. The information about the wine store appears in the psychological report on Violette, in AVP D2U8 280, p. 7. On her first marriage, see *Le Journal,* September 24, 1933.

17. *Le Journal,* September 14, 1933.

18. Marie-Noëlle Audier, "Famille et ménages à Prades (Haute-Loire) de 1714 à 1789," mémoire de maîtrise, Université de Clermont-Ferrand, 1993, 40–53; Jean Merley, *La Haute-Loire de la fin de l'Ancien Régime aux débuts de la IIIe République,* 2 vols. (Le Puy en Velay: L'Éveil de la Haute-Loire, 1974), 1: 9–27.

19. Julien Seybel, *Pont-Salomon: Village de la Haute-Loire entre les guerres* (La Séauve: Imprimerie du Velay, 1996), 54.

20. Ibid., 53–57; Yvonne Cheymol-Pialoux, *Domeyrat, mon beau village* (Brioude: Imprimerie Robert, 1984), 12–37.

21. Merley, *La Haute-Loire,* 1: 442.

22. Ibid., 1: 466–69.

23. Jean Peyrard, *La Haute-Loire d'autrefois* (Roanne: Éditions Horvath, 1982), 84–86. Many women in Prades were listed as *dentellières* in the tax rolls.

24. Merley, *La Haute-Loire*, 1: 476, 623.

25. Archives Départementales de la Haute-Loire (hereafter ADHL), 6E 176/10, January 12, 1884.

26. The rift between Félix and Baptiste is documented in AVP D2U8 380 and discussed in chapter 4.

27. ADHL 6E 176/10, January 12, 1884, and February 17, 1885.

28. Cheymol-Pialout, *Domeyrat*, 38–40.

29. ADHL 6M 184, 1926 and 1931. Prades, with a population of about 250, had 7 men working for the railway in 1926, 18 in 1931. All are listed as either *cantonnier* (digger) or *terrassier* (road worker).

30. I will refer to railway workers as "men" or "railwaymen" because in the early twentieth century only about 7 percent of the workforce of these companies were female, most of them working as crossing guards. The railway was perceived by contemporaries as a completely male environment.

31. Georges Ribeill, *Les Cheminots* (Paris: Éditions de la Découverte, 1984), 26–27; Margot B. Stein, *The Social Origins of a Labor Elite: French Engine Drivers, 1837–1917* (New York: Garland Publishing, 1987), ch. 4.

32. *Le Journal*, September 14, 1933.

33. Paul Nizan, *Antoine Bloyé* (Paris: Grasset, 1996), 34–39.

34. Ibid., 48.

35. Ibid., 60–61.

36. Ibid., 68.

37. At the time of his death, Baptiste Nozière made about 50,000 francs a year, while a beginning office worker made 10,000 to 12,000.

38. Christian Chevandier, *Cheminots en grève, ou la construction d'une identité* (Paris: Maisonneuve et Larose, 2002). The heyday of rail strikes in France was between 1891 and 1920, when about 40 percent of all railway workers belonged to a union. Union membership declined significantly after 1920. On the status of *cheminots,* see also Antoine Prost, "Mariage, jeunesse et société à Orléans en 1911," *Annales: Économies, sociétés, civilization* 36 (July-August 1981): 681.

39. Ribeill, *Les Cheminots*, 25.

40. Georges Ribeill, *Le Personnel des compagnies de chemin de fer* (Paris: Développement et Aménagement, 1980), 105, 228, 309; Ribeill, *Les Cheminots*, 97–98.

41. Nizan, *Antoine Bloyé*, 78, 85.

42. Ibid., 81–83; Valdour, *Ouvriers parisiens*, 33–40.

43. Valdour, *Ouvriers parisiens*, 28, 31, 37.

44. *Le Matin*, September 22, 1933.

45. Valdour, *Ouvriers parisiens*, 40–50.

46. Ferniot, *Pierrot et Aline*, 70, 99.

47. These details were given by Germaine's lawyer, Maurice Boitel, at the trial. Boitel mentioned that the lovers moved in together "with their parents' consent," but one wonders if the families were really consulted. The lawyer was engaged in portraying his client as a woman of irreproachable morals. "Violette Nozière en cour d'assises," *Revue des Grands Procès Contemporains* 41 (1935): 5–6.

48. Eugen Weber, *Peasants into Frenchmen: The Modernization of Rural France, 1870–1914* (Stanford, CA: Stanford University Press, 1976), 177. In one sample of railway families, 17 percent of first children were conceived out of wedlock: Stein, *Social Origins,* 227–30.

49. Jean-Marie Fitère, *Violette Nozière* (Paris: Presses de la Cité, 1975), 12–13.

50. Chevandier, *Cheminots en grève,* 91.

51. Author's interview with Simone Mayeul, March 24, 2005.

52. Couraud, *Je me souviens,* 105–6.

53. Ibid., 106; Ferniot, *Pierrot et Aline,* 33.

54. 1931 Census for the Rue de Madagascar, AVP 2Mi LN 1931/46.

55. *Détective,* no. 243, June 22, 1933.

56. The following information is from AVP 2Mi LN 1931/46.

57. Eugen Weber, *The Hollow Years: France in the 1930s* (New York: W. W. Norton, 1994), 11–14.

58. Lenard Berlanstein, *The Working People of Paris, 1871–1914* (Baltimore, MD: Johns Hopkins University Press, 1994), 142–44; Stein, *Social Origins,* 238; Delphine Gardey, *La Dactylographe et l'expéditionnaire: Histoire des employés de bureau, 1890–1930* (Paris: Belin, 2001), 265; Gérard Noiriel, *Les Ouvriers dans la société française, 19e-20e siècles* (Paris: Seuil, 1986), 125. For more general discussions, see Francis Ronsin, *La Grève des ventres: Propagande néo-malthusienne et baisse de la natalité française, XIXe–XXe siècles* (Paris: Aubier, 1980); and Jacques Dupâquier et al., *Histoire de la population française IV: De 1914 à nos jours* (Paris: Presses Universitaires de France, 1988), part 3.

59. AVP D2U8 379, August 23, 1933. This is the transcript of the police's first official visit to the apartment. The police file also includes a floor plan and photographs.

60. Bernard Marchand, *Paris, histoire d'une ville XIXe–XXe siècle* (Paris: Le Seuil, 1993), 226–44; Jean-Yves Mollier and Jocelyne George, *La Plus Longue des républiques, 1870–1940* (Paris: Fayard, 1994), 526.

61. Ferniot, *Pierrot et Aline,* 20–23, 64–65.

62. Catherine Omnès, *Ouvrières parisiennes: Marchés du travail et trajectoires professionnelles au 20ᵉ siècle* (Paris: Éditions de l'EHESS, 1997), 324.

63. Linda L. Clark, *Schooling the Daughters of Marianne: Textbooks and the Socialization of Girls in Modern French Primary Schools* (Albany: State University of New York Press, 1984), 192.

64. Stein, *Social Origins,* 219–25.

65. AVP 2Mi LN 1931/46.

66. Testimony of René Desorme, September 21, 1933, D2U8 380.

67. Edmond Goblot, *La Barrière et le niveau: Étude sociologique sur la bourgeoisie française moderne* (Paris: Presses Universitaires de France, 1967 [1925]), 23.

68. Stein, *Social Origins,* 218–19.

69. See Catherine Hodeir and Michel Pierre, *L'Exposition coloniale* (Paris: Éditions Complexe, 1991); Herman Lebovics, *True France: The Wars over Cultural Identity, 1900–1945* (Ithaca, NY: Cornell University Press, 1992); Patricia A. Morton, *Hybrid Modernities: Architecture and Representation at the 1931 Colonial Exposition, Paris* (Cambridge, Mass.: MIT Press, 2000).

70. Morton, *Hybrid Modernities,* ch. 3.

71. Ibid., 152–53; Hodeir and Pierre, *L'Exposition coloniale,* 25–26.


TWO

1. AVP D2U8 280, October 14, 1933, report on schooling by officer Coret. See also in the same file, the background and psychological report on Violette, p. 7.

2. Claude Lelièvre and Françoise Lelièvre, *Histoire de la scolarisation des filles* (Paris: Éditions Nathan, 1991), 65–95; Linda L. Clark, *Schooling the Daughters of Marianne: Textbooks and the Socialization of Girls in Modern French Primary Schools* (Albany: State University of New York Press, 1984), ch. 1.

3. Lelièvre and Lelièvre, *Histoire de la scolarisation,* 106–7; Rebecca Rogers, *From the Salon to the Schoolroom: Educating Bourgeois Girls in Nineteenth-Century France* (University Park: Penn State University Press, 2005), 205–6.

4. Clark, *Schooling the Daughters,* 119–22.

5. AVP D2U8 379, August 26, 1933; AVP D2U8 380, October 13, 1933, and December 18, 1933.

6. Delphine Gardey, *La Dactylographe et l'expéditionnaire: Histoire des employés de bureau, 1890–1930* (Paris: Belin, 2001); Siân Reynolds, *France between the Wars: Gender and Politics* (London: Routledge, 1996), 92–94.

7. Valdour, *Ouvriers parisiens,* 65–67, 69, 98.

8. Anne-Marie Sohn, *Chrysalides: Femmes dans la vie privée, XIXe-XXe siècles,* 2 vols. (Paris: Publications de la Sorbonne, 1996), 1: 342–46.

9. Ibid., 1: 345.

10. On the opening up of the professions to (mostly upper-class) women and the notion of "a diploma as a dowry," see Juliette Rennes, *Le Mérite et la nature: Une controverse républicaine, l'accès des femmes aux professions de prestige, 1880–1940* (Paris: Fayard, 2007).

11. The details are from Violette's account when she was questioned on September 9, 1933: see AVP D2U8 379. The "growth problems" are from her mother's account, September 1, 1933, D2U8 379.

12. Psychological report in AVP D2U8 380, pp. 38–39.

13. Ibid., p. 8.

14. AVP D2U8 379, deposition of Claude Joly, whose daughter attended the school with Violette.

15. On the origins and status of *cours secondaires* for girls, see Françoise Mayeur, *L'Enseignement secondaire des jeunes filles sous la Troisième République* (Paris: Presses de la Fondation Nationale des Sciences Politiques, 1977), 144–61. A report on Violette's secondary schooling is in AVP D2U8 380, October 14, 1933.

16. AVP D2U8 380, deposition of Raymond Rierciardelli, October 7, 1933.

17. Ibid., deposition of Arsène Chausse, September 19, 1933.

18. Ibid., Rierciardelli deposition. The 1926 census lists Raymond's family as four grown children, all engaged in wage labor, with a widowed mother: AVP 2Mi LN 1926.

19. AVP D2U8 379, September 12, 1933; *Paris-Soir,* September 12, 1933; *Le Petit Parisien,* September 11, 1933; *L'Œuvre,* September 12 and 13, 1933.

20. AVP D2U8 379, deposition of Germaine Nozière, September 25, 1933; the same file contains a long undated account by Germaine that also describes the scene.

21. *L'Œuvre,* September 13, 1933; *Le Journal,* September 13, 1933.

22. AVP D2U8 380, October 14, 1933.

23. *Le Petit Parisien,* September 3, 1933.

24. William Reddy, *The Invisible Code: Honor and Sentiment in Postrevolutionary France, 1814–1848* (Berkeley: University of California Press, 1997), ch. 2.

25. Debora Silverman, *Art Nouveau in Fin-de-Siècle France: Politics, Psychology and Style* (Berkeley: University of California Press, 1989), ch. 8.

26. Mayeur, *Enseignement secondaire,* 238.

27. Ibid., 182–87; Lelièvre and Lelièvre, *Histoire de la scolarisation,* 127–28.

28. Mayeur, *Enseignement secondaire,* 188.

29. Lelièvre and Lelièvre, *Histoire de la scolarisation,* 131; Reynolds, *France between the Wars,* 45–47.

30. Mayeur, *Enseignement secondaire,* 194; Catherine Ponard, "Le Lycée Fénelon, 1883–1913," mémoire de maîtrise, Université de Paris VII, 1986.

31. Sohn, *Chrysalides,* I: 74–81.

32. Simone de Beauvoir, *Mémoires d'une jeune fille rangée* (Paris: Gallimard Folio, 1972), 54, 71ff, 101, 113, 114ff, 136. Translations from this work are my own. For additional details, see Deirdre Bair, *Simone de Beauvoir: A Biography* (New York: Simon and Schuster, 1990), chs. 2–5.

33. Weber, *Hollow Years*, 11–14, 80–84.

34. Mary-Louise Roberts, *Civilization without Sexes: Reconstructing Gender in Postwar France, 1917–1927* (Chicago: University of Chicago Press, 1994), 1–151; see also Reynolds, *France between the Wars*.

35. Victor Margueritte, *La Garçonne* (Paris: Flammarion, 1922); see especially the illuminating analysis in Roberts, *Civilization*, ch. 2.

36. Roberts, *Civilization*, 46–47.

37. Bair, *Simone de Beauvoir*, ch. 1.

38. Beauvoir, *Mémoires*, 59, 135; Bair, *Simone de Beauvoir*, 40–41, 52–53.

39. Beauvoir, *Mémoires*, 91, Bair, *Simone de Beauvoir*, 82.

40. Bair, *Simone de Beauvoir*, 75; Beauvoir, *Mémoires*, 136, 231.

41. Bair, *Simone de Beauvoir*, 42.

42. Berthe Bernage, *Le Savoir-vivre et les usages du monde* (Paris: Gautier-Languereau, 1928), 199.

43. Ibid., 43, 64; Beauvoir, *Mémoires*, 32.

44. Beauvoir, *Mémoires*, 145.

45. AVP D2U8 380, Testimony of Arsène Chausse, September 19, 1933.

46. Beauvoir, *Mémoires*, 126.

47. Beauvoir, Mémoires, 307, 247; Bair, *Simone de Beauvoir*, 80.

48. Beauvoir, *Mémoires*, 244, 247.

49. Ibid., 306, 338.

50. Ferniot, *Pierrot et Aline*, 13–14.

51. Ibid., 14.

52. Ibid., 76.

53. Ibid., 77–78.

54. Ibid., 78–79.

55. Sohn, *Chrysalides*, 1: 401–6.

56. Ibid., 1: 460–71.

57. Ibid., 1: 500.

58. Sohn, *Chrysalides*, 2: 570ff.

59. Beauvoir, *Mémoires*, 118–19.

60. Sohn, *Chrysalides*, 2: 579.

61. Ibid., 2: 580–90.

62. Ibid., 2: 594–601.

63. Marcel Pagnol, *Marius* (Paris: Fasquelle, 1931), 218–23.

64. Ibid., 222.

65. Hélène du Taillis in *L'Œuvre des Femmes*, September 2, 1933.

66. *Paris-Soir*, August 26, 1933.

67. AVP D2U8 379, Deposition of Angèle Bourdon, August 23, 1933.

68. AVP D2U8 380, September 21, 1933.

69. AVP D2U8 379. The events of the fall of 1932 are detailed in Germaine Nozière's deposition of September 25, 1933, to Judge Lanoire. They are also re-

counted in a long, undated memorandum by Germaine in the same dossier, which includes the quote about begging on her knees.

70. Ibid., Germaine Nozière's deposition.

71. Ibid., and Violette's account of the episode in her deposition of September 13, 1933, AVP D2U8 379.

### THREE

1. "Family Romances," in Sigmund Freud, *Collected Papers,* ed. James Strachey (New York: Basic Books, 1959), 5: 74–78.

2. Ibid., 77–78.

3. AVP D2U8 380, Deposition of Antoinette Prades, September 6, 1933.

4. *L'Œuvre,* September 13, 1933; *Le Journal,* September 13, 1933.

5. AVP D2U8 380, Report of Drs. Claude, Crouzon, and Truelle, November 6, 1933, pp. 18–19.

6. AVP D2U8 380, Deposition of Lucien Balmain, October 3, 1933.

7. Gaston Jacobs, *Le Métro de Paris: Un siècle de matériel roulant* (Paris: La Vie du Rail, 2001), 6–10.

8. Paul Cohen-Portheim, *The Spirit of Paris* (London: B. T. Batsford, 1937), 99–101. The book was originally published in German in 1930. The quote about Vaugirard is from Valdour, *Ouvriers parisiens,* 101.

9. André Demangeon, *Paris: La ville et sa banlieue* (Paris: Bourrelier, 1946), 19; Bernard Marchand, *Paris, histoire d'une ville XIXe–XXe siècles* (Paris: Seuil, 1993), 207.

10. Demangeon, *Paris,* 20–27. More generally, see Nancy Green, *Ready-to-Wear and Ready-to-Work: A Century of Industry and Immigrants in Paris and New York* (Durham, NC: Duke University Press, 1997); and Gérard Noiriel, *Le Creuset français: Une histoire de l'immigration, XIXe–XXe siècles* (Paris: Seuil, 1988).

11. Valdour, *Ouvriers parisiens,* 89–90, 130–31; Valdour, *De la Popinq',* 54–56.

12. Valdour, *De la Popinq',* 111–13.

13. Marchand, *Paris,* 255; "Les Garnis parisiens dans l'entre-deux guerres," in Alain Faure, Claire Lévy-Vroélant, and Sian Paycha, *Garnis et meublés à Paris et dans sa région, 1850–1996: Grandeur et décadence d'un hébergement ambigu* (PUCA, June 1999), www2.urbanisme.equipement.gouv.fr/puca2/dal/dtl/agar4_2.htm.

14. In contrast, Barbara Ehrenreich, who conducted the same sort of experiment as Valdour in the United States in the 1990s, found housing to be by far the biggest expense for the poor. *Nickel and Dimed: On (Not) Getting By in America* (New York: Metropolitan Books, 2001).

15. Noiriel, *Les Ouvriers,* 150.

16. Valdour, *De la Popinq'*, 63–69.

17. Charles Sowerwine, *France since 1870: Culture, Politics and Society* (London: Palgrave, 2001), 74–88; Noiriel, *Les Ouvriers*, 99–105, 160–175.

18. Valdour, *De la Popinq'*, 47, 52–53; Valdour, *Ouvriers parisiens*, 71–72, 141.

19. Valdour, *Ouvriers parisiens*, 51, 75–76.

20. Eric Mension-Rigau, *Aristocrates et grands bourgeois: Éducation, traditions, valeurs* (Paris: Plon, 1994), 17. On the survival of the French aristocracy, see Arno Mayer, *The Persistence of the Old Regime: Europe to the Great War* (New York: Pantheon, 1981), 102–9.

21. For a fuller discussion of these themes, see Sarah Maza, *The Myth of the French Bourgeoisie: An Essay on the Social Imaginary, 1750–1850* (Cambridge, MA: Harvard University Press, 2003), especially the conclusion.

22. Beauvoir, *Mémoires*, 180–81.

23. Ibid., 181–83.

24. Ibid, 270.

25. Berthe Bernage, *Brigitte, jeune femme* (Paris: Gautier-Languereau, 1946 [1929]), 115.

26. Beauvoir, *Mémoires*, 249–50.

27. Ibid., 309–12; Bair, *Simone de Beauvoir*, 109–10.

28. Colin Crisp, *Genre, Myth and Convention in the French Cinema, 1929–1939* (Bloomington: Indiana University Press, 2002), ch. 3. More generally, see Pierre Birnbaum, *Le Peuple et les gros: Histoire d'un mythe* (Paris: Grasset, 1979).

29. Most notably Pierre Bourdieu, in such works as *La Distinction: Critique sociale du jugement* (Paris: Minuit, 1979), or *La Noblesse d'État: Grandes écoles et esprit de corps* (Paris: Minuit, 1989).

30. Goblot, *La Barrière et le niveau*, 2

31. Ibid., 5, 24.

32. Ibid., 60.

33. Mension-Rigau, *Aristocrates*, 190–210; Baronne Staffe [Blanche Soyer], *Usages du monde: Règles du savoir-vivre dans la société moderne* (Paris: G. Havard, 1899), 127–38; Berthe Bernage, *Le Savoir-vivre et les usages du monde* (Paris: Gautier-Languereau, 1928), 51, 135–37.

34. Staffe, *Usages du monde*, 130–31; Bernage, *Le Savoir-vivre*, 104.

35. Goblot, *La Barrière*, 9–10.

36. Bernage, *Le Savoir-vivre*, 54.

37. Peter Brooks, *The Novel of Worldliness: Crébillon, Marivaux, Laclos, Stendhal* (Princeton, NJ: Princeton University Press, 1969), chs. 1 and 2.

38. Maurice Halbwachs, *Les Classes sociales* (Paris: Tournier et Constans, 1937), 105–7.

39. Bernage, *Le Savoir-vivre*, 72.

40. Ibid., 36–42; Bair, *Simone de Beauvoir*, 52.

41. Bernage, *Le Savoir-vivre*, 35.

42. The literature on this point is more voluminous for earlier periods, especially the Belle Époque. See Jill Harsin, *Policing Prostitution in Nineteenth-Century Paris* (Princeton, NJ: Princeton University Press, 1985); Hollis Clayson, *Painted Love: Prostitution in French Art of the Impressionist Era* (New Haven, CT: Yale University Press, 1991); Jann Matlock, *Scenes of Seduction: Prostitution, Hysteria and Reading Difference in Nineteenth-Century France* (New York: Columbia University Press, 1994); Lenard Berlanstein, *Daughters of Eve: A Cultural History of French Theater Women from the Old Regime to the Fin de Siècle* (Cambridge, MA: Harvard University Press, 2001); Mary Louise Roberts, *Disruptive Acts: The New Woman in Fin-de-Siècle France* (Chicago: University of Chicago Press, 2002).

43. Axel Marsden, *Chanel: A Woman of Her Own* (New York: Henry Holt, 1990); Edmonde Charles-Roux, *L'Irrégulière ou mon itinéraire Chanel* (Paris: Grasset, 1994).

44. Antoine Prost, "Les Peuples du 18e arrondissement en 1936," in Jean-Louis Robert and Danielle Tartakovsky, *Paris le peuple, 18e–20e siècles* (Paris: Publications de la Sorbonne, 1999), 59–76.

45. Jules Romains, *Les Hommes de bonne volonté*, 4 vols. (Paris: Flammarion, 1958), 1: 117–18.

46. Cohen-Portheim, *Spirit of Paris*, 37, 39.

47. Ibid., 40–41; Évelyne Cohen, *Paris dans l'imaginaire national de l'entre-deux-guerres* (Paris: Publications de la Sorbonne, 1999), 237. The quote about Picard is from Robert Brasillach, *Les Sept Couleurs et Le Marchand d'oiseaux* (Paris: Plon, 1970), 313–14.

48. Jean-Claude Caron, *Les Étudiants de Paris et le quartier latin, 1814–1851* (Paris: Armand Colin, 1991).

49. Cohen, *Paris*, 236; Eugen Weber, *Action Française: Royalism and Reaction in Twentieth-Century France* (Stanford, CA: Stanford University Press, 1962), 54–55, 297–301, 365–69.

50. Jean-Edouard Goby, "Souvenirs d'un étudiant à Paris vers 1930," *La Revue du Caire* 74 (January 1945), 191–216.

51. *Paris-Guide et annuaire France-Amérique* (Paris: Éditions France-Amérique), 125–30; Goby, "*Souvenirs,*" 192, 213.

52. AVP D2U8 379, deposition of Georges Legrand, August 30, 1933; deposition of Roger Endewell, September 2, 1933; deposition of Bernard Piébourg, September 12, 1933; deposition of Aimé Tessier, September 19, 1933; deposition of Jean Leblanc, October 9, 1933.

53. *Paris-Soir,* August 30, 1933.

54. Ibid.; *L'Œuvre*, September 13, 1933.

55. See Simone de Beauvoir's remarks, quoted in ch. 2; and Cohen-Portheim, *Spirit of Paris*, 88.

56. Jerrold Seigel, *Bohemian Paris: Culture, Politics and the Boundaries of Bourgeois Life, 1830–1930* (New York: Viking, 1986), 39–42.

57. *Le Journal*, August 31, 1933.

58. Cohen-Portheim, *Spirit of Paris*, 30. See also Alain Meyer and Christine Moissinac, *Représentations sociales et littéraires, centre et périphérie: Paris, 1908–1939* (Paris: IAURIF, 1979), 114–22.

59. Cohen-Portheim, *Spirit of Paris*, 87.

60. André Breton, *Nadja*, trans. Richard Howard (New York: Grove Press, 1960), 64–65; Marc Polizzotti, *Revolution of the Mind: The Life of André Breton* (New York: Farrar, Strauss and Giroux, 1995), 264–76.

61. John Richardson, *A Life of Picasso: The Triumphant Years, 1917–1932* (New York: Knopf, 2007), 323.

62. AVP D2U8 379, deposition of Lucien Balmain, October 3, 1933.

63. AVP D2U8 380, letter from Mahmoud Adari to the judge, September 6, 1933; and deposition, October 12, 1933.

64. AVP D2U8 379, deposition of Jacques Fellous, September 2, 1933; *Le Petit Parisien*, September 3, 1933; *L'Œuvre*, September 3, 1933.

65. AVP D2U8 380, report of Inspectors Verrier and Lelièvre, September 4, 1933; and deposition of Robert Isaac Atlan, September 6, 1933; *L'Œuvre*, September 7, 1933; *Le Petit Parisien*, September 7, 1933; *Le Journal*, September 7, 1933.

66. *Le Petit Parisien*, September 13, 1933.

67. The essay, dated October 26, 1932, is preserved in AVP D2U8 380.

68. Interview of Simone Mayeul, March 24, 2005.

69. Helen Harden Chenut, *The Fabric of Gender: Working-Class Culture in Third Republic France* (University Park: Pennsylvania State University Press, 2005), 225–28, 245.

70. Pierre MacOrlan, *Le Printemps* (Paris: NRF, 1930), 89–90.

71. Mary Lynn Stewart, *Dressing Modern Frenchwomen: Marketing Haute Couture, 1919–1939* (Baltimore, MD: Johns Hopkins University Press, 2008); Chenut, *Fabric of Gender*, ch. 7; Nancy Green, *Ready-to-Work and Ready-to-Wear: A Century of Industry and Immigrants* (Durham, NC: Duke University Press, 1997).

72. Steven Zdatny, *Fashion, Work and Politics in Modern France* (New York: Palgrave MacMillan, 2006), 56–110; *Petit Écho de la Mode*, January 1, 1933.

73. Valerie Steele, *Paris Fashion: A Cultural History* (New York: Oxford University Press, 1988), 246–47; Marylène Delbourg-Delphis, *Le Chic et le look: Histoire de la mode féminine et des moeurs de 1850 à nos jours* (Paris: Hachette,

1981), 148–51; Maggy Rouff [Maggy Besançon de Wagner], *La Philosophie de l'élégance* (Paris: Éditions littéraires de France, 1942), 63.

74. Clothing details from AVP D2U8 379, deposition of Germaine Nozière, September 25, 1933; deposition of Zoe Pillot, September 2, 1933; deposition of Madeleine Debize, August 26, 1933; and deposition of Violette Nozière, August 28, 1933.

75. Bernard Marrey, *Les Grands Magasins des origines à 1939* (Paris: Picard, 1979); Michael Miller, *The Bon Marché: Bourgeois Culture and the Department Store, 1869–1920* (Princeton, NJ: Princeton University Press, 1981).

76. Jacques Valmy-Baisse, *Les Grands Magasins* (Paris: Gallimard, 1927), 14.

77. Thérèse Bonney and Louise Bonney, *A Shopping Guide to Paris* (New York: McBride, 1929), 120–22.

78. MacOrlan, *Le Printemps,* 143–44.

79. Richard Martin, *Cubism and Fashion* (New York: Metropolitan Museum of Art, 1998).

80. *Le Petit Écho de la Mode,* November 6, 1932, and December 4, 1932; *Le Jardin des Modes,* March 15, 1932.

81. *L'Œuvre,* September 7, 1933.

82. *Le Petit Écho de la Mode,* December 4, 1932; *Le Jardin des Modes,* February 15, 1933.

83. *Le Jardin des Modes,* April 15, 1932.

84. *Le Petit Écho de la Mode,* January 22, 1933, September 3, 1933; *Le Jardin des Modes,* April 15, 1933.

85. Zdatny makes this point, citing the influential work of historians like Anne Hollander, Valerie Steele, and Mary-Louise Roberts. *Fashion, Work and Politics,* 75.

86. These examples are from the fashion magazines cited above, and Delbourg-Delphis also notes that fashions of the early thirties were strict and "sculptural," with femininity confined to the details: *Le Chic et le look,* 134–36.

87. Stewart, *Dressing Modern Frenchwomen,* ch. 1.

88. Steele, *Paris* Fashion, 245–53; Yvonne Deslandres and Florence Muller, *Histoire de la mode au XXe siècle* (Paris: Somogy, 1986), 88–168; Bonney and Bonney, *Shopping Guide,* 43.

89. Steele, *Paris fashion,* 260–61.

90. Dominique Sirop, *Paquin* (Paris: Adam Biro, 1989); Steele, *Paris Fashion,* 256–58.

91. Bonney and Bonney, *Shopping Guide,* 43, 45.

92. Stewart, *Dressing Modern Frenchwomen,* 97–98.

93. Robert Forrest Wilson, *Paris on Parade* (Indianapolis, IN: Bobbs Merrill, 1925), 42.

94. Stewart, *Dressing Modern Frenchwomen*, 94, 98; Sirop, *Paquin*, 17.

95. Wilson, *Paris on Parade*, 44.

## FOUR

1. My account of this period is based primarily on Germaine Nozière's deposition to Judge Lanoire on September 25, 1933, and her long memorandum of September 19, 1933, both in AVP D2U8 379. Germaine's lawyer, Maurice Boitel, reiterated the account in his speech at the trial. See "Violette Nozière en Cour d'Assises," *Revue des Grands Procès Contemporains* 41 (1935): 8–10.

2. AVP D2U8 379, deposition of Henri Deron, September 2, 1933.

3. AVP D2U8 379, Germaine's undated memorandum.

4. Ibid.

5. *Le Petit Parisien*, August 29, 1933.

6. *Détective*, no. 253, August 31, 1933.

7. AVP D2U8 379, deposition of Angèle Bourdon, August 30, 1933; D2U8 380, deposition of Madeleine Debize, October 13, 1933.

8. AVP D2U8 380, deposition of Madeleine Feydit, October 7, 1933.

9. "Violette Nozière en Cour d'Assises," 10.

10. *Le Journal*, September 4, 1933; *Le Petit Parisien*, September 5, 1933; *Le Matin*, September 5, 1933; D2U8 379, depositions of Antoinette Prades, Joseph Boissier, and Clémence Vigouroux, September 6, 1933.

11. For a particularly revealing description of Dabin, see *L'Œuvre*, September 6, 1933, which contains the remark about "une certaine séduction un peu spéciale"; see also *Le Petit Parisien*, September 5, 1933. The exchange during the trial is in "La Condamnation à mort de Violette Nozière," in Geo London, *Grands Procès de l'année 1934* (Paris, 1935), 141.

12. *Détective*, no. 258, October 5, 1933.

13. Ibid.

14. *Le Petit Parisien*, August 31, 1933.

15. *Détective*, no. 258, October 5, 1933.

16. Jean Dabin, *Remarques sur l'esprit de contradiction* (Paris: Revue Moderne des Arts et de la Vie, 1931), 5, 9, 11.

17. AVP D2U8 380, deposition of Georges Legrand, known as Willy, October 13, 1933.

18. Weber, *Action Française*, 262–67.

19. AVP D2U8 379, deposition of Jean Dabin, September 4, 1933.

20. *Le Populaire*, September 2, 1933; AVP D2U8 379, deposition of Bernard Van de Velde, November 10, 1933.

21. AVP D2U8 379, depositions of Jean Dabin, August 30, 1933, and September 4, 1933; *Détective,* no. 258, October 5, 1933. The following details are also from Dabin's accounts in these sources.

22. The following details are from Germaine Nozière's two accounts of the summer's events, her memorandum of September 19, 1933, and her deposition of September 25, 1933, both in AVP D2U8 379.

23. Both the original letter and the copy are in AVP D2U8 380, appended to the interviews conducted in Prades on September 6, 1933.

24. AVP D2U8 379, deposition of Violette Nozière, September 9, 1933.

25. AVP D2U8 380, deposition of André Malbois, September 8, 1933.

26. AVP D2U8 379, deposition of Violette Nozière, August 28, 1933.

27. AVP D2U8 379, deposition of Germaine Nozière, August 26, 1933. The lunch menu is from *Le Populaire,* August 25, 1933.

28. AVP D2U8 379, letter from Violette, August 21, 1933.

29. The following account is drawn from the depositions by Violette on August 28 and September 9, 1933, in AVP D2U8 379; and December 16, 1933, in D2U8 380; and by Germaine on August 26, September 19, and September 25, 1933, in D2U8 379; and December 18, 1933, in D2U8 380.

30. Germaine's memorandum of September 19, 1933, in AVP D2U8 379.

31. The letter as transcribed instructs the patients to take the medicine "avant *que* de vous coucher" instead of "avant de vous coucher," a mistake commonly made by less educated people.

32. Psychological report by Drs. Claude, Crouzon, and Truelle, November 6, 1933, 26–27, in AVP D2U8 380.

33. The account is from her deposition of August 28, 1933, AVP D2U8 379.

34. AVP D2U8 380, reports by Dr. Charles Paul, August 24, 1933.

35. AVP D2U8 379, deposition of Madeleine Debize, August 26, 1933.

36. AVP D2U8 379, deposition of Violette Nozière, August 28, 1933.

37. AVP D2U8 379, deposition of Zoe Tesseydre, September 2, 1933.

38. *Paris-Midi,* August 25, 1933.

39. AVP D2U8 379, depositions of Madeleine Debize, August 26, 1933, Raoul Terrey and Stéphan Aram, August 27, 1933, and Violette Nozière, August 28, 1933.

40. AVP D2U8 379, deposition of Violette Nozière, August 28, 1933; Marcel Guillaume, *Mes Grandes Enquêtes criminelles: De la bande à Bonnot à l'affaire Stavisky* (Paris: Éditions des Équateurs, 2005), 348–49.

41. AVP D2U8 379, report of Inspector Félix Le Guillou de Penanros, August 23, 1933.

42. *Le Petit Parisien,* August 24, 1933; *Le Journal,* August 24, 1933.

43. *Le Journal,* August 24, 1933; articles in *L'Œuvre* and *Paris-Soir,* August 24, 1933.

44. *Le Journal,* August 25, 1933.

45. *L'Œuvre, Le Populaire,* and *Paris-Midi,* August 25, 1933.

46. *Le Petit Parisien,* August 25, 1933. The same newspaper carried rumors of suicide on August 27 and 28. *Paris-Soir,* August 29, 1933.

47. *Paris-Midi,* August 29, 1933.

48. *Le Petit Parisien,* August 26, 1933. The store was at 66 Rue de la Chaussée d'Antin, near the Galeries Lafayette.

49. *Le Petit Parisien,* August 27, 1933; *Action Française,* August 27, 1933.

50. AVP D2U8 379, deposition of Jean-François Pierre, September 2, 1933.

51. Ibid.; AVP D2U8 379, depositions of Louis Sellier and Jeanne Aubert, September 6, 1933.

52. AVP D2U8 379, undated police report on Violette Nozière's whereabouts on the nights of Saturday, August 26, and Sunday, August 27.

53. AVP D2U8 379, deposition of Pierre Gourcerol, September 9, 1933.

54. Ibid.; AVP D2U8 379, deposition of André de Pinguet, September 6, 1933.

55. *Le Journal,* August 29, 1933.

56. *Paris-Soir,* August 30, 1933.


FIVE

1. Florentin Raoul, *Le Parricide au point de vue medico-légal* (Lyon: A. Storck, 1901), 48–53. For a general discussion of this literature, see Sylvie Lapalus, *La Mort du vieux: Une histoire du parricide au XIXe siècle* (Paris: Tallandier, 2004), ch. 2.

2. Raoul, *Le Parricide,* 25.

3. Robert A. Nye, *Crime, Madness, and Politics in Modern France: The Medical Concept of National Decline* (Princeton, NJ: Princeton University Press, 1984), esp. chs. 4–5.

4. Gustave Asselin, "L'État mental des parricides," (medical thesis, Bordeaux, 1902), 11–30.

5. Élisabeth Cullère, *Du Parricide en pathologie mentale au point de vue nosologique* (Paris: Arnette, 1925), 98–101. Oddly enough, given the subject, the topic and some of the case studies were provided by Cullère's father, also a medical doctor, whom she acknowledges gratefully.

6. Asselin, "L'État mental," 130–33; Maximilian Mittelman, *Le Parricide et son étiologie* (Paris: Picard, 1936), 18–19. According to Raoul, there were eighty-nine rural parricides as opposed to forty-eight urban ones between 1889 and 1899: *Le Parricide,* 22.

7. *Le Populaire,* August 31, 1933.

8. *Le Matin,* August 29, 1933.

9. Biographical details from Laurent Joly's preface to Guillaume, *Grandes Enquêtes*, 7–31.

10. Ibid., 20. See also Francis Lacassin, *La Vraie Naissance de Maigret: Autopsie d'une légende* (Paris: Éditions du Rocher, 1992), esp. 137–38.

11. Guillaume, *Grandes Enquêtes*, 353–55. Elements of Guillaume's account had already appeared in *Détective*, no. 254, September 7, 1933.

12. Guillaume, *Grandes Enquêtes*, 356.

13. AVP D2U8 379, deposition of Violette Nozière, September 9, 1933.

14. AVP D2U8 379, deposition of Violette Nozière, August 28, 1933.

15. On the circulation and political leanings of 1930s newspapers, see Raymond Manevy, *La Presse de la Troisième République* (Paris: J. Forêt, 1955), 244–45; Claude Bellanger, *Histoire générale de la presse française*, 5 vols. (Paris: Presses Universitaires de France, 1972), 3: 449–583.

16. Reference in all cases is to the August 30, 1933, issue.

17. Benjamin Martin, *Crime and Criminal Justice under the Third Republic* (Baton Rouge: Louisiana State University Press, 1990), 2–20; Anne-Marie Sohn, "Les Attentats à la pudeur sur les fillettes et la sexualité quotidienne en France (1870–1939)," *Mentalités* (1989): 71–112.

18. Jean-Marc Berlière, *Le Crime de Soleilland: Les journalistes et l'assassin* (Paris: Tallandier, 2003).

19. *Détective*, no. 128, April 9, 1931.

20. Sohn, "Les Attentats," 83–90.

21. William H. Sewell, *Work and Revolution in France: The Language of Labor from the Old Regime to 1848* (Cambridge: Cambridge University Press, 1980), 224–25. On the social incidence of incest in late twentieth-century America, see Diana E. H. Russell, *The Secret Trauma: Incest in the Lives of Girls and Women* (New York: Basic Books, 1986), ch. 8.

22. *Détective*, no. 236, May 4, 1933.

23. *Détective*, no. 395, May 28, 1936.

24. *Détective*, no. 163, December 10, 1931.

25. Stefano Maffei, *The European Right to Confrontation in Criminal Proceedings: Absent, Anonymous, and Vulnerable Witnesses* (Groningen: Europa Law Publishing, 2006), 12–17.

26. *Le Petit Parisien*, September 2, 1933. Similar versions appeared that day in all the big daily papers.

27. *Paris-Midi*, September 2, 1933; *L'Humanité*, September 2, 1933.

28. *Le Petit Parisien*, September 1, 1933.

29. *Le Populaire*, September 1, 1933; *Paris-Soir*, September 1, 1933.

30. *Le Journal*, September 4, 1933.

31. AVP D2U8 380, depositions of Joseph Boissier, Baptiste Pélisse, Alfred Terisse, and Félix Nozière, September 6, 1933; *Le Petit Parisien*, September 4, 1933.

32. *Paris-Soir,* August 31, 1933.

33. AVP D2U8 379, deposition of Claude Joly, September 6, 1933; D2U8 380, depositions of Henri Duclos, Armand Rigolet, Paul Boulesteix, Paul Barbier, Joseph Dedouche, Georges Bassi, Joseph Sessau, Arsène Chausse, and Léopold Biard, September 12, 1933; deposition of Gaetan Besset, September 15, 1933; depositions of Dominique Tomasi and Arsène Chausse, September 19, 1933; deposition of Émile Mall, September 21, 1933; deposition of Pierre Pont, September 28, 1933; deposition of Gaetan Besset, September 29, 1933; *L' Œuvre,* September 16, 1933.

34. Martin, *Crime and Criminal Justice,* ch. 4.

35. Details from Lanoire's professional file, Centre des Archives Contemporaines—Fontainebleau, dossier 19770067, piece 260.

36. Ibid.

37. AVP D2U8 379, deposition of Violette Nozière, September 9, 1933.

38. AVP D2U8 379, deposition of Pierre Camus, September 12, 1933.

39. AVP D2U8 380, deposition of Jean Leblanc, October 9, 1933.

40. *L'Intransigeant,* September 14, 1933; *L'Œuvre,* September 14, 1933.

41. *Paris-Soir,* September 11, 1933; *L'Œuvre,* September 10, 1933.

42. AVP D2U8 379, deposition of Violette Nozière, September 9, 1933.

43. *Le Populaire,* September 10, 1933.

44. AVP D3U8 379, undated search report; D2U8 380, forensic report by Dr. Charles Sannié, October 9, 1933.

45. AVP D2U8 380, deposition of Violette Nozière, September 26, 1933.

46. *Le Populaire,* September 13, 1933; *L'Intransigeant,* September 14, 1933; *Paris-Soir,* September 14, 193; *La République,* September 13, 1933; *L'Œuvre,* September 14, 1933.

47. *Le Petit Parisien,* September 12, 1933.

48. *Paris-Midi,* September 13, 1933.

49. *L'Œuvre,* September 15, 1933.

50. AVP D2U8 379, deposition of Germaine Nozière, September 25, 1933.

51. *L'Œuvre,* September 16, 1933.

52. Ibid.; *Paris-Midi,* September 16, 1933; *Le Petit Parisien,* September 16, 1933; *Le Populaire,* September 17, 1933; *Le Journal,* September 17, 1933.

53. AVP D2U8 379, letter from Germaine Nozière to Judge Lanoire, September 19, 1933.

54. *Paris-Soir,* August 28, 1933.

55. *Paris-Soir,* September 5, 1933.

56. *L'Humanité,* August 26, August 31, and September 2, 1933.

57. Boitel's declaration was made to *Le Journal* on September 9, 1933; Action Française itself revealed on September 16 that Boitel was judicial counselor to the CGTU, and *L'Humanité* referred to him the same day as "our comrade."

58. *L'Humanité,* September 17, 1933.

59. AVP D2U8 380, letter from Violette Nozière to Judge Lanoire, October 19, 1933.

60. AVP D2U8 380, report of Dr. Charles Paul, August 24, 1933; D2U8 379, reports from Germaine Dubost, Suzanne Aucuit, and Marie Bernard, nurses at Hôpital Saint-Antoine, October 27, 1933. They testified that the wound was very slight, that it was almost healed by the time she arrived at the hospital, and that her poor state was due to psychological rather than physical trauma.

61. AVP D2U8 379, deposition of Violette Nozière, August 28 and September 9, 1933.

62. AVP D2U8 379, deposition of Jean Dabin, September 4, 1933.

63. *L'Intransigeant,* September 23, 1933.

64. *Le Petit Parisien,* September 12, 1933.

65. *Paris-Soir,* September 20, 1933; *L'Œuvre,* September 20, 1933.

66. *Le Petit Parisien,* September 16, 1933; *L'Œuvre,* September 17, 1933; *Le Journal,* September 17, 1933.

67. *Le Journal,* September 19, 1933; *La République,* September 20, 1933.

68. *Le Petit Parisien,* September 18, 19, and 20, 1933.

69. AVP D2U8 380, report of Inspectors Goret and Verrières, October 11, 1933.

70. AVP D2U8 380, deposition of Violette Nozière, September 26, 1933; additional information in her letter to the judge, September 27, 1933.

71. AVP D2U8 380, report of Inspectors Goret and Verrières, October 11, 1933.

72. AVP D2U8 380, undated.

73. AVP D2U8 380, September 21, 1933.

74. *Le Matin,* September 22, 1933; *L'Intransigeant,* September 23 and October 2, 1933.

75. AVP D2U8 380, deposition of Violette Nozière, September 26, 1933.

76. *Le Petit Parisien,* September 15, 1933.

77. Demartini, "L'Affaire Nozière," 200–201.

78. The earliest and most famous argument against the Wasserman Reaction was that of the bacteriologist and philosopher of medicine, Ludwik Fleck, in 1935, who challenged the traditional prejudices linked to syphilis, which had led physicians to overlook the false positives: Ludwik Fleck, *Genesis and Development of a Scientific Fact,* trans. Fred Bradley and Thaddeus J. Trenn (Chicago: University of Chicago Press, 1979).

79. *Police Magazine,* April 18, 1937.

80. E. Sue Blume, *Secret Survivors: Uncovering Incest and Its Aftereffects in Women* (New York: Random House, 1990), ch. 4.

81. Ibid., chs. 7–13; Russell, *The Secret Trauma,* chs. 9–14; Judith Lewis Herman, *Father-Daughter Incest* (Cambridge, MA: Harvard University Press, 1981), ch. 6.

82. AVP D2U8 380, depositions of Violette Nozière, December 16 and 20, 1933.

83. *L'Œuvre,* September 24, 1933; see also *Le Petit Parisien* and *Le Journal* on the same day.

84. Archives de la Préfecture de Police, Police Judiciaire—Assasinats, 1933, Dossier Nozière.

85. It is in file AVP D2U8 380, along with the many other letters sent to the judge. The pronouns used in the letter make it clear that the writer is male.

86. For a fuller discussion of the movie, see chapter 10.

87. AVP D2U8 380, deposition of Violette Nozière, December 16, 1933.

88. In the sequel to Pagnol's *Marius,* the play and movie *Fanny* (both 1932), Fanny discovers that she is pregnant by Marius, who has departed for a life at sea. She reluctantly agrees to marry the elderly Panisse, who knows that the child is not his but offers to conceal the truth and raise it as his own.


SIX

1. All the letters are in AVP D2U8 380. They are unclassified, and most are unsigned. Dates, signatures, and other details are given when available. The "I would feel bad . . ." letter is signed "Émile X."

2. Written from Lyon, September 16.

3. André Lang in *Gringoire,* September 1, 1933.

4. Luc Boltanski et al., *Affaires, scandales, et grandes causes: De Socrate à Pinochet* (Paris: Éditions Stock, 2007).

5. David Bien, *The Calas Affair: Persecution, Heresy, and Toleration in Eighteenth-Century Toulouse* (Princeton, NJ: Princeton University Press, 1960).

6. The literature on the Dreyfus affair is abundant. The fullest and most authoritative recent treatment is Jean-Denis Bredin, *The Affair: The Case of Alfred Dreyfus,* trans. Jeffrey Mehlman (New York: George Braziller, 1986). The most recent shorter treatment is Louis Begley, *Why the Dreyfus Affair Matters* (New Haven, CT: Yale University Press, 2009).

7. Annie Cohen-Solal, *Sartre, 1905–1980* (Paris: Gallimard, 1985), 694.

8. *Le Populaire,* September 2, 1933; *Le Journal,* September 10, 1933; *L'Œuvre,* September 10, 1933.

9. *Détective,* no. 265, November 23, 1933.

10. Charles Rearick, *The French in Love and War: Popular Culture in the Era of the World Wars* (New Haven, CT: Yale University Press, 1997), 53–62;

Adrian Rifkin, *Street Noises: Parisian Pleasure, 1900–1940* (Manchester: Manchester University Press, 1993), ch. 2; Louis-Jean Calvet, *Chanson et société* (Paris: Payot, 1981), ch. 5.

11. Simone Berteaut, *Piaf,* trans. Jane Guicharnaud (New York: Harper and Row, 1972), 20–29, quote p. 28.

12. *L'Intransigeant,* September 22, 1933.

13. "Violette Nozières, assassin de ses parents," Éditions Marcel-Robert Rousseaux, 1933.

14. "Violette Nozières l'assassin," Éditions Marcel-Robert Rousseaux, 1933.

15. *Paris-Soir,* August 26, 1933.

16. *Détective,* no. 254, September 7, 1933.

17. *Paris-Midi,* August 31, 1933.

18. Jean-Louis Bory, "Le Mystère de la femme en noir," *Le Nouvel Observateur,* May 13–21, 1978.

19. *Paris-Soir,* August 26, 1933.

20. *Le Journal,* August 26 and 31, 1933.

21. The first letter is dated September 15, 1933, unsigned; the second is undated and signed "B.L."; the third was written from the suburb of Drancy and dated August 8, no doubt erroneously for September 8.

22. "Autour de l'affaire Nozières" (editorial), *Paris-Midi,* September 8, 1933.

23. Letter from Gustave Lautel, born in the Tarn in 1906, son of an electrician, living at 43 Rue de Montcalm in the eighteenth.

24. September 18, 1933.

25. Report of Inspector Verrier, October 18, 1933.

26. Report of Inspector Goret, October 23, 1933.

27. Letter of September 19, 1933; and report by Inspector Verrier, October 26, 1933.

28. "Émile, où-es tu?" Éditions Marcel-Robert Rousseaux, 1933.

29. Undated letter signed "Lucie"; unsigned letter from a woman, September 19, 1933; unsigned, undated letter, handwritten in block capitals; letter signed "Maigne"; undated, unsigned letter.

30. Paul Garnier, "Les Hystériques accusatrices," *Bulletin médical* 54 (1903): 629–30.

31. Ernest Dupré, *La Mythomanie: Étude psychologique et médico-légale du mensonge et de la fabulation morbides* (Paris: Jean Gainche, 1905), 1–18.

32. René Charpentier, *Les Empoisonneuses: Étude psychologique et médico-légale* (Paris: Steinheil, 1906), 80–94.

33. Stephen Séguinot, "La Médicine devant la justice: Affaire La Rancière, 1834–1835" (doctoral thesis in Medicine, Paris, 1929).

34. *Paris-Soir,* September 15, 1933.

35. Sherry Turkle, *Psychoanalytic Politics: Jacques Lacan and Freud's French Revolution*, 2d ed. (London: Free Association Books, 1992), 3–41; on psychoanalysis in the United States, see Nathan Hale, *Freud and the Americans: The Beginnings of Psychoanalysis in the United States, 1876–1917* (New York: Oxford University, 1971), and Elizabeth Lunbeck, *The Psychiatric Persuasion: Knowledge, Gender and Power in Modern America* (Princeton, NJ: Princeton University Press, 1994); on France, see Élisabeth Roudinesco, *La Bataille de cent ans: Histoire de la psychanalyse en France* (Paris: Éditions Ramsay, 1982).

36. Turkle, *Psychoanalytic Politics*, 36–37.

37. Editorial by Emmanuel Car, *Détective*, no. 257, September 28, 1933.

38. *L'Œuvre*, September 15, 1933.

39. *L'Œuvre*, September 17, 1933; *Détective*, no. 259, October 12, 1933.

40. Magnus Hirschfeld, "En marge de l'affaire Nozières: Le démon de la sexualité," *Vu*, September 6, 1933.

41. On Freud, see the controversial work of Jeffrey Moussaieff Masson, *The Assault on Truth: Freud's Suppression of the Seduction Theory* (New York: Farrar Strauss and Giroux, 1984); and for perspective on the debate, see Janet Malcolm, *In the Freud Archives* (New York: New York Review of Books, 1997).

42. Rachel Edwards and Keith Reader, *The Papin Sisters* (Oxford: Oxford University Press, 2001), 13; Sophie Darblade-Mamouni, *L'Affaire Papin* (Paris: Éditions de Vecchi, 2000), 89–92.

43. AVP D2U8 380, psychiatric report on Violette Nozière, November 6, 1933, 1. See the interview of Dr. Truelle about the panel's mandate in *L'Intransigeant*, September 18, 1933.

44. AVP D2U8 380, psychiatric report, 7–34, quotes pp. 16 and 34.

45. Ibid., 43.

46. Ibid., 55, 57

47. Ibid., 58–59, 79.

48. Ibid., 75–76.

49. Sohn, *Chrysalides*, 1: 396–406.

50. AVP D2U8 379, report of Inspector Le Guillou de Penanros, August 23, 1933.

51. First letter undated; handwritten letter dated September 22; typewritten letter dated September 16.

52. M.G., Neuchâtel, October 7, 1933; "Une Mère de Famille," September 27, 1933; "Une Vieille Maman"; "Impressions sur l'affaire Nozière."

53. *Détective*, no. 263, November 9, 1933.

54. *La Française*, September 30, 1933.

55. AVP D2U8 379, report of Inspector Le Guillou de Penanros, August 23, 1933; *Paris-Soir*, August 26, 1933.

56. AVP D2U8 380, September 21, 1933.

57. *Paris-Soir,* August 30, 1933; *Détective,* no. 253, August 31, 1933; and no. 255, September 14, 1933.

58. "A Newspaper Reader," August 31, 1933.

59. Alphonse Desqueyrat, *Les Classes moyennes* (Paris: Éditions Spes, 1939), 37.

60. Lucien de Chilly, "La Classe moyenne en France après la guerre: Sa crise, causes, conséquences, remèdes" (University of Paris Law Faculty Thesis, 1924), 20–23.

61. See, for instance, *Le Journal,* August 27, 1933; quote from *Le Populaire,* August 31, 1933.

62. "Quartier Latin, 1932," daily report in *L'Intransigeant,* October 11–20, 1932.

63. Ibid., October 11, 1932.

64. Ibid., October 19, 1932.

65. Editorial by André Lang, *Gringoire,* September 15, 1933.

66. Editorial by Clément Vautel, *Le Journal,* September 3, 1933.

67. *Paris-Midi,* September 15, 1933.

68. *Le Peuple,* September 14, 1933; *L'Intransigeant,* September 20, 1933; *L'Ère Nouvelle,* September 14, 1933.

69. *L'Œuvre,* September 4 and 8, 1933.

70. *L'Humanité,* September 17, 1933.

71. *Le Populaire,* September 2, 1933.

72. *Le Peuple,* September 3, 1933; *L'Œuvre,* August 27, 1933.

73. Louis Laloy, "Le Mauvais Étudiant," in *L'Ère Nouvelle,* September 14, 1933.

74. One letter to Lanoire, undated, runs thus: "Violette had hidden nothing from her cherished love, who was in fact nothing more than a vulgar pimp dressed as a gentleman. He knew she would inherit 160,000 francs. He even dangled marriage before her. He was in fact the son of a station worker." Another, dated September 13: "How much responsibility must be borne by that fake professor? Crimes, as you know, are not committed by those who carry out the ultimate gesture, but by those who set them up."

75. *Le Populaire,* September 3, 1933.

76. Laloy in *L'Ère Nouvelle,* September 14, 1933.

77. August 30, 1933.

78. *L'Œuvre,* September 3 and 4, 1933.

79. Victor Turner, *The Ritual Process: Structure and Anti-Structure* (Chicago: University of Chicago Press, 1969), 95, 102–8.

80. Carolyn Dean, *The Frail Social Body: Pornography, Homosexuality and Other Fantasies in Interwar France* (Berkeley: University of California Press, 2000), 146–59, quote p. 147.

81. *L'Humanité,* September 16, 1933.

82. *Le Petit Parisien,* September 3, 1933; *L'Œuvre,* September 3 and 7, 1933.

83. The lack of commentary on Violette's interracial affairs as such is fascinating but difficult to contextualize absent any scholarly synthesis about attitudes toward blacks and Arabs in Paris and France at the time. On the one hand, female miscegenation with members of "inferior" races was denounced in scholarly studies and official reports as medically and morally deplorable, though the debate focused more on the colonies and concerned the genetic outcome rather than sexual encounters per se. Affairs between (French or American) black men and white women were common in Montmartre at the time, and the French response to them was apparently quite tolerant, certainly compared to contemporary American attitudes. Both Arabs and blacks represented a tiny minority of immigrants to France between the wars and, in that respect, may have not been seen as much of a collective threat to French womanhood. See Elsa Camscioli, *Reproducing the French Race: Immigration, Intimacy, and Embodiment in the Early Twentieth Century* (Durham, NC: Duke University Press, 2009); Tyler Stovall, "Murder in Montmartre: Race, Sex and Crime in Jazz-Age Paris," in Françoise Lionnet and Shu-mei Shih, eds., *Minor Transnationalism* (Durham, NC: Duke University Press, 2005), 143–46; and Stovall, *Paris Noir: African-Americans in the City of Light* (New York: Houghton Mifflin 1996), 19–20; Gérard Noiriel, *Le Creuset français: Histoire de l'immigration XIXe-XXe siècles* (Paris: Le Seuil, 1988), 256–57, and tables in Appendix.

84. *Le Matin,* September 6, 1933.

85. *Le Populaire,* August 31, 1933

86. *Détective,* no. 255, September 14, 1933; *Marianne,* September 9, 1933.

87. André Lang in *Gringoire,* September 22, 1933.

88. "A Newspaper Reader," August 31, 1933.

89. Pierre Drieu la Rochelle, "Le Cas de Violette Nozières," *Marianne,* September 6, 1933.

SEVEN

1. The quote is from the classic 1955 essay by Raymond Borde and Étienne Chaumeton, "Towards a Definition of Film Noir," excerpted in a translation by Alain Silver in Alain Silver and James Ursini, eds., *Film Noir Reader* (New York: Limelight, 1996), 22.

2. Maria Tatar, *Lustmord: Sexual Murder in Weimar Germany* (Princeton, NJ: Princeton University Press, 1995); Judith Walkowitz, *City of Dreadful Delight: Narratives of Sexual Danger in Late Victorian London* (Chicago: University of Chicago Press, 1992).

3. Georges Auclair, *Le Mana quotidien: Structures et fonctions de la rubrique des faits-divers* (Paris: Anthropos, 1970), 91–100. Other important works on the

*fait divers* include Marine M'sili, *Le Fait-divers en République: Histoire sociale de 1870 à nos jours* (Paris: CNRS Éditions, 2000); Annik Dubied, *Les Dits et les scènes du fait divers* (Geneva: Droz, 2004); Franck Évrard, *Fait divers et littérature* (Paris: Nathan, 1977); David H. Walker, *Outrage and Insight: Modern French Writers and the Fait Divers* (Oxford: Berg, 1995); Dominique Kalifa, *Crime et culture au XIX siècle* (Paris: Perrin, 2005), chs. 6, 9.

4. Before the case, the paper's circulation was 30,000; the Troppmann case multiplied that figure tenfold, on some days taking it to half a million. Michelle Perrot, "Fait divers et histoire au XIXe siècle," *Annales: Économies, Sociétés, Civilisations* 38 (July–August 1983): 913. Dominique Kalifa, *L'Encre et le sang: Récits de crime et société à la Belle Époque* (Paris: Fayard, 1995) 11, 20; Vanessa R. Schwartz, *Spectacular Realities: Early Mass Culture in Fin-de-Siècle Paris* (Berkeley: University of California Press, 1998), 34–40.

5. Perrot, "Fait divers," 911–12.

6. Anne-Emmanuelle Demartini, *L'Affaire Lacenaire* (Paris: Aubier, 2001).

7. The classic account of this stage in the history of perceptions of criminality is Louis Chevalier, *Classes laborieuses et classes dangereuses à Paris pendant la première moitié du XIXe siècle* (Paris: Hachette, 1984).

8. Kalifa, *L'Encre et le sang,* chapter 7; Marcel Montarron, *Histoire du "milieu" de Casque d'Or à nos jours* (Paris: Plon, 1969), 19–35; Jérôme Pierrot, *Une Histoire du Milieu* (Paris: Denoël, 2003), ch. 1.

9. Marcel Montarron, "La Guerre du crime," *Détective,* no. 391, April 21, 1936.

10. The classic analysis of melodrama as a genre is Peter Brooks, *The Melodramatic Imagination: Balzac, Henry James, Melodrama and the Mode of Excess,* 2d ed. (New Haven, CT: Yale University Press, 1995). See also Julia Przybos, *L'Entreprise mélodramatique* (Paris: José Corti, 1987); and Ben Singer, *Melodrama and Modernity* (New York: Columbia University Press, 2001).

11. Jonathan Eburne, *Surrealism and the Art of Crime* (Ithaca, NY: Cornell University Press, 2008), 195.

12. See, for instance, James R. Lehning, *The Melodramatic Thread: Spectacle and Political Culture in Modern France* (Bloomington: Indiana University Press, 2007).

13. Robert Wohl, *The Generation of 1914* (Cambridge, MA: Harvard University Press, 1979), Introduction and ch. 1; Eugen Weber, *The Hollow Years: France in the 1930s* (New York: Norton, 1994), ch. 5. It is interesting to note that a similar interest in private crime flourished in Spain at the height of the Franco regime, from the 1950s to the 1970s, when most political and ideological life was stifled by repression and censorship: see Marie Franco, *Le Sang et la vertu: Fait divers et franquisme* (Madrid: Casa de Velázquez, 2004).

14. The NRF group actually included only two men of Protestant descent, André Gide and Jean Schlumberger, but was regularly derided by critics as a

collection of "clergymen," "Latter-day Saints," and so on. See Alan Sheridan, *André Gide: A Life in the Present* (Cambridge, MA: Harvard University Press, 1966), 366.

15. Pierre Assouline, *Gaston Gallimard: Un demi-siècle d'édition française* (Paris: Balland, 1984), 33–96, quote about Gallimard and Gide p. 96, Gide on Proust p. 58.

16. For details on the Kessel family, see Yves Courrière, *Joseph Kessel ou sur la piste du lion* (Paris: Plon, 1985).

17. Assouline, *Gallimard*, 208–9.

18. The claim of a readership of one million is in issue no. 72, March 13, 1930, and again in no. 413, September 24, 1936.

19. *Détective*, no. 52, October 24, 1929, and no. 122, February 26, 1931. The official press run in 1933 was only 292,000, but since several people probably read each paper, the publishers' claims of a readership of one million may not have been that far off the mark: see Catherine Maisonneuve, "*Détective*, le grand hebdomadaire des faits-divers de 1928 à 1940" (mémoire de maîtrise, Université de Paris, 1974), 63–64. On the magazine's imitators, see Sigrid Hueber, "Les Magazines de faits divers dans les années trente" (mémoire de maîtrise, Université de Versailles, 2004). On the launching of *Détective*, see also Raymond Manévy, *Histoire de la presse, 1914–1939* (Paris: Corréa, 1945), 226–30.

20. Assouline, *Gallimard*, 212–13.

21. Christian Delporte, *Histoire des journalistes en France, 1880–1950* (Paris: Seuil, 1999), 236–40; Pierre Assouline, *Albert Londres: Vie et mort d'un grand reporter* (Paris: Balland, 1989); Marcel Montarron, *Tout ce joli monde* (Paris: Table Ronde, 1965), 13.

22. Montarron, *Tout ce joli monde*, 11.

23. *Détective*, no. 13, January 24, 1929; no. 16, February 14, 1929; no. 17, February 21, 1929; and no. 30, May 23, 1929.

24. *Détective*, no. 90, July 17, 1930; no. 96, August 28, 1930; and no. 213, November 24, 1932.

25. "The Mysteries of Dijon" appeared in no. 59, December 12, 1929.

26. Walker, *Outrage and Insight*, ch. 3.

27. *Détective*, no. 1, November 1, 1928.

28. See, for instance, issue no. 216, December 15, 1932; and no. 218, December 29, 1932.

29. *Détective*, no. 180, April 7, 1932; and no. 212, November 17, 1932.

30. *Détective*, no. 239, May 25, 1933; no. 241, June 8, 1933; and no. 300, July 26, 1934.

31. *Détective*, no. 116, January 15, 1931.

32. *Détective*, no. 418, October 29, 1936.

33. Pierre Darmon, *Landru* (Paris: Plon, 1994). For an analysis of the cultural significance of the Landru phenomenon, see Robin Walz, *Pulp Surrealism:*

*Insolent Popular Culture in Early Twentieth-Century Paris* (Berkeley: University of California Press, 2000), ch. 3.

34. The following account is drawn from Sophie Darblade-Mamouni, *L'Affaire Papin* (Paris: Éditions de Vecchi, 2000); Paulette Houdyer, *L'Affaire Papin: Le diable dans la peau* (Le Mans: Cénomane, 1988); and Rachel Edwards and Keith Reader, *The Papin Sisters* (Oxford: Oxford University Press, 200), ch. 1.

35. Darblade-Mamouni, *L'Affaire Papin,* 92–93; Edwards and Reader, *The Papin Sisters,* 15–16.

36. Suzanne Normand, "À Propos des soeurs Papin," *Marianne,* October 11, 1933.

37. Simone de Beauvoir, *La Force de l'âge* (Paris: Gallimard, 1960), 151–52.

38. *L'Intransigeant,* September 29, 1933; *Vu,* October 4, 1933; *Détective,* no. 224, February 9, 1933; *Le Journal,* September 30, 1933.

39. Georges Imam, "La Rage au cœur," *Candide,* September 21, 1933.

40. "Le Procès des soeurs Papin," *Revue des Grands Procès Contemporains* 41 (1935): 559.

41. Sarah Maza, *Servants and Masters in Eighteenth-Century France: The Uses of Loyalty* (Princeton, NJ: Princeton University Press, 1983), 100.

42. "Le Procès des soeurs Papin," 575–76, 590; Darblade-Mamouni, *L'Affaire Papin,* 60–61.

43. Darblade-Mamouni, *L'Affaire Papin,* 79–89.

44. On debates among the audience during the trial, see *Paris-Midi,* September 31, 1933; Beauvoir, *La Force de l'âge,* 152; Janet Flanner, *Paris Was Yesterday, 1925–1939* (New York: Harcourt Brace Jovanovich, 1988), 101.

45. For an excellent discussion of the intellectual and artistic legacy of the Papin case, see Edwards and Reader, *The Papin Sisters,* chs. 2–4. On the Parker and Hulme affair, see Julie Glamuzina and Alison J. Laurie, *Parker and Hulme: A Lesbian View* (New York: Firebrand Books, 1991). The Parker-Hulme case was the basis for Peter Jackson's 1994 film "Heavenly Creatures."

46. Edwards and Reader, *The Papin Sisters,* ch. 2.

47. Beauvoir, *La Force de l'âge,* 152; Flanner, *Paris Was Yesterday,* 103.

48. Flanner, *Paris Was Yesterday,* 158.

49. The following account is drawn from Maurice Garçon, *Histoire de la justice sous la IIIe République,* vol. 3 (Paris: Fayard, 1957), 131–34; and *Détective,* no. 229, March 16, 1933.

50. Flanner, *Paris Was Yesterday,* 164.

51. *Revue des Grands Procès Contemporains* 41 (1935): 318–19.

52. Edward Berenson, *The Trial of Madame Caillaux* (Berkeley: University of California Press, 1992).

53. On crimes of passion, see Joëlle Guillais, *La Chair de l'autre: Le crime passionnel au XIXè siècle* (Paris: O. Orban, 1986); and Ruth Harris, *Murders*

*and Madness: Medicine, Law and Society in the Fin-de-Siècle* (New York: Oxford University Press, 1989).

54. Garçon, *Histoire de la justice*, 106–12.

55. The following account of Dufrenne's life appeared in most of the major papers after his murder. See, in particular, *Paris-Midi*, September 25, 1933; and *Le Populaire*, September 26, 1933. More generally, see the excellent account and analysis of the case by Florence Tamagne, "Le 'Crime du Palace': Homosexualité, medias, et politique dans la France des années 1930," *Revue d'Histoire Moderne et Contemporaine* 53 (2006): 129–49.

56. Geo London, *Les Grands Procès de l'année 1933* (Paris: Éditions de France, 1934), 116–18.

57. *Paris-Midi*, September 25, 1933.

58. London, *Les Grands Procès*, 116.

59. *Détective*, no. 156, March 10, 1933. Florence Tamagne, *A History of Homosexuality in Europe: Berlin, London, Paris, 1919–1939* (New York: Algora Publishing, 2006), 336–37.

60. *Détective*, no. 389, April 9, 1936. For further coverage of the Leplée murder, see no. 390, April 16, 1936.

61. *Le Populaire*, September 29, 1933.

62. *L'Intransigeant*, September 27, 1933; *Paris-Midi*, October 6, 1933.

63. Florence Tamagne, *A History of Homosexuality in Europe: Berlin, London, Paris, 1919–1939* (New York: Algora Publishing, 2006), 336–37; Scott Gunther, *The Elastic Closet: A History of Homosexuality in France, 1942-Present* (London: Palgrave, 2009), 14–24; Carolyn Dean, *The Frail Social Body: Pornography, Homosexuality and Other Fantasies in Interwar France* (Berkeley: University of California Press, 2000), ch. 4; Tamagne, "Le 'Crime du Palace,'" 130–33.

64. London, *Les Grands Procès*, 105–7.

65. *Paris-Midi*, September 30, 1933.

66. *Détective*, no. 390, April 16, 1936.

67. Walker, *Outrage and Insight*, 3–8; Évrard, *Fait divers et littérature*. Dostoyevsky based *Crime and Punishment* on the deeds of the nineteenth-century French criminal Lacenaire; Dreiser drew the plot of *An American Tragedy* from the 1906 crime of Chester Gillette; and Oates's *Black Water* is a fictional rendering of the drowning of Mary-Jo Kopechne at Chappaquiddick.

68. Michel Winock, *Le Siècle des intellectuels* (Paris: Seuil, 1999), chs. 13, 17, 25, 31. The following discussion of Gide and Mauriac is heavily indebted to Walker's excellent analysis in *Outrage and Insight*, ch. 4.

69. Cited in Walker, *Outrage and Insight*, 53. See also Emily Apter, "Allegories of Reading/Allegories of Justice: The Gidean Fait-Divers," *Romanic Review* 80 (November 1989): 560–70.

70. Sheridan, *André Gide*, 389.

71. André Gide, *Ne jugez pas* (Paris: Gallimard, 1969). In the preface to his souvenirs from the Assizes Court, he writes: "Sitting on the jury bench you repeat to yourself the words of Christ: *Judge not.*"(9)

72. Gide, *Ne jugez pas,* 233.

73. Ibid.; Apter, "Allegories of Reading," 564–65; Jean Paulhan, *Entretiens sur des faits divers* (Paris: Gallimard, 1984), 28.

74. Paulhan, *Entretiens,* 7, 26–28, reference to *Détective,* no. 41, August 15, 1929.

75. Ibid., 49.

76. François Mauriac, *Thérèse Desqueyroux* (Paris: Grasset, 1989), 25–27. See Walker's analysis of the novel in this perspective, *Outrage and Insight,* 59–66.

77. Mauriac, *Thérèse Desqueyroux,* 74, 109.

78. Ibid., 116–17.

79. Ibid, 133.

80. Apter, "Allegories of Reading," 567.

81. Stephen Kern, *A Cultural History of Causality: Science, Murder Novels, and Systems of Thought* (Princeton, NJ: Princeton University Press, 2004), advances another argument about the change in understandings of causality from the Victorian to the modernist period. Rather than ascribing everything to the Great War, Kern proposes that the evolution of both technologies and theories of knowledge over a broad range of disciplines made for an overabundance of explanation, which undermined previous certainties about causal links.

82. The following analysis is drawn from Auclair, *Le Mana quotidien;* Paulhan, *Entretiens;* Évrard, *Fait divers et littérature;* Maurice Merleau-Ponty, "Sur les faits divers," in *Signes* (Paris: Gallimard, 1960), 389; and Fernande Schulman, "Regard sur le fait divers" *Esprit* 39 (1971): 244–52.

83. Beauvoir, *La Force de l'âge,* 168–69.

84. Ibid., 150–51, 153, 361.

85. The most thorough treatment of the Stavisky affair is Paul F. Jankowski, *Stavisky: A Confidence Man in the Republic of Virtue* (Ithaca, NY: Cornell University Press, 2000).

EIGHT

1. On Émile, see *L'Humanité,* October 2, 1933; and *Le Journal,* October 15, 1933. *L'Humanité, Le Journal,* and *Le Petit Parisien* all carried similar accounts of the October 18 hearing on the front page of their October 19, 1933, editions.

2. Jacques Niger, *Le Secret de l'empoisonneuse: Le crime de Violette Nozières, son arrestation, ses complices, enquête très complète* (Paris, 1933), 3, 30. The pamphlet cost two francs, slightly more than an issue of *Détective.*

3. Jean Pidault and Marc-Ivan Sicard, *L'Affaire Nozières: crime ou châtiment?* (Paris, 1933), 47, 99–100, 104.

4. *Détective,* no. 270, December 28, 1933; and no. 309, September 27, 1934.

5. Mark Polizzotti, *Revolution of the Mind: The Life of André Breton* (New York: Da Capo Press, 1997), 93.

6. José Pierre, ed., *Violette Nozières: Poèmes, dessins, correspondance, documents* (Paris: Terrain Vague, 1991), 14. This edition is a reprint with a preface and supporting documents of the 1933 collective work, *Violette Nozières,* published in Brussels in 1933 under the imprint Nicolas Flamel. The Pierre edition will hereafter be cited as *Violette Nozières.*

7. Gérard Durozoi, *Histoire du mouvement surréaliste* (Paris: Hazan, 1997), 8–50.

8. The following account is based on Polizzotti, *Revolution of the Mind,* chs. 1–4 and passim; and Henri Béhar, *André Breton: Le grand indésirable* (Paris: Fayard, 2002), chs. 1–4.

9. Jean-Charles Gateau, *Paul Éluard ou le frère voyant* (Paris: Robert Laffont, 1988), 80.

10. Ibid., chs. 1–12.

11. Ibid., 74, 257–59; Polizzotti, *Breton,* 298.

12. Gateau, *Éluard,* 170–71, 177–78.

13. Polizzotti, *Breton,* 150, 236–38.

14. André Breton, *Manifestoes of Surrealism,* trans. Richard Seaver and Helen R. Lane (Ann Arbor: University of Michigan Press, 1969), 123.

15. Ibid., 161–63.

16. Durozoi, *Histoire,* 167, 242, 262; Carolyn J. Dean, *The Self and Its Pleasures: Bataille, Lacan, and the History of the Decentered Subject* (Ithaca, NY: Cornell University Press, 1992), 123–99.

17. Louis Aragon, "A Man," *Little Review* (Winter 1923–24), 21.

18. Jonathan Eburne, *Surrealism and the Art of Crime* (Ithaca, NY: Cornell University Press, 2008), ch. 1.

19. Robin Walz, *Pulp Surrealism: Insolent Popular Culture in Early Twentieth-Century Paris* (Berkeley: University of California Press), 76–77.

20. Eburne, *Art of Crime,* ch. 3.

21. Mary Ann Caws et al., eds., *Surrealism and Women* (Cambridge, MA: MIT Press, 1991); Katharine Conley, *Automatic Woman: The Representation of Woman in Surrealism* (Lincoln: University of Nebraska Press, 1998); Whitney Chadwick, ed., *Mirror Images: Women, Surrealism, and Self-Representation* (Cambridge, MA: MIT Press, 1998).

22. Polizzotti, *Breton,* 20–21; Bram Dijskstra, *Idols of Perversity: Fantasies of Feminine Evil in Fin de Siècle Culture* (New York: Oxford University Press, 1986); Celia Rabinowitz, *Surrealism and the Sacred: Power, Eros, and the Occult in Modern Art* (Boulder, CO: Westview Press, 2002), ch. 11.

23. Conley, *Automatic Woman*, 10, 20.

24. André Breton, *Nadja*, trans. Richard Howard (New York: Grove Press, 1960), 159–60.

25. Conley, *Automatic Woman*, 14–20.

26. Durozoi, *Histoire*, 165–66;

27. Breton, *Nadja*, 42.

28. Ibid., 49.

29. Polizzotti, *Breton*, 264–85.

30. For an insightful treatement of the book's themes, see Roger Cardinal, *Breton: Nadja* (London: Grant and Cutler, 1986); on the press run and critical reception, see Polizzotti, *Breton*, 300–302.

31. *Violette Nozières*, 7; Polizzotti, *Breton*, 393; Béhar, *Breton*, 299.

32. The scanty surviving correspondence about the volume is reprinted in *Violette Nozières*, 53–80.

33. Anne-Emmanuelle Demartini and Agnès Fontvieille, "Le Crime du sexe. La Justice, l'opinion publique et les surréalistes: Regards croisés sur Violette Nozières," in Christine Bard et al. eds., *Femmes et justice pénale XIXe-XXe siècle* (Rennes: Presses Universitaires de Rennes, 2002), 251. My discussion here does not include the poems by René Char and Maurice Henry, which do not make direct reference to the case.

34. *Violette Nozières*, 33. All translations of the poems are my own.

35. Ibid., 18

36. Ibid., 17, 35

37. Ibid., 29.

38. Conley, *Automatic Woman*, 46.

39. *Violette Nozières*, 19.

40. Ibid., 39–40, poem by Benjamin Péret.

41. Ibid., 33, 35, 39.

42. The poster, much reproduced in recent years, was the work of Pierre Fix-Masseau, probably in collaboration with Adolphe Cassandre. Both artists produced classic Art Deco travel posters, such as Cassandre's 1935 frontal view of the French ocean liner Normandie.

43. *Violette Nozières*, 18, 35.

44. Ibid., 42–43.

45. Ibid., 22, 39.

46. Eburne, *Art of Crime*, 209.

47. *Violette Nozières*, 18–19; Demartini and Fontvieille, "Le Crime du sexe," 251.

48. Steven Harris, *Surrealist Art and Thought in the 1930s: Art, Politics, and the Psyche* (Cambridge: Cambridge University Press, 2002), 123–27, 209.

49. Durozoi, *Histoire*, 221; Meredith Etherington-Smith, *Dalí* (London: Sinclair-Stevenson, 1993), 201–6.

50. Harris, *Surrealist Art and Thought*, 49–79; Eburne, *Art of Crime*, 157–76.

51. *Le Surréalisme au Service de la Révolution* 5 (May 1933): 28. I am using the translation in Eburne, *Art of Crime*, 182. Scholarly attention to the Surrealist role in the Papin case has mostly focused on Jacques Lacan's early work on paranoia. See Eburne, *Art of Crime*, 176–93; Edwards and Reader, *The Papin Sisters*, 31–56; Christopher Lane, "'The Delirium of Interpretation': Writing the Papin Affair," *differences: A Journal of Feminist Cultural Studies* 5 (Summer 1993): 24–37.

52. Neil Baldwin, *Man Ray: American Artist* (New York: Clarkson N. Potter, 1988), ch. 1.

53. Durozoi, *Histoire*, 224ff; Harris, *Surrealist Art and Thought*, 4.

54. Durozoi, *Histoire*, 225.

55. Harris, *Surrealist Art and Thought*, 11–12, 160–63.

56. Ibid., 35–48; Durozoi, *Histoire*, 226–29.

57. Rabinowitz, *Surrealism and the Sacred*, 171–85.

58. Ibid., chs. 1–3; Durozoi, *Histoire*, 226; Harris, *Surrealist Art and Thought*, 152–63; Elizabeth Deeds Ermarth, *Sequel to History: Postmodernism and the Crisis of Representational Time* (Princeton, NJ: Princeton University Press, 1992), 91–124; Jerrold Seigel, *The Private Worlds of Marcel Duchamp: Desire, Liberation and the Self in Modern Culture* (Berkeley: University of California Press, 1995), ch. 5.

59. Breton, *Nadja*, 52.

60. *Violette Nozières*, 18, 27, 40–41.

61. Sigmund Freud, *The Uncanny*, trans. David McClintock (New York: Penguin Books, 2003), 124. See the discussion of this text in Rabinowitz, *Surrealism and the Sacred*, 15–19. Neither Rabinowitz nor other scholars who evoke Freud's text in connection with Surrealism offer any evidence of direct use or quotation by the French Surrealists.

62. Freud, *The Uncanny*, 129–30.

63. The two double portraits—the second one, of the women in prison, is a photomontage—appeared of the back page of *Le Surréalisme au Service de la Révolution* 5 (1933). See the discussion of the image in Eburne, *Art of Crime*, 176–79.

64. The last quote is from Péret's poem in *Violette Nozières*, 40.

65. Durozoi, *Histoire*, 234–36; Eburne, *Art of Crime*, 162–72.


NINE

1. AVP D2U8 380, December 16, 1933.

2. *La République*, December 17, 1933.

3. Julian Jackson, *The Popular Front in France: Defending Democracy, 1934–38* (Cambridge: Cambridge University Press, 1988), ch. 1.

4. Alexander Werth, *France in Ferment* (London: Jarrolds, 1934), chs. 7–8, 13; Charles Sowerwine, *France since 1870: Culture, Politics and Society* (London: Palgrave, 2001), 144–47.

5. *Le Petit Parisien, L'Œuvre,* and *Paris-Soir* all ran accounts of the case on October 9, 1934. The wardrobe dilemma was reported in *Le Journal* on October 7. The Neuvy story ran in *Paris-Soir* on October 11.

6. Geo London, *Grands Procès de l'année 1934* (Paris: Éditions de France, 1935), 137–38. The writer and journalist Geo London was in the courtroom for *Le Journal* and later published yearly collections of his reports on big trials, which contain much more information than most newspaper pieces; *Paris-Soir,* October 12, 1934.

7. *Paris-Soir,* October 12, 1934.

8. Gordon Wright, *Between the Guillotine and Liberty: Two Centuries of the Crime Problem in France* (New York: Oxford University Press, 1983), chs. 7 and 8.

9. Benjamin F. Martin, *Crime and Criminal Justice under the Third Republic: The Shame of Marianne* (Baton Rouge: Louisiana State University Press, 1990), 142, 145, 169, 178.

10. Ibid., 181–82.

11. AVP D2U8 380, "Extrait des minutes de la Cour d'Appel de Paris," July 2, 1934.

12. Martin, *Crime and Criminal Justice,* 144.

13. Ibid., 183–90.

14. Emmanuel Bourcier, "Si vous étiez juré dans l'affaire Nozière," *Journal de la Femme,* October 7, 1933.

15. *Paris Midi* and *L'Œuvre,* October 11, 1934.

16. AVP D2U8 380, "Assises de la Seine, Acte d'Accusation," February 27, 1934.

17. Martin, *Crime and Criminal Justice,* 179.

18. London, *Grands Procès,* 139–40.

19. The following account of the October 10 proceedings is drawn from ibid., 140–47; the October 11 issues of *Paris-Midi, Le Populaire,* and *L'Œuvre;* and the October 12 issue of *Le Journal.*

20. The prosecutor followed Peyre's comment about Dabin being a law student with the remark "*In partibus!*" *In partibus* is used in the Roman Catholic Church to describe bishops who are appointed without a see, a reference to Dabin's absence from his law classes. The joke suggests the complicity—as well as class and professional solidarity implicit in the mastery of Latin—between prosecutor and judge. London, *Grands Procès,* 141.

21. *Le Populaire,* October 11, 1934.

22. *L'Humanité,* October 11, 1934.

23. The account of Germaine's interrogation is based on London, *Grands Procès,* 148–51; and the October 12, 1934, issues of *Le Petit Parisien, Le Populaire,* and *L'Œuvre.*

24. The exchange appears in this form in London, *Grands Procès,* 150, and in similar or slightly different versions in the various newspaper accounts.

25. *Le Petit Parisien,* October 12, 1934.

26. *Paris-Soir,* October 13, 1934.

27. Ibid.; London, *Grands Procès,* 155.

28. "Violette Nozière en Cour d'Assises," 14–15.

29. The account that follows is based on ibid., 156–63; and the October 13, 1934, issues of *Paris-Midi, Paris-Soir, Le Petit Parisien, Le Populaire, L'Œuvre,* and *Le Journal.*

30. "Violette Nozière en Cour d'Assises," 14.

31. Ibid., 8.

32. Ibid., 25.

33. Ibid., 160–61. London's text contains brief excerpts from Gaudel's speech, no full copy of which appears to exist.

34. Jean-Charles Roman d'Amat and Michel Prévost, *Dictionnaire de biographie française* (Paris: Letouzey and Ané, 1948), vol. 15; *Bulletin de l'Association Amicale des Secrétaires et Anciens Secrétaires de la Conférence des Avocats à Paris* 51 (1965): 131–32.

35. On October 7, 1934, an article in *Le Journal* mentioned that he withdrew "for reasons of personal convenience that do honor to his character."

36. Yves Ozanam, "Des Combats de l'extrême-droite aux honneurs du bâtonnat: Émile de Bruneau de Saint-Auban," in Annie Deperchin et al., eds., *Figures de justice: Études en l'honneur de Jean-Pierre Royer* (Lille: Centre d'Histoire Judiciaire, 2004), 337–50.

37. The official court newspaper recorded that speeches were given by Vésinne-Larue, Vincey, and Saint-Auban, but no other paper or account mentions that the latter spoke, much less what he said. *Gazette des Tribunaux,* October 14–16, 1934.

38. *Candide,* October 5, 1933.

39. Ibid.

40. *L'Œuvre,* October 11, 1934.

41. Details on Vésinne-Larue are from a typescript obituary, "Ordre des Avocats à la Cour de Paris, cérémonies du souvenir," November 10, 1976, Bibliothèque de l'Ordre des Avocats, Paris, communicated to me by M. Yves Ozanam; and the personal recollections of the lawyer's younger cousin, Philippe de Vésinne-Larue, shared with me in conversation on July 12, 2009.

42. The detail about the lawyer being possibly in love with his client was provided by Philippe de Vésinne-Larue, who reported that this was a speculation he heard frequently in his family.

43. Letter of October 20, 1933, from the archives of the Bibliothèque de l'Ordre des Avocats, communicated by M. Yves Ozanam. The "honorarium," undoubtedly a token amount, would probably have come from the pittance she was paid for her work as a prisoner.

44. *Paris-Soir,* October 9, 1934.

45. London, *Grands Procès,* 162.

46. *Discours prononcé par Monsieur le Bâtonnier Jean Lemaire à la séance solennelle de rentrée des la conférence des avocats à la cour de Paris le 28 Novembre 1969* (Paris: Barreau de Paris, 1970), 66–69; Jacques Nobecourt, *Le Colonel de La Rocque ou les pièges du nationalisme chrétien* (Paris: Fayard, 1996), 351–52.

47. London, *Grands Procès,* 161; *Le Journal,* October 13, 1934.

48. London, *Grands Procès; Paris-Midi, L'Œuvre,* and *Le Journal,* October 13, 1934.

49. On the absence of incest as a crime in French law, see Demartini, "L'Affaire Nozière," 193.

50. *Paris-Soir,* October 13, 1934.

51. *Le Journal,* October 13, 1934; and London, *Grands Procès,* 162.

52. *L'Œuvre* and *le Populaire,* October 13, 1934.

53. Frédéric Pottecher, *Les Grands Procès de l'histoire* (Paris: Fayard, 1981), 297–98.

54. *L'Œuvre* and *Le Populaire,* October 13, 1934.

55. *Paris-Midi,* October 13, 1934.

56. *Le Journal* and *Paris-Midi,* October 13, 1934.

57. *Le Populaire,* October 13, 1934. When the journalist mentioned Doumer and Barthou, he wrote: "To cite to Maître Vincey examples that will show this clearly, I am choosing men whom he no doubt reveres." Did the writer know of Vincey's right-wing extremism, and was he being sarcastic?

58. Flanner, *Paris Was Yesterday,* 159–60. The comment about Violette's never having met a member of the government followed from the contrast Flanner was setting up between Violette and Germaine d'Anglemont, whose longtime lover was a member of the chamber.

59. See Judith Thurman, *Secrets of the Flesh: A Life of Colette* (New York: Ballantine Books, 1999).

60. *L'Intransigeant,* October 13, 1934.

61. *L'Ère Nouvelle,* October 16, 1934.

62. Laloy published Colette's letter in *L'Ère Nouvelle,* October 25, 1934.

63. *Revue des Grands Procès Contemporains* 41 (1935): 28–29.

64. Ibid., 33–34.

65. Ibid., 35–37. In the remainder of his speech (38–43), the lawyer challenged the medical experts, arguing that they based their conclusions on very short meetings with his client, and that in any event they were assigned by the prosecution.

66. It is technically possible that Vésinne-Larue, as coeditor of the *Revue des Grands Procès Contemporains,* changed the contents of his speech when it was published. Given the proximity of the publication to the time of the trial, one assumes that it would have been risky to do so, since readers of the publication could well have been present in the courtroom.

67. Claude Chevaley in *L'Œuvre,* April 4, 1937.

68. See, for instance, *Le Populaire,* October 13, 1934.

69. On the end of the trial, see *Le Populaire, le Journal, L'Œuvre,* and *Le Petit Parisien,* October 13, 1934.

70. These details are recorded in the written sentence of October 12, 1934, preserved in the Archives Nationales, Centre des Archives Contemporaines 19850797, Article 44 no. 8546 S 34. Violette was also condemned to pay 13,996.25 francs for trial expenses, and an additional 62.50 for postage.

71. *Vu,* October 17, 1934.

TEN

1. All these letters are in Violette's posttrial judicial dossier in the Archives Nationales, Centre des Archives Contemporaines—Fontainebleau, call number 19850797, Article 44, Dossier 8546 S 34, hereafter cited as AN 8456 S 34. Germaine d'Anglemont had not been acquitted but was sentenced to two years' prison for the shooting of her lover, as indicated in chapter 7 above.

2. Ibid. Jury's letter dated October 15; president of Assizes's, October 26; Gaudel's, November 23.

3. Charles Sowerwine, *France since 1870: Culture, Politics and Society* (London: Palgrave, 2001), 30–32. These laws are known informally as the Constitution of 1875, though they were not technically a new constitution.

4. Alexander Werth, *France in Ferment* (London: Jarrolds, 1934), 118–19.

5. *Détective,* no. 107, November 13, 1930. See also *Le Journal,* March 7, 1936.

6. Archives d'Ille-et-Vilaine (hereafter AIV) 278 W395, dossier 6805 no. 9517. According to incomplete prison records, Germaine visited four times in 1934 and Vésinne-Larue once in 1935.

7. *Le Journal,* March 7, 1936.

8. Paul Jankowski, *Stavisky: A Confidence Man in the Republic of Virtue* (Ithaca, NY: Cornell University Press, 2002), 235–37.

9. *Détective,* no. 430, January 21, 1937.

10. *Paris-Soir,* April 2, 1937.

11. *L'Œuvre,* April 3, 9, and 13, 1937.

12. *Le Journal,* September 17, 1937.

13. *L'Œuvre* and *Paris-Midi,* October 29, 1937.

14. Undated report from after his death on Dabin's life in hospital and the absence of conversations in Archives de la Préfecture de Police the Paris, Police Judiciaire (hereafter APP-PJ) 1933, dossier Nozière. AN 8456 S 34, documents from October 1937 to August 1938.

15. AIV 278 W 395, dossier 6805 no. 9517. A log of Violette Nozière's earnings was opened at the Rennes prison on May 14, 1940.

16. *Paris-Match,* December 10, 1966.

17. AIV 278 W395, dossier 6805 no. 9517, letters and reports from August 2 to 6, 1938; Thiebauld letters of February 7 and 13, 1939.

18. Sowerwine, *France in Modern Times,* ch. 14; Robert O. Paxton, *Vichy France: Old Guard and New Order, 1940–1944* (New York: Columbia University Press, 1972), ch. 2. Miranda Pollard, *Reign of Virtue: Mobilizing Gender in Vichy France* (Chicago: University of Chicago Press, 1998); Julian Jackson, *France: The Dark Years, 1940–1944* (Oxford: Oxford University Press, 2001), ch. 7; Nicholas Atkins, "*Ralliés* and *résistants:* Catholics in Vichy France, 1940–44," in Kay Chadwick, ed., *Catholicism, Politics and Society in Twentieth-Century France* (Liverpool: Liverpool University Press, 2000), 97–118.

19. AN 8456 S 34, letter of February 18, 1939.

20. Ibid., documents from 1941 and 1942.

21. AIV 278 W395, dossier 6805 no. 9517, report of December 28, 1943.

22. Ibid., "Procès-verbal d'un arrêté d'interdiction," March 30, 1944.

23. AN 8456 S 34, documents of September and October 1945.

24. *France-Dimanche,* June 15, 1947.

25. APP-PJ 1933, dossier Nozière, report in the context of Violette Nozière's 1952 rehabilitation request; photograph in *France-Soir,* February 23, 1952.

26. Explanation of the juridical status of *réhabilitation* in *L'Aurore,* March 25, 1953.

27. *Le Matin* and *Le Parisien Libéré,* February 26, 1953.

28. *Paris-Jour,* November 29, 1966.

29. Ibid., November 29, 1966.

30. *France-Soir,* February 26, 1963.

31. *France-Soir,* March 26, 1963; Violette gave a similar statement to *L'Aurore,* March 25, 1963: "Personally I'm indifferent. I paid. I began this quest for rehabilitation for my children, who know nothing about my past, so that they would not have to blush on my account or to suffer someday because of this ancient affair." See also *Paris-Jour,* March 25, 1963.

32. *France-Soir,* March 26, 1963.

33. *Paris-Match,* December 10, 1966.

34. Ibid.; *Paris-Jour,* November 30, 1966.

35. *Paris-Jour,* November 30, 1966.

36. *L'Aurore,* November 29, 1966; *Paris-Jour,* November 30, 1966.

37. Interview of Claude Chabrol and Isabelle Huppert in *Ouest-France,* June 14, 1978. In another interview, Chabrol said that Isabelle Huppert suggested that he make a movie about the character, but since at the time Huppert was twenty-four, Brasseur would seem the much likelier source. *La Dépêche du Midi,* May 29, 1978.

38. Jean-Marie Fitère, *Violette Nozière* (Geneva: Presses de la Cité, 1975). The other book-length treatment of the case is Véronique Chalmet, *Violette Nozières: La fille aux poisons* (Paris: Flammarion, 2004), which is also well documented but much more heavily fictionalized.

39. Chabrol told a reporter for *Le Républicain Lorrain* (May 21, 1978) that he had used Fitère's book "completely and shamelessly."

40. *Le Provençal,* May 25, 1978; *Ouest-France,* May 22 and June 14, 1978.

41. *La Dépêche du Midi,* May 28, 1978.

42. *Ouest-France,* May 23, 1978.

43. *France-Soir,* March 11, 1978.

44. *Ouest-France,* June 14, 1978.

CONCLUSION

1. The mythological framing of the affair is developed in Demartini, "L'Affaire Nozière," 190–91. On the reference to the tale "Peau d'âne," see Agnès Fontvieille, "La Question de l'énonciation dans le poème de Paul Éluard publié dans le recueil surréaliste *Violette Nozières," Le Gré des langues* 15 (1999): 90–111.

2. Marina Warner, *From the Beast to the Blonde: On Fairy Tales and Their Tellers* (New York: Farrar Strauss Giroux, 1994), chs. 19–21.

3. "Une Violette Nozières d'autrefois: Béatrice Cenci," *L'Intransigeant,* September 16, 1933; "Plaidoyer pour une parricide: Béatrice Cenci, Rome 1599," a series in *Vu,* October 4, 17, and 24, 1934.

4. Percy Bysshe Shelley, *The Cenci: A Tragedy in Five Acts* (New York: Phaeton Press, 1970), 3–4.

5. Before the case, for instance, it was the object of an extended narrative in *Détective,* no. 162, December 3, 1931.

6. Antonin Artaud, *The Cenci,* trans. Simon Watson Taylor (New York: Grove Press, 1970), x.

7. Pierre Drieu La Rochelle, "Le Cas de Violette Nozières," *Marianne,* September 6, 1933.

8. Kalifa, *Crime et Culture,* 145.

9. Simone de Beauvoir explained in her memoirs that in the early 1930s the French Left was especially blinded by its commitment to pacifism after the carnage of 1914–18, with even prominent Jewish figures like Emmanuel Berl preaching appeasement. *La Force de l'âge* (Paris: Gallimard, 1960), 168–73. I would like to thank Sarah Farmer for alerting me to the issue of the problematic "interwar" label.

# INDEX

Abd el-Krim, Muhammad, 208
Action Française, 54, 65, 89–90, 129,
  164. *See also* Camelots du Roi ("King's
  Hawkers")
*Action Française* (right-wing newspaper),
  65, 114, 210
Adari, Mahmoud, 69, 71
affairs, scandals contrasted with, 142, 144
Alexander I, king of Yugoslavia, 230
Algeria, 26, 143, 242, 264, 268
anarchists, 210
Anglemont, Germaine d' (Armande
  Huot), 190–92, 195, 233, 259, 317n58,
  318n1
anti-Semitism, 81, 201, 246–47
*Antoine Bloyé* (Nizan), 14
"Apaches," 176
Aragon, Louis, 126, 178, 205, 209, 210, 221
Aram, Stéphane, 100
aristocracy, 59, 61, 104, 169, 246, 248;
  Beauvoir family and, 37, 43, 57; fake
  nobility, 190–91; gallantry as norm, 168;
  military vocation and, 105; murder
  cases and, 114; Paquin fashion house
  and, 81. *See also* class divisions
Arnal, Louis, 10

Arp, Hans, 219
Artaud, Antonin, 280
Asselin, Gustave, 108
Atlan, Robert Isaac, 70, 91, 127, 167, 243
Auclair, Georges, 200
*Aurore, L'* (newspaper), 273

Baker, Josephine, 5
Balmain, Lucien, 52, 67, 69
Balzac, Honoré de, 195
*Barrière et le niveau, La [Barriers and
  Levels]* (Goblot), 59
Barthes, Roland, 200
Barthou, Louis, 230, 252, 317n57
Baudelaire, Charles, 210
Beach, Sylvia, 65
Beauvoir, Françoise de, 38, 41, 57–59
Beauvoir, Georges de, 41, 42–43
Beauvoir, Hélène de, 39, 40, 41
Beauvoir, Simone de, 5, 46, 282; bourgeois
  and noble family background, 39, 57;
  childhood of, 37–43, 57, 58, 62; on
  Hitler's rise to power, 201, 321n9; at La
  Coupole café, 100; on Papin sisters, 186,
  189, 190; as reader of *Détective* magazine,
  181; on women in Surrealism, 211

Danan, Alexis, 250

Danjou, Henri, 179

Daudet, Léon, 210

Daudet, Philippe, 210

death penalty, 110, 200, 204; abolition of, 115, 231; execution of women, 231, 246; Germaine's decision to prosecute and, 127; for parricide, 107; in prerevolutionary France, 188; restoration of civil rights and, 271; Violette's sentence, 256, 258–60

Debize, Madeleine, 30–31, 41, 49, 73, 151, 282; café meeting with Violette after crime, 2, 99, 100; road trip in Bugatti and, 91; at trial of Violette, 243; Violette's impersonation of, 104

"degeneracy" thesis, 108–9, 154, 155

Deibler, Anatole, 231

Demartini, Anne-Emmanuelle, 135

Dentz, Gen. Henri, 248

department stores, 72, 74–76, 174, 212

Deron, Dr. Henri, 84–86, 94; imaginary sister of, 86, 92–93, 101, 241; at trial of Violette, 238; Violette's forged letter from, 96–97, 129, 239

Deron, Janine, 86

Derval, Blanche, 212

Desbouis family, 9, 268–69

Desnos, Robert, 207

*Détective* magazine, 161, 168, 201; advertisements in, 181, 225; crime reporting in, 182–83; Dufrenne case in, 194, 195; history of, 177–79; incest tales in, 116–17; on mythomania diagnosis, 155–56; Nozière case as scandal and, 144; on Papin sisters, 186, *187;* photomontage in, 97, *98, 187;* readership, 179, 180–82, 196, 308n19; romance of crime and, 176; series on women's jails, 261; staff of reporters, 179–80; surrealistic objects in, 224–25; Violette on cover of, *119.* See also *faits divers* journalism

Didier, Père, 116

Dior, Christian, 81

"Donkey-Skin" fairy tale, 279–80

Dos Passos, John, 178

Dostoyevsky, Fyodor, 195, 310n67

Doumer, Paul, 252, 260, 317n57

Dreiser, Theodore, 138, 195, 310n67

Dreyfus affair, 2, 3, 17, 81, 202; anti-Semitism and, 247; Camelots du Roi and, 65; divisions in French society over, 142, 230; juridical rehabilitation of Alfred Dreyfus, 270; Nozière case compared with, 143, *143,* 263, 272, 279; political violence of 1930s and, 230; Zola's intervention in, 142, 226

Drieu La Rochelle, Pierre, 173, 178, 181, 281

Drumont, Édouard, 247

Duchamp, Marcel, 205, 222

Duchemin, A. M., 35

Dufrenne, Oscar, 141, 192–95, 201, 203

Dumas, Alexandre, 192, 195

Dupré, Ernest, 154

Eburne, Jonathan, 177, 217

École Sophie Germain, 30, 32

École Universelle, 49, 84

Electra complex, 155

Éluard, Paul, 214, 217, 226; as only child, 207, 213; on Papin sisters, 222; poem on Violette, 215–16, 273, 279

Émile, Monsieur, 132–35, 138, 195, 228, 264, 282; in cartoon, 167, *168;* in Chabrol film, 276; Communist view of, 238; letter signed by, 134, 253; letters to Judge Lanoire about, 150–52; rumors about discovery of, 203; sightings of, 193, 271; song about, 152; suicide of Émile Violette, 262; in Surrealists' *Violette Nozières,* 225; trial of Violette and, 229, 236, 241, 245, 257; as Violette's "protector," 132, 133, 135, 236, 253, 271

Endewell, Roger, 66, 67, 123, 243

*Ère Nouvelle, L'* (newspaper), 163–64, 165, 253

Ernst, Max, 207, 217, 219

Eugénie, Empress, 80

everyday life, violence in, 222, 281

*faits divers* journalism, 175, 177, 192, 201–2, 224, 280–82; Chabrol films and, 274; cross-class appeal of, 195; *Détective* magazine and, 179, 180, 182–83; literature and, 196–200; myth and the sacred in relation to, 200–201; Papin sisters and, 184, 190; poetic imagination

and, 200; political events as competition for, 229. *See also* newspapers
fashion, 71–78, *74–75, 77, 79*, 81–83. See also *premières*
Faulkner, William, 178
Faure, Félix, 17
Fellous, Jacques, 69–70, 91, 92, 167, 243
"Female Hysterical Accusers" (Garnier), 153
feminism, 37, 41, 160, 210, 226
*femmes fatales*, 174, 210, 211, 213, 280
Ferry Laws (1881–82), 29
Feydit, Madeleine, 86
film noir, 19, 74, 174, 199
Fitère, Jean-Marie, 274, 283n1
Flanner, Janet, 5, 189, 190, 252, 254, 317n58
Foire du Trône, 7–8
"Forbidden Fruit" (*Détective* magazine article), 116
*Fountain* (Duchamp), 205, 222
*Française, La* (feminist magazine), 160
France: *affaires* tradition, 142–43; bourgeois class identity in, 59–63; class divisions in, 58; conquest of Algeria, 26; criminal justice system, 122, 231–32; demographics, 20; penal code, 157, 256; small families and only children in, 20, 32, 60, 206; women's vote in, 78, 172; in World War II, 260, 265, 268. *See also* Third Republic
*France-Soir* (newspaper), 271, 272
Franco, Francisco, 265
French language, 9, 11
French Revolution, 6, 9, 29, 107, 194, 232
Freud, Sigmund, 50–51, 155–56; Breton's interest in, 206, 208–9, 225; on "family romances," 50; seduction theory, 156; on uncanny *(Unheimlich)*, 225
Freudianism, 156, 206, 281

Gabin, Jean, 15, 87
Gajiecky, Betty, 34, 51
Galeries Lafayette department store, 73, 74, 75, 76, 99, 103
Gallimard, Gaston, 178–80
Garçon, Maurice, 192
*Garçonne, La* (Margueritte), 38–39
Gare de Lyon, 8, 16, 27, 211
Garnier, Paul, 153

*garnis* flophouses, 6, 55
Garric, Robert, 58, 59
Gaudel (prosecutor), 241, 245–46, 247, 249, 259–60
Gaulle, Charles de, 143, 268
Genet, Jean, 181, 189
Géraud, Henri, 117, 170, 204, 247; career of, 246; on Monsieur Émile, 132–33, 135
Germany, 17, 29, 175, 247
Giacometti, Alberto, 223
Gide, André, 26, 174, 181, 200, 307n14; *faits divers* journalism and, 196–97; *Nouvelle Revue Française* (NRF) and, 178
*Gift* (Ray), 222, *223*
girls, 144, 163, 228, 260; clothes/fashion and, 4, 57, 76, 83; education of, 3, 29–30, 32, 33, 35–36, 41, 282; First World War and attitudes toward, 38–39; incest and sexual molestation of, 114–17, 136, 156, 279–80; in literature, 198, 212; mythomania attributed to, 154, 155; sexual behavior of, 37–38, 40, 43, 45–47; social class and, 37–40, 42–43, 45–47, 62; street songs and, 145, 146
Goblot, Edmond, 59–60, 61
Goby, Jean-Édouard, 65, 66
Goret, Inspector, 133
Goretta, Claude, 275
Gorguloff, Paul, 204, 246, 260
Goulue, La ("the She-Glutton"), 8
Gourcerol, Pierre, 105
*Grand Illusion* (Renoir film), 59
*Gringoire* (newspaper), 169
Gripois, Inspector, 110, 241
Guedet, Inspector, 102
*gueules noires* ("black mugs"), 15
Guillaume, Marcel, 110, 112, 113, 135, 238; on incest allegations, 136, 236; memoirs of, 262–63
Guirschovitz, Jacob Wulf, 151

Halbwachs, Maurice, 61
Haussmann, Baron Georges-Eugène, 6, 68
Hemingway, Ernest, 100, 178
Henry, Maurice, 226
Hézard, Alcime (maternal grandfather of V.N.), 9, 285n11

Hézard, Philomène Boutron (maternal grandmother of V.N.), 9, 120, 285n11
Hirschfeld, Magnus, 156
Hitchcock, Alfred, 274
Hitler, Adolf, 173, 201, 219, 247, 265, 281
Hogarth, William, 192
homosexuality, 166–67, 192–95
Hoover, Herbert, 26
housing conditions, 55
Hugo, Valentine, 219
Hulme, Juliet, 189
*Humanité, L'* (Communist newspaper), 16, 56, 130; on "confrontation" between Violette and mother, 120; on Dabin, 164, 167; on Papin sisters, 186, 222; on sexual abuse accusations, 113–14; Surrealism and, 221; trial of Violette and, 238, 242. *See also* Communist Party, French
Huot, Armande. *See* Anglemont, Germaine d'
Huppert, Isabelle, 174, 273, 275, 320n37
"hysteria," 108, 153

Imam, Georges, 186
incest, 114, 115–17, 135–36, 152, 227, 238; "Donkey-Skin" fairy tale and, 279–80; Freud's seduction theory and, 156; "hysteria" and, 153; medical specialist opinions on Nozière case, 156; Papin sisters and, 189; psychology of incestuous relationships, 136, 215–16; silence in press about, 170; witnesses to, 123; women's stories told in letters to judge, 170–72. *See also* Nozière, Jean-Baptiste, incest allegations against
Indochina, 26
International Colonial Exposition, 26, 208, 221
*Intransigeant, L'* (newspaper), 126, 134, 162–64, 186, 194, 252

Jack the Ripper, 175
Jacob, Isaac, 81
*Jardin de Modes, Le* (fashion magazine), 78, *79,* 80
Jaurès, Jean, 17, 210, 246
Jean, Marcel, 219

Jews, 54, 55, 70, 81, 151, 178; Parisian intellectuals, 178, 198; Stavisky affair and, 202
*Journal, Le* (newspaper), 56, 163, 179; on Dabin's return from Algeria, 264; on Monsieur Émile, 262; on Papin sisters, 186; reference to Dreyfus affair, 143, *143;* on sexual abuse accusations, 113; stories on Violette's crime, 101–2, 103, 105; trial of Violette and, 230, 250; on Violette's arrest, 106

Kalifa, Dominique, 281
Kessel, Georges, 178–79
Kessel, Joseph, 178–79
Kessel, Lazare, 178
Kessel, Samuel, 178
Kesselman, Wendy, 189
Klimt, Gustav, 211
Kohn-Abrest, Dr. (expert in poisons), 240

Laborie, Paul, 195
Lacan, Jacques, 189, 200, 219
La Capoulade café, 87
Lacenaire, Pierre, 176
La Coupole café, 2, 100
Lafayette, Marquis de, 6
*Lafcadio's Adventures* (Gide), 196, 197
Laloy, Louis, 253
Lamirand, Georges, 58
Lancelin, Geneviève, 184, 185
Lancelin family, 184–85, 189
Landru, Henri, 174, 183–84, 209, 274
Landry, Ernest, 19
Lanoire, Judge Edmond, 110, 112, 113, 257; assumptions about case, 134, 147; biography and career of, 122–23; in cartoon, 167, *168;* completion of investigation, 228–29, 234; Dabin questioned by, 131; death of, 277; Germaine's decision to prosecute and, 127–28; incest allegations and, 137; issue of Violette's paternity and, 138; Monsieur Émile witness and, 132, 134–35; psychiatric evaluation of Violette and, 157; Violette's "confrontation" with mother and, 117, 118

100; police investigation of crime and, 121–22; pornography stash, 125, 157; in public opinion, 158, 161; Surrealist denunciation of, 215; syphilis diagnosis of Violette and, 85, 136, 137, 170, 236, 255; Violette's affair with Dabin and, 95–96, 137, 254, 255; Violette's sexual/romantic affairs and, 33, 254

Nozière case/affair, 57, 117, 128, 203–4, 283n1; amnesia concerning, 2–3; class divisions and, 163, 167, 168–69; culture of crime narratives and, 174, 177; *faits divers* journalism and, 190, 201, 280–82; in historical perspective, 3, 281–82; memories of, 273–77; mythical dimension of, 279–80; Papin case and, 189, 190; police officials, 110; public appetite for crime and, 195; public opinion and, 141, 147–50; reputation of Latin Quarter and, 66; rumors concerning, 131–32, 134, 137–38; as scandal and affair, 144, 172; Surrealist investment in, 213–14, 226–27

Nozière family, 11–12, 109, 125, 244, 253, 284n1; gossip about, 120; hypothesis about Violette's paternity, 137–39; neighbors of, 41–42; newspaper accounts of, 101–2; in public opinion, 160–61; social isolation of, 16, 62

Nuremberg Rally, 3, 114, 281

Oates, Joyce Carol, 195–96, 310n67

Oedipal complex, 155

*Œuvre, L'* (Socialist newspaper), 16, 167, 281; campaign to reopen Nozière case, 263, 264; on "cleaning up" of Latin Quarter, 166; on crowds outside prison, 144; on Dabin, 164, 165; on incest accusations, 113, 124, 126, 137–38; trial of Violette and, 234, 241, 242, 243–44, 250, 255

office workers, 19, 45, 59, 201, 241; *dactylo* (typist-secretary), 30–31; on juror list for Violette's trial, 232; as readers of *Détective* magazine, 181, 182; salaries of, 15, 181, 286n37; single children of, 20, 30; smartly dressed, 57; white-collar workers, 7, 30, 36, 162; women as, 30–32, 39, 63

Oppenheim, Méret, 210, 224

Paalen, Wolfgang, 224

Pagnol, Marcel, 46, 302n88

Palais du Café, 66, 67, 94, 100

Papin, Christine and Léa, 141, 174, 184–86, *187*, 188–90, 195; Chabrol film about,

274; *faits divers* journalism and, 184; "magical mentality" and, 201; psychiatric evaluation of, 157, 241; Redureau affair and, 196–97; Surrealist interest in, 189, 219, 222, 226, 314n51, 314n63

Papin, Clémence, 184, 189

Papin, Émilia, 184

Papin, Gustave, 184, 189

Paquin, Isidore, 81, 82

Paquin, Jeanne Becker, 81, 82, 83

Paquin couture house, 52, 67, 72, 80, 81–82, 90

"Paranoid Portrait of Violette Nazière [Nozière]" (Dalí), 219, *220*

Paris: Belle Époque street gangs, 176; Champ de Mars, 104–5; class divisions in, 52–53, 63–64; housing shortage in, 23–24; metro system, 53–54; Opéra neighborhood, 68–69, 99, 138; right-wing violence (Feb. 6, 1934), 3, 229–30, 260; "station neighborhoods," 16; Universal Exposition, 81; villagelike *quartiers* of, 27; working-class districts and culture, 53, 54–57. *See also* Bois de Vincennes; Gare de Lyon; Latin Quarter

Paris, arrondissements of: tenth, 193, 212; eleventh, 43, 55, 115; twelfth, 5–9, 16, 18, 26, 42, 53; thirteenth, 16, 17, 31, 53, 54–55, 89; fifteenth, 54; sixteenth, 85

Paris Commune (1871), 6, 9, 53, 65, 229

*Paris-Jour* (newspaper), 272, 273

*Paris-Match* (newspaper), 273

*Paris-Midi* (newspaper), 102–3, 114, 118, 126, 163; on Pinguet, 148–49; public opinion about case and, 147; racist caricatures, 167, *168–69;* trial of Violette and, 234, 251

*Paris-Soir* (newspaper), 102, 106; on clemency for Violette, 264; Guillaume's memoirs in, 263; on Haguenau prison, 261; on mythomania diagnosis, 155; on possibility of accomplice, 129; public opinion about case and, 147; on sexual abuse allegations, 124, 126; trial of Violette and, 230, 231, 242, 250; on Vésinne-Larue, 248

Parker, Pauline, 189

parricide, in history, 107–9, 279, 280, 298n6
Patou, Jean, 80
patrimony, family *(patrimoine)*, 162
Paul, Dr. (forensic specialist), 240
Paul, Henri, 118
Paulhan, Jean, 197–98, 200
peasants, 37, 109, 116
Péchenot, Robert, 115
Péguy, Charles, 180
Penanros, Le Guillou de, 101
Péret, Benjamin, 216, 217, 222, 225, 226, 227
Perret, Pierre, 151–52
Pétain, Marshal Philippe, 208, 231, 246, 265, 266, 267–68
*Petit Écho de la Mode, Le* (fashion magazine), 77, 78
*Petit Journal, Le* (newspaper), 56
*Petit Parisien, Le* (newspaper), 16, 18, 56, 140, 167; on "confrontation" between Violette and mother, 118; *faits divers* format and, 175, 307n4; Galeries Lafayette advertisements in, 76; on hypnotism rumors, 132; on incest accusations, 113, 126; in literature, 199; stories on Violette's crime, 101, 103; on Violette's various identities, 70–71
*Peuple, Le* (newspaper), 163, 164
Peyre, Counselor, 230, 236, 237, 257, 315n20; attitude toward witnesses, 242, 243; Germaine's testimony and, 239–40
Pezinet, Louis, 132
photography, 209
Piaf, Édith, 145, 194
Picasso, Pablo, 26, 68
Picpus, village of, 6, 7
Pidault, Jean, 204, 214
Piébourg, Bernard, 66–67, 95, 236, 241, 243
Pierre, Jean-François (jazz musician), 103–4, 141, 167, *168*
pimps, 165–66, 176, 204
Pinguet, Count André de, 105–6, 148–49, 167, 168–69, *169*, 282
Plantin, Pierre, 12
Plateau, Marius, 210
PLM (Paris-Lyon-Marseille) railway line, 8–9, 10, 12, 51, 97; annual vacation for workers of, 25; Baptiste Nozière's

devotion to, 61; management-level personnel of, 90
Poiret, Paul, 80
*Populaire, Le* (newspaper), 125, 164, 165; on Dufrenne case, 194; on Pinguet, 168; trial of Violette and, 236, 237, 240–41, 243, 250
Popular Front, 3, 230, 260, 284n2; collapse of, 227, 265; right-wing riots (February 1934) and, 202
pornography, 125, 157
Porte de Charenton, 25, 27
Prades, village of, 10–13, 15, 286n29; reaction to Violette's crime in, 121; size of population, 19; vacations in, 25; Violette in, 87
*premières* (top saleswomen in fashion), 71–72, 80, 82–83, 90, 105
Pre-Raphaelites, 211
Prince, Albert, 263
prostitutes/prostitution, 16, 19, 44, 67, 138; courtesan's ascent and decline, 192; fake titles of nobility and, 190–91; "genteel," 69; male, 192, 195; perceived as carriers of pollution, 166; stories in *Détective* magazine, 182; trial of Violette and, 234
Protestants, 142, 178, 307n14
Proust, Marcel, 178, 195
psychoanalysis, 155, 157, 208

Queneau, Raymond, 207

Radical Republican Party, 193
railways and train imagery, 8, 12–13, 89, 90, 216–17. *See also* Gare de Lyon; PLM (Paris-Lyon-Marseille) railway line
railway workers, 31, 286n30; families of, 20, 24–25; fictionalized account in *Antoine Bloyé*, 14; incomes of, 15, 286n37; politics of, 16–17; social isolation of, 15–16; union membership, 15, 286n38; urban gardens of, 25
rape, 154, 170, 227; absence of witnesses to, 123; in the name *Violette*, 18, 214, 216. *See also* incest
Ray, Man (Emmanuel Radnitsky), 210, 214, 217, 224, 225
Raynal, David, 246

*223;* fantasies of sadistic transgression and, 174; Freud and, 206, 208–9, 225, 314n61; manifestos of, 205, 207, 208; Papin sisters and, 189, 219, 222, 226, 314n51, 314n63; as readers of *Détective* magazine, 181; tribute to Violette, 204–5; "Truth about the Colonies" exhibition and, 26. See also *Violette Nozières* (Surrealist collaboration)

*Surrealism in the Service of the Revolution,* 207, 221, 224

Tahra Bey, Fakir (Louis Pezinet), 132
Tanguy, Yves, 219
Terrey, Raoul, 100
Tesseydre, Zoé, 99–100
Tessier, Aimé, 66, 67, 124, 243
*Thérèse Desqueyroux* (Mauriac), 198–200
Thiebauld, Emmanuel, 266
Third Republic, 17, 26, 46; corruption among leaders of, 177; criminal procedure in, 122, 232; crisis of, 230; death penalty under, 231; female education in, 29, 35–36; office of president in, 260; politicians murdered, 246; sexual molestation of girls in, 114; white-collar workers in, 30
Toklas, Alice B., 5
Tomasi, Dominique, 121
Toulon, Pierre, 18, 43
Toulouse, Henri, 156
Toulouse-Lautrec, Henri de, 8
Tourneux, Albert, 7
Tourneux, Aline, 24, 43–45, 46
Tribout, Achille, 116
Troppmann, Jean-Baptiste, 175, 183, 307n4
Truelle, Victor, 157, 188, 241, 251
"Truth about the Colonies, The" (exhibition), 26
Tunisia, 69

unions, 15, 17, 57, 201
"Unripe Fruit, The" (*Détective* magazine article), 116–17

Valdour, Jacques, 54–56
Valéry, Paul, 197–98

Varna, Henri, 193
Véronal (sleeping drug), 84–85, 144
Verrier, Inspector, 110, 152
Verrières, Inspector, 133
Vésinne-Larue, René de, 117, 153, 244, 246, 260, 268; concluding speech at trial, 250–51, 253–56, 257, 318nn65–66; death of, 277; devotion to Violette's defense, 248, 249, 271, 317n42; Germaine's testimony at trial and, 240; incest allegations and, 253–54; journalists and, 247; life and career of, 248; medical specialists' testimony, 241, 318n65; petitions for appeal of sentence and, 256, 259; in photograph of trial, *235;* post-release life of Violette and, 270; Vichy regime and, 266–67; visits to Violette in prison, 261, 318n6
Vichy regime, 202, 227, 266
*vicieuse* (prone to sexual vice), 37
Villain, Raoul, 246
Vincey, Jean, 246, 248–49, 251–52, 254, 256, 317n57
*Violette Nozière* (Chabrol film, 1978), 174, 273–77
*Violette Nozière* (Fitère), 274
*Violette Nozières* (Surrealist collaboration), 214–17, *218,* 219, *220,* 222, 284n1; everyday objects in, 225; politics of, 226–27; publication prevented by police, 214, 256
Vionnet, Madeleine, 80, 83
Voltaire, 142, 143, 173
Vreeland, Diana, 73
*Vu* (newspaper), 156, 186

Walter, Marie-Thérèse, 68
Wasserman Reaction (test for syphilis), 136, 301n78
white-collar workers, 30, 36, 162
Willy (Georges Legrand), 66, 236; in Chabrol film, 276; conclusion of Violette's trial and, 256; Dabin and, 87, 89; money owed to by Violette, 94; road trip in Bugatti and, 91; at trial of Violette, 241, 243

women: bourgeois charity causes, 58; class mobility and, 63; in crowd outside prison, 144; of eighteenth-century salons, 35–36; fashion and, 72, 75–78, 77, 79, 80–83; female education in Third Republic, 29, 35–36; fluid status of, 4; letters written to Judge Lanoire, 159–60, 170–72, 173; office workers, 30–32, 39, 63; parricides, 108; prisons for, 180, 261; Surrealist movement and, 209–13; trial of Violette and, 231, 233; visiting rituals of bourgeoisie, 42, 62; in workforce, 20, 24, 286n30; World War I and, 38

working class, 3, 10; education and, 32, 39; fashion and working-class women, 72, 75–76; jury service and, 232; middle-class fear of crime and, 176; Parisian neighborhoods of, 6–8, 30, 53, 54–57, 63; politics and, 17–18; railwaymen as labor aristocracy, 15; sexual crimes among, 114–15; sexual propriety norms in, 37, 43, 45–47. *See also* class divisions

World War I (the Great War), 17, 18, 62, 122, 281, 321n9; Breton's service in, 206; fascination with crime in wake of, 174, 176, 177; French losses in, 20, 38; generation born during, 162; logic of causality and, 200, 311n81; loosening of sexual mores after, 115; Mata Hari spy case, 149; right-wing veterans of, 248; sexual propriety norms and, 46

World War II, 260

Worth, Charles, fashion house of, 80, 81, 82

youth, 47, 196; anxieties about, 162, 164, 166; bourgeois (upper-middle-class), 65, 165, 204; fashion and, 80; of Latin Quarter, 66, 163, 164; middle-class, 34; psychiatry and, 156; Republican Youth, 43, 44; right-wing (Camelots du Roi), 65, 129; street gangs of Belle Époque, 176; Vichy regime and, 266

Zola, Émile, 53, 142, 173, 195, 226

Text: 11.25/13.5 Adobe Garamond
Display: Adobe Garamond
Compositor: Westchester Book Group
Indexer: Alexander Trotter
Printer/binder: Sheridan Books, Inc.